Faith-based Identity and Curriculum in Catholic Schools

Faith-based Identity and Curriculum in Catholic Schools examines the relationship between faith-based education and whole curriculum at a time when neo-liberal ideologies and market values are having a disproportionate influence on national education policies.

Topics addressed include current challenges and dilemmas faced by Catholic Education leadership; Catholic social teaching and its implications for whole curriculum; the opinions of teachers in Queensland Catholic schools regarding faith-based school identity with particular reference to whole curriculum; an associated comparison of these opinions teachers with those of their USA peers; school identity and Catholic social teaching in Ontario Catholic schools; an action research approach to the integration of Catholic social teaching in Queensland Catholic schools; longitudinal study of the views of pre-service teachers at a Catholic university regarding the purposes and characteristics of Catholic schools.

Bringing together professionals and academics from across the world, *Faith-based Identity and Curriculum in Catholic Schools* will inspire Catholic and other faith-based educators to appreciate the importance and potential of the integration of faith-based perspectives such as countercultural Catholic social teaching across the school curriculum in an educationally appropriate manner.

Jim Gleeson, inaugural Professor of Identity and Curriculum in Catholic Education at Australian Catholic University, Brisbane (2013–2018), holds postgraduate qualifications in philosophy, theology and education. He is widely published and his research interests include curriculum policy/development/evaluation and faith-based education. Having started out as a secondary teacher Jim worked as a teacher educator, Department Head and Senior Lecturer at University of Limerick.

Peta Goldburg rsm, foundation Chair of Religious Education at Australian Catholic University, holds qualifications in music education, theology and religious education. She has worked extensively in primary, secondary and tertiary education sectors. Peta has led syllabus development in Religious Education and Study of Religion in Queensland for 15 years and her textbooks are used throughout Australia.

Faith-based Identity and Curriculum in Catholic Schools

Edited by
Jim Gleeson and Peta Goldburg

LONDON AND NEW YORK

First edition published 2020
by Routledge
2 Park Square, Milton Park, Abingdon, Oxon, OX14 4RN

and by Routledge
52 Vanderbilt Avenue, New York, NY 10017

Routledge is an imprint of the Taylor & Francis Group, an informa business

© 2020 selection and editorial matter, Jim Gleeson and Peta Goldburg; individual chapters, the contributors

The right of Jim Gleeson and Peta Goldburg to be identified as the authors of the editorial material, and of the authors for their individual chapters, has been asserted in accordance with sections 77 and 78 of the Copyright, Designs and Patents Act 1988.

All rights reserved. No part of this book may be reprinted or reproduced or utilised in any form or by any electronic, mechanical, or other means, now known or hereafter invented, including photocopying and recording, or in any information storage or retrieval system, without permission in writing from the publishers.

Trademark notice: Product or corporate names may be trademarks or registered trademarks, and are used only for identification and explanation without intent to infringe.

British Library Cataloguing-in-Publication Data
A catalogue record for this book is available from the British Library

Library of Congress Cataloging-in-Publication Data
A catalog record has been requested for this book

ISBN: 978-0-367-19383-6 (hbk)
ISBN: 978-0-429-20208-7 (ebk)

Typeset in Bembo
by Cenveo® Publisher Services

Contents

Editors' biographies	vii
List of contributors	ix
Acknowledgements	xi

Introduction   1
JIM GLEESON

1 **Critical challenges and dilemmas for Catholic Education leadership internationally**   11
JIM GLEESON

2 **Catholic social teaching**   31
PETA GOLDBURG RSM

3 *Laudato Si'*: **Some curriculum and pedagogical implications**   63
JIM GLEESON AND PETA GOLDBURG RSM

4 **Catholic social teaching should permeate the Catholic secondary school curriculum: An agenda for reform**   86
GERALD GRACE

5 **Teaching for a just world: Social justice and human rights perspectives across the curriculum**   98
NINA BURRIDGE

6 **The distinctive nature of Catholic Education in Ontario: Catholic perspective integrated across the formal curriculum**   113
KATHARINE STEVENSON AND MICHAEL PAUTLER

vi Contents

7 **The identity of Catholic schools as seen by teachers in Catholic schools in Queensland** 133

JIM GLEESON, JOHN O'GORMAN AND MAUREEN O'NEILL

8 **The characteristics of Catholic schools: Comparative perspectives from the United States and Queensland, Australia** 162

JIM GLEESON, JOHN O'GORMAN, PETA GOLDBURG RSM
AND MAUREEN O'NEILL

9 **Longitudinal study of the attitudes of pre-service teachers at an Australian Catholic University to key aspects of faith-based education: Some conundrums to ponder** 188

JIM GLEESON AND MAUREEN O'NEILL

10 **Curriculum, culture and Catholic Education: A Queensland perspective** 218

JIM GLEESON, JOHN O'GORMAN AND MAUREEN O'NEILL

11 **The integration of Catholic social teaching across the curriculum: A school-based action research approach** 244

JIM GLEESON

12 **Identity and Curriculum in Catholic Education: Main lessons and issues arising** 274

JIM GLEESON

Appendices

Appendix 1 Identity of Catholic schools: Outcome (criterion) variables 296

Appendix 2 Identity of Catholic schools: Regression analysis tables 298

Appendix 3 Identity and curriculum in Catholic Education: Survey of teachers' opinions regarding certain aspects of Catholic Education 311

Appendix 4 Survey of student teachers' opinions and attitudes regarding Catholic Education 321

Index 329

Editors' biographies

Professor Jim Gleeson Having worked as a post-primary teacher in Dublin and his native Tipperary, Jim spent much of his professional life as a teacher educator at University of Limerick (UL) (1981–2011). He was on the External Evaluation Team for the EU Transition from School to Adult and Working Life Projects (1979–1982) and served as Leader of the SPIRAL Transition Project at Shannon Curriculum Development Centre (1983–1987), External Evaluator of the European Studies (Ireland and Great Britain) Project (1988–1991) and National Council for Curriculum and Assessment Education Officer for the Leaving Certificate Applied (1992–1995). During his time at UL, Jim was Head of the Education Department (1991–1995), Course Leader – Master's in Educational Management (1993–2011) and Irish Universities Association nominee on the Teaching Council of Ireland (2005–2012). He completed a 5-year contract as inaugural Professor of Identity and Curriculum in Catholic Education at Australian Catholic University, Brisbane, in 2018. Jim holds undergraduate and postgraduate degrees in Philosophy, Theology and Education from the National University of Ireland and the Pontifical University. His PhD is from the University of East Anglia (Centre for Applied Research in Education) and his main research interests include curriculum development and evaluation; education and curriculum policy; faith-based education; and teacher education. He is married to Anne and they have an adult son, James.

Professor Peta Goldburg rsm After graduating from the Queensland Conservatorium of Music with a Bachelor of Arts (Music Education) in 1979, Peta was the music specialist at Biggera Waters State School (1980–1982). In 1983, she joined the Brisbane Congregation of the Sisters of Mercy and after novitiate she was Head of Creative Arts at All Hallows' School Brisbane where she taught music, drama, Religious Education and Study of Religion (1986–1993). Peta holds a Bachelor of Arts (Music Education) from the Queensland Conservatorium of Music, a Graduate Diploma in Religious Education from McAuley College, Brisbane, an

MA (Theology) from the University of Queensland, a Master of Religious Education degree from Australian Catholic University (ACU) and a PhD from the University of Newcastle. For over 20 years, she has played a significant role in syllabus development for the Queensland Studies Authority (QSA) now the Queensland Curriculum and Assessment Authority (QCAA) in particular as a member of the expert writing team for Study of Religion 2017, Chair of the Study of Religion Syllabus Committee 2001 and 2008; and Chair of Religion and Ethics Syllabus Review Committee 2013–2014. In 2012 and 2013 she was a member of the expert panel for the development of Civics and Citizenship for Australian Curriculum, Assessment and Reporting Authority (ACARA). In 1995 Peta joined the staff of ACU and has fulfilled a variety of roles including Course Coordinator, Head of School: Religious Education, Associate Dean Catholic Identity and Partnerships, and Director Postgraduate Education. She is a skilled educator having been awarded ACU Excellence Teaching Award (2005), Fellow of the Australian College of Educators (FACE) in 2006, Carrick Citation for Excellence in Teaching and Curriculum Development (Australian Government award) 2006 and Life Membership of the Australian Association for Religious Education (2011).

Contributors

Professor Nina Burridge is an Associate Professor in the Faculty of Arts and Social Sciences at the University of Technology Sydney. Her main research interests and publications centre on indigenous education, women's empowerment, social justice and human rights within Australia and in international contexts. Nina recently co-authored a report on *Human Rights Education in the School Curriculum* for the Department of the Attorney General of Australia.

Professor Gerald Grace KSG, KHS, FSES is the Director of the Centre for Research and Development in Catholic Education (CRDCE) and Editor of the journal *International Studies in Catholic Education* (ISCE) at St Mary's Catholic University, Twickenham, London, UK. He has taught at Kings College, London, Cambridge University, Victoria University of Wellington, New Zealand and the University of Durham (where he was Head of the School of Education). He founded CRDCE at the University of London, Institute of Education in 1997 (the first such centre in Europe) and launched ISCE in March 2009 (as the first international and interdisciplinary journal of Catholic education). His publications include *School Leadership: Beyond Education Management* (1995), *Catholic Schools: Mission, Markets and Morality* (2002) and *The International Handbook of Catholic Education*, 2 vols (2007). His latest book, *Faith, Mission and Challenge in Catholic Education* was published by Routledge in 2016 (hardback) and in 2017 (paperback). In 2014 he received a KSG from Pope Francis for his 'Services to Catholic education, nationally and internationally'.

Professor John O'Gorman is a former Pro Vice Chancellor at Australian Catholic University, was the Foundation Dean of the Faculty of Health and Behavioural Sciences at Griffith University and is a Professor Emeritus of both institutions. He is an organisational psychologist, a Fellow of the Australian Psychological Society, and a former editor of the *Australian Journal of Psychology*. He co-authored *Psychological Testing and Assessment* published by Oxford University Press, and was a co-editor of the five-volume Sage series on *Work and Organisational Psychology*.

Dr Maureen O'Neill has worked as a P-12 teacher throughout Australia. She holds a PhD from the University of the Sunshine Coast and has worked as lecturer, tutor and researcher at undergraduate and postgraduate levels across a range of disciplines. Maureen was the Research Assistant for the Identity and Curriculum in Catholic Education Project at Australian Catholic University.

Michael Pautler has been a Catholic educator in Ontario for nearly 40 years and has worked as teacher, consultant, Principal, Superintendent of Education and as Director of Education for three Catholic District School Boards in Ontario. In 2013, he was appointed as the Executive Director of the Ontario Institute for Catholic Education (ICE). ICE works in partnership with organisations that promote, maintain and steward publicly funded Catholic education across the province, with a particular emphasis on religious education curriculum and other subject areas as they relate and intersect with Catholic teaching. His current work supports Faculties of Education, Catholic Partner organisations and the 29 Ontario Catholic District School Boards to encourage and provide leadership development and adult faith formation opportunities.

Katharine Stevenson has been a Catholic educator in Ontario for more than 25 years. She has served as an elementary teacher, a secondary Religious Education teacher, a Religious Education curriculum consultant, and is currently a secondary school Principal. Katharine holds a Master of Religious Education and a Master of Arts in Theology from the Toronto School of Theology. She is a curriculum developer, a published author and a frequent contributor to the Institute for Catholic Education. Katharine is a tireless advocate of the valuable and distinctive role of Catholic education in the educational landscape of Ontario. She and her husband are the proud parents of two active teenage boys.

Acknowledgements

The Chair in Identity and Curriculum in Catholic Education was established at Australian Catholic University with the generous support, over a 5-year period (2013–2018), of the Archdiocese of Brisbane, the Catholic Education Offices in the Queensland dioceses of Brisbane, Cairns, Rockhampton, Toowoomba and Townsville, Queensland Catholic Education Commission, Sisters of Mercy Brisbane, Edmund Rice Trust and Presentation Sisters.

The authors wish to acknowledge the active support of the volunteer teachers from the following schools who participated in the project's action research activities with such commitment and enthusiasm: Assisi Catholic College, Upper Coomera; Holy Spirit Catholic School, Bray Park; Our Lady of the Angels Catholic Primary School, Wavell Heights; St Anthony's Catholic Primary School, Alexandra Hills; St Columban's College, Caboolture; St Ita's Catholic Primary School, Dutton Park; St Joseph's Tobruk Memorial School, Beenleigh. Further information on the activities of the participating teachers is available at 'action research activities' on the project website at http://www.acu.edu.au/1280444

Our thanks are also due to the following colleagues who kindly reviewed the previously unpublished chapters of this book:

Professor Brendan Bartlett,
Faculty of Education and Arts, Australian Catholic University

Emeritus Professor Terence Lovat,
University of Newcastle

Dr Joanne O'Flaherty,
School of Education, University of Limerick

Introduction

Jim Gleeson

The Catholic Church operates the world's largest non-governmental school system, amounting to some 45,000 secondary schools, 95,000 primary schools and almost 1,400 Catholic universities across over 90 countries. Operating as they do within an environment characterised by secularisation, detraditionalisation and pluralisation (Pollefeyt & Bouwens, 2010; Taylor, 2007), Catholic schools are challenged to adapt to changing anthropological (Lane, 2015; Pope Francis, 2015), ecclesiological (Boeve, 2005), scientific (Treston, 2001) and educational landscapes (Ball, 2012; Belmonte & Cranston, 2009; Lingard, 2010; Pollefeyt & Bouwens, 2010).

The current publication arose out of one such effort at adaptation, the Identity and Curriculum in Catholic Education initiative, a joint undertaking involving Australian Catholic University (ACU) and a wide range of Queensland Catholic Education and Religious Institute partners (see Acknowledgements). Before introducing this initiative further, it is important to locate it in the broader context of current neoliberal education policy and practice.

The wider educational environment

The prevailing educational environment, with its emphasis on market values, performativity, employment-related skills and competences, consumer choice and increased state control over curriculum content and assessment impacts on schooling practices in many ways. The associated curriculum discourse is highly technicist and instrumental and the proliferation of standardised testing programmes such as the Organisation for Economic Cooperation and Development's Programme for International Student Assessment (PISA) and Australia's National Assessment Plan – Literacy and Numeracy (NAPLAN) has resulted in considerable tension between education as a public good and a competitive private commodity, between 'having an education' and 'being an educated person' and between the role of the teacher as technician and professional. For example, Polesel, Rice, and Dulfer (2014) concluded from their national study of over 8,000 Australian educators that the high stakes NAPLAN testing regime 'distorts teaching practices, constrains the curriculum and narrows students' educational experiences' (p. 640). Such developments have a damaging and corrosive effect on teacher's autonomy and professional identity (Sachs & Mockler, 2012) and on the culture of schools (Hargreaves, 2003). These external influences are considered in some detail in Chapter 1 of this book.

Lingard (2010) argues that the impetus for the introduction of a national curriculum in Australia has come from global economic imperatives, and the Catholic Education Commission of New South Wales (2014, p. 6) describes the Australian Curriculum as 'an essentially instrumental view [that] does not describe the benefits of schooling in terms of the holistic growth of each individual student ... [nor does it] articulate a view of Australian students in terms of their overall development'. The independent reviewers of the national curriculum (Australian Government, 2014, p. 27) characterised it as a 'utilitarian and technocratic approach to the purpose of education' before going on to state that 'for Catholic educators [this view] has always been seen, at best, as a partial description of the desirable outcomes of schooling and, at worst, as a depiction of a lack of understanding of human dignity' (p. 95).

Catholic Education

The Congregation for Catholic Education (CCE) is critical of the growing popularity of a 'merely functional view of education' (CCE, 2014, para 12) and concerned about the hegemony of market values in education and the associated temptation for governments to simply respond to 'the demands deriving from the ever-changing economic situation' (CCE, 2014, para 64). The Congregation's primary concern is with the preservation of the unique climate of Catholic school communities, one where 'evangelical identity' (CCE, 2014, para 13) is expressed when the 'principles of the gospel become [the school's] internal motivation and final goal' (CCE, 1997, para 34).

In the prevailing neoliberal environment however, Catholic schools in Australia and elsewhere are increasingly challenged to maintain their overall identity, character and ethos 'in a changing religious and social reality [and to] prove their validity as viable educational institutions, as well as satisfy the requirements of the Church, while simultaneously responding to government accountability and Church expectations' (Belmonte & Cranston, 2009, p. 296). Writing in the *International Handbook of Catholic Education*, Croke (2007, p. 823) expresses concern regarding the changing profile of the student population, suggesting that the 'authenticity of the [modern Australian] Catholic school [is problematic due to] an annually increasing proportion of non–Catholic students, along with students from mainly middle class Catholic families whose adhesion to their Faith is weak' (Croke, 2007, p. 823). Such concerns were confirmed in a study of Catholic schools in Brisbane, which found that upwardly socially mobile parents, regardless of their religion, are enrolling their children in Catholic secondary schools 'for predominantly pragmatic rather than religious reasons [with a resulting] marked decline in religious commitment' (Dowling, Beavis, Underwood, Sadeghi, & O'Malley, 2009, p. 38), which suggests that 'as society is becoming more secular, Catholic schools are becoming more popular than ever' (p. 6).

Croke (2007) believes that the Australian Bishops are right to be concerned about the level of religious understanding and commitment of the next generation of Catholic school teachers while Pascoe (2007, p. 793) portrays Australian Catholic Education as being caught on the horns of a dilemma where schools emphasise 'the education of the whole person, faith and Religious Education, pastoral care and learning outcomes' when talking to parents, while focusing on issues such as legislative compliance, good governance, accountability and formal agreements in their dealings with government representatives.

This changed environment has important implications for the whole curriculum beyond Religious Education (D'Orsa, 2013; Gleeson, 2015; Institute for Catholic Education, 1996). The CCE defines the fundamental characteristics of the Catholic school in terms of the 'integral education of the human person through a clear educational project … [involving] ecclesial and cultural identity [and] love [and] service to society' (CCE, 1997, #9.3). Lane (1991) proposes that 'the Catholic school seeks to integrate the curriculum, to unify faith and culture, and to bring together the different pieces of the school programme into a higher synthesis that influences the social and spiritual formation of pupils' (p. 12). Arguing for the integration of Catholic social teaching (CST) across the formal school curriculum, Grace (2013, p. 99) suggests that 'Catholic educational institutions at all levels have failed to provide curriculum mediations of this teaching as a crucial part of the formation of Catholic youth'.

The Identity and Curriculum in Catholic Education initiative

Against this background, the Chair of Identity and Curriculum in Catholic Education was established at the McAuley (Banyo) Campus of ACU in 2010 with the generous support, over a 5-year period (2013–2018), of the donors mentioned earlier in the Acknowledgements. The ACU information package used during the search exercise stated that the Chair would, *inter alia*,

- research how the school curriculum can be developed to achieve the goals of Catholic Education;
- inform curriculum development and identify how curriculum can be shaped and implemented;

- identify schools and teachers where innovative approaches to Catholic informed curriculum in different discipline areas, for example literature, science, economics, the arts and
- identify barriers to integrating a Catholic worldview in the curriculum and possible solutions.

It is not unusual to find that curriculum development initiatives are driven by a small number of strategically well-placed 'significant' individuals. The establishment of the Chair was driven by three such individuals who concurrently filled key leadership positions during the first decade of the 21st century – Professor Marie Emmitt, Dean of the Faculty of Education and Arts at ACU from 2004 to 2014); David Hutton, Executive Director of Brisbane Catholic Education (BCE) (1998–January, 2013) and Mike Byrne, Executive Director of Queensland Catholic Education (2006–2016).

Professor Emmitt (personal communication) recalls that she commenced discussion regarding the establishment of the Chair with David Hutton, Executive Director of Brisbane Catholic Education, and ACU Vice Chancellor Professor Peter Sheehan AO in 2007. After Professor Sheehan's retirement she subsequently engaged with the new Vice-Chancellor at ACU, Professor Greg Craven, as well as Archbishop Bathersby of Brisbane. David Hutton (personal communication) recalls that there had been

> … some debate about the focus of the Chair. Initially it was suggested that it might focus on social justice, however after some time it was agreed that it should centre round Identity and Curriculum in Catholic Education. The logic behind this decision was that much academic attention had been given to Religious Education and leadership in Catholic schools, however there was a need for research into how Catholic identity and ethos permeated and was enacted in the general curriculum of the school.

Speaking at the formal launch of the Chair in 2010, Professor Emmitt explained the rationale for the establishment of the Chair:

> We surveyed Catholic universities world-wide and found no Chair focusing on curriculum and Catholic Education. There are Chairs in Religious Education and Catholic Education but none focusing on curriculum and identity in Catholic Education …. Certainly, Catholic schools have excellent Religious Education programs; they have rich social justice programs; they have rich liturgical programs; and the schools are noted for their caring and supportive environments and strong values-based education. However, generally these programs exist around the traditional school curriculum which is the state-mandated curriculum. The content of what is to be taught every day in schools has largely been ignored from a Catholic perspective.

Professor Emmitt also made reference to the timeliness of infusing Catholic perspectives alongside the mandated state and national goals at a time when a national curriculum was being developed for the first time. She went on to highlight the importance of addressing

> ... contemporary moral, ethical, religious and political questions, not only in the context of Religious Education classes, but also in all disciplines, for example English, maths, the sciences, the arts ... issues such as social justice and equity, sustainable patterns of living, working for peace within a context of understanding and respecting difference of culture, religion and other perspectives and world views.

Her bold vision was of a curriculum that would 'need to be counter cultural, even radical, with a strong critical and questioning approach related to the big issues that face the individual and society'.

Mike Byrne, Executive Director of Queensland Catholic Education Commission, spearheaded the fundraising initiative and, as David Hutton recalled, 'eventually the Queensland Catholic Education Offices and the Archdiocese of Brisbane came on board with significant funding. In addition, the Sisters of Mercy (Brisbane), the Queensland Presentation Sisters and Edmund Rice Education also offered financial support'.

When coming up with a title for the Chair, these leaders wisely eschewed the problematic and commonly used notion of 'Catholic curriculum'. The adjectival use of Catholic in this way offers a hostage to fortune in a system that is very heavily subsidised by public funding and where curriculum is centrally prescribed, while also inferring the existence and/or desirability of a 'Protestant curriculum', a 'Muslim curriculum' and so on.

Key aspects of the Chair's brief, italicised below, included engagement with contemporary culture and the explicit integration of CST and social justice principles – what was effectively a curriculum development project.

- Catholic school teachers *engaging with contemporary culture* from an informed Catholic perspective.
- Curriculum that is infused with Catholic theology and teaching in *explicit and authentic* ways.
- Curriculum that addresses large societal challenges such as *social justice and equity, sustainable patterns of living and working for peace* in more powerful ways.
- A forum that shares best practice in *integrating CST* in the classroom and co-curricular activities.

Having been appointed in January 2012 with a fixed-term 5-year contract, due to delays with Australian Immigration Professor Gleeson did not assume the position until February 2013. Unfortunately, David Hutton's term of office as Executive Director of Brisbane Catholic Education had just concluded, while Professor Emmitt's period of office as Executive Dean, Faculty of Education and Arts, elapsed soon afterwards. The impact of these changes is considered in Chapter 12.

Project management, governance and evolution

Although answerable to the Executive Dean of the Faculty of Education and Arts, the University organogram positioned the Chair in a small self-standing unit called 'Catholic Identity and Partnerships' rather than the School of Education. The Chair's assigned supervisor at ACU was Dr Peta Goldburg, Professor of Religious Education. Professor Goldburg, who had been supportive of the 'curriculum and Catholic perspectives' concept from when it was first mooted, was Chair of the Project Advisory Committee. As the scale of project activities escalated she became increasingly involved in the day-to-day work of the project. While this was not recognised as part of her official workload at the university, her expertise in Religious Education was invaluable and she has devoted long hours to providing professional development for participating teachers with regard to CST, working with action research teachers and supporting and advising the Chair in various other ways. A Project Research Assistant, Dr Maureen O'Neill, was appointed in September 2013 on a 3-day per week contract (reduced to a casual contract in 2015).

An Advisory Committee was established consisting of senior officers or representatives of the donor institutions. The Committee's terms of reference were to provide feedback on progress reports from the Chair and to provide advice and assistance in relation to

- collating and conducting research to facilitate bringing a Catholic perspective to the formal school curriculum;
- identifying the different forms the Church's evangelising mission can take in Catholic Education and their application across the curriculum in Catholic schools;
- working with the Catholic authorities and schools to develop and implement innovative approaches to Catholic-informed curriculum in different disciplines and
- evaluating possible strategies and processes that will facilitate the integration of a Catholic perspective across the curriculum.

As sometimes happens with new initiatives, interest began to wane after the first year and this was reflected in attendances at meetings of the Advisory Committee whose last meeting was in June 2015.

It was clear from the beginning that the meanings of 'curriculum integration/fusion' and 'Catholic perspectives' needed to be clearly defined. Reminiscent of Chesterton's views on Christianity, it might be said that

Introduction 7

curriculum integration is one of the great educational ideas that, for a variety of reasons, has rarely been implemented. As reported in Chapter 10, it was decided to adopt Drake's (2012) four component model integration ladder. As already observed, the Chair's brief made specific reference to CST and it was decided to 'operationalise' Catholic perspectives in these terms. This decision was informed, *inter alia*, by concerns regarding the impact of market ideologies on Catholic schools (Gleeson, 2015) as explicated in Chapter 1, by the thinking of Professor Gerald Grace (2013) at the Institute for Education in London on the relevance of CST to the school curriculum and by the work of the Ontario Institute for Catholic Education and its District Boards on the integration of CST across the curriculum in their schools since 1996 (Institute for Catholic Education, 1996).

Given the Chair's previous experience with enacting curriculum development change in Ireland and the United Kingdom, it was his belief from the very outset that the most effective response to the brief would involve an action research approach with teachers in their schools and classrooms. With that in mind it was decided, with the support of the Advisory Committee, to undertake reconnaissance, always the first stage of action research. The Committee provided support for the design and dissemination of a survey that sought to establish the views of teachers in Queensland Catholic schools with respect to the faith-based identity, purposes and characteristics of these schools and the integration of Catholic perspectives across the curriculum (Gleeson, O'Gorman, Goldburg, & O'Neill, 2018; Gleeson, O'Gorman, & O'Neill, 2018; Gleeson & O'Neill, 2017a). A longitudinal study of the associated attitudes and beliefs of ACU pre-service teachers was also conducted (Gleeson & O'Neill, 2017b) and case reports on approaches to embedding social justice across the curriculum in two Religious Institute schools were prepared.[1]

While finding schools and teachers for the planning and implementation phases of the action research proved difficult, some 30 volunteers from seven schools (including two secondary schools) eventually engaged in the project, some more actively than others. We are greatly indebted to all these teachers. As may be seen by visiting the action research part of our website,[2] (and from reading Chapter 11), the outcomes of this action research were very positive and provide valuable lessons for future attempts to integrate Catholic perspectives and/or CST across the curriculum beyond RE.

Overview of this publication

This publication draws together the main activities, outcomes and lessons of the Identity and Curriculum in Catholic Education project (2013–2018) under one cover. The central focus of the book is the relationship between the faith-based identity of Catholic schools and the formal curriculum of these schools. This relationship is of great interest, not only to Catholic educators, but also to other faith-based education systems and the wider education community.

The primary focus of Part 1 is on the relevance of CST to modern education systems. Catholic Education policymakers, scholars and practitioners are challenged in Chapter 1 to consider the ever-increasing global impact of neoliberal ideologies and market values on national education policies (Rizvi & Lingard, 2010). When such global forces are tempered by local influences, the resulting process of 'glocalisation' (Priestley, 2002) can afford schools the opportunity to preserve their unique identities. Countercultural CST has the potential to be a key agent in the 'glocalisation' of Catholic schools. Chapters 2–4 provide a general introduction to CST followed by two chapters focusing on the implications for education of two recent and particularly relevant Papal Encyclicals, *Laudato Si'* and *Caritas in Veritate*. The obvious potential for the systematic integration of human rights across the curriculum is discussed in Chapter 5. Ontario Catholic schools have moved beyond the rhetoric to actually implementing the integration of Catholic perspectives across the curriculum and their approach is set out in Chapter 6.

The findings of the research conducted by the Identity and Curriculum in Catholic Education project are presented and discussed in Part 2 (Chapters 7–12). Chapter 7 reports on a large-scale mixed methods study of the opinions, attitudes and beliefs of teachers in Queensland Catholic schools regarding the identity, purpose and characteristics of Catholic schools. Chapter 8 draws on this data to compare the ratings of teachers in Catholic schools in Queensland and the United States (Convey, 2012) for the perceived importance of given characteristics of Catholic schools. The findings of a longitudinal study of the opinions and attitudes of pre-service teachers at an ACU regarding the purposes and characteristics of Catholic schools are presented in Chapter 9. The views of Queensland teachers regarding the planned integration of curriculum perspectives across the curriculum form the basis of Chapter 10. The aforementioned action research in seven Queensland Catholic schools, where volunteer teachers sought to integrate various CST principles in their teaching of particular curriculum units, is the focus of Chapter 11. The main lessons of the Identity and Curriculum in Catholic Education Project are synthesised in Chapter 12 and their wider implications are considered.

The co-editors are aware that most readers are more likely to read individual chapters or sections of this type of book on a needs basis rather than from beginning to end and it is hoped that the inevitable repetition across some chapters will not upset readers unduly. Such repetition arises because more than half of these chapters had already been published in refereed journals and are reproduced here, sometimes with relevant updates, with the permission of the journal editors. Since it was necessary to include certain aspects of the same contextual material in each of these papers, some repetition is inevitable when all papers are collected into one volume. While most papers are formatted in APA, please note that previously published papers are formatted in the style required by the journal in which they were originally published.

Notes

1. Section B at https://www.acu.edu.au/625130.
2. See project website under action research activities at http://www.acu.edu.au/1280444.

References

Australian Government. (2014). *Review of the Australian Curriculum: Final Report*. Canberra: Australian Government Department of Education.

Ball, S. J. (2012). *Global Education, Inc: New policy networks and the neo-liberal imaginary*. Routledge.

Belmonte, A., & Cranston, N. (2009). The religious dimension of lay leadership in Catholic schools: Preserving Catholic culture in an era of change. *Catholic Education: A Journal of Inquiry and Practice, 12*(3), 294–319.

Boeve, L. (2005). Religion after detraditionalization: Christian faith in a post-secular Europe. *Irish Theological Quarterly, 70*(2), 99–122. doi: 10.1177/002114000507000201.

Catholic Education Commission, NSW (2014). Submission to the Review of the Australian Curriculum. Sydney: Catholic Education Commission.

Congregation for Catholic Education (CCE). (1997). *The Catholic school on the threshold of the third millennium*. London: Catholic Truth Society.

Congregation for Catholic Education (CCE). (2014). *Educating today and tomorrow, A renewing passion, Instrumentum laboris*. London: Catholic Truth Society.

Convey, J. J. (2012). Perceptions of Catholic identity: Views of Catholic school administrators and teachers. *Catholic Education: A Journal of Inquiry and Practice, 16*(1), 187–214.

Croke, B. (2007). Australian Catholic schools in a changing political and religious landscape. In *International handbook of Catholic education – Challenges for school systems in the 21st century* (pp. 811–834). Dordrecht: Springer.

D'Orsa, T. (2013). Catholic curriculum: Re-framing the conversation. *International Studies in Catholic Education, 5*(1), 68–82. doi: 10.1080/19422539.2012.754589.

Dowling, A., Beavis, A., Underwood, C., Sadeghi, R., & O'Malley, K. (2009). *Who's coming to school today? Final report*. Brisbane: ACER, Brisbane Catholic Education.

Drake, S. (2012). *Creating standards-based integrated curriculum*. Thousand Oaks, CA: Corwin Press.

Gleeson, J. (2015). Critical challenges and dilemmas for Catholic education leadership internationally. *International Studies in Catholic Education, 7*(2), 145–161. doi: 10.1080/19422539.2015.1072955.

Gleeson, J., O'Gorman, J., Goldburg, P., & O'Neill, M. M. (2018). The characteristics of Catholic schools: Comparative perspectives from the USA and Queensland, Australia. *Journal of Catholic Education, 21*(2), 76–106.

Gleeson, J., O'Gorman, J., & O'Neill, M. (2018). The identity of Catholic schools as seen by teachers in Catholic schools in Queensland. *International Studies in Catholic Education, 10*(1), 44–65.

Gleeson, J., & O'Neill, M. (2017a). Curriculum, culture and Catholic education: A Queensland perspective. *Curriculum Perspectives, 37*(2), 121–133.

Gleeson, J., & O'Neill, M. (2017b). Student-teacher's perspectives on the purposes and characteristics of faith-based schools: An Australian view. *British Journal of Religious Education, 40*(1), 55–69.

Grace, G. (2013). Catholic social teaching should permeate the Catholic secondary school curriculum an agenda for reform. *International Studies in Catholic Education, 5*(1), 99–109.

Hargreaves, A. (2003). *Teaching in the knowledge society*. New York, NY: Teachers College.

Institute for Catholic Education. (1996). *Curriculum matters: A resource for Catholic educators*. Toronto: Author.

Lane D. A. (2015). *Catholic education in the light of Vatican II and Laudato Si'*. Dublin: Veritas

Lane, D. A. (1991). *Catholic education and the school. Some theological reflections*. Dublin: Veritas.

Lingard, B. (2010). Policy borrowing, policy learning: Testing times in Australian schooling. *Critical Studies in Education, 51*(2), 129–147. doi: 10.1080/17508481003731026.

Pascoe, S. (2007). Challenges for Catholic education in Australia. In G. Grace & S. J. Joseph O'Keefe (Eds.), *International handbook of Catholic education – Challenges for school systems in the 21st century* (pp. 787–810). Dordrecht: Springer.

Polesel, J., Rice, S., & Dulfer, N. (2014). The impact of high-stakes testing on curriculum and pedagogy: A teacher perspective from Australia. *Journal of Education Policy, 29*(5), 640–657. doi: 10.1080/02680939.2013.865082.

Pollefeyt, D., & Bouwens, J. (2010). Framing the identity of Catholic schools: Empirical methodology for quantitative research on the Catholic identity of an education institute. *International Studies in Catholic Education, 2*(2), 193–211. Retrieved from https://doi.org/10.1080/19422539.2010.504034

Pope Francis. (2015). *Encyclical letter Laudato Si' on care for our common home*. Strathfield: St. Pauls.

Priestley, M. (2002). Global discourses and national reconstruction: The impact of globalization on curriculum policy. *The Curriculum Journal, 13*(1), 121–138. doi: 10.1080/09585170110115295.

Rizvi, F., & Lingard, B. (2010). *Globalizing education policy*. London: Routledge.

Sachs, J., & Mockler, N. (2012). Performance cultures of teaching: Threat or opportunity? In C. Day (Ed.), *International handbook on teacher and school development* (pp. 33–43). Abingdon: Routledge.

Scanlan, M. (2013). The grammar of Catholic schooling and radically 'Catholic' schools. *Catholic Education: A Journal of Inquiry and Practice, 12*(1), 25–54.

Taylor, C. (2007). *A secular age*. Cambridge, MA: Harvard University Press.

Treston, K. (2001). *Emergence for life not fall from grace*. Brisbane: Morning Star Publishing.

Chapter 1

Critical challenges and dilemmas for Catholic Education leadership internationally[1]

Jim Gleeson

Introduction

Catholic Education systems face a number of challenges today, including church/state relations, the relationship between faith and culture, the meaning of Catholic identity, declining levels of religious observance and the aging profile of religious teaching communities. Conscious of the tendency for Catholic Education systems to focus on their own uniqueness, the author addresses a challenge of a different order, one that arises from the hegemony of scientific-technical reason and market-driven neoliberal values, a hegemony that militates against gospel values. The chapter considers appropriate responses to this ideology from the perspectives of curriculum policy and practice and the social values of the gospels, particularly the option for the poor. It is based on the author's keynote address at the 2013 Australian Catholic University (ACU) Catholic Leadership Conference and reflects his familiarity with education systems in Ireland and Australia.

Grace's (1989) fundamental question remains valid – 'Education: Commodity or Public Good?' While Grace's main focus was on the value of a liberal education, it was not long before the discourse of the neoliberal ideology came to dominate. Today the term neoliberal has come to be 'used so widely and so loosely that it is in danger of becoming meaningless' (Ball, 2012, p. 3). For the purposes of this chapter, it refers to the adoption of private and social enterprise approaches to publicly funded education systems, often referred to as the new managerialism.

The hegemony of scientific-technical reason means that, redolent of the Christian existentialist philosopher Gabriel Marcel, issues of great human significance are portrayed as problems that can be solved by the relevant experts. The emphasis is on performance indicators and on finding the most economic and effective solutions to such problems, as instanced, for example, by Dubai Knowledge Village (DKV).[2] This culture of pragmatism, predicated on what Habermas (1972) calls the 'technical paradigm', is characterised by value neutrality and declining levels of critical public debate. Within the prevailing environment of enterprise and competition, there is a premium on individual rights to property ownership, legal protection and market freedom, while civic society, community values, social democracy and citizenship rights are eschewed. The focus is on collective responsibility, national identity and the pursuit of self-interest facilitates what Sennett (1998, p. 26) calls 'the corrosion of character'.

Neoliberal policies and education

Modern education systems are characterised by an undue emphasis on the relationship between education and economic growth and a growing obsession with performativity and league tables:

> … the global policy convergence in schooling has seen the economisation of schooling policy, the emergence of human capital and productivity rationales as meta-policy in education, and new accountabilities, including high-stakes testing and policy, as numbers, with both global and national features. (Lingard, 2010, p. 136)

This 'new orthodoxy in education' (Ball, 1998) questions the very aims and purposes of public education. It identifies education as the key instrument for producing the new global citizen and as a major component of economic globalisation, while teachers are viewed, in an environment that is devoid of trust, as productive workers deprived of professional autonomy. The outcomes of this new managerialist approach are evident in the annual Organisation for Economic Co-operation and Development (OECD) production, *Education at a Glance*, with its myriad of league tables that facilitate contractual rather than professional accountability[3] (Gleeson & Ó Donnabháin, 2009). Within this environment, the growing power and influence of the modern state in education is legitimated by economic concerns. As former Australian Prime Minister Gillard stated:

> Put simply, we cannot have the strong economy we want tomorrow, unless we have the best of education in our schools today. That is why the plan that I am announcing today is a plan for our schools to be in the world's top five by 2025. (The Australian, 2013, April 14)

This is to ignore Brown and Lauder's (2012) conclusion that 'the human capital theory on which official policy discourse is based is fundamentally flawed because it assumes that all can capitalise on the demands for knowledge and skills, because they are key to increasing productivity and products' (p. 6). Nor does it take cognisance of Wolf's (2002) observation that 'our preoccupation with education as an engine of growth has only narrowed the way we think about social policy' (p. 251).

This new managerialist culture redefines knowledge and education within 'the legitimate framework of public choice and market accountability' (Lynch, Grummel, & Devine, 2012, p. 4). The associated growth in policy entrepreneurship is reflected in the emergence of major international education consultancy businesses and transnational advocacy networks such as the Atlas Economic Research Foundation, the Liberty network and Tooley's Templeton Foundation (Ball, 2012). Such networks facilitate policy borrowing (Lingard, 2010) and constitute a new form of governance, what Ball (2012) calls 'a market of authorities' (p. 9). This means that 'the boundaries between state, economy and civil society are being blurred [while] multilateral agencies, NGOs and business interests and influences can separately or together constitute a powerful policy alternative to state "failure"' (Ball, 2012). The activities of such networks are heavily focused on developing countries and their policies are 'typically discussed and portrayed within a paradigm of progressive policy solutions, vulnerable constituencies and community empowerment related to human rights and environmental issues in particular' (Ball, 2012, p. 12).

The World Trade Organization's General Agreement on Trade and Services (GATS) regards education and other public services as marketable goals where 'the student is defined as an economic maximiser, governed by self-interest [and] and capable of making market-led choices' (Lynch et al., 2012, p. 14). In this environment, education is perceived as a consumable good rather than 'a key instrument in protecting people's human rights' (Lynch et al., 2012). Some 10 years ago, Merrill Lynch estimated that the global market in educational services was worth $111 billion a year outside of the United States with a 'potential consumer base of 32 million students' (Spring, 2009, p. 84). This market ideology is portrayed 'as a natural way of doing things' (Gandin, 2006, p. 192), while social policy decisions in education are increasingly being defined by powerful intergovernmental organisations, such as the United Nations, OECD, the World Bank and the International Monetary Fund (Ball, 2008; Ditchburn, 2012; Spring, 2009).

Impact on education practice

The neoliberal agenda impacts on the practice of schooling in many ways. The emphasis is on measurable outputs, employment-related skills and competences, consumer choice, increased state control over curriculum content and assessment and standardised testing. The associated curriculum discourse is highly technicist, standardised and universalistic in character, with the definition, selection and structuring of legitimate knowledge being externally prescribed and prioritising the self-realisation of the individual child. Curriculum is seen in terms of product rather than process, something that the teacher must 'deliver', rather like the mail or the milk. For example, Michael Barber's (former Head of the UK Prime Minister's Delivery Unit) address to the African Development Bank in March 2010 was titled 'An Introduction to Deliverology' (Ball, 2012, p. 108).

Au (2013) sees *No Child Left Behind* (NCLB) in the United States, with its roots 'in the logics of competition and markets of neoliberal capitalism', as the prelude to their recently introduced Common Core State Standards (CCSS). He argues that Obama's 'Race to the Top' means that NCLB is more deeply entrenched than ever, with test score results being used as the main justification for charter schools[4] which are undermining both public and Catholic education systems.

From an Australian perspective, Lingard (2010) sees the recent introduction of their national curriculum as part of a nation-building exercise involving the alignment of curriculum with global economic imperatives. From the perspective of neighbouring New Zealand, an early adopter of the neoliberal agenda, Dale (2000) argued that the popularity of standardised models of education meant that the school curriculum had become 'a ritual enactment of worldwide educational norms and conventions rather than instrumental choice of individual societies to meet various local requirements' (p. 431).

There has been a proliferation of standardised testing programmes such as the OECD's Programme for International Student Assessment (PISA), the National Assessment Plan – Literacy and Numeracy (NAPLAN) in Australia and NCLB. This has resulted in a wide variety of tensions between, for example educational quality and [e]quality, education as public good and competitive private commodity, 'having an education' and 'being an educated person', the role of the teacher as technician/professional.

The spread of this ideology has also had regrettable implications for schools, as reflected in Hargreaves (2003) study of the influence of neoliberal reforms on the highly progressive, student-centred, Blue Mountain School in Ontario. He concluded that inflexibly mandated, standardised reform measures impacted on all aspects of the school's work and culture and 'chipped steadily away at Blue Mountain's distinctive approach to teaching and learning' (Hargreaves, 2003, p. 146).

> In its short history, Blue Mountain has built a strong and enviable reputation for caring, among pupils and staff alike. But the secure selves and relationships on which effective caring depends are being consistently undermined by the effects of large-scale, standardized reform. (p. 151)

One of the defining characteristics of neoliberal policies has been an emphasis on outcomes-based education (OBE). The shortcomings of this approach have been well documented (Gleeson, 2013; Hussey & Smith, 2002; Stenhouse, 1975). While OBE is appropriate for training and instruction, it fails to recognise the importance of induction into the thought processes of the disciplines (Stenhouse, 1975), a process that draws on the essential nature of these disciplines and/or on child-centred ethical/pedagogical principles.

There is a growing realisation that PISA[5] results exert enormous and disproportionate influence on education policy. Almost 100 high-ranking international educationalists including many well-known professors of education called on the PISA director to halt the next round of testing (*The Guardian*, UK, 6 May 2014). Their overall concern is that PISA is a form of 'educational colonialism', heavily influenced by psychometricians, statisticians and economists, that harms our children, impoverishes our classrooms, further increases stress levels in schools and endangers the well-being of students and teachers.

They identified a number of particular causes for anxiety including the resulting escalation in standardised testing, the associated reliance on quantitative measures, the limitations of the actual instruments themselves, the obsession with short-term 'fixes' to help a country climb the rankings quickly, the backwash effect on physical, moral, civic and artistic education and the associated neglect of personal development, growth and well-being.

Noting the planned introduction of PISA testing to Africa, the authors suggest that OECD has formed alliances with multinational for-profit companies (policy entrepreneurs) that stand to gain financially from elementary education there. As they scathingly point out, 'comparing developing countries, where 15-year-olds are regularly drafted into child labour, with first-world countries makes neither educational nor political sense'.

The authors challenge the role of the OECD directly in their concluding paragraph:

> OECD's narrow focus on standardised testing risks turning learning into drudgery and killing the joy of learning. As PISA has led many governments into an international competition for higher test scores, OECD has assumed the power to shape education policy around the world, with no debate about the necessity or limitations of OECD's goals. We are deeply concerned that measuring a great diversity of educational traditions and cultures using a single, narrow, biased yardstick could, in the end, do irreparable harm to our schools and our students.

Not all critics of the prevailing ideology of standardised testing are academics. We have recently seen a significant *volte-face* on the part of the Editorial Board of the *New York Times* (July 2013) on this issue. While defending the NCLB Act as an exercise in school accountability, they acknowledge that 'it has become clear to us over time that testing was being overemphasized – and misused – in schools that were substituting test preparation for instruction'.

This ideology is based on certain principles that are at variance with those that underpin faith-based educational systems. Some of the countercultural possibilities of these systems are now considered.

Faith-based education and the neoliberal agenda

In his analysis of the impact of globalisation on education policy and practice, Spring (2009) notes that 'some religious and indigenous groups are major dissenters to the world culture and the materialism embodied in the human capital and progressive education models' (p. 144). Spring's (2009) examples include Gandhi's Sarvodaya, state-supported Islamic Education with its holistic vision of knowledge and education expounded by Al Zeera and liberation theology which seeks to 'free humans from the spiritual vacuum caused by political and economic repression' (p. 161). The Peruvian theologian Gutierrez saw liberation theology, influenced by Paolo Freire,[6] as creative, fruitful and ultimately political: 'liberation theology's educational programmes were practised by the Sandinista National Liberation Front in Nicaragua which overthrew the dictatorship of the Somoza dynasty in 1979 and in neighbouring El Salvador by National Liberation Front' (Spring, 2009, p. 166).

Strong religious faith 'is not an "add-on" to the rest of life, but something that has an influence on the way that the whole of life is lived [which makes it] inevitable that those starting new schools should see the nature of the curriculum as one of the central features that they wished to control and develop' (Walford, 2002, p. 404). For example, Hewer (2001) emphasises that 'the whole of education in the Muslim world is seen as a faith-centred integrated ... Islamic system that brings out profound challenges to any idea of a "value-neutral" concept of education' (pp. 522–523).

While recognising that the Muslim ideal involves the integration of faith across the whole curriculum, Walford (2002) notes that the shortage of Muslim teachers and the cost of curriculum development make this difficult in practice. Although acknowledging that some Christian Evangelical groups have devoted considerable energy to curriculum, he concludes that their 'practical attempts to design a curriculum that rejects humanism and secularism and, instead, reflects Christianity have met with various degrees of success' (Walford, 2002, p. 408). He offers the example of the Christian Schools Trust Curriculum Team for Science which offered alternative values to the 'idols of science, technology and economic growth ... [found] in secular textbooks and syllabi' (Walford, 2002, p. 411).

Taking a less extreme example, it is noteworthy that the first principle of the Norwegian core curriculum is that of 'the spiritual human being [based on] fundamental Christian and humanistic values'. The Royal Ministry of Education (1997) declares that

> our Christian and humanistic tradition places equality, human rights and rationality at the fore. Social progress is sought in reason and enlightenment, and in man's ability to create, appreciate and communicate. Together, this interwoven tradition provides us with unwithering values both to orient our conduct and to organize our communities. (p. 7)

Their other key curriculum principles are part of this piece – the creative human being, the working human being, the liberally educated human being, the social human being, the environmentally aware human being and the integrated human being.

The Vatican's Congregation for Catholic Education (CCE) has consistently adopted a holistic, integrated approach to education. For example, it has commented critically on the 'noticeable tendency to reduce education to its purely technical and practical aspects' (CCE, 1997, p. 10) and defined its educational project as a 'synthesis between culture and faith' (p. 14). It sees the fundamental characteristics of the Catholic school in terms of the 'integral education of the human person through a clear educational project of which Christ is the foundation … [involving] ecclesial and cultural identity … love [and] service to society' (CCE, 1997, p. 4). While acknowledging that 'we live in a knowledge-based society', the CCE (2013, p. 66) encourages Catholic schools 'to go beyond knowledge and educate people to think, evaluating facts in the light of values'.

The most recent CCE (2014) document again calls for a holistic, integrated education in a context where 'contemporary educators have a renewed mission, which has the ambitious aim of offering young people an integral education as well as assistance in discovering their personal freedom, which is a gift from God' (p. 10). In a clear reaction to neoliberal values, it warns against simply responding to 'the demands deriving from the ever-changing economic situation. Catholic schools think out their curricula to place centre-stage both individuals and their search for meaning … What is taught is not neutral, and neither is the way of teaching it' (CCE, 2014, p. 64). Reminiscent of Stenhouse (1975), the CCE (2014) notes that education goes well beyond instruction, and comments critically on the 'merely functional view of education' taken by the European Union, OECD, World Bank and on the instrumental and competitive emphases found in the education policies of several countries with their 'instrumental reason and competitiveness … [concerned with] the market economy and the labour market' (p. 12).

Writing in an Irish context, Tuohy (2013) argues that Catholic education 'goes beyond training in skills and the competition for qualifications. It helps individuals to seek wholeness, truth and hope in their lives [and] sees the person as essentially social, and therefore promotes a sense of community based on solidarity, the promotion of justice and making a difference' (p. 121).

While the CCE (1977) recognised that 'education is an important means of improving the social and economic condition of the individual and of peoples', it also argued that 'the Church should offer its educational services first to the poor or those deprived of family help or affection, or those far from the faith' (p. 68). Failure would contribute towards the perpetuation of privilege, 'and could thereby continue to favour a society which is unjust' (CCE, 1977). The CCE (2014) declared that 'the kind of education that is promoted by

Catholic schools is not aimed at establishing an elitist meritocracy' (p. 12), while the CCE (2013) proposed more recently that the curriculum of Catholic schools must address 'the unequal distribution of resources, poverty, injustice and human rights denied' (p. 66).

The remaining sections of this chapter will address two challenges: bringing a Catholic perspective to the whole curriculum and giving witness to the gospel value of justice, fairness and equality.

Curriculum integration: Bringing a faith-based perspective to the curriculum of Catholic schools

Curricula are never value free (Cornbleth, 1990; Grundy, 1987) and, as noted earlier, denominational school groups wish to see their own particular perspective reflected in their curricula. From the Evangelical Christian perspective, Walford (2002) suggests that Christian definitions of school subjects 'offer a coherence to the entire school curriculum that is usually absent (or certainly not made explicit but is actually in the form of secularism, individualism and so on)' (p. 412). Hewer (2001) argues that every aspect of study in a Muslim school 'should be permeated by Islamic values and the divinely ordained harmony should be brought out by the educational process'. This argument is frequently made from a Catholic perspective, for example Davis and Franchi (2013) and Arthur (2013), with the latter suggesting that

> religion cannot be separated or divorced from the rest of the curriculum, nor can religious education be seen as the raison d'etre of the Catholic school. The idea that the school subjects that make up the curriculum (excluding religious education) are value-free and therefore somehow separate from the Catholic faith is clearly contrary to the Catholic worldview (Arthur, 2013, p. 86).

The CCE (1977) suggests that 'all academic subjects can contribute to the development of a mature Christian' (p. 37), while Groome (2003) argues that the 'distinctive characteristics of Catholicism should be reflected in the whole curriculum of Catholic schools' (p. 107). Murray (1991), former Catholic Bishop of Limerick, identified five key elements of a philosophy of education: wholeness, which requires the education of the whole person; truth, which requires open expression of the values that underpin the work of the school; awakening the minds of students to economic, cultural, racial and religious injustices; respect for the honest, systematic and respectful search for truth and freedom to challenge and develop the artistic, imaginative, innovative and creative capacities of the pupil. Arguing that increased attention to science and technology must not lead to the neglect of the humanities, he flags the danger of reducing education to producing good material for the workplace or good citizens for the state rather than promoting 'the integral development of good people capable of living a fully human life' (Murray, 1991, p. 23). Murray's (1991) response, along with some other Irish colleagues, is to advocate curriculum integration:

> Education should lead to the integration of what is learned, breaking down traditional subject demarcations, overcoming fragmentation and encouraging dialogue between disciplines ... [and] address the integral development of the person: aesthetic, creative, critical, cultural, emotional, intellectual, moral, physical, political, social and spiritual. (p. 20)

> RE alone does not make the Catholic school ... The Catholic school seeks to integrate the curriculum, to unify faith and culture, and to bring together the different pieces of the school programme into a higher synthesis that influences the social and spiritual formation of pupils. (Lane, 1991, p. 12)

> The issue of depth and integration of learning is a constant challenge – a counter-cultural demand in an approach dominated by a 'surfing' mentality.[7] (Tuohy, 2013, p. 121)

The CCE (2014) also recognises the importance of an interdisciplinary approach to knowledge:

> ... each discipline is not an island inhabited by a form of knowledge that is distinct and ring-fenced; rather, it is in a dynamic relationship with all other forms of knowledge, each of which expresses something about the human person and touches upon some truth. (p. 67)

Arguing that Catholic social teaching should permeate the Catholic secondary school curriculum, Grace (2010, 2013) suggests that 'Catholic educational institutions at all levels have failed to provide curriculum mediations of this teaching as a crucial part of the formation of Catholic youth' (2013, p. 99). Drawing on the countercultural teaching of *Caritas in Veritate*, he identifies some key relevant issues including religious, moral and cultural; economic, business and enterprise and social, environmental and political. To this author's knowledge, individual Australian schools and Edmund Rice Education Australia are responding impressively to this call.[8]

It is, however, one thing to promote the notion of curriculum integration and another to implement it. While Beane (1997) and Morris (2003) have identified some nine different forms of curriculum integration, these can be reduced to three broad modes. In the multidisciplinary approach, subject disciplines continue to be taught separately with a particular theme being infused where possible. The interdisciplinary approach uses subject disciplines as tools for the study of particular problems, themes or questions. In the transdisciplinary approach, students' interests and questions become the main focus while subject boundaries are further blurred (Drake, 2012;

Drake & Burns, 2004). Gehrke (1998) sees the multi- and interdisciplinary approaches as being closely related insofar as the 'subject areas never lose their distinctive forms [and the] integrity of the disciplines is the chief concern' (p. 255), whereas the alternative transdisciplinary or 'unified studies' approach begins from 'consideration of life experiences and individual and societal needs [where] the integrity of the learner's experience, not the discipline, is the chief concern' (p. 256).

The work of the Ontario Institute of Catholic Education is regarded as one of the best examples of curriculum development and integration in Catholic schools (Arthur, 2013, p. 94). The Institute for Catholic Education (1996, p. 25) has identified three related contexts for Catholic education:

- Philosophical, based on revealed wisdom, commitment to learning excellence and a search for the common good.
- Theological, characterised by a Christ-centred faith, an incarnational anthropology, a sacramental worldview and an ecclesial sense of community.
- Curricular tasks.

Their curricular tasks fall into three categories:

- Subject specific (separation) where religion is a course of study like other academic disciplines.
- Whole-school (permeation) where the emphasis is on the role and influence of the Catholic school's culture in learning, for example pastoral care, parish and school celebrations, nurturing spirituality and outreach programmes.
- Cross-curricular (inter- and transdisciplinary) integration which brings together traditional subjects to meaningfully address themes, skills and role performance.

The Institute for Catholic Education (1996) proposes that 'curriculum integration carries within it the capacity to develop curriculum that visibly demonstrates the Catholic character of learning' (p. 26) and to provide 'an authentic fit' between the knowledge, values and skills of, for example religion and science; religion and social studies and religion and business. It recognises that integration involves 'a critical perspective on social and global issues so that curriculum is transformative and functions as a vehicle for social and personal change based on principles of justice and the view of the learner as agent of change'. It warns against superimposing/forcing religious concepts and ideas into subject areas in the name of integration, with little regard for the integrity of the academic discipline because this simply produces superficial and trivial links.

The Institute for Catholic Education (1997) has defined a common set of Catholic Graduate Expectations that include discerning believer; effective communicator; reflective, creative and holistic thinker; lifelong learner; caring family member; commitment to the common good and responsible citizen. It has also produced written guidelines for writing curriculum for Catholic schools and has established regional Curriculum cooperatives which use these guidelines to create teacher resources for educators wishing to integrate Catholic perspectives across the formal curriculum using both multi- and interdisciplinary models of integration. The supports provided for the integration of a Catholic perspective in Ontario include the following:

- Course profiles (by grade and subject), developed in conjunction with the Ministry of Education, involve the fusion of their Graduate Expectations with the Ontario Ministry of Education expected learning outcomes for specific subjects to create resources for teachers in Catholic classrooms – a form of multidisciplinary integration.
- Catholic critical literacy materials that provide support for teachers wishing to address Catholic Social Teaching in their own subjects, for example option for the poor and vulnerable; stewardship of creation and community and the common good. This also involves multidisciplinary integration.
- Catholic Curriculum Maps (Catholic Curriculum Corporation, 2006) facilitate the integration of the expected learning outcomes of the catechetical programme across the whole curriculum. A particular Catholic social teaching is taken as the key theme for each year group and a common set of 'essential questions' provides a Catholic focus for all subject areas. The use of key themes and essential questions means that, depending on the teachers involved, this approach has the potential to be interdisciplinary. Drake (2012) argues that curriculum mapping facilitates accountability in relation to the achievement of standards while helping to 'create a seamless curriculum' (pp. 39–51).

The maps and profiles continue to be revised in order to keep in step with provincial curriculum revisions and it appears that teachers have begun to take ownership of this process to the point where they need less guidance from the centre. This elaborate plan for the integration of a Catholic perspective is focused thematically around their Catholic Graduate Expectations, Catholic Social Teaching and essential questions grounded in faith formation.[9]

Drake and Burns (2004) argue that, when teachers become more familiar with a standards-based approach, they are enthusiastic about integrating areas of curriculum and 'their perception of interdisciplinary curriculum shifts dramatically' (pp. 2–3). While Catholic schools in the United States operate in a rather different environment, standards play a key role in their education policy and Catholic educators have developed a set of national standards and benchmarks for effective Catholic Elementary and Secondary schools.

CCSS have been adopted by 100 Catholic dioceses across 35 states and, according to Shimek (2014), the National Catholic Education Association is satisfied that this does not 'in any way compromise the Catholic identity or educational program of a school'. There is no guarantee however that their introduction will facilitate an integrated approach. Based on survey responses from 3,389 teachers in Catholic schools across the United States, Convey (2012) found that that the integration of Catholic teachings into the curriculum had an average ranking of fifth (of 12 possible characteristics of the Catholic school). This item also showed the greatest variation among responding teachers and administrators, receiving higher ratings from administrators and more experienced teachers than from other respondents.

Notwithstanding its focus on skills, the prevailing neoliberal ideology provides a particularly hospitable environment for the preservation of clear subject boundaries, the great barrier to curriculum integration. As noted by Lam, Alviar-Martin, Adler, and Sim (2013), 'as the push for accountability and standardised testing increased, the voices supporting integrated curricula receded' (p. 23). The net result is that 'the tenacity of subject-based curricula has been reinforced by global trends toward neoliberalism [which] forwards essentialist and perennialist agendas, embodied in standards-based reforms, high-stake examinations, accountability and ranking, and discourses focused on excellence' (Lam et al., 2013, p. 25).

As noted earlier, the prevailing neoliberal climate is characterised by increased emphasis on parental choice. This raises big questions for schools with a mission to give witness to gospel values.

Gospel values in a neoliberal environment: What is happening to 'the option for the poor'?

Market values and gospel values cannot coexist happily, and the adoption of neoliberal values has clear implications for education equality and justice. According to Maddox (2014):

> Choice has widened the gaps between the wealthy and the rest, and also hammered in some religious wedges … Today's neoliberal outsourcing push sees around 40 per cent of Australian children in education that is not free, although governments subsidise some of the costs. The latter constituency is growing with enrolments in independent schools growing by 35 per cent; and Catholic school enrolments by 11.6 per cent during the first decade of the new millennium. (pp. xi–xii)

This leads her to conclude that 'the overall makeup of Australian education is shifted away from the all-in-this-together ideal that inspired the founders of Australia's free and secular public system towards one where children are once again segregated by income, culture and religion'

(Maddox, 2014, pp. 86–87). Lye and Hirschberg (2012) found that fees charged by non-government schools in the Australian state of Victoria have been 'increasing at a very high rate along with the number of students attending these schools [with] more and more of the expense for secondary school education [being] borne directly by the parents of the students' (p. 11). The upshot is that Catholic schools in Victoria are becoming more privileged:

> Independent schools attract the more affluent families with the highest [Index of Community Socio-Educational Advantage] on average followed by Catholic and then Government schools which have minimal fees [and] consequently family income is not a barrier to enrol. (Lye & Hirschberg, 2012, p. 11)

In their study of students attending Catholic schools in Brisbane, Dowling, Beavis, Underwood, Sadeghi, and O'Malley (2009, p. 6) draw attention to the apparent contradiction that 'as society is becoming more secular, Catholic schools are becoming more popular than ever'. They concluded that the parents of children attending Catholic schools in Brisbane were strongly influenced by neoliberal thinking insofar as they 'have a pragmatic view of Catholic education and are most concerned about quality instruction and training for employment' (Dowling et al., 2009, p. 114).

As noted by Tuohy (2008), 'when the Catholic school is seen to be very successful, the motivation for seeking places may be more related to the quality of general education than to the desire for a particularly Catholic ethos' (p. 11). The Brisbane findings regarding the growing popularity of Catholic schools support Tuohy's argument – 'while parents provide numerous reasons for sending their children to non-government schools, the desire for a specifically religious education does not appear to be dominant, even amongst Catholic schools' (Dowling et al., 2009, p. 20). Teachers in Catholic schools are expressing concerns that parents see Catholic education as a more affordable version of private schooling (Gleeson & O'Neill, 2018). These market-driven trends have obvious implications for equity and fairness in the school system.

According to Australia's National Catholic Education Commission (2013, p. 86), 53% of the cost of educating a student in Catholic Education in 2011 came from federal government, 18% from state funds and 29% from private income (mainly school fees). Research conducted by the Australian Scholarship Group (ASG) concludes that primary school fees in Catholic schools in metropolitan Australia for 2014 average $3,600 per child as against $485 in government schools and $10,300 in independent schools (many of which are faith-based). They found that the average fees at secondary level are $9,000 in Catholic schools, $980 in government schools and $18,000 in independent schools.

Catholic schools are becoming 'schools of choice' for middle class non-Catholics with over 40% of secondary school students being non-Catholic. The Australian Catholic Bishops Conference (2013) pointed out that only 53% of Catholic students attended Catholic primary or secondary schools. According to McLaughlin and Standen (2013), only one in three low-income Catholic children in Australia attends a Catholic School as against almost 60% of children from high-income families. Their review indicates concern on the part of some members of the Australian Catholic hierarchy:

> Archbishop Barry Hickey of Perth, in an interview with the West Australian newspaper, stated that 'in accepting government grants, the Church's role as an advocate of the poor can be blunted'. (McLaughlin & Standen, 2013)
>
> Catholic schools are overly expensive, and the church has become too middle-class. (Bishop Kevin Manning in an interview with Sarah Price, *Sydney Morning Herald*, 19 August 2007)
>
> Poorer Catholic children are increasingly attending State schools [and] increasing accessibility for all students remains a significant challenge in some places. (Catholic Bishops of New South Wales and ACT, 2007, p. 8)

Tuohy (2008) argues that, in the Irish context, 'the marketing of many Catholic schools, especially fee-paying schools … sits uncomfortably with the Church's stated pursuit of the common good' (p. 131). Noting that upwardly mobile parents in England have been putting their children forward for late baptisms and relocating home in order to qualify for admission to Catholic schools, he recalls instances in Ireland where, 'when the Catholic school is faithful to an inclusive enrolment, parents with high social capital leave the catchment area for schools with a less varied intake' (Tuohy, 2008).

It is important to acknowledge the current tendency in Vatican documents to define poverty in spiritual rather than material terms.

> [The poor today are] those who have lost all sense of meaning in life and lack any type of inspiring ideal, those to whom no values are proposed and who do not know the beauty of faith, who come from families which are broken and incapable of love, often living in situations of material and spiritual poverty; slaves to the new idols of society, which, not infrequently, promises them only a future of unemployment and marginalisation. (CCE, 1997, Section 15)

While the CCE (2013, p. 66) acknowledges that the curriculum must address 'the unequal distribution of resources, poverty, injustice and human rights denied', it goes on to suggest the adoption of 'a broad and developed vision of poverty, in all its various forms and causes'. The following year, *Instrumentum Laboris* called for 'missionary openness towards new forms of poverty' (CCE, 2014, p. 14).

Space allows for only a brief comment on the relationship between consumer choice and education equality. It is regrettable that the significant media attention afforded PISA results focuses mainly on country rankings while ignoring the findings of the PISA meta-analysis (OECD, 2010). This latter analysis reveals some interesting characteristics of high-performing countries:

- Levels of student differentiation between and within schools are low.
- Levels of competition between schools are low.
- The disciplinary climate and teacher-student relations are good.

While the priority afforded disciplinary climate, positive relationships and caring in Australian Catholic schools is widely recognised (Gleeson & O'Flaherty, 2014; Dowling et al., 2009, p. 3), levels of between-schools competition for enrolments are uniquely high with 96% of students enrolled in schools that are in competition with at least one other school. The PISA meta-analysis finds that such competition is generally unrelated to overall student performance once socio-economic background is taken into account. In the case of Australia (OECD, 2010, p. 74), however, when socio-economic background is taken into account, the average reading performance of students attending schools that are in competition for enrolment is 24 points lower than in schools that are not in competition. The Save Our Schools (2010, December 17) movement concludes that the 'availability of choice and competition, a key principle of neoliberal policy, has not improved overall school results in the Australian situation and between-schools competition has brought average results down when socio-economic differences are taken into account'.

Conclusion

As noted by Spring (2009), 'the spiritual nature of religions creates a tension with the materialistic values embedded in human capital theory with its emphasis on economic growth and increasing personal income' (p. 175). From an Irish perspective, Lynch et al. (2012) observe that the Catholic Church has not overtly spoken out against neoliberalism and that 'the Church's concerns have been with retaining their schools rather than challenging new managerialism' (p. 36). Tuohy (2008) concludes that there is greater agreement on the purpose than the identity of Irish Catholic schools in a context where 'public policy in education is more in tune with Catholic social teaching than is the practice of many [Catholic] schools' (Tuohy, 2008, p. 131). Along similar lines, Lynch et al. (2012) contend the Irish church has not addressed the issue of how its values will be expressed in its schools: 'Despite its concern for disadvantaged people … the Catholic Church continued to uphold the elite and socially selective schools that they operate in the second-level sector' (Lynch et al., 2012, p. 36).

The challenges identified in this chapter have important implications for the identity of the Catholic school. Ireland is not atypical in this respect and Dunne (2006) summed up the main options for Catholic education there as follows:

- 'Cut one's losses with schools altogether' (Dunne, 2006, p. 212) and have parishes take on their current catechetical roles.
- 'Step back and ask quite radically what a Catholic education might look like [and] work out its practical implications' (Dunne, 2006). This would require stronger commitment and painful choices on the part of parents and a willingness to forego the luxury of having both 'the right peers and the right points [and would result in] fewer Catholic schools but ones of greater integrity' (Dunne, 2006).
- Challenge the dominant instrumentalist, technicist and ethos of schooling by adopting an overtly political role where schools become 'loci not so much of catechesis as of evangelisation in the broad sense' (Dunne, 2006).
- The status quo.

Catholic Education finds itself between the rock of the gospels and the hard place of neoliberal market values. Given the human propensity to fear change, the growing demand for places in Catholic schools and the changing profiles of both students and teachers in these schools, some version of the status quo is likely to prevail. The environment, however, continues to change with non-Catholics making up 28% of secondary staff in New South Wales in 2006, 24% of students in Catholic schools across Australia being categorised as non-Catholic (Dowling et al., 2009, p. 23), while these expansionary trends continue.

Is it possible to reconcile the prevailing neoliberal culture with gospel values in a context where the Catholic Church is inevitably influenced by prevailing societal values? Hughes (2011), for example reports that 'Australian Christians are divided on most economic issues in similar ways to the wider society' (p. 8). He found that 50% of church attenders favoured increases in social spending as against 46% of the overall population, while 21% of attenders (almost one-third in the case of Catholics) favoured reducing taxes as against 26% of the overall population. Noting that many active Catholics are not familiar with Catholic social teaching,[10] Hughes (2011) concluded that 'the consistent alignment of church attenders with other sectors of the population suggests that their opinions are often shaped largely by culture' (p. 12).

Dunne's countercultural options have the potential to address the disjuncture between gospel values and the prevailing neoliberal values of modern education systems. The OECD (2003) *Schooling for the Future* study recognises the need for new thinking regarding the future viability of the 'robust bureaucratic school' and its associated structures. Some of their suggested systemic alternatives would facilitate the integration of gospel values across the formal as well as the informal school curriculum and their application to school admission policies. This would be consistent both with recent Church statements on education and with the inclusion of a Catholic world view across the whole curriculum of Catholic schools. Any such move will demand strong leadership, intensive professional development and enormous courage, as well as shrewd political negotiation with respect to the all-important matter of funding.[11]

Notes

1. *This paper, originally published in International Studies in Catholic Education, 2015, Vol. Vol. 7, No. 2, pages 145–161, is reproduced here with the kind permission of the Editor.*
2. DKV is the world's only free zone area dedicated to human resource management and learning excellence. Established in 2003 as part of TECOM Investments, DKV aims to develop the region's talent pool and establish the UAE as a knowledge-based economy. With over 500 business partners, DKV offers human resource management, consultation, training and personal development programmes.
3. Contractual models of accountability are measurement-driven and concerned with standards and results, whereas responsive or professional accountability is 'more concerned with processes than outcomes, and with securing involvement and interaction to obtain decisions that meet a range of needs and preferences' (Glatter, 2003, p. 53).
4. Charter schools in the United States are subject to fewer rules, regulations, and statutes than traditional state schools. While they receive less public funding than public schools, as non-profit entities, they can receive donations from private sources. The number of American charter schools has been growing exponentially to some 6,400 in 2013–2014.
5. The PISA is an international survey under the auspices of the OECD. It is conducted every 3 years and aims to evaluate education systems by testing the skills and knowledge of 15-year-old students in reading, mathematics and science. Students representing more than 70 economies have participated in this assessment to date.
6. Paulo Freire's (1921–1997) best known work, *Pedagogy of the Oppressed*, was published in 1968 against the backdrop of gross inequality in Brazil. Other works include *Education, the Practice of Freedom* (1976); *The Politics of Education: Culture, Power, and Liberation* (1985) and *Politics and Education* (1998).
7. As in surfing the Internet for quick-fire answers to complex questions.
8. Edmund Rice Education Australia schools are involved in their Curriculum of Justice and Peace project where the focus is on the development of transformative and liberating curriculum. Other religious institute schools highlight the importance of social justice issues by drawing on the charism of their founder.
9. One of the seven Ontario Catholic schools' Graduate Expectations is the development of responsible citizens who give 'witness to Catholic social teaching by promoting peace, justice and the sacredness of human life'. Their curriculum mapping work involves the integration of all ten principles of Catholic social teaching into the formal school curriculum, grounded in their Religious Education and Family Life programme.
10. See also Grace (2013, p. 99).
11. The author is indebted to Katharine Stevenson, Ontario Catholic Education Institute and to Professor Denis McLaughlin and Dr Phil Standen, Australian Catholic University, for their valuable comments on an earlier draft of this chapter.

References

Arthur, J. (2013). The de-Catholicising of the curriculum in English Catholic schools. *International Studies in Catholic Education, 5*(1), 83–98.

Au, W. (2013). Coring social studies within corporate education reform: The common core state standards, social justice, and the politics of knowledge in US schools. *Critical Education, 4*(5).

Australian Catholic Bishops Conference. (2013). A profile of the Catholic community in Australia March 2013. *Australian Catholic Bishops Conference pastoral research office.* Melbourne: Australian Catholic University. Retrieved from www.catholic.org.au

Ball, S. J. (1998). Big policies/small world: An introduction to international perspectives in education policy. *Comparative Education, 34*(2), 119–130.

Ball, S. J. (2008). *The education debate.* Bristol: The Policy Press.

Ball, S. J. (2012). *Global education Inc.: New policy networks and the neo-liberal imaginary.* London: Routledge.

Beane, J. A. (1997). *Curriculum integration: Designing the core of democratic education.* New York, NY: Teachers College Press.

Brown, P., & Lauder, H. (2012). The great transformation in the global labour market. *Soundings, 51*(51), 41–53.

Catholic Bishops of New South Wales and ACT. (2007). *Catholic schools at a crossroads.* Pastoral letter of the Bishops of New South Wales and the ACT.

Catholic Curriculum Corporation. (2006). *Catholic curriculum maps: Foundational support for Catholic teachers, user guide.* Toronto: Ontario Catholic Education Institute.

Congregation for Catholic Education (CCE). (1977). *The Catholic school.* Vatican City: Author.

Congregation for Catholic Education (CCE). (1997). *The Catholic school on the threshold of the third millennium.* Vatican City: Author.

Congregation for Catholic Education (CCE). (2013). *Educating to intercultural dialogue in Catholic schools. Living in harmony for a civilization of love.* Vatican City: Author.

Congregation for Catholic Education (CCE). (2014). *Educating today and tomorrow, A renewing passion, instrumentum laboris.* Vatican City: Author.

Convey, J. J. (2012). Perceptions of Catholic identity: Views of Catholic school administrators and teachers. *Catholic Education: A Journal of Inquiry and Practice, 16*(1), 187–214.

Cornbleth, C. (1990). *Curriculum in context.* London: Falmer.

Dale, R. (2000). Globalisation, and education: Demonstrating a 'common world educational culture' or locating a 'globally structured educational agenda'! *Educational Theory, 50*(4), 427–448.

Davis, R. A., & Franchi, L. (2013). A Catholic curriculum for the twenty-first century? *International Studies in Catholic Education, 5*(1), 36–52.

Ditchburn, G. M. (2012). The Australian curriculum: Finding the hidden narrative? *Critical Studies in Education, 53*(3), 347–360. doi: 10.1080/17508487.2012.703137.

Dowling, A., Beavis, A., Underwood, C., Sadeghi, R., & O'Malley, K. (2009). *Who's coming to school today? Final report.* Brisbane: ACER, Brisbane Catholic Education.

Drake, S. (2012). *Creating standards-based integrated curriculum.* Thousand Oaks: Corwin Press.

Drake, S., & Burns, R. (2004). *Meeting standards through integrated curriculum.* Alexandra: Association for Supervision and Curriculum Development.

Dunne, J. (2006). The Catholic school, the democratic state and civil society: Exploring the tensions. In E. Woulfe & J. Cassin (Eds.), *From present to future: Catholic education in Ireland for the new century* (pp. 190–229). Dublin: Veritas.

Gandin, L. A. (2006). Creating real alternatives to neo-liberal policies in education: The citizen school project. In M. W. Apple & K. L. Buras (Eds.), *The subaltern speak: Curriculum, power and educational struggles* (pp. 217–241). New York, NY: Routledge.

Gehrke, N. J. (1998). A look at curriculum integration from the bridge. *The Curriculum Journal, 9*(2), 247–260.

Glatter, R. (2003). Governance, autonomy and accountability in education. In M. Preedy, R. Glatter, & W. Christine (Eds.) *Strategic leadership and educational improvement* (pp. 44–74). London: Open University Press/Paul Chapman.

Gleeson, J. (2013). The European credit transfer system and curriculum design: Product before process? *Studies in Higher Education, 38*(6), 921–938. doi: 10.1080/03075079.2011.610101.

Gleeson, J., & Ó Donnabháin, D. (2009). Strategic planning and accountability in Irish education: Strategy statements and the adoption and use of performance indicators. *Irish Education Studies, 28*(1), 27–46.

Gleeson, J., & O'Flaherty, J. (2014, April 6). *Teachers' perceptions of moral education in Catholic secondary schools in Australia and Ireland.* Unpublished paper read at Annual Conference of American Educational Research Association, Philadelphia.

Gleeson, J., & O'Neill, M. (2018). Study of beliefs and attitudes of teachers in Catholic schools in Queensland. *International Studies in Catholic Education, 10*(1), 44–65.

Grace, G. (1989). Education: Commodity or public good? *British Journal of Educational Studies, 37*(3), 207–221. doi: 10.1080/00071005.1989.9973812.

Grace, G. (2010). Renewing spiritual capital: An urgent priority for the future of Catholic education internationally. *International Studies in Catholic Education, 2*(2), 117–128.

Grace, G. (2013). Catholic social teaching should permeate the catholic secondary school curriculum: An agenda for reform. *International Studies in Catholic Education, 5*(1), 99–109.

Groome, T. (2003). What makes a school Catholic? In T. H. McLaughlin, J. O'Keefe, & B. O'Keeffe (Eds.), *The contemporary catholic school: Context, identity and diversity* (pp. 111–129). London: Routledge.

Grundy, S. (1987). *Curriculum: Product or praxis.* London: Falmer.

Habermas, J. (1972). *Knowledge and human interests.* London: Heinemann.

Hargreaves, A. (2003). *Teaching in the knowledge society.* New York, NY: Teachers College.

Hewer, C. (2001). Schools for Muslims. *Oxford Review of Education, 27*(4), 515–527. doi: 10.1080/03054980120086211.

Hughes, P. (2011). *Christian faith and the economy in a globalised world.* Nunawading: Christian Research Association.

Hussey, T., & Smith, P. (2002). The trouble with learning outcomes. *Active Learning in Higher Education, 3*(3), 220–233.

Institute for Catholic Education. (1996). *Curriculum matters: A resource for Catholic educators.* Toronto, ON: Author.

Lam, C. C., Alviar-Martin, T., Adler, S. A., & Sim, J. B. (2013). Curriculum integration in Singapore: Teachers' perspectives and practice. *Teaching and Teacher Education, 31*, 23–34.

Lane, D. A. (1991). *Catholic education and the school. Some theological reflections.* Dublin: Veritas.

Lingard, B. (2010). Policy borrowing, policy learning: Testing times in Australian schooling. *Critical Studies in Education, 51*(2), 129–147. doi: 10.1080/17508481003731026.

Lye, J. N., & Hirschberg, J. G. (2012). *What is a high school worth? A model of Australian private secondary school fees.* Research Paper Number 1161, University of Melbourne Department of Economics.

Lynch, K., Grummel, B., & Devine, D. (2012). *New managerialism in education. commercialisation, carelessness and gender.* New York, NY: Palgrave Macmillan.

Maddox, M. (2014). *Taking god to school. The end of Australia's egalitarian education?* Sydney: Allen and Unwin.

McLaughlin, D., & Standen, P. (2013, August 12). *The rise and demise of Australian Catholic Education?* Unpublished paper read at Australian Catholic School Leadership Conference, Sydney.

Morris, R. C. (2003). A guide to curricular integration. *Kappa Delta Pi Record, 39*(4), 164–167.

Murray, D. (1991). *A special concern.* Dublin: Veritas.

National Catholic Education Commission. (2013). Australian Catholic schools 2012: Annual report. Retrieved from www.ncec.catholic.edu.au

Organisation for Economic Co-operation and Development (OECD). (2003). *Schooling, life-long learning, and the future.* Paris: OECD.

Organisation for Economic Co-operation and Development (OECD). (2010). PISA 2009 results: What makes a school successful? Resources, policies and practices (IV). Retrieved from http://dx.doi.org/10.1787/9789264091559-en

Save Our Schools. (2010, December 17). Media release: PISA study says that competition between schools lowers student achievement in Australia.

Sennett, R. (1998). *The corrosion of character.* New York, NY: Norton.

Shimek, J. J. (2014). Catholic schools can use common Core. *Journal Interactive. Milwaukee.*

Spring, J. (2009). *Globalisation and education: An introduction.* New York, NY: Routledge.

Stenhouse, L. (1975). *An introduction to curriculum research and development.* London: Heinemann.

The Australian. (2013, April 14). Prime Minister Julia Gillard outlines splurge on schools as part of Gonski education funding reforms.

The Royal Ministry of Education. (1997). *Core curriculum for primary, secondary and adult education in Norway.* Oslo: Norwegian Board of Education.

Tuohy, D. (2008). Catholic schools: Schools for Catholics? *Studies: An Irish Quarterly Review, 97*(386), 125–136.

Tuohy, D. (2013). Governance in education – A church ministry of the future. In *Catholic schools – faith in our future* (pp. 113–126). Dublin: Association of Management of Catholic Secondary Schools.

Walford, G. (2002). Classification and framing of the curriculum in evangelical Christian and Muslim schools in England and the Netherlands. *Educational Studies, 28*(4), 403–419.

Wolf, A. (2002) *Does education matter? Myths about education and economic growth.* London: Penguin.

Chapter 2

Catholic social teaching

Peta Goldburg rsm

Introduction

Grounded in the Bible and developed in the light of experiences of people in many different cultures, Catholic Social Teaching (CST) provides a set of key principles and guidelines for action which can be used to evaluate situations, policies and approaches used in contemporary society and offers valuable insights regarding the intersection between faith, society and politics. Many social encyclicals have drawn criticism from some politicians, journalists and theologians who insist that the Church should not interfere in secular matters. However, the Second Vatican Council (1965), in the Pastoral Constitution on the Church in the Modern World (*Gaudium et Spes*), clearly articulated the right and duty of the Church to comment on worldly affairs because it is essentially concerned with the spiritual and material well-being of all people (para 76). With human dignity as its measure, the church's statements on social issues have, for more than 100 years, critiqued society and offered advice about social and economic structures without aligning with any specific political party or ideological movement. CST challenges people to develop an authentic faith-based response to changing social, political, cultural and economic conditions.

This chapter provides an introduction to CST, beginning with a brief exploration of social justice as articulated in the Bible and developed through the relatively modern corpus of writing which has become known as CST.

Justice in Scripture

The teachings in the Torah (Genesis, Exodus, Leviticus, Numbers, and Deuteronomy), the pronouncements of the biblical prophets and the Good News of Jesus all proclaim God's radical concern for justice. Ancient Israel's relationship with God began when God liberated the people from slavery in Egypt and led them to the Promised Land. God and the people entered into covenants as agreements that would maintain justice among the newly liberated people (Exodus 20:1–17). The covenant with Moses and its commandments set out ideal principles of social and economic interaction, and the legal codes in the Torah were covenantal customs, laws and measures designed to guide social and economic life in Israelite society. The books of the Hebrew prophets, Isaiah, Jeremiah, Amos, Hosea, Micah and Ezekiel frequently speak out against fraudulent practices that harm the weakest members of Israelite society – widows, orphans, the poor and outcasts – and called for a new order regulated by social concern and harmony.

The teachings of Jesus in the New Testament, drawing on the rich heritage of the Jewish Scriptures, proclaim that he came ' … to bring good news to the poor … liberty to captives … and to let the oppressed go free' (Luke 4:18–19) and he identified himself with the hungry and the stranger (Matthew 25:45). Many of the stories about Jesus in the gospels promote a vision of the Reign of God where justice will prevail. Jesus' ministry of justice includes acts of healing, feeding, reconciliation and restoring right relationships. The theme of justice is continued in the Letters of Paul where he urges the emerging Christian communities to share their resources, money and talents so that all might thrive. The Old and New Testaments provide a foundation for CST and practice in numerous ways.

The understanding of justice presented in the Scriptures is much broader than our contemporary understanding of legal justice or social justice. In the Old Testament, more than one Hebrew word is used for justice. But when translated into English, terms such as *mispat* and *sedaqah* are more commonly written as 'loving-kindness', 'mercy', 'righteousness' and 'steadfast love'. In the New Testament, when the Greek word *dikaiosyne*, righteousness, is used, the sharper requirement of justice is diminished. Christian righteousness requires that people live in a way that is consistent with the death and resurrection of Jesus and with new life in the Spirit. The word justice, from the Latin word *ius* which means 'right', concerns rights along with the duties which correspond to those rights. One's duty to respect another person flows from the other's right to life in all its fullness. Social justice requires an understanding of the distinction between society and the nation-state. Society is the total network of social, political, economic, cultural and religious relationships which are necessary for full human development, whereas the nation-state is commonly the centre of power that governs society. The extent to which the state should intervene in the life of its citizens should be balanced, enabling individuals and small group action over and against governmental intervention. The state should only intervene when lesser bodies cannot fulfil the task required by the common good. Justice demands that all people practise social responsibility. This requires people to work for social change through large institutions, including government, to change the structures that perpetuate poverty and prevent people from flourishing.

Catholic social teaching

CST, a relatively recently identified corpus of Church teachings, consists of encyclicals (letters to the whole Church) published by popes, documents from Bishops' conferences and encompasses Catholic social thought, a broader concept that includes the reflection of theologians and people engaged in social justice movements of the church.

CST is inseparable from Catholic understandings of the human person and human dignity where people are made in the image and likeness of God (Genesis 1:27), redeemed by Jesus Christ and, therefore, worthy of respect as members of the human family. According to CST, the quality of life in society and the justice of its *modus operandi*, the orientation of its structures and systems (political, legal, economic, social educational and religious) either enhance or diminish the full human development of each person.

Charles (1998) distinguishes four sources of inspiration and motivation for CST: Scripture, apostolic tradition as articulated by theologians and popes, the experience of the Church as the People of God, and relevant findings of the human and social sciences. More recently, six particular influences have been identified: the teachings of the Second Vatican Council (especially *Gaudium et Spes* and *Dignitatis Humanae*); papal encyclicals addressing social, economic, cultural, political and environmental issues; collegial teaching, including pastoral letters from Bishops; insights of liberation theologians; insights from Catholic and other NGOs; and the scholarly and academic analysis and evaluation of CST (Hornsby-Smith, 2006).

History and development

Officially classified as the first social encyclical, *Rerum Novarum*, was promulgated by Pope Leo XIII in May 1891. This document was not developed in isolation but rather is the product of the two preceding decades where clergy and laity worked to translate the Gospel message into the daily life of society at the time of the Industrial Revolution. Several events across the world influenced Pope Leo XIII to adopt the official position articulated in *Rerum Novarum*. Msgr Ketteler, Bishop of Mainz, played a significant role in the emerging Catholic social movement by encouraging progressive social legislation calling for state intervention to defend workers against the abuses of liberalism. His campaigning led to the passing of a series of social laws by an alliance of German Catholic and Socialist politicians. The pilgrimages of *La France du Travail* (working France) to Rome brought to the notice of the Pope exploitation of workers in factories. In the United States, Cardinal Gibbons of Baltimore established the first American workers' organisation, the Knights of Labor; and Cardinal Manning, Archbishop of Westminster, UK, supported the London dock strike which had repercussions throughout Europe (Aubert & Boileau, 2003). Written in response to rapid social changes, *Rerum Novarum* is grounded in a theological and philosophical anthropology of the human person which stresses people's relationship with all other human beings, especially those in most need. This communitarian anthropology underpins contemporary Catholic understandings of the state, justice, human rights, private property and the preferential option for the poor.

While *Rerum Novarum* is regarded by some as the beginning of CST, Schuck (2013) suggests a threefold phase of development for CST, namely, pre-Leonine, from the pontificate of Benedict XIV in 1740–1877; Leonine, from the pontificate of Leo XIII in 1878–1958; and post-Leonine, from the accession of Pope John XXIII in 1958 to the pontificate of Pope John Paul II (1978–2005).

The pre-Leonine period was punctuated by significant upheavals and even violence marking the end of feudalism and absolute monarchs, the onset of the Industrial Revolution, the French Revolution, socialist revolutions, the unification movements in Italy and Germany, and the Enlightenment. During these turbulent times, several popes were imprisoned by Napoleonic armies, Pope Gregory XVI (1831–1846) condemned the notion of freedom of conscience in religion, and Pope Pius IX (1846–1878) spoke out against liberal culture. At the same time, Catholic social movements such as the Society of St Vincent de Paul in France and the German Centre Party or Catholic Centre Party were developing. A tradition of encyclical writing was initiated by Pope Benedict XIV in 1740 and from then to the election of Pope Leo XIII in 1878 seventy-seven encyclicals were promulgated.

Shuck's Leonine period, from the election of Pope Leo XIII in 1878 through to the death of Pope Pius XII in 1958, was marked by antagonism between the Catholic Church and the European nation-states, aggressive colonial expansion in Asia and Africa, the Great Depression, two World Wars, the Russian Revolution, and the Cold War. Throughout this period, as well as having a preoccupation with moral issues and religious and moral authority, the Church broadened its outreach to the world. During this period the Church had nine popes and they wrote 185 encyclicals, many of which were focused on social matters. Two popes, namely Pius X and Pius XI, encouraged Catholic Action by the laity, and in Belgium, the Young Christian Worker (YCW) movement was founded and rapidly expanded across the world.

The calling of the Second Vatican Council (1962–1965) marked a watershed moment between the pre-Leonine and Leonine periods and had significant and continuing influence on the pontificates of Popes John XXIII, Paul VI, and John Paul II. During this period, the world experienced unprecedented economic growth, the collapse of the Soviet Bloc, and the Church was challenged by feminist and liberation theology, and ever-increasing global poverty.

Since the mid–1980s, CST has tried to articulate a path between state-imposed socialism and liberal capitalism and has insisted that the needs of people should come before the needs of the economy rather than vice versa. CST documents respond to world situations and challenge people to move from an immediate response in charity to action which responds in justice. However, acts of charity are often individual or private acts addressing an immediate need and responding to symptoms of injustice and inequality. Actions of justice are public, collective acts addressing longer-term need and the root causes of injustice. Acting for justice can be controversial and often requires working for social change. CST, rather than being a static body of doctrine, is a dynamic process which responds to changing circumstances and includes social doctrine, social teaching and social ethics. Indeed, on certain matters, such as democracy, co-ownership and human rights, earlier positions have been reversed.

Ways of approaching Catholic Social Teaching

Brady (2008) has identified four approaches to the study of CST. The first method is to read the social encyclicals and related documents in their entirety. While this is a worthwhile and valuable process, it takes significant time, and, for the novice reader, the texts can be quite theologically dense. The second method is to study excerpts from the documents which can provide a focused perspective on specific issues such as work, the poor or the environment. The third method is to read summaries of and commentaries on the encyclicals. This can be helpful in providing an analysis and critique of the documents but also requires engagement with primary source materials. The fourth method is predicated on the principles or themes of CST which, over time, have been identified by scholars as a means of understanding the documents and social traditions of the Church. This approach provides a general overview of the documents and enables readers to engage with some of the primary source materials and commentaries in order to gain deeper understanding. The number of CST principles identified in this way depends on the scholars who are analysing the documents. Some identify just six principles while others have identified seven, nine and even ten principles, depending on how they classify the ideas when looking at the CST documents as a body of literature.

Table 2.1 lists various expressions of the principles of CST generated by different scholars or social justice agencies of the Catholic Church. Each listing has 'human dignity' at its core, with principles such as the common good, solidarity, the preferential option for the poor and stewardship of creation being common to all. Additional principles can be seen as subsets or extensions of the aforementioned principles.

CST does not occur in a vacuum; it responds to the 'signs of the times' and to the prevailing social, economic and political environment. While the

36 Peta Goldburg rsm

Table 2.1 Expressions of Catholic Social Teaching

Six principles (Caritas, 2018)	Seven principles (US Conference of Bishops, 2018)	Nine principles (Massaro, 2016)	Ten principles (Centre of Concern, 2018)
Dignity of the human person	Dignity of the human person	Dignity of every person and human rights	Dignity of human person
Common good	Common good	Solidarity, common good and participation	Community and the common good
Preferential option for the poor	Preferential option for the poor	Option for the poor and vulnerable	Option for the poor
Stewardship of creation	Stewardship of creation	Dignity of work, rights of workers	Stewardship of creation
Solidarity	Solidarity	Colonialism and economic development	Global solidarity
Subsidiarity and participation	Subsidiarity and participation	Subsidiarity and the role of government	Role of government and subsidiarity
	Economic justice	Family life	Economic justice
	Promotion of peace	Peace and disarmament	Promotion of peace
		Property ownership in modern society, rights and responsibility	Participation in society
			Dignity of work

theological foundations of CST have remained constant, each generation has to interpret and re-fashion CST to meet the needs of each new age.

Table 2.2 provides a summary of eight social encyclicals that have been published, beginning with *Rerum Novarum* (1891) and concluding with the most recent social encyclical, *Laudato Si'* (2015). The Apostolic Letter, *Octogesima Adveniens* (1971), was published to mark the 80th anniversary of *Rerum Novarum*.

This chapter is structured around six principles of CST, identified in Table 2.1: dignity of the human person, the common good, preferential option for the poor, stewardship of creation, solidarity and subsidiarity and participation. What follows is an exploration of these principles and how they have been expressed and developed in various CST documents across the last 100 years.

Dignity of the human person

The principle of the dignity of the human person, encompassing the sanctity of human life, underpins all CST. Every person, regardless of race, gender, religion, health, intelligence, economic status or any other differentiating

Table 2.2 Social encyclicals (1891–2015)

Latin title	English title	Year	Source/author	Major issues	Key ideas
Rerum Novarum	The Condition of Labour	1891	Pope Leo XIII	Industrialisation, poverty	Workers' rights, just wages
Quadragesimo Anno	Reconstruction of Social Order	1931	Pope Pius XI	Great depression, communism, fascist dictatorships	Subsidiarity, equitable relationship between labour and capital
Pacem in Terris	Peace on Earth	1963	Pope John XXIII	Arms race, nuclear war	Human rights and social responsibility
Populorum Progressio	The Development of Peoples	1967	Pope Paul VI	Widening gap between rich and poor	Authentic development
Octogesima Adveniens (Apostolic Letter)	On the 80th Anniversary of Rerum Novarum	1971	Pope Paul VI	Urbanisation, social problems, new poor	Political action to combat injustice
Laborem Exercens	On Human Work	1981	Pope John Paul II	Workers as instruments of production	Underemployment; dignity of work
Centesimus Annus	On the One Hundredth Anniversary of Rerum Novarum	1991	Pope John Paul II	Collapse of Communism in Eastern Europe	Consumer greed and the knowledge economy
Caritas in Veritate	Charity in Truth	2009	Pope Benedict XVI	Global financial crisis	Ethical renewal
Laudato Si'	Praise be to You or On Care of Our Common Home	2015	Pope Francis	Ecology and poverty	Anthropocentrism as source of ecological crisis, excessive consumerist lifestyle

characteristic, is worthy of respect. The dignity of each person can only be protected if human rights are protected. Every person has the right to life and to those things which are essential to human decency, such as food, shelter, clothing, employment, health care and education. Corresponding to these rights are duties and responsibilities which encompass each other, our families and the wider society.

Human dignity emerges from the fundamental belief that everyone is created in God's image and likeness (Genesis 1:26–27). Human life is sacred because the human person is the clearest reflection of God in the world. Because people are made in the image and likeness of God, they have transcendent worth and value that comes from God. Human dignity, therefore, is inalienable: it is an essential part of every human being and it can never be separated from other aspects of the human person. Consequently, each person is valuable and worthy of respect and each person should not simply be able to live but she/he should also be allowed to flourish.

The Catechism of the Catholic Church (CCC, 2003) expands this understanding of human dignity when it states:

> Being in the image of God the human individual possesses the dignity of a person, who is not just something, but someone. He (sic) is capable of self-knowledge, of self-possession and of freely giving him/herself and entering into communion with other persons. And she/he is called by grace to a covenant with his Creator, to offer him/her a response of faith and love that no other creature can give in his/her stead. (para 357)

In *Rerum Novarum* (1891), Pope Leo XIII draws attention to the inherent dignity of the human person when he focuses on the inhumane treatment of workers resulting from practices caused by the expansion of industry during the Industrial Revolution:

> … it has come to pass that working men have been surrendered, isolated and helpless, to the hardheartedness of employers and the greed of unchecked competition …. (para 3)

> … oppressed workers, above all, ought to be liberated from the savagery of greedy men, who inordinately use human beings as things for gain. Assuredly, neither justice nor humanity can countenance the exaction of so much work that the spirit is dulled from excessive toil and that along with it the body sinks crushed from exhaustion. (para 59)

As a remedy for this inhumane treatment, Pope Leo XIII provides a set of guidelines for work and working conditions, including periods of rest for workers, and recommends that the nature of the work required should take account of circumstances, including time, place, season as well as the health and strength of the person. He even suggests that, for health reasons, people working in mines should have shorter hours of work (Pope Leo XIII, 1891, para 42). He advocates that workers should be paid a 'just wage for a just day's work' and that workers have the right to form associations/unions to negotiate just working conditions.

While Pope Leo XIII is openly critical of the effects of economic liberalism, he rejects a socialist solution and promotes the notion of an economic society that includes the right to private property. *Rerum Novarum* supports human dignity by upholding the rights of workers in demanding: a fair day's wage for a fair day's work, keeping Sunday as a day of rest, limiting the length of the work day, recognising the difficulty of various jobs, forbidding the labour of children and protecting the rights of all citizens, in particular the weakest. *Rerum Novarum* (Pope Leo XIII, 1891) established the position of the Church on issues pertaining to the proper relationship between labour and capital and called for 'some opportune remedy ... for the misery and wretchedness pressing so unjustly on the majority of the working class' (para 3). The encyclical gave greater impetus to existing Catholic labour movements and developed a theory of rights which highlighted the transcendent worth of people as exhibited in statements such as 'Man (sic) precedes the State' (Pope Leo XIII, 1891, para 68).

A different perspective on the dignity of the human person is presented in the encyclical, *Pacem in Terris* (Peace on Earth), promulgated by Pope John XXIII in April 1963, within weeks of the Cuban missile crisis. After the Second World War, there were conflicts across the globe: the Cold War between the Soviet Union and the United States, the spread of communism in Europe and Asia, the Korean War and the Berlin Wall dividing East and West Germany. In Cuba, Fidel Castro overthrew the dictator, Batista, and nationalised American firms in order to keep their profits in Cuba. The United States retaliated by imposing a trade embargo on Cuba and then Russia stepped in to purchase Cuban exports. The relationship between Cuba and Russia grew stronger and, by 1962, Russia had a nuclear missile base in Cuba. The United States said it would not invade Cuba if Russia withdrew its nuclear missiles. A very tense period of history followed when the world was on the brink of nuclear war, and this was not settled until Russia and the United States signed the Nuclear Test Ban Treaty in 1963.

Breaking with tradition, the encyclical was not just addressed to 'Venerable Brethren, the Patriarchs, Primates, Archbishops, Bishops and other ordinaries' (Pope Pius XI, 1931) but also to 'men and women of good will' (Pope John XXIII, 1963). Pope John XXIII appeals to the anthropological principle that every human being is gifted with intelligence and free will and that she/he has 'rights and duties, which together flow as a direct consequence from his/her nature. These rights and duties are universal and inviolable, and therefore altogether inalienable' (Pope John XXIII, 1963, para 9). Pope John XXIII not only affirmed the work of the United Nations, particularly its Universal Declaration of Human Rights, but he also 'elevated the promotion of human rights to a first order priority in the mission of the Catholic Church to the world' (Cortright, 2014, p. 36).

Pacem in Terris is the first encyclical to present a sustained discussion of human rights in the context of CST and the last encyclical to employ an exclusively natural law approach (Curran, 1991). Referring to the Universal Declaration of Human Rights and the United Nations (Pope John XXIII, 1963), the encyclical states

> ... It is a solemn recognition of the personal dignity of every human being; an assertion of everyone's right to be free to seek out the truth, to follow moral principles, discharge the duties imposed by justice, and lead a fully human life. (para 142–144)

As a member of the human family, each person has rights and duties, and *Pacem in Terris* (Pope John XXIII, 1963) provides a comprehensive list of 27 specific rights, beginning with the right to live and to have a livelihood (para 11), the right to moral and cultural values (para 12–13), the right to worship according to one's conscience (para 14), the right to choose freely one's state in life (para 15–17), the right to emigrate and immigrate (para 25) and concluding with the right to participate in public affairs and contribute to the common good (para 26–27). The document not only establishes a strong case for religious liberty, but also sets human dignity at the centre of CST by linking it with human rights.

Four years later, in 1967, *Populorum Progressio* (On the Development of Peoples) was promulgated by Pope Paul VI to address the world economy and its effect on people across the world. This social encyclical links the theme of authentic development to human dignity, saying ' ... development cannot be limited to mere economic growth. In order to be authentic, it must be complete: integral, that is, it has to promote the good of every person and the whole of humanity' (Pope Paul VI, 1967, para 14).

Pope John Paul II further develops the concept of human dignity in *Laborem Exercens* (On Human Work) promulgated in 1981 for the 90th anniversary of *Rerum Novarum*. The encyclical begins with an exhortation on Christian anthropology, focused on people created in the image of God. The main idea developed throughout the text concerns the affirmation of the dignity of workers: 'Work is in the first place "for the worker" and not the worker "for work". Work itself can have greater or lesser objective value, but all work should be judged by the measure of dignity given to the person who carries it out' (Pope John Paul II, 1981, para 6).

Laborem Exercens (1981) presents a sustained reflection on the meaning of human work and reflects John Paul's early life and experience in Poland under Communist rule. Pope John Paul II highlights the obligations that employers should have towards workers. Workers, he says, are much more than cogs in a wheel. Human dignity is specifically addressed when he raises the issue of meaningful work for people with disabilities, stating:

> The various bodies involved in the world of labour, both the direct and the indirect employer, should therefore by means of effective and appropriate measures foster the right of disabled people to professional training and work, so that they can be given a productive activity suited to them ... Each community will be able to set up suitable structures for finding or creating jobs for such people both in the usual public or private enterprises, by offering them ordinary or suitably adapted jobs, and in what are called 'protected' enterprises and surroundings ... they are full-scale subjects of work, useful, respected for their human dignity and called to contribute to the progress and welfare of their families and of the community according to their particular capacities. (Pope John Paul II, 1981, para 22)

The encyclical also includes strong statements about underemployment, unemployment and the rights of migrant workers, noting the obligation to 'provide unemployment benefits, that is to say, the duty to make suitable grants indispensable for the subsistence of unemployed workers and their families, is a duty springing from the fundamental principle of the moral order in this sphere, namely, the principle of the common use of goods or, to put it in another and still simpler way, the right to life and subsistence' (Pope John Paul II, 1981, para 18).

On the 100th anniversary of *Rerum Novarum*, Pope John Paul II, in *Centesimus Annus* (1991), raised concerns related to increasing technology in the workforce, highlighting the importance of people over machines. He was particularly concerned with rapid consumerism whereby people have developed a need for instant gratification:

> Thus a great deal of educational and cultural work is urgently needed, including the education of consumers in the responsible use of their power of choice, the formation of a strong sense of responsibility among producers and among people in the mass media in particular, as well as the necessary intervention by public authorities ... It is not wrong to want to live better; what is wrong is a style of life which is presumed to be better when it is directed towards 'having' rather than 'being', and which wants to have more, not in order to be more but in order to spend life in enjoyment as an end in itself. (Pope John Paul II, 1991, para 36)

He calls for a change in mentality whereby people share the goods of the world in order for all to prosper.

In the most recent social encyclical, *Laudato Si'* (2015a), Pope Francis identifies anthropocentrism as detrimental to human dignity and he challenges the contemporary consumerist lifestyle, calling it the 'seedbed for collective selfishness' (para 104).

The principle of the dignity of the human person is the cornerstone on which CST is built and from which all other principles emerge.

The common good

As human beings made in God's image, we are both sacred and social people and we achieve our fulfilment within community. The good of each person in society is intimately connected to the good of the wider group. Human beings are social by nature and need others in order to thrive. Consequently, how society, including its economy, law and policy, is organised directly affects human dignity and how individuals can grow and flourish within community. While love of neighbour is very important, it also requires people to have a broader view of life and to take responsibility for contributing to the good of the whole of society, namely, to contribute to the common good.

Rerum Novarum (Pope Leo XIII, 1891), through the lens of work and workers, provides an insight into the common good:

> ... The foremost duty, therefore, of the rulers of the State should be to make sure that the laws and institutions, the general character and administration of the commonwealth, shall be such as of themselves to realise public well-being and private prosperity ... since it is the province of the commonwealth to serve the common good. (para 32)

The common good concerns the welfare of the whole of society and requires a foundation of basic rights which are a minimum standard for life in society.

In *Quadragesimo Anno*, issued in the midst of the Great Depression when wealth was becoming more concentrated in the hands of few, Pope Pius XI (1931) said,

> ... the riches that economic-social developments constantly increase ought to be so distributed among individual persons and classes that the common advantage of all ... will be safeguarded; in other words, that the common good of all society will be kept inviolate. (para 57)

Mater et Magistra (Pope John XXIII, 1961) extends understanding of the common good to an international level stating that 'the avoidance of all forms of unfair competition between the economies of different countries; the fostering of mutual collaboration and good will; and effective co-operation in the development of economically less advanced communities' (para 80) should be a priority. *Pacem in Terris* (Pope John XXIII, 1963) links the common good with the protection of human rights (para 60) and encourages people to work together across national and international boundaries to promote justice and the common good (para 53). For Pope John XXIII, the whole purpose of political authority concerns the promotion of the common good.

The Second Vatican Council (1965) emphasised the social nature of humanity, saying

> ... it grows increasingly true that the obligations of justice and love are fulfilled only if each person, contributing to the common good, according to his/her own abilities and the needs of others, also promotes and assists the public and private institutions dedicated to bettering the conditions of human life. (para 30)

Here, the common good is expanded to include all elements of social life and involves the whole of humankind (Second Vatican Council, 1965, para 26).

Throughout the pontificate of Pope John Paul II, the tensions of the Cold War highlighted the need for people to work towards the achievement of an international common good. He identifies the positive role democracy can play in promoting and protecting the common good. In *Sollicitudo Rei Socialis* (Pope John Paul II, 1987), the environment is included in understandings related to the common good for the first time:

> ... natural resources are limited; some are not ... renewable. Using them as if they were inexhaustible, with absolute dominion, seriously endangers their availability not only for the present generation but above all for generations to come ... We all know that the direct or indirect result of industrialization is, ever more frequently, the pollution of the environment, with serious consequences for the health of the population. (para 34)

Later, in *Centesimus Annus* (Pope John Paul II, 1991), consumerism and ecological devastation are connected and presented as obstacles to the pursuit of the common good:

> ... it is the task of the State to provide for the defence and preservation of common goods such as the natural and human environments, which cannot be safeguarded simply by market forces ... the State and all of society have the duty of defending those collective goods which, among others, constitute the essential framework for the legitimate pursuit of personal goals on the part of each individual. (para 40)

Pope Francis (2015a) takes the idea further in *Laudato Si'*, encouraging people to engage in public life, work for the common good, recognise the dignity of all people and work for those on the margins of society. One of the key points of *Laudato Si'* (Pope Francis, 2015a) is that we are all interconnected and interrelated (para 16, 91, 92, 120, 137, 141, 240) with relationality coming before individuality.

Pope Benedict XVI, in *Caritas in Veritate* (2009), says that

> To love someone is to desire that person's good and to take effective steps to secure it. Besides the good of the individual, there is the good that is linked to living in society: the common good. It is the good of 'all of us', made up of individuals, families and intermediate groups who together constitute society … To desire the common good and strive towards it is a requirement of justice and charity (caritas). (para 7)

Pope Benedict XVI (2009) reminds readers that 'Love – caritas – is an extraordinary force which leads people to opt for courageous and generous engagement in the field of justice and peace' (para 1). Hollenbach (2011) criticises Benedict's treatment of the relationship between love and justice saying, '[t]he precedence granted to charity (caritas) over justice risks downplaying the work of justice to a lower spiritual plane than the love-as-gift that the encyclical strongly and repeatedly stresses' (p. 174). Dorr (2012), however, suggests that Pope Benedict is not opposing one to the other nor is he suggesting that love is an alternative to justice, but that love demands that we be just and that we treat people equitably.

The principle of the common good recognises that all people contribute to life in society and that they must share in the mutual benefits of life in that society for the overall functioning of a just society. The common good is not utilitarian in nature; it is focused on the good of the whole community, rather than 'the greatest good for the greatest number of people'. As Pope John Paul II (1987) clearly states, '[the common good] is the good of all and of each individual, because we are all really responsible for all' (para 38). This clearly demonstrates that the meaning of the common good has expanded from its initial understandings in early CST documents to now include transnational and global realities of the whole human family.

Preferential option for poor

The preferential option for the poor is an essential part of society's effort to realise the common good, and the common good can only be achieved if the needs of the poor and those on the margins of society are considered. God's love is universal, so the principle of the preferential option for the poor reminds people to prioritise those who are in most need.

The Preferential Option for the Poor is grounded in the biblical traditions of the Church. Indeed, in the Old and New Testaments, we learn that a society is judged according to its treatment of the poor. God's covenant with Israel was dependent on the way the community treated the poor, the widow, the orphan and the stranger (Exodus 22:20–26; Leviticus 19:9–10;

Deuteronomy 16:11–12; Isaiah 1:16–17). In the New Testament, Jesus proclaims that he has been anointed to bring the Good News to the poor (Luke 4:1–22) and, in Matthew's gospel, we are told that at the last judgement people will be judged according to how they respond to the hungry, the thirsty, the prisoner and the stranger (Matthew 25:31–46).

A basic test for society concerns how well it treats its most vulnerable members. CST reminds people that the poor and vulnerable should be the highest priority for all members of society. In 1986, the United States Catholic Bishops, in *Economic Justice for All* (EJA), argued that the poor have the single most urgent economic claim on the conscience of the nation (para 58). Solidarity with the poor establishes a fundamental demand around the recognition of the full human dignity of the poor and their situation as children of God.

In *Rerum Novarum*, referred to by some as the 'workers' charter' (Aubert & Boileau, 2003, p. 143), Pope Leo XIII (1891) called on the state to provide protection and assistance for the poor:

> … the richer class have many ways of shielding themselves and stand less in need of help from the State; whereas the mass of the poor have no resources of their own to fall back upon, and must chiefly depend upon the assistance of the State. (para 37)

Over the next 50 years, the Church was somewhat reluctant to endorse state intervention in social and family matters, even though it criticised the injustices of the liberal capitalist system. Nevertheless, Pope Pius XI (1931) draws attention to the needs of the poor when he says,

> … since manufacturing and industry have so rapidly pervaded and occupied countless regions … the number of the non-owning working poor has increased enormously, and their groans cry to God from the earth. Added to them is the huge army of rural wage workers, pushed to the lowest level of existence and deprived of all hope of ever acquiring 'some property in land,'[43] and, therefore, permanently bound to the status of non-owning worker unless suitable and effective remedies are applied. (para 59)

Pope John XXIII makes a significant contribution to expanding understandings of CST in his two major encyclicals on social issues, *Mater et Magistra* (1961) and *Pacem in Terris* (1963). In *Mater et Magistra*, he expresses his distress about the plight of poverty-stricken workers who are forced to move away from their farms into overcrowded cities (para 123) and he calls on wealthy nations to fulfil their obligation towards the poor:

> … The solidarity which binds all men (sic) together as members of a common family makes it impossible for wealthy nations to look with indifference upon the hunger, misery and poverty of other nations whose

citizens are unable to enjoy even elementary human rights ...We are all equally responsible for the undernourished peoples. [Hence], it is necessary to educate one's conscience to the sense of responsibility which weighs upon each and every one, especially upon those who are more blessed with this world's goods. (para 157–158)

While Pope John XXIII was deeply concerned about the plight of poor people, he did not specifically address the option for the poor as it is understood today. The closest he comes to criticism of either the excesses of capitalism or socialism occurs in *Pacem in Terris* (Pope John XXIII, 1963) when he says,

> ... considerations of justice and equity can at times demand that those in power pay more attention to the weaker members of society, since these are at a disadvantage when it comes to defending their own rights and asserting their legitimate interests. (para 56)

Four years later, in 1967, when *Populorum Progressio* (On the Development of Peoples) was promulgated by Pope Paul VI, the focus was the world economy and its effect on people. The document, building on earlier encyclicals, further develops the ideas of the rights of workers to a just wage, job security, reasonable working conditions and the right to join workers' associations. It also highlights the fact that 'excessive economic, social and cultural inequalities among peoples arouse tensions and conflicts and are a danger to peace' (para 76) and it has a focus on those who seek to escape hunger, poverty and disease. It calls for wealthy nations to hear the cry of the poor and respond lovingly:

> ... the superfluous wealth of rich countries should be placed at the service of poor nations. The rule which up to now held good for the benefit of those nearest to us, must today be applied to all the needy of this world. (Pope Paul VI, 1967, para 49)

Each nation, therefore, needs the social and economic structures necessary to achieve growth.

Pope Paul VI identifies a new range of social problems that stem from urbanisation, which he calls the 'new poor', in his Apostolic Letter, *Octogesima Adveniens* (1971). The 'new poor' include the elderly, people with disabilities and those marginalised by society. The Church, he says,

> ... directs her attention to these new poor – the handicapped and the maladjusted, the old, different groups of those on the fringe of society, in order to recognise them, help them, defend their place and dignity in a society hardened by competition and the attraction of success. (Pope Paul VI, 1971, para 15)

He decries large urban areas where huge numbers of people live in substandard conditions. Pope Paul VI (1971) expanded the understanding of charity (*caritas*) when he said, in

> teaching us charity, the Gospel instructs us in the preferential respect due to the poor and the special situation they have in society: the more fortunate should renounce some of their rights so as to place their goods more generously at the service of others. (para 23)

While these earlier encyclicals addressed issues of the poor, an explicit articulation of the preferential option for the poor emerged at the Conference of Latin American Bishops held in Medellin, Colombia, in 1968. Latin America, during the 1960s, was characterised by a mixture of poverty, inequality, corruption, political instability and illiteracy. Government policies of the period focused on economic growth which benefitted only the elite while the majority of Latin Americans lived in dehumanising poverty. In response to the dire situation of the time, Latin American theologians, including Gustavo Gutierrez, Juan Segundo and Lucio Gera (Kirwan, 2012), developed a process of theological and pastoral reflection which denounced the causes of underdevelopment identifying it as 'social sin'. For liberation theologians, the option for the poor 'is grounded in a new appreciation of the "exceptionality" of God's partisan action in history on behalf of the oppressed' (Kirwan, 2012, p. 250). Throughout Latin America, Catholics began to re-read and reinterpret the Scriptures and to identify God as being on the side of the poor. The Medellin conference brought the importance of the preferential option for the poor to the world's attention.

After the Medellin conference, the well-known *See, Judge, Act* method, popularised by Cardinal Joseph Cardijn of Belgium prior to the Second Vatican Council, was further developed into an instrument which enabled the grounding of social analysis in an understanding of people's lived realities. Medellin also tested Vatican II's vision of Church as the 'people of God' by placing it in the concrete realities of Latin America where most people experienced severe poverty. If the Church was to respond in Latin America, it could only do so by listening to the diversity of voices and experiences of the people. The voice of the poor transformed the Church in the light of the Gospel by calling for the creation of conditions in which all people could flourish.

Pope John Paul II, in *Solicitudo Rei Socilais* (1987), described the preferential option for the poor as having 'world-wide dimensions, embracing the immense numbers of the hungry, the needy, the homeless, those without medical care, and those without hope' (para 42). Today, when Pope Francis speaks about a church for the poor, he is reiterating the message of CST, particularly the preferential option for the poor and the teachings of Latin American theology. In *Laudato Si'*, he links inhumane living conditions with the treatment of the planet: '[t]his is why the earth herself, burdened and laid waste, is among the most abandoned and maltreated of our poor' (Pope Francis, 2015a, para 2). He also says, 'our world has a grave social debt toward the poor who lack access to drinking water, because they are denied the right to a life consistent with their inalienable dignity' (Pope Francis, 2015a, para 30).

The preferential option for the poor requires people to stop thinking of them as a burden and to see working for and with the poor as an opportunity for moral, cultural and economic growth and advancing human flourishing.

Stewardship of creation

The first Genesis creation account (Genesis 1:1–2:4) contains a profound message about stewardship: God created the world and entrusted it to human beings. For the Christian tradition, the earth is sacred and a gift of God and therefore care of the earth is a requirement of faith. Mistreatment of the natural world not only damages creation but also diminishes our dignity as human beings. The Catholic tradition calls people to protect the dignity of all and it is impossible to do so if people do not care for creation. For Catholic Christians, care of the environment is a response to a sacramental vision of the world where God is present in all things.

Stewardship is a central motif in both the Old and New Testaments. In the Old Testament, stewardship is about generosity, hospitality and care of the earth as articulated in the book of Leviticus:

> Speak to the people of Israel and say to them: When you enter the land that I am giving you, the land shall observe a Sabbath for the Lord. For six years you shall sow your field, and for six years you shall prune your vineyard, and gather in their yield; but in the seventh year there shall be a Sabbath of complete rest for the land, a Sabbath for the Lord: you shall not sow your field or prune your vineyard. And you shall hallow the fiftieth year and you shall proclaim liberty throughout the land to all its inhabitants. It shall be a jubilee for you: you shall return, every one of you, to your property and every one of you to your family. That fiftieth year shall be a jubilee for you: you shall not sow, or reap the after-growth, or harvest the unpruned vines. For it is a jubilee; it shall be holy to you: you shall eat only what the field itself produces. (Leviticus 25:2–4, 10–12)

In the New Testament, stewardship of creation involves appreciating the God-given beauty of nature, protecting and preserving the environment, respecting human life and doing all that can be done to enhance the gift to life and developing the world through human effort.

'Stewardship of creation' is a relatively new concept in CST that first emerged in Pope Paul VI's Apostolic Letter, *Octogesima Adveniens* (1971). While the letter was predominantly focused on the problem of rapid and uncontrolled urbanisation, there was nevertheless a section devoted to environmental issues:

> Man (sic) is suddenly becoming aware that by an ill-considered exploitation of nature she/he risks destroying it and becoming in his/her turn the victim of this degradation. Not only is the material environment becoming a permanent menace – pollution and refuse, new illness and absolute destructive capacity – but the human framework is no longer under humankind's control, thus creating an environment for tomorrow which may well be intolerable. This is a wide-ranging social problem which concerns the entire human family. The Christian must turn to these new perceptions in order to take on responsibility, together with the rest of humankind, for a destiny which from now on is shared by all. (Pope Paul VI, 1971, para 21)

Herein, the dangers of environmental degradation are articulated along with the call for humankind to share responsibility for doing something to remedy the situation. Later, in 1971 at the World Synod of Bishops in Rome, the document, *Justitia in Mundo* (Synod of Bishops, 1971), was issued; it focused on the structural roots of injustice, including environmental degradation caused by the rich taking advantage of the earth.

The theological foundations for stewardship of creation were explicated by Pope John Paul II in his first social encyclical, *Redemptor Hominis* (1979), when he linked the Genesis creation account with the incarnation of Jesus the Christ. He called on people not only to restore a broken humanity but also to restore a broken natural world. *Redemptor Hominis* (Pope John Paul II, 1979) presents a clear statement of environmental concern and critiques existing practice:

> … Man(sic) often seems to see no other meaning in his/her natural environment than what serves for immediate use and consumption. Yet it was the Creator's will that humankind should communicate with nature as an intelligent and noble 'master' and 'guardian', and not as a heedless 'exploiter' and 'destroyer'. (para 15)

The theological foundations for stewardship of creation are extended in *Laborem Excercens* (Pope John Paul II, 1981) where humankind is described as being a co-creator with God and consequently responsible for the preservation of the earth:

> The word of God's revelation is profoundly marked by the fundamental truth that humankind, created in the image of God, shares by their work in the activity of the Creator and that, within the limits of their own

human capabilities, humankind in a sense continues to develop that activity, and perfects it as she/he advances further and further in the discovery of the resources and values contained in the whole of creation. (para 25)

In *Sollicitudo Rei Socialis* (Pope John Paul II, 1987), human flourishing is linked to relationships with all living things, and ecological responsibility is not merely an optional extra but the very way in which humankind expresses the image of God. In this encyclical, three ideas are emphasised: humankind's connection with the whole of creation, preservation of the world for future generations and the serious impact of industrialisation on creation:

> ... one must take into account the nature of each being and of its mutual connection in an ordered system, which is precisely the cosmos ... natural resources are limited; ... Using them as if they were inexhaustible, with absolute dominion, seriously endangers their availability not only for the present generation but above all for generations to come ... We all know that the direct or indirect result of industrialization is, ever more frequently, the pollution of the environment, with serious consequences for the health of the population. (Pope John Paul II, 1987, para 34)

The idea of ecological consequences is further developed in *Centesimus Annus* (Pope John Paul II, 1991), particularly the anthropocentric view that emphasises human control and power over the earth. Unbridled consumerism is severely criticised, especially when humanity 'consumes the resources of the earth ... in an excessive and disordered way' (Pope John Paul II, 1991, para 37). The idea of social ecology is also developed in response to the serious problems of modern urbanisation and the need for urban planning so that peoples' lives are enhanced rather than diminished.

Pope John Paul II developed a unique approach to ecological issues through his interpretation of human ecology which focuses on the ontological conditions required for human flourishing. He called people to ecological conversion and the ethical mandate of responsible stewardship tying ecological conversion to mercy in the natural world as well as to inter-human relationships: 'dominion over the earth ... leaves no room for mercy' (Pope John Paul II, 1980, para 2).

Today, with our heightened awareness of interdependence, we are even more aware of how environmental problems affect everyone. The conditions of the poor are often entwined with environmental issues which are likely to be the direct or indirect result of industrialisation. As Pope Francis (2015a) reminds us in *Laudato Si'*, the deterioration of the environment and of society affects the most vulnerable people on the earth:

> Both everyday experience and scientific research show that the gravest effects of all attacks on the environment are suffered by the poorest. For example, the depletion of fishing reserves especially hurts small fishing

communities without the means to replace those resources; water pollution particularly affects the poor who cannot buy bottled water; and rises in the sea level mainly affect impoverished coastal populations who have nowhere else to go. The impact of present imbalances is also seen in the premature death of many of the poor, in conflicts sparked by the shortage of resources, and in any number of other problems which are insufficiently represented on global agendas. (para 48)

The Catholic Christian tradition is guided by some fundamental principles with respect to how people engage with the environment and exercise stewardship. Of prime importance is the interrelatedness of human beings and the rest of creation: the flourishing of all forms of human and non-human life forms is encouraged. A second principle of stewardship of creation recognises that human beings alone have the capacity for conscious self-reflection and ethical behaviour. Because God created everything and 'indeed it was very good' (Genesis 1:31), human beings strive to preserve the good of creation. Stewardship is about a way of life which responds to the God-given gifts of the environment with gratitude and therefore treats the world and the environment with respect, sharing it with others in justice.

Solidarity

As humans, we are interdependent beings, part of the Body of Christ, and therefore we are our brothers' and sisters' keepers. Within CST, solidarity outlines the social obligations of individuals, communities, institutions and nations. While the concept of solidarity is not unique to Catholic Christianity, it is a well-developed principle within CST. Pope John Paul II (1987) reminds people that love of neighbour has global dimensions:

Interdependence must be transformed into *solidarity*, based upon the principle that the goods of creation are meant for all. That which human industry produces through the processing of raw materials, with the contribution of work, must serve equally for the good of all. (para 39)

The word 'solidarity' does not appear in the Old or New Testaments, but the root of the concept is grounded in biblical understandings of justice, mercy and compassion. As noted by Beyer (2014, p. 9), Pope Pius XII, the first Pontiff to use the term 'solidarity', says that Scripture undergirds the law of 'human solidarity and charity'. The liberation theologians (Kirwan, 2012) remind people that many biblical texts point to the requirement of solidarity with the poor with particular reference to the Beatitudes (Matthew 5:1–12), emphasising the relationship between the Reign of God and solidarity with the poor.

Populorum Progressio (Pope Paul VI, 1967) introduces the idea of global solidarity and suggests that

> ... wealthy nations should give aid to and promote solidarity with developing nations; fair trading relations should be established between rich and poor nations; and that the world should focus on universal charity (*caritas*) by building a more humane world community. (para 44)

The encyclical highlights the importance of solidarity stating:

> There can be no progress towards the complete development of individuals without the simultaneous development of all humanity in the spirit of solidarity. (para 43)

Pope Paul VI (1967) also calls on people to take group and societal action for justice saying:

> Individual initiative alone and the mere free play of competition could never assure successful development. One must avoid the risk of increasing still more the wealth of the rich and the dominion of the strong, whilst leaving the poor in their misery and adding to the servitude of the oppressed. (para 33)

He also acknowledges that individual undertakings are insufficient to address systemic injustice and then stresses the importance of international cooperation.

The link between solidarity and preferential option for the poor is clearly articulated in *Sollicitudo Rei Socialis* (Pope John Paul II, 1987):

> ... solidarity is not a feeling of vague compassion or shallow distress at the misfortunes of so many people, both near and far. On the contrary, it is the firm and persevering determination to commit oneself to the common good ... because we are all really responsible for all. (para 38)

According to Beyer (2014), contemporary CST identifies three aspects of solidarity. The first aspect entails the recognition that all human beings are interdependent and that the good of the individual is predicated on the development and good of the whole of community. This requires people not only to hear the cry of the poor but also to discover the reality of the poor. The second aspect of solidarity, which is characterised by rigorous social analysis, has ethical implications for all economic, cultural, political and religious interactions. In some instances, action in solidarity is required to eliminate the cause of the suffering of others. The third aspect of solidarity focuses on social change at a structural level via social policies. Solidarity requires

Catholic social teaching 53

sustained efforts to go beyond short-term solutions and temporary aid to long-term institutional change. Solidarity also encourages mutuality because the oppressed have their own perspectives, abilities and spiritualities to share with those who seek to empower them:

> The solidarity which binds all people together as members of a common family makes it impossible for wealthy nations to look with indifference upon the hunger, misery and poverty of other nations whose citizens are unable to enjoy even elementary human rights. The nations of the world are becoming more and more dependent on one another and it will not be possible to preserve a lasting peace so long as glaring economic and social imbalances persist. (Pope John XXIII, 1961, para 157)

Such expressions of solidarity have a political edge which is evident, for example, in the formation of trade unions (e.g. 'Solidarity' in Poland in the 1980s), direct political engagement, diplomacy, protests and marches, theatre of the oppressed (Boal, 1979) and consciousness raising in education (Freire, 1970).

Pope Benedict XVI (2009) paints a complex picture of today's world where injustice abounds in the form of 'hunger, deprivation, endemic diseases and illiteracy' (para 21). Drawing inspiration from *Populorum Progressio* (Pope Paul VI, 1967), Benedict's vision of authentic development includes the active participation of all people, including their access to education and the development of a democratic society that can ensure freedom and peace. Rather like Pope Francis, he refers to ' ... the damaging effects on the real economy of badly managed and largely speculative financial dealing, large-scale migration of peoples, often provided by some particular circumstance and then given insufficient attention, [and] the unregulated exploitation of the earth's resources' (Pope Benedict XVI, 2009, para 21). He challenges people to 'liberate ourselves from ideologies, which often oversimplify reality in artificial ways' (Pope Benedict XVI, 2009, para 22) where the 'world's wealth is growing in absolute terms, but inequalities are on the increase' (para 22). He says that the world needs a new way of understanding business so that they 'assume responsibility for all the other stakeholders who contribute to the life of the business: the workers, the clients, the suppliers of various elements of production, the community of reference' (Pope Benedict XVI, 2009, para 40). He says that the 'economy needs ethics in order to function correctly – not any ethics ... but an ethics which is people-centred' (Pope Benedict XVI, 2009, para 45).

In the last section of *Caritas in Veritate* (2009), Pope Benedict XVI (see Chapter 4 of this book) addresses people's relationship with the natural environment and he reminds readers that the environment ' ... is God's gift to everyone, and in our use of it we have a responsibility towards the poor, towards future generations and towards humanity as a whole' (para 48).

Individualism, consumerism, greed, racism, sexism and the dynamics of neoliberal globalisation present obstacles to solidarity. CST suggests some ways of overcoming these obstacles in order to promote solidarity among people across the world. Given the world situation, it is crucial that those who wish to address human needs and dismantle unjust social structures share their insights and work together to make solidarity an even greater reality.

Commitment to social justice is at the heart of Catholic Christianity and central to actions for justice. Fundamental to CST is 'Christian humanism' with its emphasis on human dignity and human rights. In 2017, marking the 50th anniversary of *Populorum Progressio*, the Congregation for Catholic Education ([CCE] 2017) issued a document entitled, *Educating to fraternal (sic) humanism: Building a civilization of love*. The document challenges people to act in solidarity in order to address social justice inequities. 'Fraternal humanism' is a relatively new term used in Catholic education documents and so needs some unpacking. While 'humanism' is often associated with a philosophical and cultural movement that rejects religion, Catholic theology has, in the past, used the term 'Christian humanism' to capture the idea of looking out for the needs of others and the welfare of the whole community. *Populorum Progressio* (Pope Paul VI, 1967) calls people to 'full-bodied humanism' (para 42) which is open to the world and to others and where development of the individual entails the development of the human race as a whole. In using the term 'fraternal' (a gender exclusive term), the Congregation challenges people to cooperate for the sake of global solidarity. It says, drawing on the words of Benedict XVI (2009):

> … a new trajectory of thinking in order to arrive at a better understanding of the implications of our being one family; interaction among the peoples of the world calls us to embark upon this new trajectory, so that integration can signify solidarity rather than marginalization. (para 13)

Subsidiarity and participation

The principle of subsidiarity is one of the most fundamental principles of CST. It means that decisions should be made at the lowest level possible and the highest level necessary. The principle of subsidiarity applies to all aspects of life: government, economics, medical ethics, allocation of resources and social ethics.

The concept of subsidiarity, albeit without that name, was first introduced in *Rerum Novarum* (1891) when Pope Leo XIII argued that the state should support lower social units and not subsume them. It was further developed in *Quadragesimo Anno* (1931) by Pope Pius XI who was concerned about the common good of society, particularly in the light of increased state power and increasing individualism. He wrote

> ... Just as it is gravely wrong to take from individuals what they can accomplish by their own initiative and industry and give it to the community, so also it is an injustice and at the same time a grave evil and disturbance of right order to assign to a greater and higher association what lesser and subordinate organizations can do. For every social activity ought of its very nature to furnish help to the members of the body social, and never destroy and absorb them. (Pope Pius, 1931, para 79)

Pope Pius XI (1931) also reminds governments that the state grows rich through the work of people and therefore the distribution of wealth should serve the common good of society (para 53). He articulates a positive role for the Church in economic and social affairs and calls for a moral renovation of society through action for justice.

In *Mater et Magistra* (1961), Pope John XXIII draws attention to subsidiarity when he speaks of the need for cooperation in society, especially regarding scientific developments:

> The present advance in scientific knowledge and productive technology clearly puts it within the power of the public authority to a much greater degree than ever before to reduce imbalances which may exist between different branches of the economy or between different regions within the same country or even between the different peoples of the world ... Hence the insistent demands on those in authority – since they are responsible for the common good – to increase the degree and scope of their activities in the economic sphere, and to devise ways and means and set the necessary machinery in motion for the attainment of this end. (para 54)

Because the principle of subsidiarity is focused on the common good within a well-ordered society, it requires the state, institutions, churches and individuals to work together for the good of all. In *Pacem in Terris* (1963), Pope John XXIII highlights the positive role governments need to play in society:

> It is also demanded by the common good that civil authorities should make earnest efforts to bring about a situation in which individual citizens can easily exercise their rights and fulfil their duties as well. For experience has taught us that, unless these authorities take suitable

action with regard to economic, political and cultural matters, inequalities between the citizens tend to become more and more widespread, especially in the modern world, and as a result human rights are rendered totally ineffective and the fulfillment of duties is compromised. (para 63)

The principle of subsidiarity is closely connected to the principle of solidarity where there is a strong sense that governments should create conditions which enable human flourishing. In *Caritas in Veritate* (2009), Pope Benedict XVI says, ' ... subsidiarity respects personal dignity by recognising in the person a subject who is always capable of giving something to others' (para 57).

Subsidiarity contributes to the promotion of human dignity and the common good and is a way of protecting people from abuses by higher-level social authority. It calls on people to participate in society in order to safeguard the common good and the rights of minorities, and encourages citizens to be actively involved in the political and social reality of their country. Subsidiarity both justifies and sets limits on the activities of the state. As Pope Benedict XVI (2005) said, 'We do not need a State which regulates and controls everything, but a State which, in accordance with the principles of subsidiarity, generously acknowledges and supports initiatives arising from different social forces and combines spontaneity with closeness to those in need' (para 28). Pope John XXIII, in *Pacem in Terris* (1963), reminded all Catholics and 'men and women of good will' that it is their duty to acknowledge and respect the rights of others (para 30), collaborate mutually and wholeheartedly by contributing to the creation of civic order (para 31).

An extension of subsidiarity and the common good is seen in the principle of democratic participation. All people in society have the responsibility to contribute to and develop the communities to which they belong. Every person has the right and duty to participate in the full range of activities and institutions of social life, including political participation. Anything that blocks democratic or economic participation is a serious offence against human rights and human dignity. Employment is one of the major ways in which citizens participate in society, and many social encyclicals from *Rerum Novarum* through to *Laudato Si'* have highlighted the importance and value of work both for the individual and for the wider community.

Pope Paul VI breaks new ground in the Apostolic Letter, *Octogesima Adveniens* (1971), when he presents a theory for the role of individual Christians and local churches in responding to situations of injustice:

> It is up to the Christian communities to analyse with objectivity the situation which is proper to their own country, to shed on it the light of the Gospel's unalterable words and to draw principles of reflection, norms of judgment and directives for action from the social teaching of the Church. (para 4)

He goes on to speak out against discrimination because of race, religion, culture, gender and colour and calls for political action as well as economic action:

> Political power, which is the natural and necessary link for ensuring the cohesion of the social body, must have as its aim the achievement of the common good. While respecting the legitimate liberties of individuals, families and subsidiary groups, it acts in such a way as to create, effectively and for the well-being of all, the conditions required for attaining humanity's true and complete good, including spiritual ends … To take politics seriously at its different levels – local, regional, national and worldwide – is to affirm the duty of all people to recognise the concrete reality and the value of the freedom of choice that is offered to them to seek to bring about both the good of the city and of the nation and of all humanity. Politics are a demanding manner – but not the only one – of living the Christian commitment to the service of others. (Pope Paul VI, 1971, para 46)

According to the principle of participation, all people have the right and responsibility to participate in political institutions so that government can achieve its proper goals. One of the important functions of government is to assist citizens in fulfilling their responsibility to others in society. Everyone has the right to participate in the economic, political and cultural life of society. It is wrong for a person or group to be excluded unfairly or to be unable to participate in society. Everyone should take part in the building up of community as far as possible as this is one way that the dignity of the human person is promoted.

Pope Benedict XVI (2011) describes participation as:

> … acting in a responsible way on the basis of an objective and integral knowledge of the facts; it means deconstructing political ideologies which end up supplanting truth and human dignity in order to promote pseudo-values under the pretext of peace, development and human rights; it means fostering an unswerving commitment to base positive law on the principles of natural law. (p. 5)

Pope Francis (2015b), in his address to the joint session of the United States Congress in 2015, reminded people that

> Each son or daughter of a given country has a mission, a personal and social responsibility … A political society endures when it seeks, as a vocation, to satisfy common needs by stimulating the growth of all its members, especially those in situations of greater vulnerability or risk. (p. 1)

The social nature of humankind, articulated in the book of Genesis (Genesis 2:18), calls all people to play an integral part in the family of humanity interconnected with local, national and global life, contributing to development of society and social transformation.

Some concluding remarks

The integrity of the interrelationships between all CST principles emerges clearly from the above consideration of the dignity of the human person, common good, preferential option for the poor, stewardship of creation, solidarity, and subsidiarity and participation. Together, these principles provide a set of signposts and questions to guide people in the choices they make and actions they take when addressing justice in the world. One of the major strengths of CST is that it is humanistic, in the sense that it appeals not just to Christians but to all people. Such a strength enables a dialogue across and within various traditions, including the language of human rights. Other strengths include its emphasis on the sharing of power through participation and subsidiarity and on community solidarity and responsibility, rather than individualism.

CST provides the basis for a rigorous critique of modern-day education policy directions, as discussed in Chapter 1 of this book, and so it is particularly important for Catholic schools to apply a faith-based critique of market educational values. The most recent social encyclical, *Laudato Si'*, the focus of Chapter 3, underlines the importance and urgency of such a critique from the perspective of Catholic schooling. These concluding remarks, which are focused on the relevance of CST to education, are developed further in various chapters. The manner in which the Ontario Institute for Catholic Education and Ontario Catholic Education Districts (see Chapter 6) have been realising the potential of CST is particularly relevant.

While CST clearly has the potential to make the world a better place, one wherein peace, justice and love are the norm, it is regrettable that only a few Catholics are aware of the CST tradition. It is noteworthy that the Catholic Bishops of the United States called on educators in 1998 to serve as 'leaven in the wider society' by more overtly teaching about CST within the general curriculum of schools stating,

> There are many innovative efforts by Catholic educators to communicate the social doctrine of the Church. At the same time, however, it is clear that in some education programs Catholic Social Teaching is not really shared or not sufficiently integral and explicit. As a result, far too many Catholics are not familiar with the basic content of Catholic Social Teaching. More fundamentally, many Catholics do not adequately understand that the social teaching of the Church is an essential part of

Catholic faith. This poses a serious challenge for all Catholics, since it weakens our capacity to be a Church that is true to the demands of the Gospel. (United States Catholic Bishops, 1998)

They call on those involved in Catholic education to teach the Catholic social tradition in its fullness and identify that there is an urgent need to incorporate CST more fully and explicitly into Catholic educational programmes and integrating CST into the mainstream of all Catholic educational institutions. 'Catholic schools ... are vitally important for sharing the substance and values of CST ... the social justice dimensions of teaching are integral to Catholic education ... [and] an essential part of Catholic identity and formation' (United States Catholic Bishops, 1998). The '... values of the Church's social teaching must not be treated as tangential or optional [but]... a core part of teaching ... otherwise programs would be offering an incomplete presentation of the Catholic tradition' (United States Catholic Bishops, 1998).

The CCE (2017) document, *Educating to Fraternal (sic) Humanism* (EFH), also focuses on the relevance of CST to education when it states

> Education to fraternal (sic) humanism must make sure that learning knowledge means becoming aware of an ethical universe in which the person acts. In particular, this correct notion of the ethical universe must open up progressively wider horizons of the common good, so as to embrace the entire human family ... the specific task that education to fraternal (sic) humanism can perform is to contribute to building such a culture based on intergenerational ethics. (para 20–21)

In many Catholic schools, social justice activities are part of the broader religious life of the school and fundraising activities or food collections often take place for worthy charities. In some schools, CST is taught as part of the religious education curriculum and astute teachers make relevant links between the broader justice-based activities within the religious life of the school and teaching about justice in the religious education curriculum. Only a few teachers, however, make planned links between CST and the general curriculum.

Models of enquiry learning and frames of analysis are used in humanities subjects such as history, geography, economics and citizenship. The Cardijn *See, Judge, Act* model (Pope John XXIII, 1961, para 236) and the pastoral circle approach (Holland & Henriot, 1986), discussed in Chapters 3 and 11 of this book, provide scaffolding for the use of CST principles for decision-making processes in classroom situations. The considered selection of appropriate resources for teaching and learning provides another valuable opportunity to apply the lens of CST to teaching, learning and curriculum. This may not involve finding new materials or resources but rather asking different, more critical, questions of existing resources. CST concerns social issues; it enables students to focus their learning on the real world and to act in response to their investigations of the associated complexities and ambiguities.

It is noteworthy that, over time, CST has moved from a deductive, top-down style to a more inductive, bottom-up mode of reasoning and action, from statements about justice to providing people with ideas for the way they might go about acting for justice. The idea of *praxis* (the unique mixture of theory and action) is now an integral component of CST. In a time of rapid social change marked by apathy, CST is a vehicle through which people can engage and comment on public life and present a voice for justice. It is the Church's presentation and articulation of its reflection on human beings in society which is an essential element of faith. CST also provides principles for reflection, criteria for judgement, and guidelines for action. In education, CST can be used as a lens through which to interpret and critique the general curriculum and it offers one valuable way of developing identity within the Catholic tradition.

References

Aubert, R., & Boileau, D. (2003). *Catholic social teaching: An historical perspective*. Milwaukee: Marquette University Press.

Beyer, G. J. (2014). The meaning of solidarity in Catholic social teaching. *Political Theology*, *15*(1), 7–25.

Boal, A. (1979). *Theatre of the oppressed*. London: Pluto Press.

Brady, B. V. (2008). *Essential Catholic social thought*. New York, NY: Orbis Books.

Caritas (2018) Retrieved from https://www.caritas.org.au/learn/cst

Catechism of the Catholic Church (CCC). (2003). Retrieved from http://www.vatican.va/archive/ENG0015/_INDEX.HTM

Centre of Concern. (2018) Retrieved from https://educationforjustice.org/topics/

Charles, R. (1998). *Christian social witness and teaching: The Catholic tradition from Genesis to Centesimus Annus* (Vol. 1). Leominster: Gracewing.

Congregation for Catholic Education (CCE). (2017). *Educating to fraternal humanism: Building a civilization of love 50 years after Populorum progressio*. Retrieved from http://www.vatican.va/roman_curia/congregations/ccatheduc/documents/rc_con_ccatheduc_doc_20170416_educare-umanesimo-solidale_en.html

Cortright, D. (2014). Assessing Pacem in Terris 50 years on: A personal odyssey. *Journal of Catholic Social Thought, 11*(1), 33–46.

Curran, C. (1991). *Catholic social teaching 1891-present: A historical, theological, and ethical analysis*. Washington, DC: Georgetown University Press.

De Berri, E., Hug, J., & Henriot, P. (2003). *Catholic social teaching: Our best kept secret*. New York, NY: Orbis Books.

Dorr, D. (2012). *Option for the poor and for the earth: Catholic social teaching*. New York, NY: Orbis Books.

Freire, P. (1970). *Pedagogy of the oppressed*. New York, NY: Continuum.

Holland, J., & Henriot, P. (1986). *Social analysis: Linking faith and justice.* New York, NY: Orbis Books.

Hollenbach, D. (2011). Caritas in Veritate: The meaning of love and urgent challenges of justice. *Journal of Catholic Social Thought, 8*(10), 171–182.

Hornsby-Smith, M. P. (2006). *An introduction to Catholic social thought.* New York, NY: Cambridge University Press.

Kirwan, M. (2012). Liberation theology and Catholic social teaching. *New Blackfriars, 93*(1044), 246–258.

Massaro, T. (2012). Nine key themes of Catholic social teaching. In *Living Justice: Catholic Social Teaching in Action* (2nd ed., pp. 113–165). Lanham: Rowman & Littlefield.

Pope Benedict XVI. (2005). Encyclical letter *Deus caritas est*. Retrieved from http://w2.vatican.va/content/benedictxvi/en/encyclicals/documents/hf_benxvi_enc_20051225_deus-caritas-est.html

Pope Benedict XVI. (2009). Encyclical letter *Caritas in Veritate*. Retrieved from http://w2.vatican.va/content/benedict-xvi/en/encyclicals/documents/hf_ben-xvi_enc_20090629_caritas-in-veritate.html

Pope Benedict XVI. (2011). *Message of His Holiness Pope Benedict XVI for the celebration of the World Day of Peace.* Retrieved from http://w2.vatican.va/content/benedict-xvi/en/messages/peace/documents/hf_ben-xvi_mes_20101208_xliv-world-day-peace.pdf

Pope Francis. (2015a). Encyclical letter *Laudato si'*. Retrieved from http://w2.vatican.va/content/francesco/en/encyclicals/documents/papa-francesco_20150524_enciclica-laudato-si.html

Pope Francis. (2015b). *Address of the Holy Father to the joint session of the United States Congress.* Retrieved from http://w2.vatican.va/content/francesco/en/speeches/2015/september/documents/papa-francesco_20150924_usa-us-congress.pdf

Pope John Paul II. (1979). Encyclical letter *Redemptor hominis*. Retrieved from http://w2.vatican.va/content/john-paul-ii/en/encyclicals/documents/hf_jp-ii_enc_04031979_redemptor-hominis.html

Pope John Paul II. (1980). *Dives in misericordia*. Retrieved from http://w2.vatican.va/content/john-paul-ii/en/encyclicals/documents/hf_jp-ii_enc_30111980_dives-in-misericordia.html

Pope John Paul II. (1981). *Laborem exercens*. Retrieved from http://w2.vatican.va/content/john-paul-ii/en/encyclicals/documents/hf_jp-ii_enc_14091981_laborem-exercens.html

Pope John Paul II. (1987). Encyclical letter *Sollicitudo rei socialis*. Retrieved from http://w2.vatican.va/content/john-paul-ii/en/encyclicals/documents/hf_jp-ii_enc_30121987_sollicitudo-rei-socialis.html

Pope John Paul II. (1991). Encyclical letter *Centesimus annus*. Retrieved from http://w2.vatican.va/content/john-paul-ii/en/encyclicals/documents/hf_jp-ii_enc_01051991_centesimus-annus.html

Pope John XXIII. (1961). Encyclical letter *Mater et magistra*. Retrieved from http://w2.vatican.va/content/john-xxiii/en/encyclicals/documents/hf_j-xxiii_enc_15051961_mater.html

Pope John XXIII. (1963). Encyclical letter *Pacem in terris*. Retrieved from http://w2.vatican.va/content/john-xxiii/en/encyclicals/documents/hf_j-xxiii_enc_11041963_pacem.html

Pope Leo XIII. (1891). Encyclical letter *Rerum Novarum*. Retrieved from http://w2.vatican.va/content/leo-xiii/en/encyclicals/documents/hf_l-xiii_enc_15051891_rerum-novarum.html

Pope Paul VI. (1967). Encyclical letter *Populorum progressio*. Retrieved from http://w2.vatican.va/content/paul-vi/en/encyclicals/documents/hf_p-vi_enc_26031967_populorum.html

Pope Paul VI. (1971). Apostolic Letter *Octogesima adveniens*. Retrieved from http://w2.vatican.va/content/paul-vi/en/apost_letters/documents/hf_p-vi_apl_19710514_octogesima-adveniens.html

Pope Pius XI. (1931). Encyclical letter *Quadragesimo anno*. Retrieved from http://w2.vatican.va/content/pius-xi/en/encyclicals/documents/hf_p-xi_enc_19310515_quadragesimo-anno.html

Schuck, M. J. (2013). The Catholic Church and the movements: Revisiting the history of Catholic social thought. *Journal of Catholic Social Thought, 10*(2), 241–257.

Second Vatican Council. (1965). *Gaudium et spes*. Retrieved from http://www.vatican.va/archive/hist_councils/ii_vatican_council/documents/vat-ii_const_19651207_gaudium-et-spes_en.html

Synod of Bishops. (1971). *Justitia in mundo*. Retrieved from http://www.vatican.va/roman_curia/synod/documents/rc_synod_doc_19711130_giustizia_po.html

United States Catholic Bishops. (1986). *Economic justice for all: Pastoral letter on Catholic social teaching and the US Economy*. Retrieved from http://www.usccb.org/upload/economic_justice_for_all.pdf

United States Conference of Catholic Bishops. (1998). *Sharing Catholic social teaching: Challenges and directions*. Retrieved from http://www.usccb.org/beliefs-and-teachings/what-we-believe/catholic-social-teaching/sharing-catholic-social-teaching-challenges-and-directions.cfm

US Conference of Bishops (2018) Retrieved from http://www.usccb.org/beliefs-and-teachings/what-we-believe/catholic-social-teaching/seven-themes-of-catholic-social-teaching.cfm

Chapter 3

Laudato Si': **Some curriculum and pedagogical implications**

Jim Gleeson and Peta Goldburg rsm

Introduction

Promulgated on 18 June 2015, the social encyclical *Laudato Si'* (On Care of Our Common Home) received widespread publicity in the secular media. Building on the 1963 encyclical *Pacem in Terris* in which Pope John XXIII appealed for peace to 'all people of good will' at a time when the world was on the brink of nuclear war, Pope Francis (2015) in *Laudato Si'* addresses 'every person living on the planet' (para 3) and he identifies climate change, global poverty and deepening inequality as comparable planetary challenges. He expands on ideas presented in earlier social encyclicals of the Catholic Church drawing on the Catholic Social Teaching (CST) principles (see Chapter 2) of the dignity of the human person, the common good, subsidiarity, preferential option for the poor and stewardship of creation. What is new though is that all of these themes are interconnected and linked to the environment in *Laudato Si'*. While the popular press praised *Laudato Si'* as a document which addressed serious environmental issues of our age, it is much more than that insofar as it calls for a 'bold cultural revolution' (Pope Francis, 2015, para 114).

Key aspects of *Laudato Si'*

Pope Francis (2015) introduces a robust theology of creation and a comprehensive vision of the world encouraging people to take a global perspective rather than focusing on commitment to nationalities, ideologies, economic theories and politics. The document, six chapters in total, is structured using Joseph Cardijn's *See, Judge, Act* model from the Young Christian Worker movement of the 20th century, later expanded by the liberation theologians as the model for social analysis (Boff, 2015).

Chapter 1, the 'See' section, examines the symptoms of environmental degradation and calls on the reader to hear the cry of the poor and earth as both suffer from climate change, the impact of carbon intensive economies and the social and environmental impact of mining. Chapters 2, 3 and 4, the

'Judge' section, draw on Scriptural traditions and critique anthropocentrism, consumerism and the human roots of the ecological crisis while calling for the development of an integral ecology. Chapters 5 and 6, the 'Act' section, suggest an approach for action including international collective actions such as switching from fossil fuels to renewables, and the development of international agreements and legislation, while Chapter 6 focuses more specifically on ecological education and spirituality.

Laudato Si' clearly draws on the Catholic theological tradition as evidenced in its referencing of Saints Francis of Assisi, Bonaventure and Thomas Aquinas. Pope Francis (2015) places the encyclical within the modern, ongoing CST tradition saying this encyclical 'is now added to the body of the Church's social teaching' (para 15). He emphasises the continuing nature of the Church's social tradition referring to earlier popes who first drew attention to world challenges and ecological issues. He quotes Pope Paul VI, who in *Octogesima adveniens* (1971) alerted people to the 'tragic consequences' of environmental degradation and the '… ill-considered exploitation of nature' (para 21). He reminds people that Pope John Paul II (1991) said that we should 'safeguard the moral conditions for an authentic human ecology' (para 38) and that authentic human development presumes respect of the human person and the world and that people should 'take into account the nature of each being and of its mutual connection in an ordered system' (SRS para 34). He also refers to Pope Benedict XVI who said that the world cannot be analysed from one perspective only and that 'the deterioration of nature is closely connected to the culture which shapes human coexistence' (CV para 51). *Laudato Si'* is presented as a public examination of conscience about how people live in communion with God as well as how people live with others and all of creation.

Pope Francis (2015) acknowledges that Christians have at times in the past misinterpreted Genesis 1:28 '… Be fruitful and multiply and fill the earth and subdue it; and have dominion over the fish of the sea and over the birds of the air and over every living thing that moves upon the earth'. He acknowledges that '[w]e had never mistreated and offended our common home as much as in the last two centuries' (Pope Francis, 2015, para 53). Building on environmental theology and social teaching concerning creation, redemption and the role of humanity, *Laudato Si'* shows how the resources of the natural environment are, in their own right, important to the creation and redemption of the universe, arguing that it is essential that humanity respects creation and exercises stewardship over it.

Pope Francis (2015) speaks of 'a constant schizophrenia [resulting from] a misguided anthropocentrism' (para 118) and criticises the dominant technocratic paradigm of our modern world which results in a mindset that blinds people to the intrinsic value of other creatures and beings. Such thinking, he says, leads to exploitation of children and abandonment of the elderly. Consequently, Pope Francis (2015) argues that we need 'a distinctive way of looking at things' in order to 'resist the assault of the technocratic paradigm' (para 111).

One of the key points of *Laudato si'* is that relationality should come before individuality since we are all interconnected and interrelated (Pope Francis, 2015, paras 16, 91, 92, 120, 137, 141, 240). An important aspect of relationality which is evident in the encyclical is the kinship which exists between the human world and the natural world. Dialogue is another theme consistent throughout *Laudato Si'*. As well as calling for dialogue among the religions, Pope Francis (2015) calls for a 'new dialogue about how we are shaping our planet' (para 14). He calls for an 'intense' and 'fruitful' dialogue between religion and science (para 62), between ecology and spirituality (paras 216–221) and between politics and economics (paras 189–198). This emphasis on dialogue is intrinsic to the development of a new theological anthropology.

The entire third chapter of the encyclical is devoted to an analysis of 'the human root of the ecological crisis' (Pope Francis, 2015, paras 101/136). Pope Francis (2015) addresses the concept of authentic development which is a holistic understanding of the interaction of economies and the rights and dignity of people. 'Social love' he says, 'moves us to devise larger strategies to halt environmental degradation and to encourage a "culture of care" which permeates all of society' (Pope Francis, 2015, para 231). In the tradition of the liberationists, he points out that the global poor are materially harmed by the degradation of the planet and raises the issue of 'compulsive consumerism' (Pope Francis, 2015, para 203) which gives people the impression that they are free because 'they have ... the freedom to consume' (para 203).

Pope Francis (2015) is vehement in his critique of greed and consumerism and his focus on the poor prompts him to suggest that there should be differentiated responsibilities for the planet and that 'countries which have benefited from a high degree of industrialisation ... have a great responsibility for providing a solution to the problems they have caused' (para 170). He also identifies our misguided, modern anthropocentrism as one of the sources of the ecological crisis. *Laudato Si'* presents peace, justice and the preservation of creation as three interconnected human rights themes.

Anthropocentrism, anthropology and education

In order to understand the implications of this encyclical for education, we first of all need to consider its concerns regarding modern forms of anthropocentrism and its call for a new anthropology. Any such change is, of course, relevant to our way of knowing (epistemology) and to education and curriculum in Catholic schools.

Anthropology: The 'red thread'

Pope Francis (2015) is forthright in his condemnation of what he calls the prevailing 'tyrannical' (para 68), 'distorted' (para 69), 'excessive' (para 116) and 'misguided' (paras 119, 122) forms of anthropocentrism which compromise the 'intrinsic dignity of the world [with the result that] human beings misunderstand themselves and end up acting against themselves' (para 115). This creates an environment where technical thought is prized over reality (Pope Francis, 2015, para 106), thus shaping the lives of individuals and the workings of society (para 107) and dominating economic and political life (para 109). Drawing on Vatican II and the work of Charles Taylor (2007), Lane (2015) emphasises the importance of listening to the 'signs of the times' and highlights the significance of 'the social and cultural context in which education takes place today' (p. 28). This necessitates a move away from a form of anthropocentrism which is characterised by 'radical individualism, the myth of the self-sufficient subject, the commodification of the self through market demands, the deconstruction of the self by postmodernity, gender issues and the spiritual and cultural isolation of the self in the twenty-first century' (Lane, 2017a, p. 128). Australian readers will be more familiar with the related position adopted by Pollefeyt and Bouwens (2010).

While recognising the role of education in bringing about change (para 15), Pope Francis (2015) is adamant that no amount of education will succeed unless we come up with a new way of thinking about human beings (paras 9, 215). Noting that recent Vatican documents such as *Instrumentum Laboris* (Congregation for Catholic Education [CCE], 2014) and *Laudato Si'* (2015) recognise that anthropology is 'in crisis', Lane (2017a, p. 127) asserts that 'anthropology has the potential to be the centrepiece of Catholic education' and sees it as 'a red thread running through many areas of life: economics, ecology, ethics, education, philosophy and theology' (Lane, 2017b, p. 64). *Educating to fraternal humanism* (CCE, 2017, para 5) calls for 'the joint development of civic opportunities with an educational plan that promotes... cooperation in a united world [and this is] now an anthropological question which involves an educational component that can no longer be deferred'.

Anthropology and education

So, what is the relationship between anthropology and education? Anthropology is 'the study of what it means to be a human being, an examination of what is at the core of human identity, an examination of human flourishing' (Lane, 2017a, p. 63). This has been the core question in some of the better-known curriculum developments of the 20th century including Man (sic): A Course of Study (Bruner, 1966), the Humanities Curriculum Project (Stenhouse, 1968) and the Ontario Social Studies Curriculum (Ontario Ministry of Education, 2004). As Gonzalez (2010) reminds us, the field of 'anthropology and education [with its] deep roots in social critiques of schools and schooling... began by asking how and why do human beings educate the way they do?' (p. 249). Since education policy and practice are deeply embedded in social processes, 'basic theoretical questions cannot be decontextualised from political and applied questions' (Gonzalez, 2010, p. 249). The influence of neoliberal thinking and market values on our modern-day education systems and schools (Ball, 2012; Gleeson, 2015; Lingard, 2010) is such that, as Levinson (2005) states in his paper on the anthropology of education, 'now more than ever our schools overwhelmingly seek to create the economically competent or adaptable worker, not the democratic or intercultural citizen' (p. 329).

Anthropologists of education have been primarily concerned with advocacy around linguistic, immigration and indigenous issues. However, *Laudato Si'* (2015) and authors such as Lane (2015, 2017a, 2017b) and others are raising more fundamental issues to do with what Tillich called life's ultimate questions: 'what is meaningful, what gives life purpose, how do I discern right from wrong' (Valk, 2007, p. 273). Valk (2007) suggests that the various responses to these questions are best seen in terms of worldviews which play important and significant roles in our diverse modern society. As is the case with Catholic identities (Arbuckle, 2013), there is also multiplicity of Catholic worldviews. In a similar mode, Lane (2017a) suggests that we must revise our 'inadequate presentation of Christian anthropology' (p. 131) and 'move beyond the modern notion that one anthropology fits all' (Lane, 2017b, p. 66). This raises interesting theological questions that are beyond the scope of this chapter insofar as 'official' Catholic anthropology is predicated on a monomorphic/monolithic worldview that includes fundamental beliefs regarding original sin, natural law, sexuality, gender, the state of grace, eschatology and human destiny.

Laudato Si', knowledge paradigms and school curriculum

As part of his critique of anthropocentrism, Pope Francis (2015) calls for 'an educational programme [that] generates resistance to the assault of the technocratic paradigm' (para 111). Writing from a secular perspective, Boyte (2016) notes that '*Laudato Si'* [includes] a trenchant critique of technocracy that clearly articulates the limits of scientific and technological modes of thought [and calls for] a larger understanding of the public and human purposes and practices of knowledge-making' (p. 53) which is obviously a fundamental aspect of education. The technocratic paradigm treats education in isolation from 'its cultural and socio-cultural contexts', as if it were apolitical and value-free (Cornbleth, 1990, p. 17). It ignores questions about the nature and purpose of knowledge and treats knowledge as 'an object that can be reproduced and given to students [and whose] possession is indicated by [student performance] on a pencil and paper test' (Cornbleth, 1990, p. 18).

Boyte (2016) goes on to identify the dangers inherent in positivist approaches to knowledge when they 'become the default, unselfconscious way of seeing [and where] the economy accepts every advance in technology with a view to profit, without concern for its potentially negative impact on human beings' (p. 54). This resonates with Lane's (2017a) argument that:

> Western societies have been held captive to a market-driven capitalism and new-liberal economics [where] the dignity of the individual, the well-being of the community and earth-community, the integrity of human relationships and respect for human embodiment are of another order. (p. 71)

In sharp contrast to the technical knowledge paradigm, Confucianism viewed the school curriculum in terms of the story we tell our children about the virtuous life, while Aristotle (1980) saw it as that which is conducive 'to the good life in general' where the focus is on *phronesis* (*what* is to be done, practical wisdom) rather than *techne* (*how* something can be done) (p. 142). Another possible variation involves the replacement of the noun 'curriculum' (a course to be run) with the Latin verb *currere* (Pinar, 2004), 'the running of the course' (p. 35). These options involve the replacement of what Habermas calls the technical interest with his emancipatory interest where the dominant concerns include the distribution of power and the questioning of previously taken-for-granted assumptions (Carr & Kemmis, 1986). This involves the emancipation of the student through the process of learning, what Stenhouse (1975) calls 'a critical model, not a marking model' (p. 80) that is predicated on pedagogical and ethical principles of procedure.

Such approaches represent a transformative vision of education where the parts of society are interdependent rather than fragmented and independent, where the common good is promoted directly rather than indirectly, where government is seen as participative rather than managerial, where problems require structural transformation rather than continuous improvement and where the central values are communitarian rather than individualistic. Meanwhile the CCE (2017, para 6) calls for a fraternal (sic) humanism, 'putting the person at the centre of education, in a framework of relationships that make up a living community, which is interdependent and bound to a common destiny'.

So what is the contribution of *Laudato Si'* (2015) to resolving the dilemma presented by these conflicting theories of knowledge and educational philosophies? Boyte (2016) identifies three values that are common to civic studies and *Laudato Si'*. First, the shared emphasis on 'everyday citizens [as] primary agents of change', which reflects the Pope's involvement with the Theology of the People movement, 'the community organizing practices which empowered the poorest of people in the slums of cities like Buenos Aires' (Boyte, 2016, p. 51). Second, he believes that *Laudato Si'* is very effective in translating 'sharp disciplinary distinctions between empirical sciences (natural and social), normative fields (humanities), and action fields (the professions)' (Boyte, 2016) into mainstream public culture and intellectual life (p. 53).

Third, Boyte (2016) argues that Pope Francis' invocation of CSTs speaks to the 'growing crisis of work across the whole of modern societies [by challenging the notion of work] as a means to an end [where] people work "to live"—dictated by the narrow imperatives of profit taking' (p. 56).

Laudato Si' and Catholic Education

The CCE (1997) defines the fundamental characteristics of the Catholic school in terms of the 'integral education of the human person through a clear educational project of which Christ is the foundation ... [one that involves] love [and] service to society' (p. 4) and it criticises the 'noticeable tendency to reduce education to its purely technical and practical aspects' (p. 10). *Instrumentum Laboris* (CCE, 2014) calls for a holistic, integrated education that is focused on students' search for meaning and warns against simply responding to 'the demands deriving from the ever-changing economic situation' (para 64). Reminiscent of Stenhouse (1975), the CCE (2014, para 12) notes that education transcends mere instruction and comments critically on the 'merely functional view of education' taken by the European Union, Organisation for Economic Co-operation and Development (OECD) and the World Bank and on the instrumental and competitive emphases found in the education policies of several countries with their 'instrumental reason and competitiveness ... [and their concerns with] the market economy and the labour market'. All of this challenges us to 'redefine our vision regarding education' (CCE, 2014, para 6) and to 'express the anthropology underlining our educational vision for the 21st century in different terms' that are theocentric and characterised by truth, human relationships as a way of being and sustainable development.

While Catholic Education has often been understood as a 'synthesis between culture and faith' (CCE, 1997, p. 14), this raises the question: what culture are we talking about? Is it the prevailing neoliberal, anthropocentric culture or an emancipatory, faith-based culture? As Lane (2015) remarks, the 'disconnect between faith and contemporary culture is the greatest challenge facing Catholic education today' (p. 42). Pascoe (2007) argues that Catholic schools in Australia (and beyond) serve two masters. On the one hand, they tell potential students and parents that the purpose of Catholic schools is to educate the whole person, promote faith, provide pastoral care and achieve the prescribed learning outcomes. On the other hand, their engagements with government are likely to focus on matters such as core purpose, parent choice, legislative compliance, good governance, accountability and meeting formal agreements.

The holistic philosophy of education promoted by the Congregation and *Laudato Si'* focuses on CST principles outlined in Chapter 2, such as the common good (Pope Francis, 2015, para 204), the dignity of the human person (para 205), preferential option for the poor (para 158) and subsidiarity and participation (social responsibility; paras 206–208). Rowlands (2015) believes that Pope Francis' (2015) challenge to 'the dominant ideas of competitive individualism [is] already uttering a kind of politics and a kind of theology' that is closely related with CST as evidenced by his 'intervention on migrants … the most striking example of this prior to *Laudato Si*" (p. 418). Lane (2017b) argues that such a 'theology of anthropology [is] fast becoming the red button issue in ethics, in ecology, in gender studies, in religion and in theology … [a theology] that aims at liberation through kenosis' (p. 134).

Ormerod (2016) remarks that the 'two words which appear throughout [*Laudato Si*'] are "urgent" and "crisis"'(p. 5), adding that Pope Francis identifies a number of areas where 'significant changes in attitudes and forms of social organisation' are required: religious; moral; cultural; social, economic and political. While all of these are of immediate relevance to curriculum, education policymakers and leaders first of all must adopt a 'more critical approach' (Pope Francis, 2015, para 19) if they are to address the increased emphasis on managerialism, standardised testing and performativity (Ball, 2012; Lingard, 2010). Lane (2017b, p. 129) suggests that, if the alternative anthropology set out in *Laudato Si*', with its emphasis on interconnectedness, interrelatedness and interdependence were placed at the centre of Christian education, this would challenge the 'modern myth of unlimited human progress and growth' (Lane, 2015, p. 52) which is predicated on belief in the availability of infinite quantities of energy and resources (Pope Francis, 2015, paras 106, 78).

Laudato Si' *and cross-curricular dialogue*

Laudato Si' laments the way in which knowledge is fragmented by education systems and calls for 'dialogue among the various sciences … since each can tend to become enclosed in its own language, while specialization leads to a certain isolation and the absolutization of its own field of knowledge' (Pope Francis, 2015, para 201). This resonates with the CEE's (2014) recognition of the importance of an interdisciplinary approach to knowledge where:

> … each discipline is not an island inhabited by a form of knowledge that is distinct and ring-fenced; rather, it is in a dynamic relationship with all other forms of knowledge, each of which expresses something about the human person and touches upon some truth. (para 67)

Laudato Si' has clear implications for some of the major cross-curricular issues of our time such as sustainability, well-being and citizenship. The encyclical has received most attention for its focus on climate change and ecological issues, with its publication being welcomed by various international leaders including the UN General Secretary, Ban Ki-moon, senior World Bank figures and the European Commission, and applauded by large environmental non-governmental organisations such as Greenpeace. However, writing from the perspective of environmental science, O'Neill (2016) recognises that *Laudato Si'* is 'not a document exclusively about the environment or climate change. Rather, it addresses wider questions about relations between people and with nature, and about new ways of understanding progress and development' while drawing on scientific research to 'emphasise the scale of the environmental challenge for humanity, highlighting the disproportionate impacts on the poor' (p. 749).

Pope Francis (2015) includes ideas from Catholic thinkers such as Teilhard de Chardin, Romano Guardini, Dante Alighieri, Protestant Paul Ricoeur and Sufi Muslim Al Al-Khawwas (Boff, 2015). For example, he cites Guardini (1998) to the effect that 'the technological mind sees nature as... a cold body of facts, as a mere "given", as an object of utility, as raw material to be hammered into useful shape' (p. 82). *Laudato Si'* also cites the encyclical *Centesimus Annus* (John Paul II, 1991): 'Not only has God given the earth to man (sic), who must use it with respect for the original good purpose for which it was given, but, man too is God's gift to man. He must therefore respect the natural and moral structure with which he has been endowed' (p. 841). Pope Francis (2015) expresses the hope that environmental education will restore ecological equilibrium and establish harmony in the world (para 201) and strongly encourages education in environmental responsibility so as to promote 'ways of acting [that] directly and significantly affect the world around us [and] restore our sense of self-esteem [and] enable us to live more fully' (para 212). Anthropocentrism creates the illusion that things have value only insofar as they are ordered to human use, while ignoring the reality that, since everything is related (paras 137–138), we cannot dominate the earth.

At a time when school curricula are paying increasing attention to 'wellbeing' (Australian Curriculum, Assessment and Reporting Authority, 2012; Department of Education and Skills, 2016), such a holistic approach to education reflects the need for humanity to achieve what Pope Francis (2015) calls a 'new self-awareness' (para 203) that supports a shift away from anthropocentrism and is characterised by 'openness to others, each of whom is a "thou" capable of knowing, loving and entering into dialogue' (para 119). Annett (2016) acknowledges that:

> Pope Francis revived the ancient idea that human life is grounded in... three relationships [with God, with our fellow human beings, and with the land, namely] integral ecology – meaning that when one of these relationships is ruptured, the others are ruptured too. (p. 51)

This resonates with the assertion in *Laudato Si'* that 'there can be no ecology without an adequate anthropology' (Pope Francis, 2015, para 118). As noted by Rowlands (2015), *Laudato Si'* recognises the role of the state in facilitating ecological change and calls for a 'renewal of jurisprudence in conversation with Christian theology' (p. 418).

Whereas well-being is primarily a personal matter, citizenship has to do with societal relationships and social responsibility which have important implications for education for citizenship at local, national and global levels including the responsible use of modern technologies. Boyte (2016) argues that Francis' call for a 'healthy politics' in *Laudato Si'* is like the 'citizen politics' of faith-based communities insofar as it values 'everyday citizens as primary agents of change, developing power in settings which are often disempowering and tapping talents and energies often overlooked or discarded in conventional culture and intellectual life' (p. 51). Boyte (2016) concludes that *Laudato Si'* 'offers building blocks for an alternative understanding of democracy and its politics by emphasizing human particularity in contrast to reductionist strands of philosophy and politics' (p. 57) while Rowlands (2015) notes that *Laudato Si'* recognises the importance of 'reciprocity between citizens and between rich and poor' (p. 418) and arrives at the conclusion that the 'encyclical baptizes no form of politics we currently see on offer' (p. 419).

Laudato Si' *and individual learning areas*

Changes in our understanding of anthropology also have important implications for particular learning areas such as economics, geography, science, literature and visual arts. Francis (2015) is highly critical of 'compulsive consumerism' (para 203) where 'purchasing is always a moral – and not simply economic – act' (para 206). His concerns regarding 'environmental degradation' (Pope Francis, 2015, para 206) have widespread implications for the school curriculum, particularly for economics and geography. As previously discussed, *Laudato Si'* provides the basis for a rigorous critique of neoliberal economics from the perspectives of social justice and CST. Subjects such as science and geography have obvious relevance to environmental sustainability. Pope Francis (2015) recognises the importance of going beyond the transmission of scientific information to critiquing the 'myths' that are 'grounded in a utilitarian mindset (individualism, unlimited progress, competition, consumerism, the unregulated market)' (para 210) while Lane (2015) suggests that 'cosmology and biological evolution would be a good place to begin in addressing our common origins' (p. 50).

Given its strong focus on holistic and emancipatory education it is hardly surprising that *Laudato Si'* highlights the importance of education in the Arts and Humanities – 'if we reason only within the confines of [science], little room would be left for aesthetic sensibility, poetry, or even reason's ability to grasp the ultimate meaning and purpose of things' (Pope Francis, 2015, para 199). This resonates with Murray's (1991) suggestion that 'education should ... address the integral development of the person: aesthetic, creative, critical, cultural, emotional, intellectual, moral, physical, political, social and spiritual' (p. 20). The CCE (2014) warns against simply responding to 'the demands deriving from the ever-changing economic situation. Catholic schools think out their curricula to place centre-stage both individuals and their search for meaning ... What is taught is not neutral, and neither is the way of teaching it' (pp. 10, 64). The CCE (2014) goes on to comment critically on the 'merely functional view of education' (p. 12) taken by agencies such as the OECD and the World Bank and on the instrumental, market-driven competitive education policies of several countries.

The overall picture emerging then is one where *Laudato Si'* is of enormous relevance for education because of its challenges to the fundamental anthropological and epistemological principles on which much educational thought and policy is based and its curriculum implications both in terms of cross-curricular themes that are of considerable importance in modern society and its implications for a wide range of learning areas. Pope Francis (2015) calls for 'educators capable of... helping people, through effective pedagogy, to grow in solidarity, responsibility and compassionate care' (para 210). Given the countercultural messages of both *Laudato Si'* and CST (Chapter 2), these educators will inevitably be engaged in critical pedagogy, the focus of the final section of this chapter.

Critical pedagogy

While we tend to associate critical pedagogy with Freire (1970), Giroux (1981), Macdonald (1971) and Apple (2004), its roots can be traced to Dewey's (1916) social reconstructionist thinking, particularly his critique of acquisitive educational values and his social justice concerns. Madero (2015) reminds us that 'those within the educational field often forget that what informed Freire's thought was not only his humanist background but also his Catholic one' (pp. 122–123). In Freire's (1997) own words, 'all arguments in favour of the legitimacy of my struggle for a more people-oriented society have their deepest roots in my faith. It sustains me, motivates me, challenges me ...' (p. 104). Madero (2015) concludes that Freire, 'without being a theologian, shares the same definitions used by many of the representatives of liberation theology' (p. 126). Freire (1970) was particularly concerned to challenge 'banking' understandings of curriculum 'delivery' by providing problem-based curricula that focused on the lived concerns of students from disadvantaged communities in Brazil. Building on Freire, Macdonald (1971) sought to 'rekindle critical, democratic, practical, progressive and reconstructionist values within schools' (Schubert, 2008, p. 404).

Drawing on Bernstein (1971), Lingard and Mills (2007) assert that pedagogy needs to be located 'within considerations of curricula and the purposes of schooling' (p. 235). This approach is encapsulated in the following extract from a school principal's letter to all teachers at the beginning of the new school year:

> Dear Teacher
> I am the survivor of a concentration camp. My eyes saw what no person should witness:
> Gas chambers built by learned engineers.
> Children poisoned by educated physicians.
> Infants killed by trained nurses.
> Women and babies shot and burned by high school and college graduates.
> So I am suspicious of education. My request is: Help your students become human. Your efforts must never produce learned monsters, skilled psychopaths, educated Eichmanns. Writing and arithmetic are important only if they were to make our children more humane. (Delpit, 2006, p. xix)

Critical pedagogy is concerned with social justice issues and societal divisions that result from unequal power and undemocratic institutions (Hayes, Mills, Christie, & Lingard, 2006). Pope Francis (2015) suggests that the prevailing 'vision of "might is right" has engendered immense inequality, injustice and acts of violence against the majority of humanity, since resources end up in the hands of the first comer or the most powerful: the winner takes all' (para 82). Critical pedagogy poses the question that epitomises the emancipatory rather than the dominant technical paradigm: who benefits? As Giroux (2004) puts it, 'the fundamental challenge facing educators within the current age of neoliberalism is to provide the conditions for students to address how knowledge is related to the power of both self-definition and social agency' (p. 34). For Giroux (2004), critical pedagogues are public intellectuals who 'refuse all attempts to reduce classroom teaching exclusively to matters of technique and method' (p. 41) in pursuit of moral and political imperatives that are 'premised on the assumption that learning is not about processing received knowledge but actually transforming it as part of a more expansive struggle for individual rights and social justice' (p. 34).

This struggle means that critical pedagogues must inevitably address controversial issues in their classrooms. A matter is controversial 'if contrary views can be held on it without those views being contrary to reason' (Dearden, 1981, p. 38), for example when the evidence is insufficient to reach a decision or when the outcomes are contingent on future events. Stenhouse (1968) observed that each of the areas of study in his integrated Humanities Curriculum Project involved highly controversial value judgements, adding that 'it is just this controversial aspect of the work which offers the prospect of live significance' (p. 30).

Treatment of social justice in the classroom 'involves shifting out of "neutral", both in terms of teachers' orientation to social inequalities as well as to pedagogy' (Kelly and Brandes, 2001, p. 450). Students arrive at controversial issues, such as the treatment of refugees and the impact of proposed commercial developments on the environment, from different perspectives that are often heavily influenced by parental values and attitudes. It is important to introduce them to multiple perspectives and, to do this, the teacher has to choose between several possible classroom roles. These range from the dispassionate presentation of all views, to declaring their personal commitment to a particular position, to advocating a particular view, to one of neutral chairperson who facilitates students to arrive at their own conclusions, to devil's advocate who challenges various positions as they arise while remaining neutral. There are different nuances in each of these options and the teacher has a professional responsibility to behave in an educationally appropriate manner. Notwithstanding the general support for adoption of the role of neutral chairperson, Kelly and Brandes (2001) concluded from their study of student teachers that 'neutrality is not only undesirable but impossible' (p. 450).

Freire (1970) was particularly concerned with the pursuit of critical literacy where he combined basic literacy with the development of critical consciousness (conscientisation) and the desire to effect societal change. Ontario Catholic Education has adopted the principle that critical theological thought must be at the centre of Catholic curricula in Catholic schools (see Chapter 6, this volume). The notion of 'Catholic critical literacy' is central to their approach based on the following principles and associated questions (Institute for Catholic Education, 1996):

- All texts are constructions (What attitudes, lifestyles, interpretations and conclusions has the author built into the text? How might the texts be changed to recognise or include missing voices such as the marginalised or a faith perspective?).
- Each person interprets messages differently (How might age, culture, life experiences, faith influence how this text is interpreted?).
- Texts serve different interests (What is the author's motive/intent? Who benefits if the message is accepted? Who may be disadvantaged?).
- Each medium develops its own 'language' in order to position readers/ viewers in certain ways (How have the distinctive techniques, conventions and aesthetics been used to create meaning? Do these techniques lead the viewer to a life affirming, realistic view of the world?).

For Freire (1970), critical pedagogy is about *praxis*, that is awareness raising (conscientisation, reflection) and action. It is significant that *Laudato Si'* concludes that 'the effects of the present imbalance can only be reduced by our decisive action, here and now' (Pope Francis, 2015, para 161) and that Chapter 5 of the encyclical is called 'Lines of Approach and Action'. Giroux

(2004) believes that 'critical pedagogy proposes that education is a form of political intervention in the world that is capable of creating the possibilities for social transformation' (p. 34).

Critical pedagogy in action

Two particular praxis-based methodologies are commonly used to assist people to reflect on what is happening in society, what issues need to be addressed and what action might be taken as a result of the analysis. The methodologies offer individuals and communities a framework from which to explore the details of social issues, apply moral principles, make prudent judgements and act in light of the decisions made. Both methodologies are forms of social analysis.

Social analysis as described by Holland and Henriot (1986) is the effort to obtain a more complete picture of the social situation by 'exploring historical and structural relationships' (p. 14) by moving beyond issues, policies and structures to focus on systems in terms of levels including primary groups, local communities, nation-states and global systems. These systems are analysed in terms of time (historical analysis) and space (structural analysis). Ultimately, objective dimensions (organisations, behaviour patterns and institutions) as well as subjective dimensions (consciousness, values and ideologies) are identified and analysed in order to understand the assumptions operative in any given social situation. The questions posed attempt to uncover the underlying values that shape the perspectives and decisions.

The two methodologies discussed in this section begin from peoples' lived experiences and from the assumption that as individuals and groups we are neither objective nor blind. We come to all social analysis situations from a particular perspective and we also need to identify and include other perspectives that confront the same social situations. From a CST perspective, we need to ensure that all voices are heard in the conversation, especially the voices of the poor and marginalised. Since the values we bring to our social analysis naturally influence our decisions, both of these methodologies remind participants to apply the lens of Catholic Christianity, including Scripture, Tradition, and CST, to the decision-making process. Both models function more appropriately as ongoing spirals rather than closed circles and both provide avenues to explore issues of inequality in ways that they do not become either too abstract or too personal to be persuasive or effective. The two methodologies are: See, Judge, Act; and the Pastoral Circle.

See, Judge, Act

The *See, Judge, Act* approach was developed by the Belgian Cardinal Joseph Cardijn (1882–1967). Cardijn was influenced by social Catholicism of the late 19th century, and in the late 1920s he founded the Young Trade Unionists

(Jeunesse Sydnicaliste) later called the Young Christian Workers (Jeunes Ouvrières Chreétiennes) (Sands, 2018). He used the See, Judge, Act model with workers in factories as a means of improving their work and life situations. The approach became popular and caught the attention of Pope John XXIII who in *Mater et Magistra* (1961) endorsed the approach saying:

> There are three stages which should normally be followed in the reeducation of social principles into practice. First, one reviews the concrete situation; secondly, one forms a judgement on it in the light of these same principles; thirdly, one decides what the circumstances can and should be done to implement these principles. These are the three stages that are usually expressed in three terms: observe, judge, act. (para 236)

Cardijn summarises the approach as a '... method of education [which is] suited equally well to the masses as to the elites. It takes place in life and through life' (Sands, 2018, p. 3). Sands (2018) believes that the method is helpful because it 'first seeks to understand the communities in which it is employed ... to safeguard that what one does for social justice actively reflects the wills and wants of the community' (p. 3). See, Judge, Act involves a movement from engagement and solidarity to reflection, understanding, analysis and evaluation, to taking non-violent cooperative action to restore, alleviate or change the situation (see Figure 3.1).

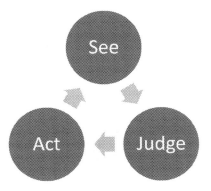

Figure 3.1 See, Judge, Act

The 'See' movement involves seeing, hearing and experiencing the lived reality of individuals and communities, naming what is happening that causes concern and carefully and intentionally examining the primary data of the situation. The 'Judge' movement requires analysis of the situation in order to make an informed judgement about it and involves two key parts: social analysis and theological reflection. The 'Act' movement requires planning in order to carry out actions aimed at transforming the social structures that contribute to suffering and injustice.

The See, Judge, Act approach is developed for classroom application in Table 3.1 (Goldburg, 2018).

Once the three-step process is completed, it is helpful to review the actions taken to see what can be learnt from the process. In reviewing these actions, the following could be considered: Did we carry out the action? Did we achieve the original purpose? Did it change the situation of the person(s) who originally brought the situation to our attention? What difficulties did we come up against? What effect did our action have on us and on others? What

Table 3.1 See, Judge, Act approach

• **See** – explore facts of events and situations

Where did it take place?
Who was involved?
What actually happened?
Who is affected and in what way/s?
How often does this occur?
How does this issue affect us locally? Globally?
How does the situation affect those involved?
What was said? Why did this happen?
Why did people act as they did?
What are the causes and consequences of what happened?
What experience or knowledge of this issue do I have?
What are my concerns or questions about this issue/situation?

• **Judge** – examine the rights and wrongs relevant to the situation, taking note of what has been examined in 'see' using the subheadings of social analysis and theological reflection.

Social analysis
Why does this situation exist?
What are the root causes?
Consider economic factors: who owns, controls, pays, gets and why?
Consider political factors: who decides, for whom? How do decisions get made? Who is left out of the process? Why?
Consider social factors: who is left out? Who is included? Why?
Consider historical factors; What past events influence the situation today?
Consider cultural factors: what values are evident? What do people believe in? Who influences what people believe?
Theological reflection
What Scripture can help us to interpret this experience?
How do biblical values help us to see their reality in a different way?
What does Catholic Social Teaching say about this issue? What key CST principles apply to this situation?

• **Act** – what action needs to be taken to change the situation? What actions need to be taken to address root causes?

Is there anything I/we can do, no matter how small, to improve the situation?
Is there anything more we need to find out?
How can we do this?
Is there anyone we can influence to improve things?
What action are we going to take?
How will the action/s transform the structure and relationship that produce this situation?

did we learn from the action? Is there anything we would do differently? Is there any further action we can take? The See, Judge, Act process is a potent way of reading the signs of the times and engaging in action for justice in a way that is transformative.

Liberation theologians, including Leonardo Boff and Clodovis Boff, used the See, Judge, Act methodology as a foundation for investigating oppression in Latin America (Sands, 2018). Later they expanded the ideas of Cardijn into what Holland and Henriot (1981) call the Pastoral Circle. The purpose of the Pastoral Circle is decision and action. Holland and Henriot (1986) identify two approaches to social analysis: an academic approach and a pastoral approach. An academic approach is detached, abstract, dissecting its elements for the purpose of understanding, while a pastoral approach looks at the reality from an 'involved, historically committed stance, discerning the situation for the purpose of action' (p. 7).

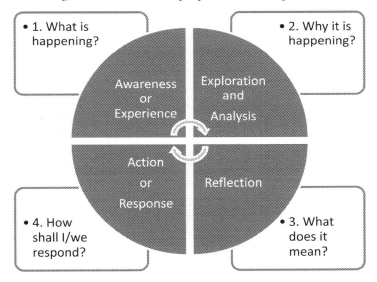

Figure 3.2 Pastoral Circle

The Pastoral Circle (Figure 3.2) consists of four movements: experience, social analysis, theological reflection and action. Holland and Henriot (1981) describe the four movements of the Pastoral Circle as follows:

- Experience – what is happening?
- Social Analysis – why is it happening and what are the root causes and values underlying the issue?
- Theological Reflection – what does it mean? In this phase a person makes judgements about the issue and its causes based on biblical and theological traditions as appropriated into their life and culture.
- Action or Response – act on the judgements made in a manner consistent with one's own moral values.

Table 3.2 Pastoral circle

Movement 1: Identify the issue or experience by asking What is happening? What is the current situation? and What is happening that we would like to investigate further?

Movement 2: Social analysis asks Why is it happening? In this stage, consider the social, cultural, economic, political, environmental and ecclesial factors that influence the situation. Some questions that may assist students to delve more deeply into the situation include the following: What is the history of the situation? What are the major structures (institutions, policies and processes) that affect the issue? What are the connections, explicit and implicit, between these structures? What is the future direction of this situation? Students are encouraged to draw conclusions considering some or all of the following: What influence do policy and economics have? What role do cultural values play in the situation? What are the causes of the situation and why? What do the people need or want? What institutions have shaped the situation for better or worse? Government? Church? Family? Community Groups? Corporations?

Movement 3: Theological reflection requires students to probe What does it mean? Some questions which focus the probing may include the following: What aspect/s of the social issue reinforces Catholic Christian values? What aspect/s of the issue undercuts Catholic Christian values? What does the Catholic Christian tradition have to say about the situation? What do we understand from Scripture about the situation? What does Catholic Social Teaching have to say? What insight might men and women through Church history bring to the situation?

Movement 4: Action or response focuses on identifying possible responses to the situation and the practical steps required to make a response. Students are encouraged to consider the following: What is a realistic action? What specific steps could I/we take? How can I/we assist people to engage in responding to the situation? (Goldburg 2018).

The framework in Table 3.2 provides a foundation for applying the Pastoral Circle to various curriculum investigations.

The Pastoral Circle is referred to by some as the 'circle of praxis' because it emphasises the ongoing relationship between reflection and action. The concept of praxis is drawn from Paulo Freire's classic *Pedagogy of the Oppressed* (1970) and is related to the 'hermeneutic circle a method of interpretation that sees new questions continually raised to challenge older theories by the force of new situations' (Holland & Henriot, 1986, p. 8). The first movement, Experience, is situated in the lived experiences of people and communities. It tries to identify what people are undergoing, feeling and responding. The second movement, Social Analysis, examines the causes, probes the consequences, delineates linkages and identifies the actors. It attempts to make sense of the experience by placing it within the broader picture and drawing connections between them. The third movement, Theological Reflection, challenges people to understand and analyse the experience in the light of faith, Scripture, CST and Church Tradition. The fourth movement, Action or Response, is designed in order to be most effective not only in the short term but also in the long term. A response of action brings about a new situation which in turn calls for further mediation through analysis, reflection and action. Thus, the Pastoral Circle is more of a pastoral spiral because each approach breaks new ground.

Both See, Judge, Act and the Pastoral Circle methods of social analysis are closely related, and both have links with faith and justice. The models presume certain theological presuppositions. That is, we have 'values' and 'biases' that come from the Catholic Christian tradition. These values and biases shape and orient the questions so that students are challenged to take action on behalf of justice and that the sharp dichotomies between sacred and secular, religious and political are rejected. Commitment to social justice and action is value-laden and if faith and culture are to interact in the manner in which the Congregation documents say they should, Catholic schools cannot be factories 'for learning various skills and competencies designed to fill the echelons of business industry' (Miller, 2015, p. 364), rather they should promote integral education enabling students to apply the principles of critique and evaluation. While the two methodologies are theological tools they are simultaneously teleological methods that aim at alleviating an issue within a community and they do so by explicitly taking sociocultural contexts into account.

Laudato Si' in the context of neoliberal education policy: Some concluding remarks

In his book, *Critical Pedagogy for Social Justice*, Smyth (2011) argues that 'one of the most salient consequences of the "technical turn" is that teachers have been forced to become complicit in the myth ... of "skills formation", within a narrow and diminished version of vocationalism' (p. 15). Redolent of Pope Francis, Smyth (2011) expresses concern regarding 'the requirement to convert schools into citadels of "consumption"... in which parents are left with no choice but to shop around for the best individual deal for their children' (p. 16) with inevitable consequences for public education.

Writing from an Australian perspective, Smyth (2011) is scathing about the pervasiveness of managerialist discourse in relation to teaching and teachers' work, discourse such as 'benchmarking, standards, competencies, performance management, performance pay, value added, best practice ... delivery targets, [and] performance indicators' (p. 15). He believes that, in this environment, teachers are neutered insofar as it 'renders them apolitical and non-partisan in a culture [where] success is based solely upon meritocratic effort [and where] the message to teachers is that they ought not to have a "social justice" agenda' (Smyth, 2011, p. 29). Drawing on the work of Giroux and others, Smyth (2011) refers to teachers as 'intellectual/political actors [in a context where] teaching is by nature a political activity' (p. 31). While this approach has obvious parallels with the approaches both of Cardijn (Sands, 2018) and Holland and Henriot (1986) introduced earlier, the introduction of CST, particularly the 'cognate' ideas and principles in *Laudato Si'*, has obvious potential to move the discourse to another level.

However, as noted by Lingard and Mills (2007), 'pedagogies alone cannot ensure socially just outcomes from schooling and socially just and inclusive practices in classrooms' (p. 237). Curriculum is a contextualised social process (Cornbleth, 1990) and the politics of federalism (Savage, 2016) provides the immediate background for the Australian Curriculum which was developed to meet 'a political deadline' with the result that 'the whole exercise [was one of] rushed compromise ... based on political or policy considerations rather than educational ones' (Australian Government, 2014, p. 224). This represents a good example of what the critical pedagogues see as 'power relations and cultural politics' (Giroux, 2004, p. 33), representing what Wrigley (2017, p. 1) calls 'canonical knowledge of academic disciplines' rather than the 'vernacular knowledge of marginalised groups [which provides the basis for] a social justice curriculum'.

The reality is that 'assessment or its narrower companion, testing' (Lingard & Mills, 2007, p. 237) has become the main driver of education policy. As suggested by Smyth (2011), this emphasis on performativity and high-stakes testing (e.g. PISA, NAPLAN) promotes the 'standardization of teaching [and] disempowers and deskills teachers [as] the content of the curriculum moves to match what the tests require' (Au, 2011, p. 30). For example, Polesel, Rice and Dulfer (2014, p. 640) concluded from their study of 8,000 Australian educators' views on the impact of NAPLAN on Australian schools and students that high-stakes testing regimes 'distort teaching practices, constrain the curriculum and narrow students' educational experiences'. Similarly, a recent study of geography and history teachers in England found that the prevailing 'technical-rational framework ... reveals a deficit in ethical responsibility brought about by the system's reliance on standardization, datafication and conformity around predetermined and externally imposed norms' (Winter, 2017, p. 70).

Just like the pervasive influence of testing and performativity, the social, environmental and educational challenges addressed in *Laudato Si'* are of serious global significance. Pope Francis (2015) expresses frustration at the weakness of the international response to the current ecological crisis – 'We lack leadership capable of striking out on new paths and meeting the needs of the present with concern for all and without prejudice towards coming generations' (para 53). If Catholic schools are to take the countercultural pathway demanded by *Laudato Si'* in their pursuit of education for social justice and if the rhetoric of the CEE with respect to holistic education and Gospel values is to become reality, they require authentic (Duignan, 2014) and transformative leadership (Brown, 2006). Scanlan's (2013) phrase 'the grammar of Catholic schooling' represents the ways in which 'certain structures became legitimized to the point that they are unquestioned' with the result that authentic responses to CST in US schools have been inhibited. *Laudato Si'* challenges senior Catholic Education leaders to interrogate the prevailing grammar of Catholic schooling.

References

Annett, A. (2016). Human flourishing, the common good, and Catholic social teaching. In J. Helliwell, R. Layard, & J. Sachs (Eds.), *World happiness report: Volume II* (pp. 38–65). New York: Columbia University Earth Institute.

Apple, M. W. (2004). *Ideology and curriculum*. New York: Routledge.

Arbuckle, G. A. (2013). *Catholic identity or identities? Refounding ministries in chaotic times*. Minnesota: Liturgical Press.

Aristotle. (1980). *The Nichomachean ethics*. (D. Ross, Trans.). Oxford: Oxford University Press.

Au, W. (2011). Teaching under the new Taylorism: High-stakes testing and the standardization of the 21st century curriculum. *Journal of Curriculum Studies, 43*(1), 25–45. doi: 10.1080/00220272.2010.521261

Australian Curriculum, Assessment and Reporting Authority (ACARA). (2012). *The shape of the Australian Curriculum. Version 4.0*. Sydney: ACARA.

Australian Government. (2014). *Review of the Australian Curriculum: Final report*. Canberra: Australian Government.

Ball, S. J. (2012). *Global Education Inc. New policy networks and the neo-liberal imaginary*. London: Routledge.

Bernstein, B. (1971) On the classification and framing of educational knowledge. In M. F. D. Young (Ed.), *Knowledge and control* (pp. 47–69). London: Collier-Macmillan.

Boff, L. (2015). *The Magna Carta of integral ecology: Cry of the earth-cry of the poor*. Retrieved from https://leonardoboff.wordpress.com/2015/06/18/the-magna-carta-of-integral-ecology-cry-of-the-earth-cry-of-the-poor/

Boyte, H. (2016). *Laudato Si'*, civic studies, and the future of democracy. *The Good Society, 25*(1), 46–61.

Brown, K. M. (2006). Leadership for social justice and equity: Evaluating a transformative framework and andragogy. *Educational Administration Quarterly, 42*(5), 700–745.

Bruner, J. S. (1966). *Toward a theory of instruction*. Cambridge, MA: Belknap Press.

Carr, W., & Kemmis, S. (1986). *Becoming critical, education, knowledge and action research*. London: Falmer.

Congregation for Catholic Education (CCE). (1997). *The Catholic school on the threshold of the third millennium*. Vatican City: CCE/Author.

Congregation for Catholic Education (CCE). (2014). *Educating today and tomorrow, a renewing passion, instrumentum laboris*. Vatican City: CCE/Author.

Congregation for Catholic Education (CCE). (2017). *Educating to fraternal humanism: Building a civilization of love 50 years after Populorum progressio*. Vatican City: CCE/Author. Retrieved from http://www.vatican.va/roman_curia/congregations/ccatheduc/documents/rc_con_ccatheduc_doc_20170416_educare-umanesimo-solidale_en.html

Cornbleth, C. (1990). *Curriculum in context*. London: Falmer.

Dearden, R. F. (1981). Controversial issues in the curriculum. *Journal of Curriculum Studies, 13*(1), 34–44.

Delpit, L. (2006). *Other people's children cultural conflict in the classroom*. New York: The New Press.

Department of Education and Skills. (2016). *Strategy statement and action plan for education (2016-2019)*. DES: Author

Dewey, J. (1916). *Democracy and education*. New York: Macmillan.

Duignan, P. A. (2014). Authenticity in educational leadership: History, ideal, reality. *Journal of Educational Administration, 52*(2), 152–172. https://doi.org/10.1108/JEA-01-2014-0012

Freire, P. (1970). *Pedagogy of the oppressed* (MB Ramos, Trans.). New York: Continuum.

Freire, P. (1997). *Pedagogy of the heart*. New York: Continuum.

Giroux, H.A. (1981). *Ideology, culture and the process of schooling*. Philadelphia: Temple University Press.

Giroux, H. A. (2004). Critical pedagogy and the postmodern/modern divide: Towards a pedagogy of democratization. *Teacher Education Quarterly, 31*(1), 31–47.

Gleeson, J. (2015). Critical challenges and dilemmas for Catholic Education leadership internationally. *International Studies in Catholic Education, 7*(2), 145–161. doi:10.1080/19422539.2015.1072955

Goldburg, P. M. (2018). *Understanding religion 10*. Cambridge: Cambridge University Press.

Gonzalez, N. (2010). Advocacy anthropology and education. *Current Anthropology, 51*(2), 249–258.

Guardini, R. (1998). *The end of the modern world*. Wilmington: ISI Books.

Hayes, D., Mills, M., Christie, P., & Lingard, B. (2006). *Teachers and schooling making a difference productive pedagogies, assessment and performance*. Sydney: Allen & Unwin.

Holland J., & Henriot, P. (1981). *Social analysis: Linking faith and justice*. Blackburn: Dove Communications.

Holland, J., & Henriot, P. (1986). *Social analysis: Linking faith and justice*. New York: Orbis Books.

Institute for Catholic Education (ICE). (1996). *Curriculum matters: A resource for Catholic educators*. Retrieved from http://iceont.ca/publications/

John Paul II. (1991). Encyclical letter *Centesimus Annus*.

Kelly, D. M., Minnes Brandes, G. (2001). Shifting out of 'neutral': Beginning teachers' struggles with teaching for social justice. *Canadian Journal of Education, 26*(4), 437–454.

Lane, D.A. (2015). *Catholic Education in the light of Vatican II and Laudato Si'*. Dublin: Veritas.

Lane, D.A. (2017a). Catholic Education in the light of Vatican II: Anthropology and Catholic Education. In *Vatican II and new thinking about Catholic Education* (pp. 123–135). Oxford: Routledge.

Lane, D.A. (2017b). Anthropology in the service of bridges to hope. In G. O'Hanlon *(Ed.), A dialogue of hope. Critical thinking for critical times* (pp. 63–77). Dublin: Messenger Publications.

Levinson, B. (2005). Citizenship, identity, democracy: Engaging the political in the anthropology of education. *Anthropology and Education Quarterly, 36*(4), 329–340.

Lingard, B., & Mills, M. (2007). Pedagogies making a difference: Issues of social justice and inclusion. *International Journal of Inclusive Education, 11*(3), 233–244. doi:10.1080/13603110701237472.

Lingard, B. (2010). Policy borrowing, policy learning: Testing times in Australian schooling. *Critical Studies in Education, 51*(2), 129–147. doi: 10.1080/17508481003731026

Macdonald, J. B. (1971). Curriculum theory. *Review of Educational Research, 64*(5), 196–200.

Madero, C. (2015). Theological dynamics of Paulo Freire's educational theory: An essay to assist the work of Catholic educators. *International Studies in Catholic Education, 7*(2), 122–133.

Miller, J. M. (2015). The Holy See's teaching on Catholic schools. In R. Topping (Ed.), *Renewing the mind A Reader in the Philosophy of Catholic Education* (pp. 357–376). Washington: Catholic University of America Press.

Murray, D. (1991). *A special concern*. Dublin: Veritas.

O'Neill, E. (2016). The pope and the environment: Towards an integral ecology? *Environmental Politics, 25*(4), 749–754. doi: 10.1080/09644016.2016.1159603

Ontario Ministry of Education. (2004). The Ontario curriculum: Grades 1–6: Social studies, and grades 7 and 8: History and geography. Ontario: Ministry of Education.

Ormerod, N. (2016). *Laudato Si'* in the context of Catholic social teaching. *St Mark's Review, 236*(2).

Pascoe, S. (2007). Challenges for Catholic Education in Australia. In G. Grace, & J. O'Keefe (Eds.), *International handbook of Catholic Education – Challenges for school systems in the 21st century* (pp. 787–810). Dordrecht: Springer.

Pinar, W. F. (2004). *What is curriculum theory?* New Jersey: Lawrence Erlbaum.

Polesel, J., Rice, S., & Dulfer, N. (2014). The impact of high-stakes testing on curriculum and pedagogy: A teacher perspective from Australia. *Journal of Education Policy*, *29*(5), 640–657. doi: 10.1080/02680939.2013.865082

Pollefeyt, D., & Bouwens, J. (2010). Framing the identity of Catholic schools: Empirical methodology for quantitative research on the Catholic identity of an education institute. *International Studies in Catholic Education*, *2*(2), 193–211.

Pope Benedict XVI. (2009). Encyclical letter *Caritas in veritate*. Retrieved from http://w2 .vatican.va/content/benedict-xvi/en/encyclicals/documents/hf_ben-xvi _enc_20090629_caritas-in-veritate.html

Pope Francis. (2015). Encyclical letter *Laudato Si'* on care for our common home. Retrieved from http://w2.vatican.va/content/francesco/en/encyclicals/documents/papa-francesco _20150524_enciclica-laudato-si.html

Pope John Paul II. (1987). Encyclical letter *Sollicitudo rei socialis*. Retrieved from http://w2.vatican.va/content/john-paul-ii/en/encyclicals/documents/hf_jp-ii _enc_30121987_sollicitudo-rei-socialis.html

Pope John XXIII. (1961). Encyclical letter *Mater et magistra*. Retrieved from http://w2.vatican .va/content/john-xxiii/en/encyclicals/documents/hf_j-xxiii_enc_15051961_mater.html

Pope John XXIII. (1963). Encyclical letter *Pacem in terris*. Retrieved from http://w2.vatican. va/content/john-xxiii/en/encyclicals/documents/hf_j-xxiii_enc_11041963_pacem.html

Pope Paul VI. (1971). Apostolic letter *Octogesima adveniens*. Retrieved from http://w2.vatican.va/ content/paul-vi/en/apost_letters/documents/hf_p-vi_apl_19710514_octogesima-adveniens.html

Rowlands, A. (2015). *Laudato Si'*: Rethinking politics. *Political Theology*, *16*(5), 418–420.

Sands, J. (2018). Introducing Cardinal Cardijn's see-judge-act as an interdisciplinary method to move theory into practice. *Religions*, *9*(4), 129.

Savage, G. C. (2016). Who's steering the ship? National curriculum reform and the re-shaping of Australian federalism. *Journal of Education Policy*, *31*(6), 833–850. doi: 10.1080/02680939.2016.1202452

Scanlan, M. (2013). The grammar of Catholic schooling and radically 'Catholic' schools. *Catholic Education: A Journal of Inquiry and Practice*, *12*(1), 25–54.

Schubert, W. H. (2008). Curriculum inquiry. In F. M. Connelly, M. F. He, & J. A. Phillion (Eds.), *The Sage handbook of curriculum and instruction* (pp. 399–419). Los Angeles: Sage Publications.

Smyth, J. (2011). *Critical pedagogy for social justice*. New York: Continuum.

Stenhouse, L. (1968). The humanities curriculum project. *Journal of Curriculum Studies*, *1*(1), 26–33.

Stenhouse, L. (1975). *An introduction to curriculum research and development*. London: Heinemann.

Taylor, C. (2007). *A secular age*. Cambridge, MA: Harvard University Press.

Valk, J. (2007). Plural public schooling: Religion, worldviews and moral education. *British Journal of Religious Education*, *29*(3), 273–285.

Winter, C. (2017). Curriculum policy reform in an era of technical accountability: 'Fixing' curriculum, teachers and students in English schools. *Journal of Curriculum Studies*, *49*(1), 55–74. doi: 10.1080/00220272.2016.1205138

Wrigley, T. (2017). 'Knowledge', curriculum and social justice. *The Curriculum Journal 29*(1), 4–24. doi: 10.1080/09585176.2017.1370381

Chapter 4

Catholic social teaching should permeate the Catholic secondary school curriculum: An agenda for reform[1]

Gerald Grace

Introduction

In their publication, *Our best kept secret: The rich heritage of Catholic social teaching*, Schultheis, De Berri and Henriot (1988) argue that such teaching, 'seems to have been forgotten, or never known, by a majority of the Roman Catholic community' (p. 3).

Reviewing the situation in 1988, the authors detailed this rich (but relatively unknown) heritage as including the Papal encyclicals of Leo XIII (1891), Pius XI (1931), Paul VI (1967) and John Paul II (1981, 1988). To this can now be added the ground-breaking encyclical of Benedict XVI, *Caritas in Veritate* (2009).

Michael Schultheis and his co-authors saw the major problem to be the lack of access by the majority of the Catholic population to the formal discourse in which Papal encyclicals are expressed. While it is undoubtedly true that the language used in the encyclicals has been an impediment, it is also true that Catholic educational institutions at all levels have failed to provide curriculum mediations of this teaching as a crucial part of the formation of Catholic youth. A great opportunity for the dissemination of the countercultural social messages of the Church has thereby been lost despite the existence of valuable sources such as Dorr (1983/2003) and Walsh and Davies (1991).

This chapter argues that Pope Benedict's encyclical, *Caritas in Veritate*: on integral human development in charity and truth, by reason of its radical observations and its timely application to contemporary world conditions, could provide the material for Catholic educators to use in a wide range of secondary school curricula subjects.

In addition to the intrinsic value of the Pope's teaching, the use of this encyclical throughout the curriculum will provide a distinctive religious, cultural and educational message which will not be found in local state secular schools.

How can the teachings of *Caritas in Veritate* permeate the curricula of Catholic schools and colleges?

From a close reading of *Caritas in Veritate*, at least three major themes can be discerned: (1) religious, moral and cultural issues; (2) economic, business and enterprise issues and (3) social, environmental and political issues.

Insofar as Catholic schools and colleges, internationally, have curricula constituted by theology and Religious Education, philosophy and ethics, personal and moral education, mathematics, business and enterprise studies, economic and social sciences, politics, environmental and physical sciences and humane subjects (literature, history, languages, geography, etc.), the potential for permeation of Catholic social teaching is considerable across many subjects.

Religious, moral and cultural issues

In this sector of the school curriculum, study sessions for senior students could be constructed as discussion topics related to specific *Caritas in Veritate* extracts, with assignment questions designed to elicit personal, critical responses from the students. Some examples would be

- 'Charity demands justice: recognition and respect for the legitimate rights of individuals and peoples. It strives to build the earthly city according to law and justice. On the other hand, charity transcends justice and completes it in the logic of giving and forgiving' (paras 6, 7).[2]

In what ways does charity 'transcend' justice?

- 'Underdevelopment is the lack of brotherhood among individuals and peoples. As society becomes ever more globalised it makes us neighbours but does not make us brothers. Reason can establish civic equalities but it cannot establish fraternity' (paras 19, 20).

Outline your understanding of the Christian doctrine of fraternity and indicate how it could be applied to international development.

- 'Today, people frequently kill in the holy name of God ... This applies especially to terrorism motivated by fundamentalism which generates grief, destruction and death and obstructs dialogue between nations' (paras 29, 33).

How would you answer the arguments of Professor Richard Dawkins that this is the inevitable outcome of religious belief?

88 Gerald Grace

- 'When he is far away from God, man is unsettled and ill at ease. Social and psychological alienation and the many neuroses that afflict affluent societies are attributable, in part, to spiritual factors' (paras 76, 88).

To what extent do you agree with this statement?

- 'The greatest service to development then, is a Christian humanism ... Openness to God makes us open towards our brothers and sisters and towards an understanding of life as a joyful task to be accomplished in a spirit of solidarity' (paras78, 91).

Does the record of Christian social action in the world support, in your view, this assertion?

Clearly, a study programme based upon this section of *Caritas in Veritate* must be based upon a resource book of readings covering issues such as conceptual distinctions of forms of charity, developing ideas of social justice, interpretations of fraternity, study of the various types of religious fundamentalism, engagement with the work of the 'new atheists', for example Dawkins (2006), and historical study of Christian social action. While this will be demanding for both teachers and students, it can be suggested that senior students in Catholic schools are likely to engage with these issues with interest and vigour. In other words, it should contribute powerfully to a renewed and better-informed Catholic social conscience among the young.[3]

Economic, business and enterprise issues

The development of curriculum subjects and curriculum materials related to the study of Economics, Finance, Business Administration and Enterprise is a growing feature of Catholic schools and colleges internationally. This reflects, in part, the expectations of government, parents and senior students that these subjects are a necessary preparation for an increasingly competitive, mobile and globalised world of international corporate business, finance and trade. The utilitarian appeal of these subjects is high.

A challenge for Catholic schools and colleges is that the addition of these subjects to the curriculum may represent an entirely secular and utilitarian cultural implant in their programmes unless these subjects are brought into an organic relation with the religious, moral and social teachings of the Church. However, is this happening? There is little evidence that this organic relation is being developed in the schools. The cultural problem here is that many writers on economics and related subjects have kept religious and moral issues outside the boundaries of their subject content and analysis. In a recent publication, *The Credit Crunch: Making moral sense of the financial crisis* (2009), Edward Hadas has argued, 'In addition to greed itself and bad ideas about human nature, one other factor may have played a role in the pre-crisis abdication of responsibility in finance. This is the refusal to take morality seriously in any economic discussions' (p. 42).[4] It must also be admitted that the 'rich heritage' of Catholic social and moral teaching relevant to these subjects has, in general,[5] been ignored in many Catholic schools internationally. That is why this present situation, marked by a global economic and financial crisis (salient in the thoughts of contemporary students) and the publication of *Caritas in Veritate* which addresses these issues from a Catholic perspective, provides an opportunity for all Catholic schools and colleges to focus upon the relevance of Catholic social teaching to contemporary conditions.

Caritas in Veritate presents an agenda of issues for discussion and reflection which all senior students in Catholic Education should encounter in their studies. The following are some examples of what Pope Benedict offers for their consideration:

- 'The world's wealth is growing in absolute terms but inequalities are on the increase. The scandal of glaring inequalities continues' (paras 22, 25).
- The conviction that the economy must be autonomous, that it must be shielded from the influences of a moral character, has led man to abuse the economic process in a thoroughly destructive way' (paras 34, 39).
- 'The market can be a negative force, not because it is so by nature, but because a certain ideology can make it so' (paras 36, 42).
- 'John Paul II taught that investment always has moral as well as economic significance' (paras 40, 47).
- 'Financiers must rediscover the ethical foundations of their activity so as not to abuse the sophisticated instruments what can serve to betray the interests of savers' (paras 65, 77).

Catholic schools and college teachers have the potential to be significant innovators in bringing together the study of economics, finance, business administration and enterprise with an in-depth understanding of Catholic religious, moral and social teaching, so that a higher-order level of knowledge and understanding can be achieved in these crucial contemporary subjects.

Caritas in Veritate could be the catalyst for this necessary cultural transformation.[6]

Social, environmental and political issues

The intrinsic appeal of social, environmental and political issues to senior students in Catholic schools and colleges is considerable.[7] They are, after all, the inheritors of a world which many of them believe is in a dysfunctional state on all three dimensions. As a generation, they are probably possessed of more information and consciousness of the nature and extent of social, environmental and political dysfunctions in the world than any previous generation. It is entirely likely that they expect their school and college programmes to engage seriously with these issues, not only in the terms of knowledge but also in suggesting what Catholic social action is needed to help a process of change and development.

In meeting these expectations, *Caritas in Veritate* has much to offer because Pope Benedict XVI shares their concerns and provides profound guidance for action and transformation:

> The crisis thus becomes an opportunity for discernment in which to shape a new vision for the future. (p. 24)

The Pope's discernment and vision is developed in a number of strong statements which have the potential to animate the consciousness and action of Catholic youth in their subsequent vocations and roles in adult life.

Such statements as

- 'The processes of globalization ... open up the unprecedented possibility of large-scale redistribution of wealth on a world-wide scale; if badly directed however, they can lead to an increase in poverty and inequality'. (paras 42, 50)
- 'Today the material resources available for rescuing peoples from poverty are potentially greater than ever before, but they have ended up largely in the hands of people from developed countries who have benefited more from the liberalisation that has occurred in the mobility of capital and labour'. (paras 42, 51)
- 'The way humanity treats the environment influences the way it treats itself ... This invites contemporary society to a serious review of its lifestyle, which, in many parts of the world is prone to hedonism and consumerism, regardless of their harmful consequences'. (paras 51, 63)
- 'Every migrant is a human person who, as such, possesses fundamental inalienable rights that must be respected by everyone and in every circumstance'. (paras 62, 75)
- 'There is urgent need of a true world political authority ... vested with the effective power to ensure security for all, regard for justice, and respect for rights'. (paras 67, 79–80)[8]

It is sometimes the case that senior students in Catholic schools and colleges begin to distance themselves from the practice and discourse of the Faith because they perceive it to be disconnected from the many challenges of the 'real world'[9] in which they live.

Detailed study of *Caritas in Veritate* has the potential to show that, on the contrary, the Christian religion in the Catholic tradition is integral to an understanding of these challenges and a valuable source of guidance in ways of responding to them. There is a Heavenly City to which all believers aspire, but there is also an Earthly City which believers are called upon to perfect by social action. As Pope Benedict expresses it:

> Development requires attention to the spiritual life ... trust in God, spiritual fellowship in Christ, reliance upon God's providence and mercy, love and forgiveness, self-denial, acceptance of others, justice and peace. All this is essential if "hearts of stone" are to be transformed into "hearts of flesh" (Ezk. 36: 26), rendering life on earth "divine" and thus more worthy of humanity. (paras 79, 92)

In other words, what is projected to contemporary youth as the 'real world' is in fact a construct of globalised materialism from which religious faith is either marginalised or represented by the media in its distorted and funda-mentalist extremes. Catholic social teaching and, in particular, the teachings of *Caritas in Veritate* show to the young the authentic face of religion and a 'real world' that can be attained by social action inspired by faith.

Catholic social teaching and the Catholic school curriculum

In 1999, Robert Davis wrote a ground-breaking chapter with the title, 'Can there be a Catholic curriculum?' His purpose was to generate a debate[10] among Catholic educators about this crucial issue at a time when both government and economic agencies internationally appeared to be dominating the content, assessment and purposes of curricula. Davis' argument was that discussion of this issue had virtually disappeared from the considerations of Catholic educators.

His thesis was that

> the price Catholic schools have had to pay for their accreditation as appro-priate centres for the 'delivery' of the modern curriculum is a restriction of their Catholicity to those features of school life where secular society is prepared to permit the manifestation of Catholic ideas – mainly wor-ship, ethos and Religious Education. (pp. 221–222)

While worship, ethos and Religious Education are clearly central to the maintenance of a distinctive Catholic educational mission, Davis was raising the question of whether this was sufficient in itself if the major part of the curriculum and discourse in the school was, in essence, secular, utilitarian and shaped by government and economic requirements.

In as far as Davis' analysis is correct, in many societies, it points to an urgent need to strengthen the Catholic cultural content of the curriculum in general to prevent a process of incorporation into a secularised and technicist educational culture.

It has been the argument of this chapter that the rich heritage of Catholic social teaching, with its implications for the teaching of many subjects in the curriculum, could provide such distinctive and countercultural material. While *Caritas in Veritate* provides the immediate stimulus to do this, the encyclical itself is built upon the insights of earlier work, especially from Pope Paul VI and Pope John Paul II. Taken together, this is a rich resource which innovative teachers can use to illuminate a range of subjects in ways which are distinctively different to those used in state secular schools. In this way, the Catholicity of the school will be strengthened not only by its worship, ethos and formal Religious Education, but by a total curriculum experience which integrates faith and learning through the agency of Catholic social teaching.

To bring about such a transformation will require school authorities to struggle for more relative autonomy in curriculum provision; it will require changes in professional preparation and continuing professional development programmes for Catholic teachers and it will require school leaders to be innovative agents of change. However, if the mission integrity[11] of Catholic schools and colleges in an increasingly secular, globalised and technicist world is to be maintained, such cultural action is essential.

Education and the formation of the Catholic social conscience

Speaking of education in *Caritas in Veritate*, Benedict XVI reminds his readers that, 'the term "education" refers not only to classroom teaching and vocational training ... but to the complete formation of the person' (paras 61, 73).

As educational discourse in contemporary society becomes increasingly dominated by the language of 'training', a Catholic educational discourse which emphasises 'formation of the person' is not only countercultural, but more humane. It insists that the ultimate goal of the educational process is the formation of good persons equipped with knowledge and skills to serve the common good motivated by faith and a Catholic social conscience.

But what is this conscience and how is it formed?

In his essays, *On Conscience* (1984/reprinted 2006), Cardinal Joseph Ratzinger argued that

> conscience signifies the perceptible and demanding presence of the voice of truth in the subject himself. It is the overcoming of mere subjectivity in the encounter ... with the truth from God. (p. 25, 2006 edition)

At the same time

> included in the concept of conscience is an obligation, namely the obligation to care for it, to form it and educate it. (p. 63, 2006 edition)

In addition to the direct teaching received by the young from their parents and attendance at Mass, Catholic schools and colleges clearly represent crucial arena for the forming and informing of conscience. The Catholic social conscience of the young will not simply result from the acquisition of knowledge about Catholic social teaching, although that is the necessary foundation. It will require the nurture of their spirituality and Christian faith by a constant interaction between such social teaching and the teaching, practice and mission of Jesus Christ and the saints. To be truly animated, such students need opportunities to be involved in Catholic social action projects in their communities and beyond. The *International Handbook of Catholic Education* (2007) records examples of such formative and practical action by Catholic schools and colleges in different parts of the world.[12] The challenge is not that such formation and expression of the Catholic social conscience is absent in Catholic Education, but rather that it is in danger of being marginalised in the contemporary pursuit of better academic and test results. The history of Catholicism is rich in the heritage of the martyrs of conscience who have shown 'obedience to the truth which must stand higher than any human tribunal'[13] (p. 26, 2006 edition). Catholic schools and colleges are not lacking in role models with which to inspire contemporary students to think and act beyond a culture of acquisitive and competitive individualism. In writing *Caritas in Veritate*, Pope Benedict XVI has given them a better vision for the future and has emphasised that love of God must always be shown in love of neighbour.

Conclusion: Catholic social teaching – a major theological and cultural resource for Catholic Education

This chapter has argued that Catholic Education internationally could be renewed and reanimated by a systematic permeation of Catholic social teaching across all subjects of the curriculum. This strategy would have many advantages. It would, first and foremost, have the potential to engage the interest and involvement of senior students at a time when many of them begin to question the relevance of their faith to contemporary challenges. It would help to inform and strengthen their Catholic social conscience as they came to understand that the teachings of Jesus Christ and the saints as mediated by the Catholic tradition of social analysis make an organic relation between faith and action in the world. At the same time, it would help to prevent both students and schools from becoming incorporated into a global culture in which 'the only criterion is practical utility and the only value is economic and technological progress'.[14]

While *Caritas in Veritate* provides the immediate stimulus for making such a cultural transformation in Catholic Education, and is strongly founded upon earlier Papal encyclicals which need to be rediscovered, the corpus of Catholic social teaching is more extensive than that provided by the Magisterium. An appendix to this chapter suggests a supplementary range of other sources which can be used by Catholic educators. However, it has to be recognised that serious cultural transformations in educational practice are not easy, especially in contemporary conditions where academic 'productivity', public accountability, market competition and value for money calculations are dominating educational institutions. As many hard-pressed school leaders and teachers will observe, measurements of Catholic social conscience are not included in school accountability processes by public agencies. So, while Catholic social teaching may be a valuable resource for Catholic school curricula, it may not 'count' in the public mechanisms for school evaluations and judgements of 'success'.

It is in situations such as this that a distinctive quality of Catholic school and college leadership must assert itself. Catholic school leaders have to 'render to Caesar', but they also have to 'render to God'. They are the guardian of the mission integrity of the schools. However, public accountability requirements are not the only impediments: there are workload and time pressures which block the path to religious, cultural and curriculum change. It is one thing to list the sources for the serious study of Catholic social teaching; it is another thing for already pressurised educators to find easy access to such sources for classroom stimulus material. A survey of the available literature, prior to the publication of *Caritas in Veritate*, suggests that one of the most useful mediating texts for school leaders and teachers is the Fourth Edition of *Catholic Social Teaching*, published by the Center of Concern in Washington in 2003. Here is, in effect, a valuable teacher's handbook which gives access to Catholic social teaching in classroom-related format.

To supplement and to background the profound insights of *Caritas in Veritate*, teachers and students can construct a term's programme focused on seven core principles of Catholic social teaching as outlined in this text: (1) The Dignity of the Human Person, (2) The Dignity of Work, (3) The Person in Community, (4) Rights and Responsibilities, (5) Option for Those in Poverty, (6) Solidarity and (7) Care for Creation. Contained within these principles are discussion and analysis topics of great potential interest, for example the common good, 'structures of sin', liberation theology, human rights, resisting market idolatry, subsidiarity, peace-making and the just war.[15]

In 1996, the Catholic Bishops' Conference of England and Wales published a ground-breaking document, *The Common Good and the Catholic Church's Social Teaching* in which they called for:

> more participation in the future development of Catholic Social Teaching so that it is properly owned by all Catholics (paras 31)

The way to ensure this ownership and the formation of a maturely developed Catholic social conscience in all members of the Church is to permeate the curriculum and the pedagogy of Catholic schools and colleges, with the rich heritage of Catholic social teaching. Catholic Bishops Conferences across the world could now give leadership in this crucial area to strengthen the religious and cultural distinctiveness of Catholic school curricula at a time when such curricula are under threat from utilitarian and secular national priorities.

Notes

1. This paper was originally published in *International Studies in Catholic Education* (2013), Vol. 5, Issue 1, pages 99–109 and it is reproduced here with the permission of the Editor of that journal. It formed the basis of Professor Grace's video presentation at the November 2017 Dissemination Conference hosted by the Identity and Curriculum in Catholic Education Project at the ACU Leadership Centre, Brisbane.
2. All quotations are taken from the 2009 edition of *Caritas in Veritate* published by The Catholic Truth Society, London and reproduced with permission.
3. It also has to be accepted that some young people will disagree with the stance taken by the Pope and the Catholic Church on these issues as part of their own individual critical development.
4. There have been some attempts to bring the Christian religion and the world of economic enterprise into dialogue, for example *Morality and the Market Place: Christian Alternatives to Capitalism and Socialism* (Griffiths, 1982), *God and the Marketplace: Essays on the Morality of Wealth Creation* (Davies, 1993), *Managing as if Faith Mattered* (Alford & Naughton, 2001) and *Globalisation for the Common Good* (Mofid, 2002). However, this literature does not seem to have affected school curricula in general.
5. This situation varies internationally. Catholic schools and colleges in the United States, especially Jesuit schools, have engaged seriously with Catholic social teaching in their curricula and in social action.
6. *Caritas in Veritate* could be the catalyst for this, but it could also help in the rediscovery of other Papal encyclicals of Catholic social teaching. It is clear that Pope Benedict XVI was deeply influenced by Pope Paul VI's encyclical, *Populorum Progressio* (1967). See pp. 11–21 of *Caritas in Veritate*.
7. See *Young Adult Catholics* (Hoge, Dinges, Johnson, & Gonzales 2001).
8. This is a clear criticism of the present effectiveness of the United Nations Organisation.
9. 'Real world' is a contemporary ideological device used to suggest that proposed alternatives to the status quo are impractical theory or naive utopias.
10. For one response to this debate, see *'Can There be a Catholic School Curriculum?'* published by the Centre for Research and Development in Catholic Education in 2007.
11. In first using the concept of mission integrity (Grace, 2002), I stressed the importance of the mission to the poor. However, mission integrity involves not only service to a particular category of students, but also a distinctive Catholic curriculum content.
12. See *International Handbook of Catholic Education* (Grace & O'Keefe, 2007), Chapters 6, 10, 22, 24, 33, 37 and 39.
13. See also the earlier statement of Father Joseph Ratzinger, when acting as theological adviser to the Second Vatican Council: 'Over the Pope as expression of the binding claim of ecclesiastical authority, there stands one's own conscience, which must be obeyed before all else, even if necessary against the requirements of ecclesiastical authority. This emphasis on the individual whose conscience confronts him with a supreme and ultimate tribunal, and one which in the last resort is beyond the claim of external social groups, even the official church, also establishes a principle in opposition to increasing totalitarianism' (Vorgrimler, 1967, 134).
14. Congregation for Catholic Education (1988, para 10).
15. *Catholic Social Teaching: Our Best Kept Secret* (De Berri, Hug, Henriot, & Schultheis, 2003, pp.18–34).

References

Alford, H. (OP), & Naughton, M. (2001). *Managing as if faith mattered: Christian social principles in the modern organisation*. Notre Dame: University of Notre Dame Press.

Benedict XVI. (2009). *Caritas in Veritate: Encyclical letter on integral human development in charity and truth*. London: Catholic Truth Society.

Congregation for Catholic Education. (1988). *The religious dimension of education in a Catholic school*. London: Catholic Truth Society.

Davies, J. (Ed.). (1993). *God and the marketplace: Essays on the morality of wealth creation*. London: Institute of Economic Affairs.

Davis, R. (1999). Can there be a Catholic curriculum? In J. Conroy (Ed.), *Catholic education: Inside out/outside in* (pp. 207–230). Dublin: Lindisfarne Books.

Dawkins, R. (2006). *The god delusion*. London: Bantam Books.

De Berri E. (SJ), Hug, J. (SJ), Henriot, P. (SJ), & Schultheis M. (SJ). (2003). *Catholic social teaching: Our best kept secret* (4th ed.). New York: Orbis Books.

Dorr, D. (1983/2003). *Option for the poor: A hundred years of Catholic social teaching* (2003 revised ed.). New York: Orbis Books.

Grace, G. (2002). 'Mission integrity': Contemporary challenges for Catholic school leaders. In K. Leithwood & P. Hallinger (Eds.), *Second international handbook of educational leadership and administration*. Dordrecht/Boston: Kluwer Academic Press.

Grace, G., & O'Keefe, J. (SJ) (Eds.). (2007). *International handbook of Catholic education* (Vol. 2). Dordrecht: Springer.

Griffiths, B. (1982). *Morality and the market place: Christian alternatives to capitalism and socialism*. London: Hodder and Stoughton.

Hadas, E. (2009). *The credit crunch: Making moral sense of the financial crisis*. London: Catholic Truth Society.

Hoge, D., Dinges, W. Johnson, M., & Gonzales, J. (2001). *Young adult Catholics: Religion in the culture of choice*. Notre Dame: University of Notre Dame Press.

John Paul II. (1981). *Laborem Exercens* [On human work] *encyclical letter*. Vatican City, Rome. Retrieved from https://en.wikipedia.org/wiki/Laborem_exercens

John Paul II. (1988). *Sollicitudo Rei Socialis* [The social concern of the church] *encyclical letter*. Vatican City, Rome. Retrieved from https://en.wikipedia.org/wiki/Sollicitudo_rei_socialis

Leo XIII. (1891). *Rerum Novarum* [On the condition of labour] *encyclical letter*. Vatican City, Rome. Retrieved from https://en.wikipedia.org/wiki/Rerum_novarum

Mofid, K. (2002). *Globalisation for the common good*. London: Shepheard–Walwyn.

Paul VI. (1967). *Populorum Progressio* [The development of peoples] *encyclical letter*. Vatican City, Rome. Retrieved from https://en.wikipedia.org/wiki/Populorum_progressio

Pius XI. (1931). *Quadragesimo Anno* [The reconstruction of the social order] *encyclical letter*. Vatican City, Rome. Retrieved from https://en.wikipedia.org/wiki/Quadragesimo_anno

Ratzinger, J. (2006). *On conscience*. San Francisco, CA: Ignatius Press.

Schultheis, M., (SJ), De Berri, E. (SJ), & Henriot, P. (SJ). (1988). *Our best kept secret: The rich heritage of Catholic social teaching*. London: Catholic Fund for Overseas Development.

Vorgrimler, H. (Ed.). (1967). *Commentary on the documents of Vatican II Vol V*. New York: Herder and Herder.

Walsh, M., & Davies, B. (1991). *Proclaiming justice and peace: Papal documents from Rerum Novarum through Centesimus Annus, North American Edition*. Mystic, CT: Twenty-Third.

Further sources for the study of Catholic social teaching

Booth, P. (Ed.). (2007). *Catholic social teaching and the market economy*. London: Institute of Economic Affairs.

Caldecott, S. (2009). *Catholic social teaching: A way in*. London: Catholic Truth Society.

Catholic Bishops' Conference of England and Wales. (1996). *The Common good and the Catholic Church's social teaching*. London: CBC.

Charles, R. (SJ). (1998). *Christian social witness and teaching* (Vol. 2). Leominster: Gracewing.

Clark, C., & Alford, H. (2009). *Rich and poor: Rebalancing the economy*. London: Catholic Truth Society.

Coleman, J., & Ryan, W. (2005). *Globalization and Catholic social thought*. Ottawa: Novalis.

Cullen, P., Hoose, B., & Mannion, G. (Eds.). (2007). *Catholic social justice: Theological and practical explorations*. London: Continuum.

Gutierrez, G. (1983). *A theology of liberation: History, politics and salvation*. London, SCM Press.

Hollenbach, D. (2003). *The common good and Christian ethics*. Cambridge: Cambridge University Press.

Hornsby-Smith, M. (2006). *An introduction to Catholic social thought*. Cambridge: Cambridge University Press.

McDonough, S. (SSC). (1990). *The greening of the church*. London: SCM Press.

Pontifical Council for Justice and Peace. (2004). *Compendium of the social doctrine of the church Vatican City*. Rome: Libreria Editrice Vaticana.

Rowland, C. (Ed.). (1999). *The Cambridge companion to liberation theology*. Cambridge: Cambridge University Press.

Chapter 5

Teaching for a just world: Social justice and human rights perspectives across the curriculum

Nina Burridge

Introduction: The purposes of education in the 21st century

Education impacts each of us in many ways and in so many facets of our lives. Our life trajectories are often shaped, not just by our capacity to succeed in examinations, but also by the values and attitudes that we learned at school. Various studies (e.g. Hattie, 2003) illustrate how the influences of teachers, peers and the education system generally are crucial to success at school and to our understanding of the world around us.

Researchers have long debated the purposes of education from the time of Socrates to the progressive education philosophy of John Dewey (1897) of the 20th century, the liberationist philosophy of the 1960s in Paulo Freire's *Pedagogy of the Oppressed* (1968) and to today's debates about the market-driven education system that favours education for 'workforce development' to meet a nation's economic needs (Ball, 2012; Lingard, 2010). Many believe that the current focus on the credentialist economic model of education is misplaced insofar as education is about much more than gaining a qualification for work, and teaching is much more than just getting students to pass their examinations.

Teaching is more than a profession; it is a way of having an impact on people and communities. When I joined the teaching profession the slogan was 'teach and make a difference'. In my role as a history teacher, I came to realise that learning about world history provided me with an understanding of society, social class and how power, politics and society interact. The capacities for empathy and critical thinking are important skills when it comes to teaching about the past. They involve the ability to imagine, to see the world in a multifaceted way and to analyse the impact when wrongs are committed and rights are infringed. Empathy and critical thinking develop the capacity to put oneself in someone else's shoes and to understand their contexts, their experiences and their rights as human beings.

The notion of teaching as a moral practice (Pring, 2001) and the teacher as an 'activist professional' (Sachs, 2000) are central to the focus in this chapter on human rights and social justice. This means viewing a teacher as a person with a moral mission to help create a better world by educating young people about issues of equity, social justice and rights, not just in their local context but also in the wider global sphere.

Nussbaum (2009, 2010, 2016) writes that the purpose of education is for 'human development', helping students to become educated in their fields and also critically aware, active participants in their communities and in global issues:

> The goal of education for human development is producing decent world citizens who can understand the global problems ... and who have the practical competence and the motivational incentives to do something about these problems. (Nussbaum, 2009, p. 6)

Education for human development competes with the more instrumentalist objectives of education. As Nussbaum (2009) points out:

> Education is often discussed in low-level utilitarian terms: how can we produce technically trained people who can hold onto 'our' share of the global market? With the rush to profitability, values precious for the future of democracy are in danger of getting lost. The profit motive suggests to most concerned politicians that science and technology are of crucial importance. We should have no objection to good scientific and technical education. But other abilities – abilities crucial both to the health of democracy and to the creation of a decent world culture and a robust type of global citizenship – are at risk of getting lost in the competitive flurry. (p. 6)

According to Nussbaum, global citizenry requires critical thinking, the capacity for Socratic dialogue, self-criticism and critical thought about one's own traditions in order to facilitate dialogue across political boundaries. It also requires the ability to understand difference, both to see oneself as a member of a heterogeneous world and to understand the history and character of diverse groups. And finally, it requires narrative imagination and empathy, the ability to be an intelligent reader of other people's stories and to think about what the inner life of another may be like (Nussbaum, 2016).

Nussbaum's philosophy provides ambitious goals for education at a time when the curriculum is already overloaded (Australian Government, 2014) and teachers feel the pressure of having to meet many expectations in relation to their roles which often go far beyond their expertise or discipline knowledge (e.g. Polesel, Rice, & Dulfer, 2014). Yet, it cannot be denied that teachers are in a position to influence the development of students not just as learners but as human beings, as citizens and members of a broader community.

Against that background, the next section of the chapter considers the purposes of education from the perspectives of social justice and human rights. This is followed by consideration of the explicit and implicit opportunities for human rights education in various subject areas based on our empirical evidence. This naturally leads on to a discussion of the classroom applications of these findings and their implications for teacher professional learning. The relevance of our findings to Catholic schools is considered followed by some concluding remarks.

Social justice and human rights in education

There is much that connects the concepts of social justice and human rights. Social justice is often defined as the aspiration for equity for all human beings in terms of the distribution of wealth, access to education, employment and social services. Social justice implies a sense of connection to the principles of egalitarianism and ethical behaviour, as well as access to and involvement in policy development and administration. A humane society is the product of a socially just society.

A socially just society presupposes that individuals and governments understand that all humans have a right to live with dignity and have their rights respected. Peaceful, rights-based solutions to conflict have often emerged in the aftermath of conflict such as World Wars. For example, the United Nations and its Universal Declaration of Human Rights (UDHR) (1948) emerged from the chaos of the Second World War. While the United Nations has been criticised as being an impotent body for its failure to stop international crises (McGreal, 2015), it has nevertheless enacted international human rights conventions, declarations and treaties that at the very least provide a focus for human rights. Individual nations have also adopted Human Rights Acts, and while Australia is one of the few democratic countries not to have introduced Human Rights legislation at the Federal level, some Australian states/territories such as Victoria and the Australian Capital Territory (ACT) have their own human rights legislation (Burridge et al., 2013). In the absence of Federal legislation, students should learn over the course of their schooling about civil and political rights; economic, social and cultural rights; humanitarian rights and various group rights (workers, women, children, minority groups, refugees, Indigenous people and people with a disability).

Human rights and the rights frameworks that are embedded in national and international human rights conventions and declarations serve as moral and legal frameworks (Australian Human Rights Commission [AHRC], 2018), which are universal and inalienable (Office of the High Commissioner for Human Rights [OHCHR], 2015a). Educating young people about international human rights frameworks and legislation is an important way of underpinning rights and freedoms in our democratic system.

Osler and Starkey (2005) emphasise the important role of education in strengthening democracy and providing young people

> ... with appropriate experiences which allow them to make sense of international politics and interdependence while at the same time enabling them to feel that they can make a difference and participate in shaping our common future. (p. 12)

As has been argued above, education is much more than what happens within the four walls of a classroom. It is also much more than assessment, measurement and international testing systems such as the Programme for International Student Assessment (PISA). It is not just about preparation for work, as emphasised by the corporate mindset of politicians and leaders of industry. It is a complex mixture of all these, but also much more. Ensuring a focus on human rights education in the school curriculum is one way to build greater emphasis on broader goals and purposes of education.

Legislative and policy frameworks

Education about human rights in schools is shaped by international legislation and Australian policy frameworks that link back to the adoption of the Universal Declaration of Human Rights (UDHR; UN General Assembly, 1948):

> Education shall be directed to the full development of the human personality and to the strengthening of respect for human rights and fundamental freedoms. It shall promote understanding, tolerance and friendship among all nations, racial or religious groups, and shall further the activities of the United Nations for the maintenance of peace. (Article 26.2)

Since 1948, the United Nations has urged countries to disseminate the Declaration and to educate people about its contents, as well as the subsequent UN human rights conventions, treaties and charters, which have all included a role for school education (OHCHR, 2004).

Recent developments in human rights education at the international level have been marked by the UN Decade for Human Rights Education (1995–2004; OHCHR, 2015b), the World Program on Human Rights Education (2005; OHCHR, 2015c) and the publication of the UN Declaration on Human Rights Education and Training (OHCHR, 2011), which stated that

> ... all educational, training, information, awareness-raising and learning activities [are] aimed at promoting universal respect for and

observance of all human rights and fundamental freedoms and thus contributing ... to the prevention of human rights violations and abuses by providing persons with knowledge, skills and understanding and developing their attitudes and behaviours, to empower them to contribute to the building and promotion of a universal culture of human rights. (p. 3)

In 2010, the Australian Labor government undertook to develop both a Human Rights Framework and action plan in response to the National Human Rights Consultation of 2009 which recommended that human rights education should be a priority in schools and government organisations in order to build a culture of rights (Commonwealth of Australia, 2009).

While the focus on human rights education is continuing at the international level and the United Nations has initiated the third phase of the World Programme for Human Rights Education (2015–2019), the Australian Government has done little to promote human rights education within our education system or within public policy frameworks. Therefore, it has been left up to individual teachers, schools and educational administrators to examine the opportunities for human rights education provided by the recently introduced national Australian Curriculum and to implement programmes, activities and classroom strategies that focus on building a rights-based culture in schools.

The remainder of this chapter will report on our study of human rights education in Australian primary and secondary schools up to 2012 and on the possibilities offered by the introduction of the Australian Curriculum around that time.

Explicit and implicit teaching of human rights in the curriculum of Australian states and territories

This section of the chapter presents the main findings from *Human Rights Education in the School Curriculum* (Burridge et al., 2013). The aim of our study was to identify explicit and implicit opportunities for human rights education in the primary and secondary school curriculum in each Australian state and territory. The key research questions included whether human rights issues were addressed explicitly or implicitly, whether topics were compulsory or elective, the availability and range of sector-specific initiatives, the impact of state and territory human rights legislation and other curricular learning opportunities. Our data collection methods involved round-table discussions and interviews as well as documentary analysis of available primary and secondary school curriculum materials. The purpose of the round-table discussions/interviews in each state and territory was to gain the perspectives of government and Independent School sectors, curriculum agencies, teacher associations and the main nongovernment groups working on human rights issues within schools. School curriculum materials were analysed to identify the curriculum subject areas that provide opportunities for students to learn about human rights issues.

Our evidence suggests that human rights education was only addressed in a relatively narrow base of subjects. While opportunities existed for students to learn about fairness and respect, these were not presented in terms of human rights education and were at the discretion of the individual teacher. There was a widely expressed view that the curriculum in all states and territories suffered from overcrowding 'as educational policy makers tried to meet political and community-based demands for additions to the curriculum that would address an ever increasing set of issues related to safety, health and well-being, emergence of social media ...' (Burridge et al., 2013, p. 58). A recurring argument in the various round-table discussions was that human rights education would only be taken seriously when it became mandatory, that is when the Australian Curriculum, Assessment and Reporting Authority (ACARA) and the various states and territories include human rights, as well as ethical understanding, as an explicit part of the Australian school curriculum.

The round-table discussions and document searches threw up a discernible difference between explicit references to human rights terminology/topics in the curriculum documents and implicit references for the capacity to cover human rights issues. The overall sense emerging from the round-tables was that 'participants referred to specific subjects without a clear understanding of the topics or issues addressed' (Burridge et al., 2013, p. 59).

As might be expected, the Years 11–12 subjects with the most explicit references to human rights humanities based included history, geography and legal studies along with politics and international studies and Aboriginal studies and society. The lower secondary years curriculum provided explicit opportunities to study a diverse set of human rights issues in history, geography, Aboriginal studies and civics and citizenship units. There was, however, no guarantee that human rights would be an essential curriculum theme even where such syllabus units were defined as mandatory.

Human rights issues were not explicitly named or addressed in any subject areas across the primary curriculum up to Year 4, while there were implicit opportunities in the Years 5 and 6 history and geography and civics and citizenship syllabuses and in the English K-6 and, in some states, in the physical development, health and physical education (PDHPE) K-6 syllabuses. The researchers concluded there is a 'gap in the current curriculum of an explicit focus on human rights education in the primary years, and particularly in early childhood education K-2' (Burridge et al., 2013, p. 60).

A summary of the main findings of our study is presented in Figure 5.1 and in the Appendix (Burridge et al., 2013, p. 65).

104 Nina Burridge

Curricular opportunities:
An analysis of the opportunities for human rights education in the school curriculum shows that:

- The Senior Years 11 to 12 provide the most explicit and implicit learning opportunities to study topics that are clearly related to human rights issues.
- Among these opportunities there is a mix of mandatory and elective topics.
- Only a small number and proportion of students are likely to study human rights issues to any significant extent across their school years.
- The study of human rights issues takes place without any clear overall definition of rights and mostly without any overarching context or link back to UN declarations, treaties, conventions, or recent Australian rights legislation.

In the senior secondary years:

- The main explicit opportunities found as a result of this study are in History, Geography, Legal Studies subjects, and in Civics and Citizenship units of study.
- A number of subjects with small enrolments and not widely available also provide explicit opportunities for teaching about human rights. These subjects are politics, society and culture, aboriginal studies, women's studies, and studies in religion.
- Implicit opportunities were found in the subjects English, science and economics and business.
- Only a few subjects, specific to a few states and territories, namely history, Australian and global politics, Australian and international politics and aboriginal studies specifically, mentioned any UN human rights declarations, treaties or conventions or Australian rights legislation.

In the junior secondary years:

- Across the Secondary Years 7 to 10, it was mostly the Year 9 and 10 curriculum that offered the main explicit opportunities for human rights teaching – in history, geography, aboriginal studies subjects and civics and citizenship units.
- Implicit opportunities occurred in English, science and economics.

In the primary years:

- Human rights issues did not appear to be explicitly mentioned. Implicit opportunities were found mostly in the Human Society and its Environment (HSIE) or its equivalent Learning Area.
- The subjects included history, geography, English, physical development health and physical education (PDHPE) and civics and citizenship units.

Figure 5.1 Explicit and implicit opportunities for treatment of human rights across the curriculum

Social justice, human rights in the Australian Curriculum

The Australian Curriculum and Reporting Authority (ACARA, 2012) began work on the development of the national curriculum in 2007/2008, and individual learning areas were developed over a number of years, beginning with English, mathematics, science and history in 2010. This complex process was undertaken in stages and the Foundation to Year 10 (K-10) curriculum is now being implemented, while Years 11 and 12 reforms are also coming on stream (ACARA, 2018).

The *Shape of the Australian Curriculum* (ACARA, 2012) identifies eight learning areas (with their respective subjects), seven general capabilities and three cross-curriculum priorities.

Two of the general capabilities are of particular importance to human rights education, namely, ethical understanding and intercultural understanding. The ACARA (2012) defines these as follows:

> Students develop *ethical understanding* as they identify and investigate the nature of ethical concepts, values and character traits, and understand how reasoning can assist ethical judgment. Ethical understanding involves students in building a strong personal and socially oriented ethical outlook that helps them to manage context, conflict and uncertainty, and to develop an awareness of the influence that their values and behaviour have on others. (p. 17)

> Students develop *intercultural understanding* as they learn to value their own cultures, languages and beliefs, and those of others. They come to understand how personal, group and national identities are shaped, and the variable and changing nature of culture. The capability involves students in learning about and engaging with diverse cultures in ways that recognise commonalities and differences, create connections with others and cultivate mutual respect. (p. 17)

The Australian Curriculum identifies three cross-curriculum priorities to be embedded across all learning areas, which are important to equip young Australians with the skills, knowledge and understanding to engage in a globalised world. These are Aboriginal and Torres Strait Islander histories and cultures, Asia and Australia's engagement with Asia, and sustainability. Participants in the human rights round-table discussions (Burridge et al., 2013 p. 61) noted that the new emphasis on science and society and on sustainability as a cross-curriculum theme provided openings for human rights to be addressed in the science curriculum.

While there are no explicit references to social justice or human rights within the cross-curriculum priorities, there are implicit understandings about culturally responsive approaches to engaging with Australia's Indigenous peoples and culture and with neighbouring countries and cultures as well as the importance of human rights and freedoms.

Round-table participants saw the introduction of national curriculum subjects as providing real opportunities to embed essential learning about rights into the national agenda for all schools insofar as 'publishers will be able to produce something for the whole nation that could be used. The little publications we've had state by state (on human rights) could be replaced because they're more economically viable' (Burridge et al., 2013, p. 60).

Participants expressed their disappointment however that, despite some advocacy from the AHRC, 'human rights education was not specifically mentioned in the overarching framework of the Australian Curriculum' (Burridge et al., 2013, p. 60). They called for the inclusion of human rights in the support documentation for the general capabilities of ethical understanding and intercultural understanding as well as all three cross-curriculum priorities.

They welcomed the inclusion of specified knowledge and understanding of Aboriginal and Torres Strait Islander cultures as an essential set of skills for accreditation in the new National Teacher Professional standards introduced by the Australian Institute for Teaching and School Leadership (AITSL, 2013). Given the diverse nature of our student population and the multicultural nature of our classrooms today, it was also seen as important to combine multiculturalism and diversity within a general human rights approach. The overall recommendation of our report was that, 'once the new national Australian Curriculum is fully developed and implemented, Australian Curriculum subjects need to be audited to determine the extent to which human rights issues have been effectively integrated into the curriculum' (Burridge et al., 2013, p. 61).

Teaching about human rights in the classroom

As human rights educators, teachers need to develop students' critical thinking skills so that they can evaluate evidence, make judgements about human rights issues in the community and develop active citizenship. Students must learn to understand differing perspectives, develop empathy, question what they are being told and ask whose agendas are and are not being served. This capacity can be developed through engaging with real-life scenarios through simulations, gaming, debates and community action beyond the classroom.

Participants identified important prerequisites to effective implementation of any human rights issues in schools. They noted the importance of pedagogical practices, that is how we teach was of equal importance to what we teach. Since students need constant engagement and technologies are constantly being upgraded, teachers need to be skilled in a variety of teaching and learning methods and to have an understanding of the cultural contexts in which they find themselves. Participants also expressed concerns about how the outcomes of human rights education could be assessed. Concerns were also raised about the importance of developing and distributing relevant resources and emphasised the value of a centralised repository for materials.

Participants emphasised that teachers needed to model human rights in order for a culture of rights to develop and for students to actively embrace new understandings about rights and bring about transformative learning. A great deal still depends on teachers' interests and commitment, as well as the kind of pedagogy and approach they used in their human rights teaching.

It is individual teachers who determine the level of detail in teaching about human rights, particularly at the 'explicit' level.

Choosing which rights to teach is a highly contested question (Cassidy, Brunner, & Webster, 2014), since political and social debate impacts variously on educators and school sectors. The existing national human rights framework provides a useful starting point for discussion. The AHRC (n.d.) has identified the following areas for investigation: civil and political rights, the right to adequate food and water, health care, education, a clean environment, welfare assistance; and humanitarian rights such as the rights of prisoners.

Our research found that teachers were often reluctant to approach controversial issues. It is clear from our round-table discussions that the context of the school often determined what issues were discussed and what texts were taught, and that many teachers did not want to put themselves into a position where they had to contradict a school's approach or its policies or come into conflict with the parent community or the school system they worked in. As noted by Branigan and Ramcharan (2012), dealing with indigenous rights/culture, women's and/or children's rights and religious freedom, as well rights pertaining to gender and sexuality poses difficult challenges for teachers in classrooms, some of whom feared that teaching children's rights may create classroom disruption.

On the other hand, there is research which indicates that if children are taught about rights and respect for rights, their attitudes to others become more positive and accepting (Tibbitts & Fernekes, 2011). Similarly, a study on values education undertaken by Education Services Australia (ESA, 2010) found that in schools where values were embedded in curriculum content and pedagogy, children exhibited 'increased empathy, tolerance, understanding and respect; increased sharing and team work; and greater willingness to tell the truth and accept responsibility for their actions ... [and] decreased playground fighting' (ESA, 2010, cited in AHRC, 2011, p.4). It was noted that, while some restorative justice programmes which operate in both private and public education systems are linked to schools that have challenging discipline-based environments, other programmes are linked to an improved understanding of children's rights.

It is important for schools to set parameters, to openly discuss issues and upskill teachers through targeted professional learning programmes and to provide them with the necessary awareness, knowledge, skills and strategies so as to effectively tackle contested issues. In this world of global connectivity, the capacity to link with schools internationally is an important aspect of human rights education. Teachers can extend their students' learning opportunities around various aspects of human rights education by building up their capacity to link with schools in other countries. The capacity to utilise social media in a safe way and connect with corresponding schools is also a valuable way to extend such collaborations. This may also enable cultural exchanges, perhaps with the support of local and international non-governmental organisations (NGOs). The Asian Education Foundation, World Vision and the United

Nations Youth Association as well as many other NGOs are already using technologies to engage with and create new global interactive opportunities.

As with all curriculum innovations, strong executive leadership that supports staff and specific programmes is essential to change in schools and participants commented on 'the difference good distributive leadership made by taking a whole-school approach to a project' (Burridge et al., 2013, p. 62). Participants also identified the importance of the role of parents and the community in human rights education. The need to engage with parents about human rights education is particularly important in schools where parents have expressed concerns about the teaching of controversial issues. Useful precedents are available in anti-bullying restorative justice projects, in Play by the Rules (2018), a national project about fair play in sport and in Fair Go Sport (Australian Sports Commission, 2010).

Social justice and social responsibility in Catholic schools

Our research identified specific opportunities for human rights education in the social justice and social responsibility syllabus in faith-based schools that champion these activities as part of their school ethos. Round-table participants

> applaud[ed] the efforts of the Catholic school system to work with social justice issues which of course are seen as being closely related to human rights education. More importantly, these projects are often linked with community groups, with NGOs and their own faith-based lay organisations and do actively engage students in their operations. (Burridge et al., 2013, p. 61)

The treatment of controversial issues can be particularly difficult in the context of faith-based schools.

A feature of the Catholic Education system is its focus on aspects of social justice and social responsibility with an emphasis on Gospel values and Catholic social teaching. Such projects are often linked with community groups, NGOs or faith-based organisations and actively engage students in their operations. One such useful resource is the *Catholic social teaching* tool kit (Caritas Australia, 2018) designed for both primary and secondary years to promote a sense of social responsibility. The Catholic social teaching themes included in the tool kit relate well to rights and responsibilities and the importance of human dignity which could be explored in English, human society and its environment (HSIE) and personal development, health and physical education (PDHPE) subjects in both the primary and secondary years.

Beyond the mandated curriculum, many Catholic schools engage in community projects that have a social justice and/or human rights focus. These range from visiting homeless shelters, women's refuges and youth agencies to global peace-based activities as well as fundraising for specific causes, such as poverty or the elimination of child labour (Burridge et al., 2013 p. 37). Catholic schools also engage in social justice activities through a number of Catholic organisations, linking students to the work of Catholic agencies such as Caritas and the St Vincent de Paul Society. Caritas Australia, the Catholic Church's international aid and development organisation, works in over 30 developing countries. Grounded in the Catholic Social Justice Teaching tradition, it supports long-term development programmes in impoverished communities in Africa, Asia, East Timor, the Pacific, Latin America and Australian Indigenous communities (Caritas Australia, 2018).

Teacher professional learning

All the round-tables identified the crucial importance of professional learning for teachers in the implementation of a human rights education strategy and in the changing context of the new Australian national curriculum. For example, teachers felt quite vulnerable in the newly mandated areas of Australian Indigenous rights and history. It was reported that teachers were hesitant to approach certain issues because they felt they lacked the skills to deal with them appropriately, and it was suggested that education departments and schools should work with professional teacher associations to provide more targeted professional learning opportunities for teachers. This was seen as particularly important in view of the changes that the Australian Curriculum would bring to schools. We found, however, that '[f]ew programmes were available or had been offered to enable and support teachers to implement the various curriculum opportunities that were already in place' (Burridge et al., 2013, p. 47).

Teacher associations are well placed to contribute to human rights education and filling the gaps in teacher knowledge and expertise about human rights issues. These associations may have the capacity to support teachers through workshops, annual conferences and the application of various communication technologies.

Teacher education providers have opportunities to focus on human rights both from a philosophy of education perspective and the development of a rights-based culture in schools and classrooms. While the deconstruction of power structures within society is often attempted through the lens of sociology of education, not all teacher education providers undertake to develop pre-service teachers' ideas about social justice and global citizenship. Providing learning experiences with a human rights focus where communication technologies, social media and interactivity are utilised is an important consideration for teacher education institutions.

Developing schools as holistic learning communities connected with the key local organisations such as NGOs who work with the homeless, women's shelters or in refugee support services enhance student learning by making it authentic and ensure that individual learning areas and subjects are not silos but linked through cross-curriculum activities. Teachers and schools should be encouraged to reach out and develop global networks to enrich the education process for their students.

Conclusion

The researchers have noted the potential opportunities provided for Human Rights Education in the curriculum along with the barriers to their realisation. While there was general support for human rights education in the round-table discussions, 'there appears to be some reluctance or ambivalence among school educators and teachers about the teaching of human rights' (Burridge et al., 2013, p. 58).

The paramount reason for educating students about human rights is to create a more socially just society and to engage students in the process of becoming active global citizens who are confident and creative, who actively engage in their communities and who 'take responsibility for their own actions, respect and value diversity and see themselves as contributors to a more peaceful and sustainable world' (Bradbury, 2013, p. 221).

Engaging students in activities that enable them to think critically about issues requires teachers to provide experiential and activity-centred learning that involves problem-solving and futuristic thinking. Such learning also involves presenting students with effective multifaceted classroom activities that involve connecting with global communities, so that they analyse and discuss the diversity of the planet in social, political and economic terms. It requires committed teachers who will assist students to investigate the challenges the world faces in times of great technological change where social media, for example, is impacting on our rights and freedoms.

The implementation of effective and worthwhile human rights programmes in schools requires commitment not just from one passionate teacher, but from the leadership team in the school to enable a whole-school approach to build a rights-based culture in the school. There is a real need to work with national and state-based curriculum bodies as well as the various school sectors to ensure that human rights, social justice and ethical behaviour are included as an explicit part of the formal school curriculum. Furthermore, it is crucial that pre-service teachers are supported with adequate and effective teacher professional learning and access to quality resources and technologies so that they become advocates for human rights education based programmes in schools. The time is now for education systems, schools and teachers to focus on building in the students of tomorrow, the aspiration and capacity to fight for a socially just world that respects human rights and the dignity of all creatures.

The overall conclusion of our study was that, insofar as Australian education systems and providers place emphasis on social justice, there is nevertheless a lack of clarity and direction when it comes to human rights education.

While we identified good opportunities at secondary level for the explicit treatment of human rights, there was an obvious gap at primary level. It is too early to comment on the Australian Curriculum, although the absence of explicit reference to human rights education there is disconcerting. Context is everything, and the failure to incorporate human rights education across the curriculum must be seen against a background of 'the lack of support by some political leaders, particularly at the national level, for the introduction of an Australian Human Rights Act' (Burridge et al., 2013, p. 58).

References

Australian Curriculum, Assessment and Reporting Authority (ACARA). (2012). *Shape of the Australian curriculum.* Sydney: Author.

Australian Curriculum, Assessment and Reporting Authority (ACARA). (2018). *Monitoring the effectiveness of the foundation – Year 10 Australian curriculum.* Sydney: Author.

Australian Government. (2014). *Review of the Australian Curriculum: Final report.* Canberra: Author.

Australian Human Rights Commission (AHRC). (n.d.). *Rights and freedoms: Right by right.* Retrieved from https://www.humanrights.gov.au/rights-and-freedoms-right-right-0

Australian Human Rights Commission (AHRC). (2011). *Human rights education in the national school Curriculum: Position Paper of the Australian Human Rights Commission.* Retrieved from http://humanrights.gov.au/education/positionpaper/index.html

Australian Human Rights Commission (AHRC). (2018). *Human rights based approaches.* Retrieved from https://www.humanrights.gov.au/human-rights-based-approaches

Australian Institute for Teaching and School Leadership (AITSL). (2013). *Insights. A unit outline and content for professional learning units to support teachers in meeting Focus Areas 1.4 and 2.4.* Victoria, TX: AITSL.

Australian Sports Commission. (2010). *Fair go, sport.* Retrieved from https://www.humanrights-commission.vic.gov.au/our-projects-a-initiatives/fair-go-sport

Ball, S. J. (2012). *Global Education Inc. New policy networks and the neo-liberal imaginary.* London, England: Routledge.

Bradbury, D. (2013). Bridges to global citizenship: Ecologically sustainable futures utilising children's literature in teacher education. *Australian Journal of Environmental Education, 29*(2), 221–237.

Branigan, E., & Ramcharan, P. (2012). Human rights education in Australia: Reflections on the meaningful application of rights and values in practice. *Journal of Human Rights Practice, 4*(2), 233–252.

Burridge, N., Chodkiewicz, A., Payne, A., Oguro, S., Varnham, S., & Buchanan, J. (2013). *Human rights education in the school curriculum.* Report compiled for the Attorney General's Department. Sydney: University of Technology.

Caritas Australia. (2018). *Educating for a just world.* Retrieved from https://www.caritas.org.au/learn/schools

Cassidy, C., Brunner, R., & Webster, E. (2014). Teaching human rights? All hell will break loose! *Education, Citizenship and Social Justice, 9*(1), 19–33. doi:10.1177/1746197913475768

Commonwealth of Australia. (2009). *National human rights consultation report.* Barton, ACT: Federal Attorney General's Department. Retrieved from http://www.ag.gov.au/

Dewey, J. (1897). My pedagogic creed. *The School Journal, LIV*(3), 77–80.

Education Services Australia (ESA). (2010). *Giving voice to the impacts of values education: The final report of the values in action schools project.* Australia: Author.

Freire, P. (1968). *Pedagogy of the oppressed.* New York: Seabury Press.

Hattie, J.A.C. (2003, October). Teachers make a difference: What is the research evidence? Paper presented at the Building Teacher Quality: What does the research tell us ACER Research Conference, Melbourne, Australia. Retrieved from http://research.acer.edu.au/research_conference_2003/4/

Lingard, B. (2010). Policy borrowing, policy learning: Testing times in Australian schooling. *Critical Studies in Education 51*(2), 129–147. doi:10.1080/17508481003731026.

McGreal, C. (2015). 70 years and half a trillion dollar later: What has the United Nations achieved? *The Guardian.* Retrieved from https://www.theguardian.com/world/2015/sep/07/what-has-the-un-achieved-united-nations

Nussbaum, M. (2009). Education for profit, education for freedom. *Liberal Education, 95*(3), 6–13.

Nussbaum, M. (2010). *Not for profit.* Princeton, NJ: Princeton University Press.

Nussbaum, M. (2016). The struggle within: Education and human development. *ABC Religion and Ethics.* Retrieved from http://www.abc.net.au/religion/the-struggle-within-education-and-human-development/10097290

Office of the High Commissioner for Human Rights (OHCHR). (2004). *Statement of the United Nations High Commissioner for Human Rights.* Retrieved from https://newsarchive.ohchr.org/EN/NewsEvents/Pages/DisplayNews.aspx?NewsID=1608&LangID=E

Office of the High Commissioner for Human Rights (OHCHR). (2011). *UN Declaration on Human Rights Education and Training.* Retrieved from https://www.ohchr.org/EN/Issues/Education/Training/Compilation/Pages/UnitedNationsDeclarationonHumanRightsEducationandTraining(2011).aspx

Office of the High Commissioner for Human Rights (OHCHR). (2015a). *Vienna Declaration and Programme of Action.* Retrieved from http://www.ohchr.org/EN/ProfessionalInterest/Pages/Vienna.aspx.

Office of the High Commissioner for Human Rights (OHCHR). (2015b). *United Nations Decade for Human Rights Education (1995–2004).* Retrieved from http://www.ohchr.org/EN/Issues/Education/Training/Pages/Decade.aspx

Office of the High Commissioner for Human Rights (OHCHR). (2015c). *World Programme for Human Rights Education (2005-ongoing).* Retrieved from http://www.ohchr.org/EN/Issues/Education/Training/Pages/Programme.aspx

Osler, A., & Starkey, H. (2005). *Changing citizenship: Democracy and inclusion in education.* Maidenhead, England: Open University Press.

Play by the Rules. (2018). *Making sport inclusive, safe and fair.* Retrieved from https://www.playbytherules.net.au/

Polesel, J., Rice, S., & Dulfer, N. (2014). The impact of high-stakes testing on curriculum and pedagogy: A teacher perspective from Australia. *Journal of Education Policy, 29*(5), 640–657. doi: 10.1080/02680939.2013.865082.

Pring, R. (2001). Education as a moral practice. *Journal of Moral Education, 30*(2), 101–112.

Sachs, J. (2000). The activist professional. *Journal of Educational Change, 1*(1), 77–94.

Tibbitts, F., & Fernekes, W. R. (2011). Human rights education. In S. Totten & J. E. Pedersen (Eds.), *Teaching and studying social issues: Major programs and approaches* (pp. 87–117). Charlotte, NC: IAP Information Age Publishing.

UN General Assembly. (1948). *Universal declaration of human rights.* New York: Author. Retrieved from https://www.un.org/en/universal-declaration-human-rights/

Chapter 6

The distinctive nature of Catholic Education in Ontario: Catholic perspective integrated across the formal curriculum

Katharine Stevenson and Michael Pautler

Introduction

A distinctively Catholic Education system has existed in Ontario for almost 200 years. For the last 30 years, Catholic schools in Ontario have been fully funded by public tax dollars, a status achieved in incremental steps over time as a result of political advocacy and court challenges. Throughout the protracted struggle to achieve equitable public funding, the Ontario Catholic Education community has consistently and creatively worked to ensure the Catholic character of Catholic schools. As one of four publicly funded education systems in Ontario today, Catholic educators are mandated to deliver the secular Ontario Ministry of Education curriculum to elementary and secondary school students from Kindergarten to Grade 12. As a Catholic institution granted authority by the Ontario Bishops, Catholic schools are also charged to deliver the Ontario curriculum with a difference, and Catholic educators accomplish this by integrating a Catholic worldview across the curriculum. Catholic educators employ religious frameworks to assist with this task. In doing so, authentic curriculum connections are made and initiatives mandated by the Ontario Ministry of Education are effectively adapted for use in Catholic schools. Catholic curriculum integration also serves to support the full development of each student in response to the challenges of the day and enables them to transform their world.

This chapter will provide a brief overview of the history of Catholic Education in Ontario. The guidance and support of Catholic Education partners such as the Assembly of Catholic Bishops of Ontario (ACBO), the Institute for Catholic Education (hereafter referred to as 'ICE') and the Catholic Curriculum Corporation (hereafter referred to as 'CCC') will be noted. An analysis of the Catholic character of curriculum will explore the way in which curriculum separation, permeation and integration contributes to distinctive Catholic curriculum. Specific examples of this Catholic character of curriculum in Ontario Catholic schools, as well as the emergence of religious frameworks to support Catholic curriculum, will be explored. Discussion will include the way in which such religious frameworks, such as a Catholic social teaching framework, serve to adapt both Ontario Ministry of Education curriculum and initiatives for use in Catholic schools.

Publicly funded Catholic Education in Ontario

Catholic Education in the province of Ontario has been publicly funded, in whole or in part, for over 175 years. While Catholic schools have existed since the 1600s, permanent government financial support was not provided until 1841. Upper Canada, as Ontario was known at that time, was settled by an English Protestant majority and a French Catholic minority, while Lower Canada (now the province of Quebec) was settled primarily by a French Catholic majority, with an English Protestant minority presence. As Upper and Lower Canada explored the possibility of political union as a defensive measure against the perceived threat of expansion by the United States, strong protection for linguistic and religious minority rights were essential to overcome the historical rivalry and suspicion between French and English. Over time, a series of legislative compromises began to enshrine strong protection for minority rights in law. The Scott Act of 1863 guaranteed Catholic schools would be governed by trustees in a manner comparable to their Protestant public school counterparts, and have a limited share of the Common School Fund of the Canadian Government. With the British North America Act of 1867, Canada became a nation and Catholic Education was constitutionally guaranteed as a minority right for French-Canadian Catholics in Upper Canada (see Article 93).

While protection of minority rights, including rights with respect to education, were entrenched in the Canadian constitution at the federal level, education is the primary responsibility of the provincial level of government, and practice regarding the public funding of Catholic schools varies widely from province to province. Ontario, with a population of approximately 13.6 million, is Canada's most populous province, and one of four of 13 Canadian provinces and territories where Catholic schools receive full (or nearly full) public funding. While rooted in history, approaches to funding have been dynamic, and have evolved over the years (Dixon, 2003).

Initially, Catholic elementary schools were afforded limited public funding, accessing only tax dollars from property owners who identified as Catholic, and financial support for Catholic secondary schools was not available at all. In incremental steps, further government funding for elementary schools was made available over time, sometimes as a result of successful court challenges, and sometimes as a result of political advocacy. Eventually Grades 9 and 10 (considered the first 2 years of secondary programme in Ontario's Kindergarten to Grade 12 system) were financially supported, but at elementary school rates, a significantly lesser level than that provided to public secondary schools. It would not be until 1984 that full funding was extended to Catholic schools through to the completion of secondary school

The distinctive nature of Catholic Education   115

(K to 12). Even then, government grants were not equitable. Catholic school systems had limited access to corporate property taxes, Catholic schools were typically funded at lesser levels, and secondary students paid tuition to supplement the costs of operating Catholic secondary schools. Completion of funding, which provided full recognition and government funding of all educational programmes, K-12, was announced in 1984 and phased in by 1987. Catholic schools are now eligible for both capital grants to support the construction and maintenance of school buildings and operating grants for instruction. This decision of the provincial government provided a stable financial foundation, and ushered in an era of rapid expansion of Catholic secondary schools, although fully equal funding was not achieved until further changes were introduced to the education funding model in 1998.

Today there are four government-funded school systems in the province of Ontario – English public, French public, English Catholic and French Catholic – and each system is funded at comparable levels.[1] Just over 2 million students attend publicly funded schools in Ontario, and English Catholic schools account for approximately one third of that number. Ontario has just over 1,500 publicly funded Catholic schools with approximately 625,000 students, operated by 29 Catholic district school boards, and employing nearly 50,000 Catholic teachers.[2]

Corresponding with the period during which Catholic schools advocated for and gradually accessed increased levels of public funding, Ontario's Catholic schools were experiencing the gradual reduction of direct participation and involvement of religious brothers, sisters and priests. Initially, almost all Catholic schools were associated with religious communities, and the presence of religious brothers, sisters and priests as teachers naturally ensured the Catholic character and ethos of the schools, as well as contributing significantly to their financial viability. By the 1960s, the presence of religious personnel had begun to diminish significantly in elementary schools as religious communities, experiencing reduced numbers of vocations, began to concentrate efforts on secondary schools. Within the span of 30 years, the presence of religious teachers and administrators in Catholic schools went from being the norm to being a rarity. With fewer community members working in secondary schools, the religious congregations were challenged to maintain the financial costs of operating schools. By the mid-1980s, when full government funding was finally achieved, the financial contributions of religious congregations ceased. Within a decade, the presence of religious personnel in Catholic schools virtually disappeared. Today, the leadership positions in Catholic school districts and Catholic schools, and the teaching positions within Catholic classrooms are filled almost exclusively by lay Catholics, and the very small number of religious sisters, brothers and priests associated with Catholic schools are most frequently to be found in roles supporting Chaplaincy teams.

While the level of direct accountability to the Ontario Ministry of Education (hereafter referred to as 'the Ministry') has increased over time,

Catholic schools continue to operate with the authority and approval of the Ontario Catholic Bishops. The ACBO includes Bishops from the 17 dioceses across the province which is home to 4 million Catholics, approximately 30% of the overall population. Diocesan boundaries do not directly correspond with the geographical boundaries of the 29 Catholic district school boards which have been established by the Ministry, nor do school boundaries necessarily correspond directly with parish boundaries. Dioceses have no direct financial or managerial responsibility for the Catholic schools within their jurisdiction, but exercise significant, if indirect, influence over the Catholic schools that operate under their authority by canon law. In this context, pastoral letters from the Bishops of Ontario to the Catholic Education community have become one mechanism by which the Bishops articulate mission and vision, offer encouragement, and influence the direction and priorities of a publicly funded school system.

A time of transition: Towards distinctive Catholic curriculum

Following the completion of funding to Catholic secondary schools, key moments would begin to shape the distinctive approach to Catholic curriculum in Ontario. The Bishops of Ontario played a key role in helping to shape this distinctive approach, even as the leadership of Catholic schools was essentially passed to the laity. In 1989, the Catholic Bishops of Ontario issued the pastoral letter, *This Moment of Promise*, and noted both the opportunities and the challenges that come with full funding. In this pastoral letter, the Bishops included key messages from Pope Saint John Paul II to the Catholic Education community. During his 1984 visit to Newfoundland, Canada, the Pope had stated, 'We must grasp firmly the challenge of providing a kind of education whose curriculum will be inspired more by reflection than by technique, more by a search for wisdom than by the accumulation of information' (ACBO, 1988, p. 16).[3] Furthermore, during his 1988 visit with the Ontario Bishops, the Pope stated, 'Even though the financial viability of Catholic schools has been guaranteed, the task remains of ensuring their Catholic character' (ACBO, 1988, p. 11). Acknowledging the challenge articulated by the Holy Father, the Bishops called for Catholic schools to be places where knowledge is transformed by the deeper search for meaning. They encouraged the Ontario Catholic Education community to embrace the challenges and opportunities of the moment to emphasise and discover new responses and new solutions. The Bishops identified a number of critical tasks that needed to be addressed, stating (in part):

> We need to develop further and to articulate a Catholic philosophy of education for our times so that our distinctive vision of education will permeate every aspect of our curriculum and all dimensions of the

The distinctive nature of Catholic Education   117

> learning process ... Efforts in developing curriculum specifically for Catholic schools should continue. Religious education should not be reduced to one course in our school. Rather, our whole educational process should become a religious activity. Faith should infuse every subject and aspect of our curriculum. (ACBO, 1988, p. 20)

Freed from the worry of financial burden, the Bishops challenged those in the Catholic Education community to establish a clear vision of Catholic Education worthy of this gift that had been received.

As a strategic response to the challenges and opportunities presented by a fully publicly funded Catholic school system, the Ontario Bishops established the ICE in 1988. The mission of ICE is to bring together, work with and assist organisations that share responsibility for English Catholic Education in their efforts to promote and maintain publicly funded Catholic schools animated by the gospel and reflecting the tenets of the Catholic faith (ICE, 2018). As a corporate entity, ICE falls under the authority of the ACBO, but broad oversight and governance is provided by a board of directors representing seven partner organisations or associations that work cooperatively in the interest of publicly funded Catholic schools. The partners include the Ontario Bishops, school trustees, directors and supervisory officers, business officials, principals and vice principals, teachers and parents. ICE also works with and supports the 29 Catholic district school boards. The broad mandate for ICE includes coordination of organisations in writing Catholic curriculum,[4] developing foundational documents in Catholic educational practice, outlining programmes for pre-service and in-service professional development for Catholic educators and leaders, commissioning research related to Catholic Education and fostering positive relationships and common vision on issues and policies that promote and protect Catholic Education. ICE has no direct responsibility for operation of schools or delivery of programmes, but serves and supports the organisations and individuals who do hold those responsibilities.

ICE, though a very small organisation, is able to function only by the collaborative efforts of all Catholic partners in Ontario. These include groups, associations and school boards who contribute voluntarily to fund the Institute, but more importantly, who support its work by making valuable human resources available. Strength of ICE, and the resultant quality of materials developed, is the ability to access and rely on the contributions of Catholic field practitioners including classroom teachers, curriculum consultants and programme coordinators who are actively engaged in the work of delivering distinctively Catholic curriculum.

One of the early tasks of ICE was to articulate a vision of who the Catholic learner was becoming. This vision identified the knowledge, skills, values and attitudes the Catholic Education community hoped to foster in students along their Catholic school journey. The *Ontario Catholic School Graduate Expectations* (ICE, 1998a) describe the learner as

- a discerning believer formed in the Catholic faith community;
- an effective communicator;
- a reflective, creative, and holistic thinker;
- a self-directed, responsible, lifelong learner;
- a collaborative contributor;
- a caring family member and
- a responsible citizen.

These seven overall expectations and the associated 52 specific expectations have provided a vision to guide educators in the design and implementation of Catholic curriculum in Ontario Catholic schools that supports the full flourishing of students – body, mind and spirit. Developed collaboratively by the education community, it is the most recognisable and well-adopted religious framework used by educators in Ontario. The *Ontario Catholic School Graduate Expectations* reflect the belief that Catholic schools are both places of learning and places of believing. 'As learners, Catholic students are encouraged by the community to cultivate their intellectual and aesthetic potentialities; as believers, they are inspired to grow in faith in the presence of Jesus Christ' (ICE, 1996a, pp. 19–20).

In order to address the mandate to coordinate the work of Catholic associations and organisations in writing Catholic curriculum within the parameters established by the Ministry, ICE developed a series of foundational documents in Catholic educational practice. In 1996, ICE published *Curriculum Matters: A Resource for Catholic Educators*. This document includes five papers intended to engage all Catholic Education stakeholders in a meaningful dialogue about 'a suitable curriculum' for Catholic schools. *Curriculum Matters* identifies the responsibility of these stakeholders 'to fashion a curriculum whose foundation rests on the distinctive characteristics of the Roman Catholic Tradition' (ICE, 1996a, p. 1). ICE then published a companion document, *Writing Curriculum for Catholic Schools: A Framework* (1996b) to translate the philosophical, theological and methodological context of Ontario Catholic Education described in *Curriculum Matters* into a practical framework for the development of Catholic curriculum.

By 1997, the Ontario educational landscape was undergoing significant reform. School boards were restructured and amalgamated into larger districts and the Ministry committed to a shared vision of educational accountability, quality, curriculum standards, and financial structure. The Ministry proposed the development of curriculum policy documents for each course of study in Ontario secondary schools with the expectation of implementation in *all* publicly funded school boards. In 1998, ICE published *Educating the Soul: Writing Curriculum for Catholic Secondary Schools*, which identified the challenges this government initiative posed to the curricular future of Catholic secondary schools. These generic curriculum policy documents for use across the province of Ontario would naturally be void of any reference to the distinctive character of Catholic curriculum, would imply the concept of Catholic character to be irrelevant, would remove the importance of values formation essential to Catholic curriculum, would reduce education to preparation for the market-place rather than a deeper vision of life and would deny religious language or symbols in favour of secularism. ICE (1998b) concluded:

> Ontario's curricula landscape as outlined in *Education Reform*, therefore, cannot be endorsed by Catholic secondary schools without destroying their self-identity. Simply stated, the challenge to Catholic secondary schools is to develop, produce and implement a curriculum for secondary schools that is Catholic in purpose and character. (p. 6)

Educating the Soul was clear to state that curriculum in Catholic secondary schools *could not* be guided solely by Ministry curriculum documents – 'To do so would be to forfeit the Catholic character of its educational mandate – a mandate that clearly states that the essence of education is that it be religious' (ICE, 1998b, p. 11). In response to concerns raised by the Catholic Education community, the government of Ontario provided financial support for the creation of Catholic curriculum for Catholic schools. Coordinated through ICE, Catholic Course Profiles were developed that infused Catholic character and values into the Ministry curriculum documents across all subject disciplines for use in Ontario Catholic secondary schools.

Understanding the Catholic character of curriculum

The work of the ICE has helped to develop an understanding of Catholic curriculum in a broad sense. *Educating the Soul* describes curriculum as

> much more than policy documents and support materials. At its core, it reveals fundamental beliefs and values about the nature, task, and specific character of the educational enterprise. It incarnates the vision of education from which it originates and the end towards which education is directed. (ICE, 1998b, p. 12)

It argues that an understanding of curriculum in the Catholic educational context as distinct from that of secular education is necessary, asserting

> [t]o limit curriculum to Ministry definitions such as 'a plan for student learning which is implemented in schools,' is to reduce curriculum to little more that society's latest educational menu, solely pragmatic and utilitarian in nature, and void of any effective and convincing interpretation of existence. (ICE, 1998b, p. 12)

Curriculum Matters (ICE, 1996a, pp. 22–28) describes three approaches to the Catholic character of curriculum – separation, permeation and integration.[5] The task of developing resources to reflect this Catholic character is brought into focus when the curriculum type is understood. First, curriculum separation refers to curriculum and programme development specifically for religious education courses or classes. 'Its primary goal is the development of religious literacy and formation and the incentive to produce such explicit religious material comes from within the Catholic community itself' (ICE, 1996a, p. 23). In Ontario Catholic schools, there are comprehensive curriculum policy documents for elementary and secondary school Religious Education and Family Life Education, and these documents guide curriculum writing for these courses. These policy documents are developed and published by ICE on behalf of and with the authority of the Bishops of Ontario. Educators who work to create religious education resources understand such writing to be explicitly religious. 'When separation is the task, the Catholic character of curriculum writing poses less of a challenge. Since Catholic schools teach religion, building curriculum materials that assist in the development of religious literacy and formation makes eminent sense' (ICE, 1996a, p. 23).

Although curriculum separation is a subject-specific task, curriculum permeation is understood as a school-wide task. 'Permeation refers to curriculum materials that address the role of the Catholic school's culture and its communal features in the process of learning' (ICE, 1996a, p. 24). This is not curriculum in the narrow sense, but understood more broadly as the purposeful experiences that contribute to the Catholic ethos of the learning environment. Curriculum permeation in Catholic schools is intentionally guided by Catholic values. It is evidenced, for example, by the social justice endeavours of the school, the signs and symbols present, the way the liturgical year is recognised and celebrated and the holistic vision of the learner. The Catholic character of curriculum permeates beyond the classroom into both the physical and the social environment of the school. Curriculum permeation is not only guided by Catholic values, but it also makes evident those values. A culture that is shaped by the values and traditions of the Catholic faith is a model to the Catholic school community of the important way in which faith should guide decisions. Curriculum permeation 'identifies the connection between faith and life, church and school, learning and the call to community service and ministry in Jesus' name' (ICE, 1996a, p. 24). In Catholic schools, the task of curriculum permeation is also explicitly religious.

Finally, *Curriculum Matters* describes the cross-curricular task of curriculum integration. Integration moves beyond specific course content 'to the connections, relationships, and life problems that exist within an increasingly complex and interdependent world' (ICE, 1996a, p. 24). Curriculum integration has the potential to be transformative when connections foster 'the

The distinctive nature of Catholic Education 121

knowledge, values and skills that bring about a critical perspective on social and global issues' (ICE, 1996a, p. 25). The primary challenge with curriculum integration is that of 'curriculum fit'. This curriculum task should serve a greater purpose than just integration itself. Curriculum writers must ensure that their attempts at integration are organic rather than being simply superimposed for the sake of connection. In the latter case, attempts at integration are inauthentic. Curriculum integration makes evident the Catholic character of curriculum when authentic connections to faith are made across the curriculum. With this intentionality, all courses of study possess a distinctive Catholic worldview. 'Problems arise when religious concepts and ideas are forced into subject areas in the name of integration with little regard for the integrity of the academic discipline itself' (ICE, 1996a, p. 25). For example, to explore current environmental issues while fostering an understanding of the call to care for creation as God's stewards is an authentic curriculum fit in a science class. In this case, the knowledge and skills of the science curriculum take on a religious dimension. Conversely, the study of the water cycle and subsequent mention that God gathered together the waters on the third day of creation is a 'superimposed' connection that appears as an add-on to the science curriculum.

The Catholic character of curriculum in Ontario Catholic schools

As previously noted, the development of both Ontario Religious Education and Family Life Education curriculum policy is overseen by ICE, as mandated by the Bishops of Ontario. All Catholic teachers in Ontario responsible for teaching Religious Education and Family Life Education courses are expected to implement the grade-specific course curriculum as outlined in these Ontario Catholic curriculum policy documents.[6] The task of *curriculum separation* is clear in this Catholic educational context. Primary resources are developed to align with Ontario Catholic curriculum policy and are approved for use by the Ontario Bishops in all 17 dioceses (e.g. *Fully Alive* is the approved programme for Grades 1–8 elementary Family Life Education; *Growing in Faith, Growing in Christ* is the approved programme for Grades 1–8 elementary Religious Education). Supplemental resources are also developed and reviewed by the Education Commission of the Bishops.

In a province with four publicly funded school systems, Ontario Catholic schools seek to consistently make evident their distinctive Catholic character. *Curriculum permeation* supports this task. All Ontario Catholic schools are guided by a vision of the learner as articulated in the *Ontario Catholic School Graduate Expectations* (as previously noted; ICE, 1998a). Since 1998, this common vision guides Ontario Catholic educators to make classroom, school, board and system decisions that will support the ongoing holistic development of each student – body, mind and spirit. An understanding of who the learner is becoming is theologically tied to an understanding of the mandate of Catholic schools. *Curriculum Matters*, states,

> ... Catholic schools must be places where students can hear Jesus' invitation to follow him, where they can receive his command to love all people, and where they can realize his presence and his promise to be with them always. Only in this way can they be nurtured and encouraged to become who they are meant to be: persons of dignity and freedom, created in the image and likeness of God as modelled in Jesus Christ. (ICE, 1996a, p. 21)

This vision of the learner within an understanding of the mandate of Catholic schools permeates all curriculum, in the broad sense of the word, when the *Ontario Catholic School Graduate Expectations* are used as a religious framework from which to approach the curriculum.[7]

The Catholic character of curriculum is further made evident through *curriculum integration*. In Ontario, all teachers are mandated to teach the Ontario curriculum as outlined in Ministry curriculum policy documents for each subject or course of study. Ontario Catholic educators are further mandated to deliver this curriculum with a difference – through the lens of faith. Catholic teachers present a Catholic worldview when authentic faith connections are made in all grades and across all subjects. *Curriculum Matters* identifies the challenge this poses as follows:

> The Ministry is producing generic, one size fits all curriculum documents for use in English language schools, whether they be public or separate ... curriculum documents will require serious modification and re-design to meet the different educational objectives which we claim distinguish us from the public school system. It is through demonstrating a unique curriculum structure and educational philosophy that Catholic Education will maintain its identity ... On this issue, our fate is in our own hands. (ICE, 1996a, p. 6)

There are few resources that seamlessly integrate secular course content with a Catholic worldview. This typically becomes the curriculum planning task of the classroom teacher. As such, Catholic educators benefit from resources that provide a religious framework from which to make authentic curriculum connections and that provide concrete examples which serve to illustrate the nature of Catholic curriculum integration.

The CCC is one of a number of Catholic educational partners committed to supporting publicly funded Catholic Education in Ontario.[8] Aided by an initial grant from the Ministry, the CCC was founded in 1992 and identifies as its mission 'Building and sustaining the Catholic capacity of educators through the development and provision of high quality Catholic curriculum, resources, support and professional development' (CCC, 2018). The CCC is similar to ICE in that it operates with limited staff to leverage and coordinate the collective efforts of Catholic educators. It is governed by a board with a representative from each of the 17-member Catholic school boards in central and south-western Ontario along with other Catholic educational partners. Catholic educators from each member Catholic school board serve on each of the four curriculum councils of the CCC (Faith in Education, Elementary, Secondary and Information, Communications, Technology). Through the guidance of the board and the work of the councils, the CCC provides professional development to Catholic educators, coordinates an annual provincial Catholic Education conference, 'When Faith Meets Pedagogy', and produces and provides 'quality Catholic curriculum resources by accessing and sharing the talents, energy and resources of various Catholic boards interested in promoting and preserving the "sacred trust" of Catholic Education' (CCC, 2018). Writing projects are proposed by member boards and others with a vested interest in the continued excellence of Catholic Education in Ontario (e.g. ICE, community organisations, publishers). CCC resources are then made freely available at their website.[9]

Catholic social teaching as a framework for distinctive Catholic curriculum

In 2005, the CCC undertook to create a framework that would assist Catholic elementary teachers to plan and implement a distinctively Catholic curriculum. The CCC assembled a team of Catholic educators representing Kindergarten to Grade 8. The religious education curriculum for each grade was used as the foundation for the framework that would develop. Most Catholic boards at the time were using the national catechetical programme of the Canadian Catholic Bishops, *Born of the Spirit* and *We Are Strong Together* (2005a and 2005b, respectively). Key concepts of the religious education programme for each grade were identified, forming the basis for essential questions, or 'big ideas'.

The curriculum writers also sought to identify an overarching Catholic theme for each grade. While exploring existing religious frameworks and considering the nature of these Catholic themes, the team reviewed the 1998 United States Catholic Bishops' statement, *Sharing Catholic Social Teaching: Challenges and Directions:*

> There are many innovative efforts by Catholic educators to communicate the social doctrine of the Church. At the same time, however, it is clear that in some educational programs Catholic social teaching is not really shared or not sufficiently integral and explicit. As a result, far too many Catholics are not familiar with the basic content of Catholic social teaching. More fundamentally, many Catholics do not adequately

understand that the social teaching of the Church is an essential part of Catholic faith. This poses a serious challenge for all Catholics, since it weakens our capacity to be a Church that is true to the demands of the Gospel. (United States Conference of Catholic Bishops, 1998)

The American Bishops go on to say, 'If Catholic education and formation fail to communicate our social tradition, they are not fully Catholic' (United States Conference of Catholic Bishops, 1998). Challenged and inspired by these words, the CCC writing team reviewed the religious education programme for each grade and ultimately identified a Catholic social teaching, aligned thematically, to become the overarching Catholic theme for each grade level.

In the Fall of 2006, the CCC published *Catholic Curriculum Maps: Foundational Support for Catholic Teachers*. Each grade-level map provided an at a glance summary of the key concepts of the religious education programme organised by strand – Sacred Scripture, Profession of Faith and Prayer/ Sacramental Life. Essential questions served to cluster the content of the religious education programme into 'big ideas' and a Catholic social teaching was identified as the overarching Catholic theme for the year. These curriculum maps were intended to serve as the lens for Catholic elementary educators to make Catholic connections across the curriculum while ensuring the religious education programme would be the foundation for such connections. As an example, the Grade 5 Catholic Curriculum Map has the essential question, 'How do I live in community?', and the Catholic social teaching principle/ theme, Community and the Common Good. A Grade 5 Catholic teacher could begin the task of curriculum integration by reviewing the mandated Ontario curriculum for opportunities to explore a Catholic understanding of the way we are called to live in community and care for the good of all. Students could read and reflect on short stories and novels that examine themes of community in literacy class, consider the role of government to establish safe communities where citizens may thrive in social studies class and consider their role within God's community of creation in science class.

In 2012, ICE released the Elementary Religious Education curriculum policy document. Though educators previously had access to a catechetical resource to support religious education classes (*Born of the Spirit* and *We Are Strong Together*), this is the first-ever comprehensive curriculum policy document for use in Ontario Catholic elementary schools that identifies what students are expected to know and do in religious education from Grades 1–8 (ICE, 2012). The *Growing in Faith, Growing in Christ* religious education programme has replaced the previous catechetical programme in order to align with the expectations of this new curriculum policy. The Catholic Curriculum Maps created using the previous catechetical programme may undergo a revision for alignment with the new curriculum policy document. Alternatively, after a decade's use, they may continue to serve as an exemplar of the way key concepts of the religious education curriculum can become animated and find relevance in other areas of the curriculum.

Perhaps the Catholic social teaching framework that continues to be used in boards and schools best illustrates the enduring utility of the Catholic Curriculum Maps project. The Curriculum Map development process was replicated for secondary school and two Catholic social teachings were chosen as Unifying Themes for each grade, 9 to 12 (ICE, 2016). This Catholic social teaching framework from Kindergarten to Grade 12 is an example of an explicit religious framework used by Catholic schools for curriculum planning. Not only does it provide a structure that allows for the intentional permeation of Catholicity throughout the learning environment, but it also aids educators in the task of curriculum integration. As previously noted, *Curriculum Matters* highlighted the difficult task of making authentic faith connections in subjects devoid of religious references. Most subject areas 'are truly secular in their worldview and knowledge; if religion is mentioned at all, it is usually as an historical reference or as a personal preference' (ICE, 1996a, p. 25). A Catholic social teaching framework used to overlay the curriculum of a particular course of study serves as a religious lens through which the curriculum is viewed in order to make evident the Catholic worldview. It serves to sharpen focus, so a Catholic educator may review course material in order to highlight particular Catholic themes or concepts.[10]

The Ontario character development initiative in a Catholic educational context

Ontario Catholic Education is accountable to a secular Ministry of Education. At all times, there exists a dual responsibility to fairly and fully implement Ministry initiatives while also clearly exerting a Catholic identity and encouraging a Catholic worldview. As one of four publicly funded education systems, Catholic Education has an obligation to demonstrate its relevance and right to exist as a separate entity and to do so requires the ability to demonstrate alignment with the Ministry expectations while maintaining a distinctiveness of approach sufficient to justify a separate school system. Some in the Catholic Education community view each new Ministry initiative with suspicion. With an ever-present political reality that calls for one publicly funded education system, there are cynics who wonder if the next Ministry initiative will be the one that will cause the Catholic educational system to stumble and say, 'We are unable to implement this in our schools'. Others in the Catholic community recognise Ministry initiatives as opportunities to say, 'We recognize the educational good in this initiative and this is how our faith perspective further supports it'. What follows are examples of the way in which the Catholic Education community has responded in faith to the Ministry initiatives.

At about the same time as the release of the CCC's Catholic Curriculum Maps, the Ministry released *Finding Common Ground: Character Development in*

Ontario Schools, K-12 (Ontario Ministry of Education, 2006). The Ministry recognised Ontario's increasing diversity and identified the need to find common ground based on shared values. What the Ministry envisioned was curriculum permeation whereby the school culture, shaped by common values, would positively form the character of students. *Finding Common Ground* states, 'Character development is not a new curriculum. Neither is it an add-on. It is embedded in all that we do in schools. It is intentionally infused in our policies, practices, programmes and interactions' (Ontario Ministry of Education, 2006, p. 3).

Those in Catholic Education found a character development initiative to be somewhat redundant given the tradition of moral education in Catholic schools. Indeed, the Ministry noted:

> Catholic schools, for example, have been founded on the basis of inculcating Catholic values and have programs in place that nurture the academic, social, emotional, physical and spiritual well-being of their students. Historically, Catholic Education has stressed community involvement as an important means for students to put beliefs into practice. (Ontario Ministry of Education, 2006, p. 8)

Yet, it was not enough for Catholic school boards to say, 'This is what we do!' As an accountability measure, the Ministry required Ontario schools and boards to provide evidence of the ways in which they addressed the key components of the Character Development Initiative, including the intentional infusion of these components 'into the policies, programmes, practices and interactions within the school and board' (Ontario Ministry of Education, 2006, p. 4).

In 2008, the Education Commission of the Ontario Bishops released a position paper intended to assist Catholic boards and schools to engage this Ministry initiative while remaining faithful to the long tradition of Catholic Education in Ontario. The Bishops suggested that the concept of virtue is central to Catholic moral theology and thus character development. In the history of the Church, 'Character formation was understood as part of the catechetical process, an integral dimension of religious education' as the baptised were supported to live a virtuous life (ACBO, 2008, p. 4). The Bishops recognised elements of 'education to virtues' when the Ministry's Character Development Initiative described developing interior traits such as 'respect, responsibility, justice and empathy' (as quoted in ACBO, 2008, p. 5). However, the Bishops noted how 'education to virtues' served a different purpose than the Ministry's Character Development Initiative. From a Ministry perspective, character development supports academic achievement, the development of the whole student in their growth as citizens and safe and orderly learning environments where students are engaged in their own learning (see Ontario Ministry of Education, 2006, p. 3). The acquisition of common values is promoted for socio-economic considerations. While the

Bishops acknowledged this as an important consideration for the just ordering of society, they were clear that it is not the ultimate purpose of character development – 'In the Catholic tradition, education to virtues is understood as an element in the full flowering of the human person' (ACBO, 2008, p. 6).

The Bishops also noted two further important distinctions between the Ministry's Character Development Initiative and the Catholic approach to virtues education. First, the Ministry called for extensive community consultation and consensus to identify mutually agreeable character attributes. In the Catholic tradition, virtues are grounded in a Christian anthropology. They are 'determined according to a vision of the human person in relationship with God in Jesus-Christ' (ACBO, 2008, p. 6). Second, there is no place for God or a spiritual approach in the Ministry's Character Development Initiative. In the Catholic tradition, '[t]he foundational virtues of faith, hope and love are directed towards God and inspired in us by God's Spirit … The development of character in the Catholic tradition is seen as a synergy between God's grace and human freedom' (ACBO, 2008, p. 6). Given these differences, the Bishops recognised the need to adapt the Character Development Initiative for use in Ontario Catholic schools.

In the final analysis, the Bishops deemed the Ministry's Character Development Initiative to be both an opportunity and a challenge for the Catholic Education community. Because it provided opportunity to better articulate how Catholic schools foster the 'full flowering' of each student and it offered a framework within which to achieve this goal, the Bishops identified the Character Development Initiative as 'a gift for our Catholic school system' (ACBO, 2008, p. 8). However, the Bishops also cautioned that this initiative must be integrated into the existing faith-based school system without compromising Catholic tradition, identity and purpose. For this reason, the Bishops encouraged Ontario boards and schools to respond to the initiative with virtues language. In so doing,

> [i]t helps us re-acquire a valuable concept in our tradition, compels us to recognise God's role in the character development of our students, and helps us focus on specific habits that foster and protect the freedom to which we are all called. (ACBO, 2008, p. 8)

Many Catholic boards and schools responded to the Ministry's Character Development Initiative by implementing a virtues framework. This typically presents as a virtue of the month that serves as a whole-school focus. Curriculum permeation is evident when a particular virtue is highlighted within the school at assemblies and liturgies, in school newsletters and on school websites, and when students are recognised for demonstrating the virtue in their relationships with others. Curriculum integration occurs when educators link curriculum with the opportunity to better understand the Catholic virtue and how it may transform actions toward the good. While still used in Catholic boards and schools today, the use of virtues as a religious framework has not been as fully developed or universally adopted as others. *Ontario Catholic School Graduate Expectations* serve as the most commonly utilised religious framework in Ontario Catholic Education. Increasingly, boards and schools have adapted the Bishops' message and have moved to a Catholic social teaching framework to focus on virtues 'in action'.

The Ontario financial literacy initiative in a Catholic educational context

A Ministry expectation for increased focus on financial literacy in Ontario schools serves to further illustrate the way Ontario Catholic Education routinely responds to Ministry of Education initiatives. In 2010, the Ministry released *A Sound Investment: Financial Literacy in Ontario Schools*, calling for educators to embed financial literacy education into the Ontario curriculum. The Ministry envisioned schools in which 'Ontario students will have the skills and knowledge to take responsibility for managing their personal financial well-being with confidence, competence, and a compassionate awareness of the world around them' (Ontario Ministry of Education, 2010, p. 4). The working group that was convened by the Ministry and charged with gathering information and conducting consultations

> ... heard that financial literacy should be linked to such concepts as compassionate citizenship, character development, and ethical decision making. Students, parents, and teachers drew a strong connection between understanding the financial implications of a decision and understanding the social, ethical, and environmental implications of that decision. (Ontario Ministry of Education, 2010, p. 18)

The Catholic Education community immediately recognised how faith must play an important role in these ethical decisions, and once again identified opportunities to approach an expectation of the secular educational authority from a distinctively Catholic perspective. With respect to financial literacy, Catholic educators considered what Scripture teaches about financial matters; what the social tradition of our Church teaches about a living wage, the dignity of work, economic justice; how we must also consider the 'wants and needs' of others and not just ourselves and how the Catholic community defines 'success'. This Ministry initiative was seen as an opportunity to model Catholic curriculum integration.

The Ministry supported this initiative by funding the development of financial literacy lessons for secondary school Religious Education courses, while the CCC supported the development of similar resources for elementary Family Life Education. The resulting documents, available online at the CCC website, serve as an important model of the way in which the Catholic social teaching framework can be used to view such secular initiatives. They demonstrate how an understanding of each Catholic social teaching can be used to ask critical questions related to financial literacy, for example

- *Human Dignity:* How do our material 'wants' compare with our spiritual 'needs'?
- *Option for the Poor and Vulnerable:* What is our moral obligation to 'the widow, the orphan, the poor'?
- *Stewardship of Creation:* How do consumer choices impact a world with limited resources?
- *Promotion of Peace:* How can financial security promote peace?
- *Community and the Common Good:* How do we ensure that the needs of the many are not given priority over those of the few?

Catholic educators are called to model such critical questions while moving students to do the same. As students begin to ask questions using their emerging Catholic worldview, '[c]urriculum now functions in a transformative way, as a vehicle for personal and social change based on the principles of justice and the view of the learner as agent-of-change' (ICE, 1996a, p. 25). In this way, the Ministry's financial literacy education initiative provides opportunity for Catholic educators to 'prepare students to live in this culture and to embrace all that is good in it' while also providing opportunity to 'be critical of those aspects of our culture which are contrary to the values of our faith tradition' (ACBO, 1988, p. 14).

Character development and financial literacy are but two examples of Ministry initiatives that are translated for use in a Catholic educational context. In both cases, a Catholic social teaching framework has proven helpful to educators who seek to authentically connect the core principles of these initiatives to the Catholic faith. This framework also supports students to make such connections and to ask critical questions, informed by faith. In doing so, teachers and students come to a deeper awareness of the way in which faith permeates all aspects of the educational enterprise.

Challenge and opportunity in Ontario Catholic Education

For nearly 200 years, Catholic Education has been part of the social and educational fabric of Ontario. Catholic schools have continued to operate with the authority and approval of the Ontario Catholic Bishops, and indeed have grown and flourished with public funding, within the cultural and educational milieu of a broader, secular environment. As one of four publicly funded education systems in Ontario, Catholic Education has an obligation to demonstrate its relevance and right to exist as a separate entity and to do so requires the ability to demonstrate alignment with the Ministry expectations while maintaining a distinctiveness of approach sufficient to justify a separate school system. As such, the Catholic Education community is called to be responsive to the challenges of each time.

Since full funding, the Ontario Bishops have employed pastoral letters to communicate with all Catholic Education partners. These letters have served to assess the cultural context of the time and offer hope and encouragement to remain true to the mission and vision of Catholic Education. A recurrent theme in each letter is one of challenge and opportunity. In the 2018 pastoral letter, *Renewing the Promise*, the Ontario Bishops write,

> Those who worked tirelessly to establish Catholic Education in Ontario nearly two hundred years ago could not have imagined our current context, with both its challenges and opportunities: accessibility to a fully funded Catholic system; the presence of a well-educated Catholic laity in Catholic school; the complexity of strengths and needs presented by a rich diversity of students; the presence of well-developed Catholic curriculum; the passionate commitment to social justice and stewardship of the environment of so many students and educators; the pressures of a culture that does not celebrate life the way we do; the omnipresence of social media; a culture that distrusts religion and religious insight; the serious ethical challenges of our time; and the social and economic pressures on families, parishes and school communities. (ACBO, 2018, p. 3)

The Bishops ask those in Catholic Education to consider how the Spirit is calling forth a response in this context – and, indeed, the Ontario Catholic Education community is committed to respond!

In the most recent pastoral letter, the Ontario Bishops offer the Emmaus story as a source of reflection. Catholic schools are not only places of teaching and learning, but must also be places where the Risen Lord is encountered each day, where individuals and communities are accompanied on their faith journey and where joyful disciples are sent forth to tell of the Good News of Jesus Christ they have received. Those in Catholic Education must practice what Pope Francis calls 'the art of accompaniment' by 'taking the time to walk alongside one another, to listen and to teach, and in so doing, to transform' (ACBO, 2018, p. 6).

When Ontario Catholic schools ensure Catholic character by infusing faith in every aspect of the curriculum, the contextual challenges of the time become opportunities to transform culture. Catholic educators, guided by the vision of the learner as articulated by the *Ontario Catholic School Graduate Expectations* (ICE, 1998a), recognise their role in developing the 'full flowering' of each student – body, mind and spirit. Curriculum integration that seeks to consistently present a Catholic worldview across all subjects enables students to become discerning believers, effective communicators, critical

The distinctive nature of Catholic Education   131

thinkers, lifelong learners, collaborative contributors, caring family members and responsible citizens. In Ontario Catholic schools, curriculum becomes responsive and a vehicle for change.[11]

Notes

1. Some Ontario Catholic educational literature makes the distinction between 'public' schools and 'separate' schools. This can be misleading as there are four publicly funded school systems. This chapter will use the term 'secular' to refer to those publicly funded English language schools that are not Catholic.
2. See website of Ontario Catholic School Trustees Association (OCSTA) at www.ocsta.on.ca. It should be noted that the vast majority of educators in elementary and secondary Catholic schools in Ontario are Catholic.
3. ACBO denotes the Assembly of Catholic Bishops of Ontario. Prior to 2009, the Bishops were the Ontario Conference of Catholic Bishops (1989).
4. The term, 'Catholic curriculum' is used widely in the Catholic Education community in Ontario. Catholic curriculum is understood as the mandated Ontario Ministry of Education curriculum taught 'with a difference' in Catholic schools when Catholic educators intentionally integrate a Catholic worldview across the curriculum.
5. These three approaches to the Catholic character of curriculum are described in the *Curriculum Matters* (ICE, 1996a) essay, *Ontario Catholic Education: Its Curricular Context*, authored by Larry Trafford. Trafford was a frequent contributor to ICE publications during the 1990s and early 2000s while working, first as a programme coordinator for Religious and Family Life Education for the Toronto Catholic District School Board, and subsequently as a professional learning officer with one of the ICE partners, the Ontario English Catholic Teachers' Association.
6. Ontario Catholic Curriculum Policy Documents are available online at the Institute for Catholic Education at http://iceont.ca.
7. For examples of Catholic curriculum developed using the *Ontario Catholic School Graduate Expectations* as a religious framework, see the CCC and the Eastern Ontario CCC resources, available online at http://catholiccurriculumcorp.org/ and http://www.eoccc.org/, respectively.
8. The CCC is a consortium of 17 member Catholic school boards in central and south-western Ontario. By virtue of its geographical location and size, the CCC is currently the most influential consortium in Ontario. Other consortia have also contributed to the development of Catholic curriculum. See, for example, the exemplary online resources of the Eastern Ontario CCC (www.eoccc.org).
9. Catholic curriculum resources developed by the CCC may be accessed at http://catholiccurriculumcorp.org/.
10. Though such a religious framework is helpful to classroom teachers responsible for the delivery of Catholic curriculum each day, it has also been used in the development of curriculum for the province. See, for example, the online resources available at the CCC or the Eastern Ontario CCC.
11. Readers may also wish to watch Katharine Stevenson's conference presentation on the project website at https://www.acu.edu.au/1341703

References

Assembly of Catholic Bishops of Ontario (ACBO). (1988). *This moment of promise*. Retrieved from http://acbo.on.ca/download/education-archives/

Assembly of Catholic Bishops of Ontario (ACBO). (2008). *Character development and the virtuous life: A position paper*. Retrieved from http://www.acbo.on.ca/englishdocs/OCCB%20position%20paper%20on%20CDI%20FINAL-%20August%202008%20.pdf

Assembly of Catholic Bishops of Ontario (ACBO). (2018). *Renewing the promise*. Retrieved from http://acbo.on.ca/download/education-archives/

British North America Act. (1867). Retrieved from http://www.legislation.gov.uk/ukpga/Vict/30-31/3/contents

Canadian Conference of Catholic Bishops. (2005a). *Born of the spirit*. Ottawa, ON: Author.

Canadian Conference of Catholic Bishops. (2005b). *We are strong together*. Ottawa, ON: Author.

Catholic Curriculum Corporation (CCC). (2006). *Catholic curriculum maps: Foundational support for Catholic teachers*. Retrieved from http://catholiccurriculumcorp.org/catholic-curriculum-maps-foundational-support-for-catholic-teachers-2006/

Catholic Curriculum Corporation (CCC). (2018). *CCC history*. Retrieved from http://catholiccurriculumcorp.org/our-organization/history/

Dixon, R. T. (2003). *Catholic Education and politics in Ontario*, Vol. 4. Toronto, ON: Catholic Education Foundation of Ontario.

Institute for Catholic Education (ICE). (1996a). *Curriculum matters: A resource for Catholic educators*. Retrieved from http://iceont.ca/publications/

Institute for Catholic Education (ICE). (1996b). *Writing curriculum for Catholic schools: A framework*. Retrieved from http://iceont.ca/wp-content/uploads/2015/08/Writing-Curriculum.pdf

Institute for Catholic Education (ICE). (1998a). *Ontario Catholic school graduate expectations*. Retrieved from http://iceont.ca/resources/ontario-catholic-school-graduate-expectations/

Institute for Catholic Education (ICE). (1998b). *Educating the soul: Writing curriculum for Catholic secondary schools*. Retrieved from http://iceont.ca/publications/

Institute for Catholic Education (ICE). (2012). *Ontario Catholic elementary curriculum policy document, Grades 1–8: Religious education*. Retrieved from http://iceont.ca/ontario-catholic-curriculum/

Institute for Catholic Education (ICE). (2016). *Ontario Catholic secondary curriculum policy document, Grades 9–12: Religious education*. Retrieved from http://iceont.ca/ontario-catholic-curriculum/

Institute for Catholic Education (ICE). (2018). *Our mission*. Retrieved from http://iceont.ca/about-us/

Ontario Conference of Catholic Bishops. (1989). *This moment of promise*. Retrieved from http://acbo.on.ca/download/education-archives/

Ontario Ministry of Education. (2006). *Finding common ground: Character development in Ontario schools, K-12*. Retrieved from http://www.curriculum.org/secretariat/files/Dec11CharacterReport.pdf

Ontario Ministry of Education. (2010). *A sound investment: Financial literacy education in Ontario schools*. Retrieved from http://www.edu.gov.on.ca/eng/Financial_Literacy_Eng.pdf

United States Conference of Catholic Bishops. (1998). *Sharing Catholic social teaching: Challenges and directions*. Retrieved from http://www.usccb.org/beliefs-and-teachings/what-we-believe/catholic-social-teaching/sharing-catholic-social-teaching-challenges-and-directions.cfm

Chapter 7

The identity of Catholic schools as seen by teachers in Catholic schools in Queensland[1]

Jim Gleeson, John O'Gorman and Maureen O'Neill

Introduction

Discussing Christian faith in the context of modern Europe, Boeve (2005) portrays the current age as one that is post-secular and characterised by detraditionalisation and pluralisation, one where Catholic education is challenged to embrace new anthropological and scientific (Lane, 2015; Pope Francis, 2015; Treston, 2001) insights and developments. This dramatically changed environment poses significant challenges for faith-based schools (Gleeson, 2015a; Rymarz, 2011; Scanlan, 2013). The Pollefeyt and Bouwens (2010) framework for Catholic institutional identity favours 'recontextualisation', far removed from traditional approaches to confessional identity and defined as 'identity construction in a pluralist perspective [which attempts] to understand the Catholic faith re-interpreted in a contemporary cultural context' (p. 202).

While Australian Catholic schools are predominantly managed and staffed by lay principals and teachers and continue to attract a significant proportion of Catholic students, the proportions of non-Catholic and/or 'unchurched' teachers and students have grown considerably (Chambers, 2012; McLaughlin, 2006). Data regarding students' and parents' reasons for school choice are available (Dowling, Beavis, Underwood, Sadeghi, & O'Malley, 2009; Goldring & Phillips, 2008), but information regarding teachers' choice of school is more difficult to find (Forsey, 2010).

Indeed, as Grace (2002) remarks, 'apart from a substantial body of scholarship in the United States, the systematic investigation of post-Vatican II schooling is remarkably undeveloped' (p. 110). An empirical study of 746 lay teachers in Catholic schools in a large US archdiocese (Tarr, Ciriello, & Convey, 1993) found that teachers with a commitment to mission were most satisfied with their school environments, and Convey's (2014) US study of 716 teachers in three Catholic dioceses also emphasised the importance of mission:

> Teachers who are highly committed to fostering the school's Catholic identity will work harder to achieve those objectives that are consistent with its Catholic mission. (p. 4)

> The motivation to teach in the school because it was a Catholic school is important for many Catholic teachers. (p. 21)

Identity, purposes and characteristics of Catholic schools

Against that background, the authors designed and disseminated a survey with the aim of establishing the opinions of teachers in Queensland Catholic schools regarding the identity, purpose and characteristics of these schools. They also conducted follow-up interviews with a sample of volunteer teachers. The main purpose of this chapter is to present and discuss the main findings of this study, having first considered these broad issues with particular reference to Catholic schooling in Australia.

Identity, purposes and characteristics of Catholic schools

The Congregation for Catholic Education (CCE, 1997) highlights the importance of the 'unique Christian school climate' (para 19) of Catholic school communities, one where 'faith, culture and life are brought into harmony' (para 11) and where the 'evangelical identity' (CCE, 2014, p. 13) of the Catholic school takes expression when the 'principles of the gospel become [the school's] internal motivation and final goal' (CCE, 1997, para 34).

Many scholars of Catholic education have highlighted the centrality of faith formation:

> [The Catholic school educates] the very 'being' of its students, to inform, form, and transform their identity and agency ... with the meaning and ethic of Christian faith ... [they become] just and compassionate disciples of Jesus [and are] personally influenced and enriched by Catholic faith. (Groome, 1996, p. 118)

> [It is the] non-negotiable duty [of a Catholic school to provide] forms of education through which the essential doctrines and devotions of Catholicism are transmitted'. (Haldane, 1996, p. 133)

> Catholic school culture is a 'Gospel Culture'. A school is authentically Catholic when a Gospel culture animates everything that transpires in the school. (Cook, 2001, p. 95)

> Catholic schools in England, USA and Australia were, in their origins, constructed and constituted as citadels and fortresses for the preservation of faith in a hostile external environment characterised by the dominant Protestant order ... (Grace, 2002, p. 7)

> A Catholic school by its very nature should have a distinct, Catholic culture [where] faith community constitutes an integral part of the school's Catholic identity. (Convey, 2012, p. 190)

Turning the rhetoric into reality is, however, increasingly problematic, and noted, for example, by Rymarz (2011):

> ... the days of uncritical, almost passive, enculturation appear to be over. For Catholic schools, strong identity is not an option as much as

The identity of Catholic schools   135

a necessity in a culture where options abound … Catholic schools face the challenge of having to articulate a message and a rationale to a more demanding and discerning audience. (pp. 7–8)

Grace (2002) contends that failure to attend to a school's distinctiveness is to risk loss of identity, while Sullivan (2000) sees such failure as 'neglect [of] the sources of our faith' which causes us to 'forget where we stand and why we … have these priorities' (p. 27). For purposes of this chapter, the identity, purposes and characteristics of Catholic schools are broadly seen in terms of faith commitment, prayer and liturgical events, religious symbols, curriculum and action for social justice.

From an Australian perspective, Dowling et al. (2009) remarked that teachers generally 'expressed strong endorsement of the importance of religious faith and practice in the life of the schools [while] only a very small proportion of staff thought that the best thing their school did was provide good academic results' (p. 4). Byrne (2005), on the other hand, concluded the Western Australia teachers in his study identified a 'gap between the reality and rhetoric of Catholic schooling' (p. 150), while Belmonte and Cranston (2009) noted that Catholic schools in Australia are increasingly challenged to

… maintain their overall character and ethos in a changing religious and social reality [and to] prove their validity as viable educational institutions, as well as satisfy the requirements of the Church, while simultaneously responding to government accountability and Church expectations. Their identity as Catholic schools is fundamental to their existence, and, when they cease to be Catholic … they cease to exist. (p. 296)

Croke (2007) suggests that the 'authenticity of the [modern] Catholic school' is problematic:

Put simply, the Australian Catholic school of the early 21st century has an annually increasing proportion of non–Catholic students, along with students from mainly middle class Catholic families whose adhesion to their Faith is weak. (p. 823)

Chambers (2012) too draws attention to increasing enrolments of students who are not Catholics, suggesting that this 'brings into question traditional assumptions about the clientele of Catholic schools, the religious activity in Catholic schools and the ecclesial nature of Catholic schools' (p. 186).

The 'tradition of thought, rituals, mores, and organizational practices' (Bryk, 1996, p. 37) represents a key aspect of Catholic schools as faith communities. As noted by Grace (2002):

Traditional Catholic liturgy … was a central part of Catholic schooling, especially where such schooling was provided by vowed religious or by teaching brothers. The rituals and devotions of the school year could generate a school ethos in which mystery, sacredness, power, symbolism and dramatic theatre could be realised over and against the prosaic routines of everyday life. (p. 64)

Flynn (1993) suggests that liturgies 'enable the [Australian] school community to celebrate its faith in Jesus Christ through prayer and the Eucharist ... [and] builds up the spirit of Christian community' (p. 50). He also highlights the importance of religious symbols that 'are visible expressions of what the school stands for [including] religious symbols, school badges and mottoes, school assemblies and graduations, school handbooks, magazines and newsletters and school uniforms' (Flynn, 1993, pp. 43–44).

The CCE (2014) is rightly critical of the growing popularity of a 'merely functional view of education' (p. 12) and concerned about the hegemony of market values in education and the associated temptation for governments to simply respond to 'the demands deriving from the ever-changing economic situation' (p. 64). Dowling et al. (2009) report that, 'when stakeholders were forced to choose the dominant thing that [Catholic] schools do best, they chose a "caring community" over academic qualities', adding that 'it may be that stakeholders believe ... that if they get the personal care of the student right, the academic results follow' (p. 4). Maltese head teachers interviewed by Mifsud (2010) felt that 'the main activity of a Catholic school is in giving a holistic education [which] forms an intrinsic aspect of the Catholic anthropological perception of the human person' (p. 54).

Such a perspective has, of course, important implications for the whole curriculum beyond Religious Education (D'Orsa, 2013; Gleeson, 2015a; Institute for Catholic Education, 1996). The CCE (1977) portrays the identity of Catholic schools as a 'synthesis of culture and faith and a synthesis of faith and life' (p. 37) and defines the fundamental characteristics of the Catholic school in terms of the 'integral education of the human person through a clear educational project ... [involving] ecclesial and cultural identity [and] love [and] service to society' (9.3). Groome (1996) argues that the 'distinctive characteristics of Catholicism itself ... should be reflected in the whole curriculum of Catholic schools' (p. 107), while Lane (1991) proposes that 'the Catholic school seeks to integrate the curriculum, to unify faith and culture, and to bring together the different pieces of the school programme into a higher synthesis that influences the social and spiritual formation of pupils' (p. 12).

The commitment of Catholic schools to action for social justice can be seen in the Congregation's recognition that 'education is an important means of improving the social and economic condition of the individual and of peoples' (CCE, 1977, p. 68) in response to 'the unequal distribution of resources, poverty, injustice and human rights denied' (CCE, 2013, p. 66). Mifsud (2010) suggests that 'the preservation of Catholic identity in Catholic schools subsists in its mission to "outreach"' (p. 54), while Grace (2002) suggests that 'there can be no authentic love of God … which is not, at the same time, linked … to loving and helping one's neighbour' (p. 205). Arguing for the integration of Catholic Social Teaching across the formal school curriculum, Grace (2013) suggests that 'Catholic educational institutions at all levels have failed to provide curriculum mediations of this teaching as a crucial part of the formation of Catholic youth' (p. 99).

Benson and Guerra (1985) found that for many Catholic teachers in the United States 'concerns for social justice … tend toward the middle of a list of 22 life goals', and Convey (2012) reports that, although US teachers in Catholic schools rated the importance of 'service' highly, they ranked it relatively low. Scanlan (2013) concludes that the 'grammar of Catholic schooling has allowed Catholic schools in the United States to become more exclusionary in recent decades, counter to the espoused values of Catholic Social Teaching' (p. 39).

Catholic schooling in Australia

Australia has a tripartite system of education (Perry & Southwell, 2014) with a strong emphasis on student choice (Organisation for Economic Co-operation and Development [OECD], 2010). As noted by Gonski et al. (2011), 'the impact of student background on educational outcomes is stronger in Australia than it is in other OECD countries. The practical effect of this rating is that across Australia, students from disadvantaged backgrounds are consistently achieving educational outcomes lower than their peers' (p. 105). Along similar lines, Perry and McConney (2010) concluded from their study of student outcomes in Australia that 'the SES context in which students find themselves is strongly and consistently associated with academic performance, across all student SES groupings'.

While Independent and Catholic schools are fee-paying, they are heavily subsidised by government, with 'enrolments in independent schools growing by 35 per cent and Catholic school enrolments by 11.6 per cent during the first decade of the new millennium' (Maddox, 2014, p. xi). The socio-educational advantage (SEA) differences noted by Gonski et al. (2011) and by OECD are clearly evident in the fact that 'the government sector educates 66% of all students [and] takes 79% of the bottom SEA quarter. The Catholic sector educates 20% of all students and takes 15% of those from the bottom SEA quarter. The independent sector educates 14% and takes 6% of those in the bottom SEA quarter' (Kenway, 2013, p. 290). The distribution of students who are Aboriginal, have disabilities and come from remote and very remote areas is similarly skewed.

There were over 1,700 Catholic schools (primary and secondary) in Australia in 2013 and 72% of their net average recurrent income came from Commonwealth and State budgets with the balance from private income (National Catholic Education Commission, 2013, p. 86). Dowling et al.

(2009) highlight a 'remarkable greening' (p. 28) as reflected in the diminishing age profile of teachers in Brisbane Catholic schools over the past 5 years as well as the growing proportion of non-Catholic teachers employed in Catholic schools. Catholic schools are attended by 22% of the school-going population and by 53% of Catholic children (Australian Catholic Bishops Conference, 2013).

As noted by Croke (2007), 'fewer Catholic families are choosing Catholic schools, even though their resources are better than ever [and] the growth in Catholic schools is being entirely sustained by middle class families of other Christian denominations, and non-Christian faiths (Muslim, Buddhist, Hindu)' (pp. 815–816). According to Dowling et al. (2009), upwardly socially mobile parents, regardless of their religion, are enrolling their children in Catholic secondary schools 'for predominantly pragmatic rather than religious reasons [with a resulting] marked decline in religious commitment' (p. 38). This throws up the apparent contradiction that, 'as society is becoming more secular, Catholic schools are becoming more popular than ever' (Dowling et al., p. 6). Remarking that some states were reviewing their fees policies to ensure that Catholic schools are open to those with limited financial resources, Pascoe (2007, p. 797) notes the Janus-like nature of Australian Catholic Education:

> In describing the nature and purpose of Catholic schools to potential students and parents, emphases are likely to be on the education of the whole person, on faith and religious education and on pastoral care and learning outcomes. In liaising with government, emphases are likely to be on core purpose, support of democratic principles and institutions, parent choice, legislative compliance, good governance, sound educational practice, commitments to accountability, and fulfilment of elements of formal agreements. (p. 793)

Catholic Education is caught on the horns of this dilemma and Croke (2007) believes that the Australian bishops are

> ... right to be concerned at the level of religious understanding and commitment of the next generation of Catholic school teachers [in a context where] Australian research on senior school students suggests that their commitment to their faith is tenuous ... while the very limited studies of those already teaching in Catholic schools have raised alarm bells in some quarters. (p. 823)

Methodology

Using a mixed methods approach the authors sought to establish the views of teachers in Queensland Catholic schools regarding the identity, purposes and characteristics of their schools, using the survey instrument in Appendix 3.

This survey, which was designed in collaboration with representatives of the five Catholic Education Offices in Queensland, included items about the importance of faith-based school identity, the characteristics of Catholic schools, reasons for working in Catholic Education and the purposes of Catholic schools (from a given list including generic and faith-based items). Compilation of the 15 given characteristics of Catholic schools involved the adaptation of Convey's (2012) study in US Catholic Schools under four main headings: faith community; prayer, liturgies and symbols; whole curriculum and community service.

The survey was set up using Qualtrics software and piloted with 88 teachers in four Catholic schools in Rockhampton. It was distributed electronically to all 6,832 teachers in Queensland Catholic schools in March 2014.[2] In order to ensure anonymity and confidentiality, participants were not asked to provide their names or the name of school where they worked. Incomplete responses were discarded, leaving a total of 2,287 responses in January 2015, an overall response rate of 33.5%.

Using the Queensland Catholic Education Commission (2012) data for teacher gender and school type, we believe that our respondents were representative of teachers in Queensland Catholic schools. In total, 72.8% of the respondents were female compared to 73.8% of all teachers in the Queensland Catholic system, and 57.6% (53.7%) of respondents taught in primary schools and 42.4% (46.3%) in secondary schools.

Respondents included a broad range of ages (modal range 40–49 years) and teaching experience (modal range 11–20 years). Half of them had taught for more than 10 years in Catholic schools. Over 80% identified as Catholic with one-third saying that religion is very important to how they live their lives (subsequently referred to as religiosity), while one-third had added professional responsibilities ranging from principal to 'position of added responsibility'. Almost two-thirds had some current or past experience of teaching Religious Education and/or Study of Religion (RE/SoR) and more than three-quarters rated their knowledge of Catholic teaching as either very good (24%) or good (53%),[3] particularly those who were Catholic, teachers of RE/SoR, had longer service in Catholic education, added professional responsibilities and for whom religion was important in how they lived their lives.

Survey data were analysed using descriptive statistics and multiple regression analysis. Predictor variables were grouped in Sets for analysis purposes as shown in Table 7.1.

A sequential (hierarchical) strategy (Cohen & Cohen, 1975) was adopted whereby entry in the regression equation started with Set 1, and the other Sets were then introduced incrementally. This allowed the additional variance to be examined at each step. Predictor Sets 1–4 were entered at the first step, followed by Set 5 at the second step, to allow testing of the statistical significance of the increment in R^2. For outcome variables that were dichotomous, logistic regression was used, with variable Sets entered hierarchically.

140   Jim Gleeson, John O'Gorman, et al.

Table 7.1 Variables used for regression analysis

Set 1	Demographics	Gender, age, level (primary/secondary), length of service, level of appointment (APPOINT)
Set 2	Role in Catholic school	Teacher of Religion, Studies of Religion (SoR), responsibility for curriculum leadership, length of service in Catholic Education (LOSCATH)
Set 3	Religion and religiosity	Nominated religion; importance of religion to 'how I live my life' (RELGIMP)
Set 4	Self-reported levels of knowledge	Three items (Catholic teaching/social teaching/moral teaching) were combined to form a single variable, KNOWTOT
Set 5	Reasons for working in Catholic schools	ENVIRO (because of Catholic School environment) COMIT (because of commitment to Catholic faith)
Set 6	Catholic purpose and identity	PURPCATH2 (faith-based school purpose) CATSCHDIF (Catholic schools are different to other schools) CATIDIMP (importance of faith-based school identity) PRACTICES (characteristics to do with school practices) PEOPLE (characteristics to do with school community)
Set 7	Integration of a Catholic perspective across the whole curriculum	INTEGR1 (perceived importance of such integration) INTEGR2 (perceived importance of planning for integration) INTEGR3 (extent to which such integration is practised)

Where an outcome (criterion) variable (see Appendix 1 for more information regarding these variables) was either continuous or an ordinal category variable, initial regression analyses used Ordinary Least Squares (OLS) regression with variables entered hierarchically as already described. Multilevel modelling was not possible since, for reasons of confidentiality, respondents were not asked to identify their schools.

The assumptions of the regression model were tested in each case, including the independence of errors in prediction in terms of the Durbin-Watson statistic, the homoscedasticity of the relationship between predictor and outcome variables in terms of plots of residuals against predicted values and the normality of the error distributions in terms of p-p plots. Statistics used to test the assumptions were within the conventional tolerances used in the literature.

Where the outcome variable was markedly skewed, conclusions from the OLS regression were checked using ordinal regression or, if the assumption of proportional odds was not met, multinomial regression. All analyses used SPSS 22. Further information regarding the regression analyses for each variable is provided in Table A1 in Appendix 2.

Results of the regression analyses were examined principally in terms of the magnitudes of the beta weights assigned to the variables in each regression model and the statistical significance of those weights, with larger weights being taken to indicate the greater importance for a variable. With such a large sample, however, statistical significance at the conventional threshold level of .05 is almost guaranteed and accordingly a more stringent criterion

The identity of Catholic schools   141

was set. With a maximum of 18 input variables a Bonferroni adjustment specifies a criterion of $.05/18 = .0028$ or $.003$ (rounded) and this was used in assessing the statistical significance of a variable in a regression model.

The authors are unaware of any similar survey with so many respondents within a Catholic education system (33.5%) and are confident in their findings. While they sought to take account of the interrelations among the various relevant factors using regression analysis, it should be noted that this is not a probability sample of the population to which we sought to generalise. Furthermore, the design was cross-sectional with all variables measured at the same point in time, and hence causal relations cannot be assumed between any of the predictors identified and the outcome variables.

Some 43 survey respondents, representing a wide range of teaching experience, volunteered for follow-up interview, and 20 (13 secondary) of these were chosen with a view to getting the widest possible range of perspectives. The purpose of these interviews was to enquire more deeply into the survey finding and each interview lasted 30–40 minutes. Data were analysed using a thematic coding approach (Miles & Huberman, 1994) with responses categorised according to emergent themes using an inductive approach and thematic analysis (Lewis, 2009). Transcripts were studied, themes were identified and answers were indexed, organised and classified consistent with the emerging themes (Creswell, 1994).

Findings

Key findings are now presented under the following headings: reasons for working in Catholic schools, faith-based identity of Catholic schools, purposes of Catholic schools and characteristics of Catholic schools. Readers will find the information regarding Sets (Table 7.1) helpful as they consider the findings and, in the interests of economy, some of the variable names used there are used later in the chapter.

Reasons for working in Catholic schools (Set 5)

When teachers were invited to choose three reasons for working in Catholic schools from a given list (see Question 8 of survey, Appendix 3), their most popular reasons were 'the environment of Catholic schools' (ENVIRO, 87%) and 'commitment to the Catholic faith' (COMIT, 62%), with 30% choosing job-related reasons such as work security and convenient location. When asked to identify their single most important reason for working in the Catholic sector, over half the respondents (56%) chose the 'environment of Catholic schools', while 27% chose 'commitment to the Catholic faith' and 17% chose job-related reasons.

Sets 1–4 variables accounted for 5% of the variance for ENVIRO and this was statistically significant ($p < .001$). Having shorter teaching service alongside longer teaching service in Catholic schools were the only statistically significant predictors of ENVIRO ($p < .003$) (see Table B2, Appendix 2). Sets 1–4 variables accounted for 47% of the variance in respect of COMIT and this was statistically significant ($p < .001$). The beta weights indicate that the statistically significant ($p < .003$) predictor variables for COMIT were being Catholic, having high levels of religiosity, having experience of teaching religion, teaching at primary level, high self-ratings for knowledge of Catholic teaching and longer service in Catholic Education (see Table B3, Appendix 2). Those who were Catholic were 14 times more likely to endorse their faith commitment as the main reason for choosing to teach in a Catholic school, and those with high levels of religiosity being more than twice as likely to endorse faith commitment. As previously explained, the ENVIRO and COMIT variables constitute Set 5 in the regression analysis.

Faith-based identity of Catholic schools (Set 6)

Two survey items feed into respondents' perspectives regarding faith-based school identity –whether Catholic schools are different to other schools and the perceived importance of the faith-based identity of Catholic schools.[4] The vast majority of respondents (93%) believed that Catholic schools are either very different (63%) or different (30%) to other schools (CATSCHDF). Sets 1–4 variables accounted for 7% of the associated variance and this was statistically significant ($p < .001$). Those most likely to say that Catholic schools are different to other schools had high levels of religiosity and considered they have a better knowledge of Catholic teaching (see Table B7, Appendix 2). When Set 5 variables were included in the regression they accounted for an additional 1% of the variance. Religiosity and knowledge of Catholic teaching remained statistically significant ($p < .003$) together with ENVIRO (see Table B7, Appendix 2).

Some 87% of respondents saw the Catholic identity of their school as either important or very important (CATIDIMP), while 7% felt it was unimportant. Sets 1–4 variables accounted for 21% of the variance and this was statistically significant ($p < .001$). The strongest predictors of these high ratings were, in order of beta weightings ($p < .003$), being Catholic, high levels of religiosity, higher levels of self-reported knowledge of the Catholic faith, being a primary teacher and having experience of teaching religion (Table B8, Appendix 2). The inclusion of Set 5 variables accounts for an additional 4% of the variance ($p < .001$) and this was also statistically significant. The strongest predictors of the importance of faith-based school identity ($p < .003$) were, in order of importance, choosing to teach in Catholic schools because of faith commitment, choosing to teach in Catholic schools because of their environment, being Catholic, high self-rated levels of knowledge of the Catholic faith, high levels of religiosity and being a primary teacher (Table B8, Appendix 2).

Overall then, when these two identity variables are taken together, three predictor variables are strong predictors of both CATSCHDF and CATIDIMP: choosing to teach in Catholic schools because of their environment and

The identity of Catholic schools   143

having high levels of religiosity and of self-reported knowledge of Catholic teaching. Strong Sets 1–5 predictors of CATIDIMP were choosing to teach in Catholic schools because of faith commitment, being Catholic and being a primary teacher.

Purposes of Catholic schools

Respondents were asked to rank five given purposes of Catholic schools in order of importance and their first three choices were weighted. The resulting cumulative scores are given in Table 7.2 along with respondents' choices of the single most important purpose.

The purpose with the highest cumulative and individual scores was 'provide a safe and nurturing environment', followed by 'provide an authentic experience of a Catholic community' and 'education in the Catholic faith and tradition', with 'academic achievement' scoring lowest. Three-quarters of respondents were positive or very positive about the effectiveness of their individual schools in achieving these various given purposes. When these purposes are categorised as either generic or faith-related (the latter are marked with an asterisk in Table 7.2), generic purposes had a slightly higher cumulative score. However, faith-based purposes had slightly higher scores when respondents were asked to nominate their single most important purpose.

Sets 1–4 variables accounted for 11% of the variance for choice of faith-related purposes (PURPCATH2) and this was statistically significant ($p < .001$). The strongest predictors of endorsement of explicitly faith-based purposes of Catholic schools ($p < .003$) were, in order of importance, being Catholic, more years teaching in Catholic schools and higher levels of religiosity (Table B4, Appendix 2). When Set 5 variables were included in the regression they accounted for an additional 3% of the variance, and the Sets 1–4 predictors just identified were 'overshadowed' by COMIT (Table B4, Appendix 2), with those choosing to teach in Catholic schools due to their faith commitment being more than twice as likely to endorse explicitly faith-related purposes of schooling.

Table 7.2 Perceived purposes of Catholic schools (N = 2,287)

Purposes	Cumulative scores	Single most important purpose % (N)
Develop active and informed citizens	2,623	18.2% (416)
Education in the Catholic faith and tradition*	2,314	19.5% (445)
Promote academic achievement	1,196	4.6% (105)
Provide an authentic experience of a Catholic community*	2,613	21.6% (492)
Provide a safe and nurturing environment	3,216	26.5% (604)
Teach Christian values*	1,729	9.7% (221)

* Denotes purposes categorised as faith-related.

Space does not allow for detailed treatment of interviewees' views regarding school purposes (Gleeson, 2015b).[5] It is noteworthy that patterns emerging from the survey recurred here, with frequent references to providing a safe and nurturing environment, an authentic experience of Catholic community and education in the Catholic faith and tradition. Indicative comments include

> The main purpose of Catholic Education is to create a supportive and safe environment built on Christian values. (Primary)

> If the child isn't feeling safe and supported and nurtured and growing, then we can't teach them. (Secondary)

> It's about the spirit of a Catholic school, [its] history and foundation wrapped up in a faith … it's bigger than just a school [and] more than an educational institution. (Secondary)

> It's evangelisation really … three per cent of our students actually attend Mass … so there's not much experience or knowledge base about what it is to be Catholic. (Primary)

Secondary teachers also emphasised values and citizenship education. Many interviewees highlighted an issue that was not explicitly included in the survey, namely the holistic nature of Catholic education, often comparing Catholic schools favourably with other systems:

> A holistic approach to a child's development is important … secular organisations really can't touch that. (Primary)

> It's a holistic education, not purely academia … looking at the student as a whole, spiritually, culturally and academically. (Secondary)

Characteristics of Catholic schools

Survey respondents were asked to rate the importance of 15 given characteristics of Catholic schools (survey Question 17, Appendix 3) and 3 points were awarded for 'essential', 2 for 'very important' and 1 for 'important'. They were also asked to use their ratings to identify the six most important characteristics in rank order. As part of the analysis these rankings were weighted, with 6 points awarded to the first ranked, 6 points to the second and so on.

The same six characteristics scored highest, in the same order, in both ratings and rankings. 'Caring community' was rated essential by 88%, with 60% ranking it as the single most important characteristic and 85% ranking it in the first three.

Using principal component analysis (PCA) and Varimax rotation on the 15 characteristics, two components (PRACTICES and PEOPLE) were identified that account for 49% of the variance between individual responses to the characteristics items. As shown in Table 7.3, most ratings and rankings were higher for PRACTICE characteristics than for PEOPLE characteristics.

The identity of Catholic schools   145

Table 7.3 Ratings and rankings of given characteristics of Catholic schools

					Rating	Ranking
Characteristics (N = 2,287)	Essential (%)	Very Important (%)	Important (%)	Unimportant (%)	Overall score (rank)	Overall score (rank)
Caring community*	88	10	2	1	6,516(1)	9,180(1)
The school is a community of faith*	58	29	11	2	5,545(2)	6,367(2)
Prayer is integral to the school's daily life for staff and students*	56	28	15	2	5,413(3)	5,921(3)
The school engages in outreach and social justice programmes*	52	35	12	1	5,421(4)	5,303(4)
Religious Education programmes present the teachings of the Catholic Church*	45	33	20	3	5,003(5)	4,136(5)
The school community celebrates school liturgies frequently*	41	37	20	2	4,967(6)	3,508(6)
Catholic symbols throughout the school*	39	27	28	6	4,565(9)	2,269(7)
The principal is Catholic	46	20	21	14	4,519(10)	2,213(8)
The teachers of RE are accredited to teach RE	45	28	21	7	4,810(7)	2,135(9)
The school has strong links with the wider Church*	33	43	21	3	4,687(8)	1,992(10)
The integration of Catholic teachings across ALL learning areas is intentionally planned	15	25	39	21	3,065(11)	1,777(11)
Annual age-appropriate religious retreats are available to students*	12	24	41	23	2,881(12)	1,504(12)
Teachers of religion are Catholic	15	22	35	28	2,819(13)	853(13)
The vast majority of teachers are Catholic	11	24	35	29	2,688(14)	507(14)
The vast majority of students are Catholic	5	17	39	39	2,018(15)	368(15)

* Denotes PRACTICE characteristics.

146 Jim Gleeson, John O'Gorman, et al.

Table 7.4 Component loadings for characteristics of Catholic schools

Items	Component 1 (PRACTICES)	Component 2 (PEOPLE)
Annual age-appropriate religious retreats are available to students	.31	.00
Catholic symbols throughout the school	.55	.32
Caring community	.50	−.07
Prayer is integral to the school's daily life for staff and students	.69	.30
Religious Education programmes present the teachings of the Catholic Church	.60	.39
Teachers of religion are Catholic	.08	.78
The principal is Catholic	.24	.71
The school community celebrates school liturgies frequently	.67	.36
The school engages in outreach and social justice programmes	.61	−.02
The school is a community of faith	.75	.21
The school has strong links with the wider Church	.65	.29
The teachers of RE are accredited to teach RE	.39	.46
The vast majority of students are Catholic	.00	.77
The vast majority of teachers are Catholic	.12	.87

As shown in Table 7.4, the components of PRACTICES included 'community of faith', prayer, school liturgies, community links, outreach and social justice, display of Catholic symbols, orthodoxy of RE programmes, caring community and school retreats. The integration of Catholic perspectives across all learning areas was not considered here since it was included as an outcome variable in Set 7.

Sets 1–4 variables accounted for 16% of the variance for PRACTICES characteristics and this was statistically significant ($p < .001$). The signs of the beta weights ($p < .003$) indicate that PRACTICES are seen as more important to the identity of a Catholic school by those who, in order of importance, consider they have a better knowledge of the Catholic faith, are non-Catholic,[6] have high levels of religiosity, are female, teach religion and who have added professional responsibilities (Table B5, Appendix 2). When Set 5 was added to the regression, this accounted for a further 1% of the variance. The overall regression remained significant with the strongest predictors of PRACTICES, in order of importance, being non-Catholic, COMIT, ENVIRO, better knowledge of the Catholic faith, high levels of religiosity, being female and having added professional responsibilities (Table B5, Appendix 2).

The PEOPLE component included the remaining five characteristics and these had to do with the Catholicity of the members of the school community – teachers, teachers of religion, principal and students and the accreditation of

The identity of Catholic schools 147

teachers of RE. As shown in Table 7.3, individual rankings and ratings for PEOPLE characteristics were relatively low.

Sets 1–4 variables accounted for 18% of the variance and this was statistically significant ($p < .001$). The signs of the beta weights indicate that PEOPLE characteristics are seen as more important by those who are Catholic, who teach at the primary level and have higher levels of religiosity (see Table B6, Appendix 2). When Set 5 variables are added to the regression, an additional 1% of the variance is accounted for and the overall regression remains statistically significant ($p < .001$). The signs of the beta weights indicate that the strongest predictor variables for PEOPLE characteristics are, in order of importance, being Catholic, COMIT and high levels of religiosity (Table B6, Appendix 2). From an overall perspective, it is noteworthy that the importance of PRACTICES is rated more highly than PEOPLE and that being Catholic and having high levels of religiosity emerge as the only statistically significant predictor variables for both characteristic variables across Sets 1–5.

While this chapter does not address teachers' attitudes to professional development, one of the more interesting findings is that those respondents who were more willing than their peers to undertake professional development in relation to the faith-based identity of their schools ($p < .001$ are those who are more willing to integrate Catholic perspectives across the curriculum, have high levels of religiosity, see the PRACTICES and/or PEOPLE characteristics of Catholic schools as important and have added professional responsibilities within the school (Table B13, Appendix 2). That is to say, they have high levels of commitment to many key aspects of the faith-based identity of Catholic schools.

Those who volunteered for interview also referred frequently to environmental and faith-related purposes and characteristics of Catholic schools in the same breath, highlighting the importance of practices such as caring communities, holistic education, faith-based and values education and family spirit:

> … care for the whole person, helping our students to achieve their best … our pastoral care is very good, particularly when families are distressed. (Primary)

> A sense of family spirit has been strong in all the [Catholic] schools I've been at …. We become pseudo-parents and pseudo-nurses … Catholic schools are a lot more pastoral … we are encouraged to build a really positive rapport with students based on Catholic values. (Secondary)

Their understanding of faith-based identity included evangelisation, prayer and liturgy, Catholic worldview, school charism and Catholic symbols. The centrality of prayer and liturgy was mentioned frequently together with the role of Catholic schools in introducing students to basic Catholic beliefs and perspectives. Many interviewees highlighted the contribution of Catholic schools to values, ethics and citizenship education, gospel values, role modelling and social justice. Some secondary teachers were at pains to point out that Catholic schools do not have a monopoly on pastoral care or values education. It is also important to note that more experienced interviewees were very conscious of declining levels of religious practice and home support, for example

> We're the face of the church to these guys ... we teachers are the priests and the brothers and the sisters ... that defines a Catholic school.

Summary of main findings

There was very strong support for the view that Catholic schools are different to other schools and for the importance of this unique identity. Survey respondents gave school environment as the most common reason for choosing to work in Catholic schools, well ahead of faith commitment and job-related issues. This pattern was reinforced by the fact that they indicated their clear preference for 'the provision of a safe and nurturing environment' when asked about the purpose of Catholic schools and when they overwhelmingly opted for 'caring community' as the most important characteristic of Catholic schools. The interview data lend further support to the perceived importance of a caring school environment. It should also be noted however that faith-based purposes and characteristics, particularly PRACTICES (which also includes 'caring community'), were highly rated and ranked.

As shown in Table 7.5 (p. 149), high ratings for religiosity (the importance of religion to how I live my life) emerge from the regression analysis as the most consistent predictor ($p < .003$) of the perceived importance of faith-based identity, purposes and characteristics of Catholic schools and also of faith-based commitment as the reason for choosing to teach in Catholic schools. Other noteworthy findings include

- Length of service in Catholic Education is a strong predictor of the perceived importance of the faith-based purpose of Catholic schools and of both commitment to the Catholic faith (COMIT) and the environment of Catholic schools (ENVIRO) as reasons for working in Catholic schools.
- High self-ratings for one's knowledge of Catholic teachings (KNOWTOT) are a strong predictor of the perceived importance of the faith-based identity of Catholic schools and of PRACTICES characteristics. It is also a strong predictor of faith commitment as a reason for teaching in Catholic schools (COMIT).
- Being Catholic is a really strong predictor of COMIT and is also a strong predictor of the perceived importance of PEOPLE characteristics and of the faith-based purpose of Catholic schools.

The identity of Catholic schools　149

Table 7.5 Summary of main survey findings

Input variables	Reasons for teaching in Catholic School		Catholic identity*		Faith-based purpose		PRACTICES characteristics		PEOPLE characteristics	
	COMIT	ENVIR	Sets 1–4	Sets 1–5	Sets 1–4	Sets 1–5	Sets 1–4	Sets 1–5	Sets 1–4	Sets 1–5
KNOWTOT	√		√	√			√	√		
APPOINT							√	√		
Primary teacher	√								√	√
Catholic	√				√			√	√	√
RELGIMP	√		√	√	√		√	√	√	√
LOSCATH	√	√			√					
RE/SoR teacher	√						√			
Female							√	√		
COMIT						√		√		√
ENVIRO				√				√		

* Catholic identity combines two parts of Question 16 (Appendix 3) – Catholic schools are different and the perceived importance of faith-based identity of Catholic schools, and the three variables identified are strong predictors of both parts. Being Catholic, a teacher of RE/SoR, and a
primary teacher as well as COMIT, and are also strong predictors of CATHIDIMP (the Catholic
identity of my school is important to me).

- COMIT trumps all Sets 1–4 variables as a predictor of the importance
  of the faith-based purpose of Catholic schools, while ENVIRO is a
  strong predictor of the perceived importance of the faith-based identity
  of Catholic schools. Both COMIT and ENVIRO are strong predictors
  of PRACTICES characteristics, while COMIT is also a strong predictor
  of PEOPLE characteristics.
- Of the Set 1 demographic characteristics, being female and having added
  professional responsibilities are strong predictors of the perceived importance of PRACTICES characteristics, while being a primary teacher is a
  strong predictor of the perceived importance of PEOPLE characteristics.

Discussion

Of the many interesting themes regarding teachers' beliefs and opinions
around Catholic education that emerge from the above data, two particularly
interesting ones are chosen for discussion here:

- The descriptive statistical findings outlined above show that respondents consistently rated the importance of a school environment that is safe, nurturing
  and caring very highly. This can be seen in their reasons for choosing to work
  in Catholic schools, in their perceptions of the characteristics of Catholic
  schools and in their support for generic purposes of Catholic schools.

- The findings of our regression analysis, summarised in Table 7.5, identify certain strong predictors for the perceived importance of the faith-based identity, purpose and characteristics of Catholic schools. Religiosity (the importance of religion to how I live my life) is the most consistently strong predictor followed by knowledge of Catholic teaching, length of service in Catholic schools and faith-based reasons for choosing to teach in Catholic schools.

The main outcomes both of the descriptive statistics and the regression analysis are now considered.

Descriptive statistics: Importance of safe and caring environment

The strong emphasis in the teacher interviews on holistic, person-centred educational values together with survey respondents' high regard for caring and nurturing school environments resonates with the thinking of McClelland (1996), McLaughlin (1996), Murray (1991) and others. Holistic education has been a prominent feature of the philosophy of Catholic education for many years (Maritain, 1943; Murray, 1991), and McLaughlin (1996) argues that the 'aspiration to holistic influence' is one of the major reasons why the Church considers that 'separate Catholic schools are such an important part of its educational mission' (p. 150). As Murray (1991), former Catholic Bishop of Limerick, argues

> ... the Catholic tradition of education involves no diminution or distortion of the aims of education. Instead it gives to the Wholeness, Truth, Respect, Justice and Freedom pursued in education a new depth, a richer possibility, a fuller understanding ... Otherwise we run the risk of reducing education to a process seeking merely to produce good material for the 'workforce' or good citizens for the state, rather than to help the integral development of good people capable of living a fully human life. (pp. 23–24)

Murray (1991) goes on to invoke the CCE statement that 'the Catholic school is committed to the development of the whole human being, since in Christ all human values find their fulfilment and unity. Herein lies the specifically Catholic character of the school' (p. 35).

Of course it is eminently reasonable to argue that providing safe and caring environments is a priority for all schools and teachers regardless of school type. For example, 'care for self/others and compassion' is among the nine defined values of the National Framework for Values Education in Australian Schools (Australian Government, 2005). As Noddings (1997) argues in her commentary on public education policy in the United States of America, 'our society does not need to make its children first in the world in mathematics and science ... our main educational aim should be to encourage the growth of competent, caring, loving, and lovable people' (p. 27).

Whereas faith-based schooling was historically understood in terms of explicit religious and moral education, new research insights are

> ... challenging some of the assumptions held by faith-based schools in earlier times that part of their system's distinctiveness was to be found around the values agenda ... [with the result that] values education is being seen increasingly to have outgrown any earlier conceptions of being exclusively germane to, much less dependent on, the faith-based setting. (Lovat & Clement, 2014, p. 567)

This illuminates the finding of Pollefeyt and Bouwens (2010) that Catholic schools are using 'values education in a Christian perspective [which] can also appeal to post-Christians, other-believers and other-minded people' (p. 200). The widening gap between the Catholic faith and contemporary culture has encouraged Catholic schools to attempt to seek a 'compromise between culture and Catholic tradition in an attempt to maintain a Catholic school identity that "keeps up with the times" and with which anybody can reconcile' (Pollefeyt and Bouwens, 2010, p. 200).

Notwithstanding the organic relationship between school environment and Catholic ethos, the importance attached by teachers in this study to generic school purposes and characteristics raises important issues for Catholic schools at a time when the CCE (1997, 2014) places heavy emphasis on faith development and Gospel values. This emerging picture is redolent of what Lane (2015) calls the 'disconnect between faith and contemporary culture ... the greatest challenge facing Catholic education today' (p. 42).

Rymarz (2010) recalls the argument of Canadian Justice Sharpe that the teacher in a Catholic school is '"a witness to the faith" [who] transmit[s] Catholic faith through example and active participation in the liturgical and sacramental life of the Church as well as through the personal relationships they form with their students' (p. 300). Rymarz (2010) suggests that the move towards generic values as 'a policy may not result in long term stability [since] these values could be well described as human or even Aristotelian values and are, therefore, common to a range of schools' (p. 305).

The changing profile of students and teachers in Catholic schools 'challenges the very nature and purpose of Catholic schools' (Chambers, 2012, p. 186) and increases the propensity for schools and education partners to see a caring and nurturing environment as the 'golden mean'. Authorities can take heart however from the finding of Gleeson and O'Flaherty (2016) that teachers in Australian Catholic schools were 'more likely than their Irish counterparts to find inspiration in school charism and to use the discourse of relationships rather than respect' (p. 52). Australian teachers were also more likely to see their roles primarily as nurturer/professionals,[7] focusing on students' holistic, moral and personal development with most survey respondents subscribing to holistic rather than instrumental educational aims and favouring collaborative over individual learning (Gleeson & O'Neill, 2015). It should also be acknowledged of course that the creation of caring and nurturing environments has not always prioritised in Catholic and other denominational schools and institutions (e.g. Coldrey, 1992).

It may, however, be a cause of some concern that teachers in Catholic schools in the United States (Convey, 2012) were far more likely than Queensland teachers to rate faith-related characteristics as essential (Gleeson, O'Gorman, Goldburg, & O'Neill, 2018; Chapter 8 of this book). For example, while 93% of US teachers rated 'school is a community of faith' as an essential characteristic of Catholic schools, only 43% of Queensland teachers did so. The more challenging and adverse circumstances under which Catholic schools and teachers operate in the United States may help explain these quite remarkable jurisdictional differences. US teachers make considerable sacrifices, in a context where, 'on average, Catholic high school teachers … were paid about 75% of prevailing local public school wages' (Bryk, 1996, p. 27).

Regression analysis: Strongest predictors of faith-based beliefs regarding Catholic Education

While simple demographic variables such as age and gender showed few significant beta weights, the religiosity of the respondents was a strong predictor of eight of the faith-based outcome measures in Table 7.5. This calls for a deeper consideration of the significance of religiosity. Three-quarters of respondents said that religion is either important or very important to how they live their lives – 77% of Catholics as against 61% of non-Catholics. The Sets 1–3 predictors of religiosity ($p < .003$) are being older, having added professional responsibilities in the school, and being a teacher of religion (see Table B15, Appendix 2). The Spearman correlation between religion and religiosity is −.11 and the Cramer's V is slightly larger at .18. This weak relationship between religion and religiosity indicates that religiosity is a substantially independent variable in its own right rather than a proxy for religion.

As noted by Holdcroft (2006) religiosity is 'synonymous with such terms as religiousness, orthodoxy, faith, belief, piousness, devotion, and holiness' (p. 89). This suggests that respondents may have interpreted that particular survey item in terms of any one or more of the following five dimensions of religiosity identified by Glock and Stark (1965) as reported by Holdcroft (2006) – experiential, ritualistic, ideological, intellectual and consequential. The intellectual dimension of religiosity, which is closely related to the ideological, has to do with knowledge of Catholic teaching, a prior condition of its acceptance. The consequential dimension, on the other hand, best fits the provision of a caring and nurturing environment. Meanwhile, the experiential dimension focuses on personal faith experience, while the ritualistic dimension involves the experience of community worship. It would be necessary, of course, to conduct a more in-depth study in order to establish what dimensions of religiosity our respondents had in mind. However, the declining church attendance rates in Australia and the strong relationships between religiosity and being older, being a teacher of religion and high levels of self-reported knowledge of Catholic teaching (see Table B15, Appendix 2) would suggest that our respondents may have been thinking of the intellectual and cognitive rather than the ritualistic and experiential aspects of religiosity.

Half the respondents had more than 10 years' experience of teaching in Catholic Education and 25% of these had 11–20 years with the remainder having more than 20. Having longer experience of teaching in Catholic schools was a strong predictor ($p < .003$) of faith-based reasons (COMIT and ENVIRO) for choosing to teach in Catholic schools and of the perceived importance of the faith-based purpose of Catholic schools. A similar pattern emerges from two US-based studies:

> Years of experience teaching in Catholic [Elementary] schools also emerges as significant predictor of Catholic school identity. (Hobbie, Convey, & Schuttloffel, 2010, p. 19)

> … the longer the teacher or administrator worked in Catholic schools, the higher the rating they gave of the essential nature of the school's faith community to its Catholic identity … it takes time and experience for teachers to grasp fully the importance of the faith community and their role in creating and sustaining it [with the result that] rapid turnover in a Catholic school may be a prescription for an unfocused Catholic environment. (Convey, 2012, pp. 208–209)

The emerging importance of length of time spent teaching in Catholic schools may be indicative of school-based socialisation experiences (Gleeson, O'Flaherty, Galvin, & Hennessy, 2015; Lortie, 1975; Morine-Dershimer & Corrigan, 1997) during a period of profound change in Australian society. Some 10 years ago, Croke (2007) expressed concerns regarding the imminent retirement of 'a generation or two of qualified teachers, many former Religious or religiously formed to some extent, whose careers have developed with the system' (p. 822). The profile of pre-service teachers at one of Australia's two Catholic universities (see Chapter 9 in this book) does nothing to alleviate these concerns. In their responses to an open-ended question about the challenges facing Catholic schooling today (Gleeson & O'Neill, 2015), many survey respondents expressed similar concerns in relation to the 'changing of the guard'.

Noting the serious decline in the numbers of 'consecrated persons' in leadership positions in Catholic schools internationally, Grace (2010) remarks that 'the spiritual capital of these religious has been passed on to a first generation of lay leaders and teachers who have experienced the formative influence of their charisms' (p. 123). Echoing the concerns of Croke (2007) that have been noted earlier, Grace (2010) identifies spiritual capital as an 'urgent priority' and calls on 'the conferences of Catholic bishops internationally … [to] place the renewal of spiritual capital in Catholic education high on their priority agendas' (pp. 123–124). This scenario is currently playing out in Queensland insofar as many Catholic schools are becoming increasingly dependent for their faith-based identity on their founding charism (Gleeson & O'Flaherty, 2016).

Teachers' self-reported knowledge of Catholic teaching was also a strong predictor ($p < .003$) of the perceived importance of the identity and characteristics (PRACTICES) of Catholic schools. As in the case of religiosity, it is somewhat difficult to comment on this outcome in view of the subjective nature of these ratings and the paucity of comparable literature. Some three-quarters of respondents rated their knowledge as good or very good, and the strongest predictors ($p < .003$) of these high scores were religiosity, length of service in Catholic education, being a teacher of religion, being Catholic and being a secondary teacher, all of which were also strong predictors ($p < .003$) of the decision to teach in Catholic Education because of one's faith commitment (COMIT).

Just over 80% of survey respondents were Catholic. It is noteworthy, if not entirely surprising, that Catholic respondents were 14 times more likely to give their faith commitment (COMIT) as the reason for choosing to teach in a Catholic school and that such commitment is a very strong predictor ($p < .003$) of the perceived importance of the faith-based purpose and characteristics of Catholic schools. It should also be noted however that being Catholic does not emerge as a strong predictor of the perceived importance of the faith-based identity of Catholic schools or of their PRACTICES characteristics. These findings should however be read in conjunction with the earlier section of this chapter dealing with secularisation, the declining rates of church attendance and the concerns expressed by commentators such as Croke (2007) and others.

With regard to school type, being a primary teacher (60% of respondents) rather than a secondary teacher was strongly associated ($p < .003$) with the decision to teach in Catholic schools because of one's faith commitment and with the perceived importance of community-related characteristics of Catholic schools (PEOPLE). Comparative studies of the beliefs and values of primary and secondary teachers are remarkably rare. It seems reasonable to suggest however that the significance of this variable may be due to the fact that Religious Education is part of the brief of most primary teachers and to the more student-centred nature of the primary curriculum by comparison with the stronger focus on subjects at secondary level (Hanewald, 2013).

Many scholars have affirmed the important part played by school principals and senior leaders in creating the environment necessary for strong Catholic identity (Ciriello, 1998; Convey, 1992; Cook & Simonds, 2011; Degenhardt & Duignan, 2010; Jacobs, 1997). Convey (2012) found that senior school leaders were more supportive than their colleagues of faith-based purposes, while Harkins (1993) reported that school principals in the United States were the most likely to rate the development of the school's faith community as essential. One-third of our respondents had added professional responsibilities, and the Spearman rank order correlation for added responsibilities and length of service in Catholic schools was statistically significant ($p < .001$). Consistent with the findings of Convey (2012), having added professional responsibilities was a strong predictor ($p < .003$) of the perceived importance of the PRACTICE characteristics of Catholic schools, suggesting a heightened awareness on the part of senior leaders of the significance of these characteristics to the faith-based identity of Catholic schools.

Concluding remarks

While many teachers' responses were consistent with Catholic Church expectations regarding the identity of Catholic schools, it is hardly surprising that considerable variance also emerged in view of the problematic nature of faith-based identity and the 'many different theological and sociological understandings of Catholic identities' (Arbuckle, 2013, p. 67). Noting the changing profile of teachers in the Catholic Education system, Rymarz (2010) remarks that 'a critical problem for Catholic schools is the serious lack of committed Catholic teachers on staff' and goes on to point out that 'there is a point ... below which the work of the Catholic school is imperiled if it does not have a sufficient number of highly committed individuals' (p. 304).

It is hoped that the current findings will assist policymakers insofar as they provide empirical evidence of the key variables that consistently make a difference to the ways in which teachers see the faith-based identity, purposes and characteristics of Catholic schools. Chief among these are high levels of religiosity, length of service in Catholic Education, having high self-ratings for knowledge of Catholic teaching, being Catholic and choosing to teach in Catholic schools because of one's faith commitment. It is a cause of some concern that just over a quarter of the respondents gave their 'commitment to the Catholic faith' as their main reason for working in Catholic schools and that respondents generally favoured generic over faith-based school characteristics and purposes. The high predictive value of religiosity underlines the timeliness of Rymarz's (2010) call for 'a mechanism to identify ... teachers already possessing a strong sense of religious commitment' (p. 307).

As Croke (2007) concludes, 'ensuring the quality of teachers, and eventually leaders, may well turn out to be the most difficult and threatening challenge to the future of Catholic schools in Australia' (p. 823). The importance of faith-based professional development is especially clear at a time when 'the value and authenticity of Catholic schools will be heavily reliant on the quality and commitment of its teachers ... [amid] widespread concerns about the capacity of many young teachers and student teachers to teach in a Catholic school, or at least to contribute meaningfully to the core religious goals of the school' (Croke, 2007, p. 822).

Catholic Education in the United States offers some valuable lessons in this respect (Krebbs, 2000; Smith & Nuzzi, 2007). Notwithstanding respondents' high self-ratings for knowledge of Catholic teaching, teacher professional development constitutes an important foundation for such theological literacy, a point that was recognised by interviewees in this study with longer experience of working in Catholic schools. Catholic school leaders are challenged to add a transformative 'theological' dimension to such professional development by the predilection of participating teachers for generic purposes and characteristics.

A number of Australian dioceses and schools have been engaging for some 10 years now with the Leuven Catholic Identity Project whose leaders have expressed concerns regarding the growing prevalence of 'horizontalisation' (settling for generic purposes and characteristics) where Catholic teaching is 'reduced to just an ethical code, which moreover is broadly shared' (Pollefeyt & Bouwens, 2010, p. 201). This raises the fundamental question: 'can one still rightly speak of a "Catholic school" when God and Jesus Christ are not being talked about?' One possible response involves the promotion of confessional identity involving high levels of religious practice and Catholic formation and stronger ties with the local parish and clergy. Pondering whether 'there is sufficient support for this identity option' (Pollefeyt & Bouwens, 2010, p. 202), they indicate their preference for 'recontextualisation', which best happens in a 'dialogue school' that is

> ... deliberately in search of a renewed Catholic profile in and through conversation with plurality [that] tries to understand the Catholic faith re-interpreted in a contemporary cultural context ... shaped by at least a significant minority of Catholics who are recognizable as such and want to enter dialogue explicitly. (Pollefeyt & Bouwens, 2010, pp. 202–203)

The scope for such dialogue is constrained however by the aforementioned dominance of market forces in current education policy and practice (CCE, 2014; Gleeson, 2015a; Lingard, 2010).

Notes

1. This revised version of our paper published in *International Studies in Catholic Education*, Vol. 10, Issue 1, pages 44–65 is reproduced with the kind permission of the Editor, Professor Gerald Grace. This version also replaces the original version on the journal website.
2. Since initial response rates were slightly lower than desirable due to technical issues associated with the use of a variety of different browsers, the research team also administered the survey at school staff meetings in 20 Brisbane diocesan schools.
3. It should be noted that these are self-ratings.
4. See survey Question 16 in Appendix 3.

The identity of Catholic schools 157

5. See http://www.acu.edu.au/775158.
6. This somewhat surprising finding may suggest that many non-Catholic teachers regard the outward signs as more important than characteristics of the community such as the religion of teachers and students. The zero-order correlation between RELIGION and PRACTICES is positive, as would be expected, that is Catholics are more likely to see the religious practices of the school as important to its Catholic identity. The change in sign is brought about by its inclusion with other variables in the regression equation.
7. This model of teacher professionalism has the development of the individual and teacher relationships with children as its primary focus. Sockett (2008) sets it alongside three other forms of professionalism: scholar-professional, clinician-professional and moral agent.

References

Arbuckle, G. A. (2013). *Catholic identity or identities? Refounding ministries in Chaotic times.* Minnesota: Liturgical Press.

Australian Catholic Bishops Conference. (2013). *A profile of the Catholic community in Australia.* Clayton, Victoria: Pastoral Research Office.

Australian Government. (2005). *National framework for values education in Australian schools.* Canberra: Commonwealth of Australia.

Belmonte, A., & Cranston, N. (2009). The religious dimension of lay leadership in Catholic schools: Preserving Catholic culture in an era of change. *Catholic Education: A Journal of Inquiry and Practice, 12*(3), 294–319.

Benson, P. L., & Guerra, M. J. (1985). *Sharing the faith: The beliefs and values of Catholic school teachers.* Washington, DC: National Catholic Educational Association.

Boeve, L. (2005). Religion after detraditionalization: Christian faith in a post-secular Europe. *Irish Theological Quarterly, 70*(2), 99–122. doi: 10.1177/002114000507000201.

Bryk, A. S. (1996). Lessons from Catholic high schools. In T. H. McLaughlin, J. O'Keefe, & B. O'Keeffe (Eds.), *The contemporary Catholic school: Context, identity and diversity* (pp. 25–41). London: Falmer Press.

Byrne, D. (2005). *The Understandings of Catholic lay secondary teachers on the nature and purpose of Catholic schooling.* Thesis submitted in partial fulfilment of requirements for the Master of Educational Management Degree, University of Western Australia.

Chambers, M. (2012). Students who are not Catholics in Catholic schools: Lessons from the second Vatican council about the Catholicity of schools. *International Studies in Catholic Education, 4*(2), 186–199.

Ciriello, M. J. (Ed.). (1998). *The principal as educational leader* (2nd ed.). Washington, DC: United States Catholic Conference.

Cohen, J., & Cohen, P. (1975). *Applied multiple regression/correlation analysis for the behavioural sciences.* Hillsdale, NJ: Erlbaum.

Coldrey, B. (1992). 'A most unenviable reputation': The Christian brothers and school discipline over two centuries. *History of Education, 21*(3), 277–289.

Congregation for Catholic Education (CCE). (1977). *The Catholic school.* London: Catholic Truth Society.

Congregation for Catholic Education (CCE). (1997). *The Catholic school on the threshold of the third millennium.* Vatican City: Author.

Congregation for Catholic Education (CCE). (2013). *Educating to intercultural dialogue in Catholic schools. Living in harmony for a civilization of love.* London: Catholic Truth Society.

Congregation for Catholic Education (CCE). (2014). *Educating today and tomorrow: A renewing passion, Instrumentum laboris.* Vatican City: Author.

Convey, J. J. (1992). *Catholic schools make a difference: Twenty-five years of research.* Washington, DC: National Catholic Educational Association.

Convey, J. J. (2012). Perceptions of Catholic identity: Views of Catholic school administrators and teachers. *Catholic Education: A Journal of Inquiry and Practice, 16*(1), 187–214.

Convey, J. J. (2014). Motivation and job satisfaction of Catholic school teachers. *Journal of Catholic Education, 18*(1), 4–25. Retrieved from http://dx.doi.org/10.15365/joce.1801022014

Cook, T. J. (2001). *Architects of Catholic culture: Designing and building Catholic culture in Catholic schools.* The NCEA Catholic Educational Leadership Monograph Series. Washington, DC: NCEA.

Cook, T. J., & Simonds, T. A. (2011). The charism of 21st-century Catholic schools: Building a culture of relationships. *Catholic Education: A Journal of Inquiry and Practice, 14*(3), 319–333.

Creswell, J. (1994). *Research design qualitative, quantitative and mixed method approaches* (2nd ed.). London: Sage.

Croke, B. (2007). Australian Catholic schools in a changing political and religious landscape. In G. Grace & J. O'Keefe (Eds.), *International handbook of Catholic education – Challenges for school systems in the 21st century* (pp. 811–834). Dordrecht: Springer.

D'Orsa, T. (2013). Catholic curriculum: Re-framing the conversation. *International studies in Catholic education, 5*(1), 68–82. doi: 10.1080/19422539.2012.754589.

Degenhardt, L., & Duignan, P. (2010). *Dancing on a shifting carpet.* Victoria: ACER Press.

Dowling, A., Beavis, A., Underwood, C., Sadeghi, R., & O'Malley, K. (2009). *Who's coming to school today? Final report.* Brisbane: ACER, Brisbane Catholic Education.

Flynn, M. (1993). *The culture of Catholic schools: A study of Catholic schools 1972–1993.* Homebush: St Pauls.

Forsey, M. (2010). Publicly minded, privately focused: Western Australian teachers and school choice. *Teaching and Teacher Education, 26*(1), 53–60.

Gleeson, J. (2015a). Critical challenges and dilemmas for Catholic education leadership internationally. *International Studies in Catholic Education, 7*(2), 145–161.

Gleeson, J. (2015b). Report on teacher interviews (April 2015). Retrieved from http://www.acu.edu.au/__data/assets/pdf_file/0006/775158/MAY1515compositeteachintvreport.pdf

Gleeson, J., & O'Flaherty, J. (2016). The teacher as moral educator: Comparative study of secondary teachers in Catholic schools in Australia and Ireland. *Teaching and Teacher Education, 55,* 45–56. Retrieved from http://dx.doi.org/10.1016/j.tate.2015.12.002

Gleeson, J., O'Flaherty, J., Galvin, T., & Hennessy, J. (2015). Student teachers, socialisation, school placement and schizophrenia: The case of curriculum change. *Teachers and Teaching, 21*(4), 437–458. doi: 10.1080/13540602.2014.968895.

Gleeson, J., O'Gorman, J., Goldburg, P., & O'Neill, M. (2018). The characteristics of Catholic schools: A comparative study of the perceptions of teachers in Catholic schools in USA and Queensland. *Journal of Catholic Education, 21*(2), 76–106.

Gleeson, J., & O'Neill, M. (2015). Report on survey of teachers' opinions regarding certain aspects of Catholic Education. Retrieved from http://www.acu.edu.au/__data/assets/pdf_file/0010/802378/draft_teacher_report.pdf

Glock, C. Y., & Stark, R. (1965). *Religion and society in tension.* San Francisco: Rand McNally.

Goldring, E. B., & Phillips, K. (2008). Parent preferences and parent choices: The public–private decision about school choice. *Journal of Education Policy, 23*(3), 209–230. doi: 10.1080/02680930801987844.

Gonski, D., Boston, K., Greiner, K., Lawrence, C., Scales, B., & Tannock, P. (2011). Review of funding for schooling. Final report. Department of Education, Employment and Workplace Relations. Retrieved from www.schoolfunding.gov.au

Grace, G. (2002). *Catholic schools: Mission, markets and morality*. London: Routledge Falmer.

Grace, G. (2010). Renewing spiritual capital: An urgent priority for the future of Catholic education internationally. *International Studies in Catholic Education, 2*(2), 117–128.

Grace, G. (2013). Catholic social teaching should permeate the Catholic secondary school curriculum an agenda for reform. *International Studies in Catholic Education, 5*(1), 99–109.

Groome, T. H. (1996). What makes a school Catholic? In T. H. McLaughlin, J. O'Keefe, & B. O'Keeffe (Eds.), *The contemporary Catholic school: Context, identity and diversity* (pp. 107–125). London: Falmer.

Haldane, J. (1996). Catholic Education and Catholic Identity. In T. H. McLaughlin, J. O'Keefe, & B. O'Keeffe (Eds.), *The contemporary Catholic school: Context, identity and diversity* (pp. 126–136). London: Falmer.

Hanewald, R. (2013). Transition between primary and secondary school: Why it is important and how it can be supported. *Australian Journal of Teacher Education, 38*(1), 62–74. Retrieved from http://ro.ecu.edu.au/ajte/vol38/iss1/5

Harkins, W. (1993). *Introducing the Catholic elementary school principal: What principals say about themselves, their values, their schools*. Washington, DC: National Catholic Educational Association.

Hobbie, M., Convey, J. J., & Schuttloffel, M. J. (2010). The impact of Catholic school identity and organizational leadership on the vitality of Catholic elementary schools. *Catholic Education: A Journal of Inquiry and Practice, 14*(1), 7–23.

Holdcroft, B. (2006). What is religiosity? *Catholic Education: A Journal of Inquiry and Practice, 10*(1), 89–103.

Institute for Catholic Education. (1996). *Curriculum matters: A resource for Catholic educators*. Toronto: Author.

Jacobs, R. M. (1997). *The grammar of Catholic schooling*. Washington, DC: National Catholic Educational Association.

Kenway, J. (2013). Challenging inequality in Australian schools: Gonski and beyond. *Discourse: Studies in the Cultural Politics of Education, 34*(2), 286–308. doi:10.1080/01596306.2013.770254.

Krebbs, M. J. (2000). Values infusion: A systematic response to Catholic identity. *Journal of Catholic Education, 3*(3). Retrieved from http://digitalcommons.lmu.edu/ce/vol3/iss3/4

Lane, D. A. (1991). *Catholic education and the school. Some theological reflections*. Dublin: Veritas.

Lane, D. A. (2015). *Catholic education in the light of Vatican II and Laudato Si'*. Dublin: Veritas.

Lewis, J. (2009). Redefining qualitative methods: Believability in the fifth moment. *International Journal of Qualitative Methods, 8*(2), 1–15.

Lingard, B. (2010). Policy borrowing, policy learning: Testing times in Australian schooling. *Critical Studies in Education, 51*(2), 129–147. doi: 10.1080/17508481003731026.

Lortie, D. C. (1975). *Schoolteacher: A sociological study*. Chicago, IL: University of Chicago Press.

Lovat, T., & Clement, N. (2014). So who has the values? Challenges for faith-based schools in an era of values pedagogy. In M. Reiss & Y. Waghid (Eds.), *International handbook of learning, teaching and leading in faith-based schools* (pp. 567–582). Dordrecht: Springer.

Maddox, M. (2014). *Taking God to school: The end of Australia's egalitarian education?* Sydney: Allen and Unwin.

Maritain, J. (1943). *Education at the crossroads*. New Haven: Yale University Press.

McClelland, V. (1996). Wholeness, faith and the distinctiveness of the Catholic school. In T. H. McLaughlin, J. O'Keefe, & B. O'Keeffe (Eds.), *The contemporary Catholic school: Context, identity and diversity* (pp. 155–161). London: Falmer.

McLaughlin, D. (2006). The dialectic of Australian Catholic education. *International Journal of Children's Spirituality, 10*(2), 215–233.

McLaughlin, T. H. (1996). The distinctiveness of the Catholic school. In T. H. McLaughlin, J. O'Keefe, & B. O'Keeffe (Eds.), *The contemporary Catholic school: Context, identity and diversity* (pp. 136–154). London: Falmer.

Mifsud, F. (2010). The community aspect of the Catholic school is the backbone of the Catholic ethos. *International Studies in Catholic Education, 2*(1), 50–63.

Miles, M., & Huberman, M. (1994). *Qualitative data analysis: A source book of new methods.* London: Sage.

Morine-Dershimer, G., & Corrigan, S. (1997). Teachers' beliefs. In H. J. Walberg & G. Haertle (Eds.). *Psychology and educational practice* (pp. 297–306). Berkeley, CA: McCutcheon.

Murray, D. (1991). *A special concern.* Dublin: Veritas.

National Catholic Education Commission. (2013). *Australian Catholic schools 2012: Annual report.* Retrieved from www.ncec.catholic.edu.au

Noddings, N. (1997). A morally defensible mission for schools in the 21st century. In E. Clinchy (Ed.), *Transforming public education: A new course for America's future* (pp. 27–37). New York: Teachers College Press.

Organisation for Economic Co-operation and Development (OECD). (2010). *PISA 2009 results: What makes a school successful? Resources, policies and practices (IV).* Retrieved from http://dx.doi.org/doi:10.1787/9789264091559-en

Pascoe, S. (2007). Challenges for Catholic education in Australia. In G. Grace & J. O'Keefe (Eds.), *International handbook of Catholic education – Challenges for school systems in the 21st century* (C. 787–810). Dordrecht: Springer.

Perry, L., & McConney, A. (2010). School socio-economic composition and student outcomes in Australia: Implications for educational policy. *Australian Journal of Education, 54*(1) 72–85.

Perry, L. B., & Southwell, L. (2014). Access to academic curriculum in Australian secondary schools: A case study of a highly marketised education system. *Journal of Education Policy, 29*(4), 467–485. doi: 10.1080/02680939.2013.846414.

Pollefeyt, D., & Bouwens, J. (2010). Framing the identity of Catholic schools: Empirical methodology for quantitative research on the Catholic identity of an education institute. *International Studies in Catholic Education, 2*(2), 193–211.

Pope Francis. (2015). *Encyclical letter Laudato Si' on care for our common home.* Strathfield: St. Pauls.

Queensland Catholic Education Commission. (2012). *Queensland Catholic Schools 2012.* Brisbane: Queensland Catholic Education Commission.

Rymarz, R. (2010). Religious identity of Catholic schools: Some challenges from a Canadian perspective. *Journal of Beliefs & Values, 31*(3), 299–310. doi: 10.1080/13617672.2010.521006.

Rymarz, R. (2011). The future of Catholic schools in a secular culture of religious choice. *Journal of Religion and Society, 13*, 1–12.

Scanlan, M. (2013). The grammar of Catholic schooling and radically 'Catholic' schools. *Catholic Education: A Journal of Inquiry and Practice, 12*(1), 25–54.

Smith, P. A., & Nuzzi, R. J. (2007). Beyond religious congregations: Responding to new challenges in Catholic education. In G. Grace & J. O'Keefe (Eds.), *International handbook of Catholic education – Challenges for school systems in the 21st century* (pp. 103–124). Dordrecht: Springer.

Sockett, H. (2008). The moral and epistemic purposes of teacher education. In M. Cochran-Smith, S. Feiman-Nemser, & D. J. McIntyre (Eds.), *Handbook of research on teacher education: Enduring questions in changing contexts* (pp. 45–65). New York: Routledge, Association of Teacher Education.

Sullivan, J. (2000). Catholic education: Distinctive and inclusive. *Journal of Religious Education, 48*(1), 26–31.

Tarr, H. C., Ciriello, M. J., & Convey, J. J. (1993). Commitment and satisfaction among parochial school teachers: Findings from Catholic education. *Journal of Research in Christian Education, 2*(1), 41–63.

Treston, K. (2001). *Emergence for life not fall from grace*. Brisbane: Morning Star Publishing.

Chapter 8

The characteristics of Catholic schools: Comparative perspectives from the United States and Queensland, Australia[1]

Jim Gleeson, John O'Gorman, Peta Goldburg rsm and Maureen O'Neill

The identity of faith-based schools is coming under growing pressure in an increasingly secularised society that is dominated by market values (Ball, 2012; Gleeson, 2015; Lingard, 2010) and is characterised by detraditionalisation and pluralisation (Boeve, 2005). Within this new environment, faith-based education in Catholic schools is challenged to embrace changing anthropological (Francis, 2015; Lane, 2015), ecclesiological (Boeve, 2005) and scientific (Treston, 2001) landscapes. For example, the Centre for Academic Teacher Training of the Faculty of Theology of the Catholic University of Leuven (Belgium) has responded to such challenges by developing 'a new empirical methodology to frame the identity structure of Catholic educational organizations' (Pollefeyt & Bouwens, 2010, p. 193).

Against that background, Catholic schools are facing something of an identity crisis. Youniss (2000) noted that Catholic schools in the United States often bear little resemblance to their predecessors insofar as they 'charge high tuition, place academic achievement first, are staffed by lay teachers, and have significant non–Catholic enrolment [and] … resemble only vaguely the system of Catholic schooling that developed over the past 150 years' (p. 9). While Belmonte and Cranston (2009) insist that the identity of Catholic schools is 'fundamental to their existence, and when they cease to be Catholic, for all purposes they cease to exist' (p. 296), they recognise that Catholic schools in Australia have to serve many masters, so that

> … challenged to maintain their overall character and ethos in a changing religious and social reality [they] must prove their validity as viable educational institutions, as well as satisfy the requirements of the Church, while simultaneously responding to government accountability and Church expectations. (Belmonte & Cranston, 2009, p. 296)

The main purpose of this chapter is to compare the opinions of teachers in Catholic schools in the United States (Convey, 2012) and Queensland

(Gleeson, O'Gorman, & O'Neill, 2018) with respect to the importance of given characteristics of Catholic schools. The empirical findings are prefaced by consideration of the identity and characteristics of Catholic schools and a general comparison of Catholic Education in the two jurisdictions. The discussion of findings attempts to explain the extraordinary inter-jurisdictional differences that emerge from the empirical data.

Identity and characteristics of Catholic schools

The identity of Catholic schools is integrally associated with the transmission of the Catholic faith. According to the Second Vatican Council, the Catholic school 'strives to relate all human culture eventually to the news of salvation, so that the light of faith will illumine the knowledge which students gradually gain of the world, of life, and mankind' (Abbott, 1966, p. 646). The Congregation for Catholic Education (CCE, 1997) identified the fundamental principles of Catholic schools in terms of cultural identity, integral all-round Christocentric education and service to society so that, 'from the first moment that a student sets foot in a Catholic school, he or she ought to have the impression of entering a new environment, one illumined by the light of faith, and having its own unique characteristics' (p. 25).

This current comparison of teachers' perceptions of the importance of given characteristics of Catholic schools is grounded in Convey's (2012) model of Catholic school identity, as shown in Figure 8.1.

Convey (2012) sees the institutional identity of schools as being primarily driven by the people who belong to school communities – school principals, senior leaders, teachers and students. School leaders are responsible for shaping a school culture that reflects Catholic identity. While recognising that each school has its own unique culture and traditions, Convey (2012) saw the

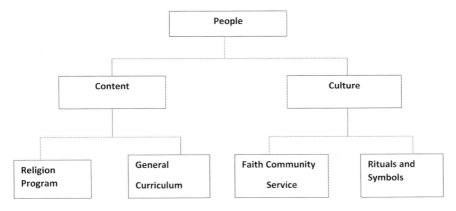

Figure 8.1 Components of Catholic school identity. Reproduced from Convey (2012). Used with permission

common institutional culture of Catholic schools in terms of faith community, service, rituals and symbols. The formal curriculum, traditionally seen in terms of a selection from the culture made on the basis of ideology (Lawton, 1975) and the story we tell our children about the good or virtuous life (Trant, 2007), consists of the general curriculum and Religious Education (RE). In the following sections, we explore each of these elements of Catholic identity.

Content: Curriculum

The CCE (1977) defines the specific mission of the Catholic school in terms of 'a critical systematic transmission of culture in the light of faith and the bringing forth of the power of Christian virtue by the integration of culture with faith and faith with living' (para 49). Many Congregation statements are clearly of relevance to the school curriculum well beyond RE. The CCE (1997) sees the 'integral education of the human person through a clear educational project ... [involving] ecclesial and cultural identity ... love [and] service to society' (p. 4) as a fundamental characteristic of the Catholic school and encourages Catholic schools 'to go beyond knowledge and educate people to think, evaluating facts in the light of values' (CCE, 2013, p. 66).

The CCE (2014) challenges 'contemporary educators [to] have a renewed mission [with] the ambitious aim of offering young people an integral education' (p. 10) and warns against simply responding to 'the demands deriving from the ever-changing economic situation' (p. 64). It comments critically on the 'merely functional view of education' taken by the European Union, Organisation for Economic Co-operation and Development (OECD), World Bank and on the prevalence of 'instrumental reason and competitiveness ... [concerned with] the market economy and the labour market' (CCE, 2014, p. 12) found in many developed countries. What is important for them is that Catholic schools 'think out their curricula to place centre-stage both individuals and their search for meaning [since] what is taught is not neutral, and neither is the way of teaching it' (CCE, 2014, p. 64). Many Catholic academics, including Murray (1991), Lane (1991), Grace (2010), Davis and Franchi (2013) and Arthur (2013), have expressed concerns about neoliberal influences on education and advocated curriculum integration rather than separation, as does Ontario's Institute for Catholic Education (1996).

Culture: Faith community and service

The Second Vatican Council defined the *proper function* of the Catholic school as the creation of 'a special atmosphere animated by the Gospel spirit of freedom and charity, to help youth grow' (Abbott, 1966, p. 646). Francis and Egan (1990) noted the strong historical support for the Catholic school as a faith community, while Groome (1996) argued that the 'very nature and purpose [of the Catholic school] calls it to be a community of Christian faith'

(p. 116). The CCE (1997) portrayed the Catholic school as a place 'in which faith, culture and life are brought into harmony'.

Drawing on the work of Coleman, Hoffer, and Kilgore (1982), Convey (2012) argued that a 'Catholic school by its very nature should have a distinct Catholic culture' and pointed out that

> ... research has shown that good Catholic schools have a 'sense of community,' which has a positive effect on the quality of life in the school and contributes to its effectiveness ... The school's faith community is a functional community that produces social capital and is a major contributor to the effectiveness of the school. It's the faith community of the school that constitutes an integral part of the school's Catholic identity. (p. 190)

In light of the growing diversity of Catholic school communities, the modern Catholic school can no longer rely on the faith-based identity of parents and students to create institutional Catholic identity (Croke, 2007; NCEA, 2017).

From the cultural perspective of service, the CCE (2013) recognised the important role of education in improving the social and economic conditions of people's lives in declarations such as 'the kind of education that is promoted by Catholic schools is not aimed at establishing an elitist meritocracy' (p. 12) and proposed that the curriculum of Catholic schools must address 'the unequal distribution of resources, poverty, injustice and human rights denied' (p. 66). Scanlan (2011) highlighted the potential for linking Catholic identity and inclusivity, while Grace (2010, 2013) argued that Catholic social teaching should permeate the Catholic secondary school curriculum in three key areas: (a) religious, moral and cultural; (b) economic, business and enterprise and (c) social, environmental and political. The Institute for Catholic Education (1996) of Ontario regards curriculum as 'transformative ... [a] vehicle for social and personal change based on principles of justice and the view of the learner as agent-of-change' (p. 26).

We now turn to the role of the symbols, rituals and liturgies in expressing the faith and culture of Catholic school communities.

Culture: Symbols, rituals and liturgies

Drawing on James Joyce's experience of Catholic education in his *Portrait of an Artist as a Young Man*, Grace (2002) explained how

> Traditional Catholic liturgy ... was a central part of Catholic schooling, especially where such schooling was provided by vowed religious or by teaching brothers. The rituals and devotions of the school year could generate a school ethos in which mystery, sacredness, power, symbolism and dramatic theatre could be realised over and against the prosaic routines of everyday life. For some ... this encounter was compelling. (p. 64)

Grace's (2002) research with UK head teachers found 'much disjuncture between the liturgical life of Catholic secondary schools ... and the liturgical culture of parishes and churches' (p. 220), while Flynn (1993), in his Australian study, identified school-based liturgies as the occasion where 'the school community celebrate[s] its faith in Jesus Christ through prayer and the Eucharist ... [and] builds up the spirit of Christian community' (p. 50). Flynn (1993) also highlighted the importance of 'religious symbols [as] visible expressions of what the school stands for [including] school badges and mottoes, school assemblies and graduations, school handbooks, magazines and newsletters and school uniforms' (pp. 43–44). Writing about Catholic elementary schools in the Midwestern United States, Scanlan (2011) described the use of icons, crucifixes and regular Catholic rituals, such as daily school prayer, monthly masses and prayer services as 'ubiquitous' practices (p. 306).

Summary

This brief treatment of the content and culture of Catholic schools resonates with McLaughlin's (2000) conclusion that the aim of Catholic schools is to

> ... generate a challenging, authentic educational environment, faithful to the Catholic tradition of offering a synthesis of faith and culture, which, while promoting integral human growth, provides a catalyst for students to take the opportunity to initiate or continue a personal relationship with Christ, that witnesses its practical expression in an active, inclusive, care for others, while confronting contemporary injustices in economic and social structures. (p. 111)

Catholic Education in Australia and the United States

Having considered the generic features of Catholic Education, we now consider some particular features of Catholic education in American and Australia in order to set the scene for the comparison of teachers' ratings of the importance of given characteristics of Catholic schools, the primary focus of this chapter.

Catholic Education in Australia

The 2016 census[2] classified 23% of the Australian population as Catholic, while 30% returned as 'no religion'. Wilkinson (2013) found that some 11% of Australian Catholics attended Mass each week in 2011, while the Australian Catholic Bishops Conference (2013) reported a Mass attendance rate of one-eighth on a typical weekend in 2011. This percentage has been falling fairly steadily since its peak in the mid-1950s.

Historically, the teaching force in Australian Catholic schools consisted mainly of religious (priests, female religious and brothers) who 'ensured that the learning environments, both in the formal curriculum and extra-curricular activities, were permeated by religious practices' (O'Donoghue & Burley, 2008, p. 184). However, most teachers in Australian Catholic schools today are laypeople (Hansen, 2001), and Rossiter (2013) has highlighted how school charisms 'maintain some sense of historical continuity with the distinctive spirituality and mission of their founding religious orders' (p. 9).

Following an arrangement between the government and the Catholic Church in the early 1970s (Maddox, 2014), Australian Catholic schools are independent and autonomous. Teachers' salaries are on par with the state sector and the National Catholic Education Commission (2013) reported that in 2011, 53% of the cost of educating a student in a Catholic school was covered by federal funds, 19% from state government funds and 28% from private sources, mainly through school fees.

Research conducted by the Australian Scholarship Group (ASG) found that 2014 annual primary school fees in Catholic schools in Metropolitan Australia averaged AUD 3,600 per child, AUD 485 in government schools and AUD 10,300 in Independent schools. The average annual fees at secondary level were AUD 9,000 in Catholic schools, AUD 980 in government schools and AUD 18,000 in Independent schools. Maddox (2014) noted that 'the overall makeup of Australian education is shift[ing] … with children [being] once again segregated by income, culture and religion' (pp. 86–87), with Catholic schools becoming the 'schools of choice' for middle class non-Catholics, who constitute over 40% of Catholic secondary school students. The Australian Catholic Bishops Conference (2013) reported that only 53% of Catholic students attended Catholic schools, and Croke (2007) noted that

> … fewer Catholic families are choosing Catholic schools, even though their resources are better than ever [and] the growth in Catholic schools is being entirely sustained by middle class families of other Christian denominations, and non-Christian faiths (Muslim, Buddhist, Hindu). (pp. 815–816)

According to a study of students attending Catholic schools in Brisbane, 'as society is becoming more secular, Catholic schools are becoming more popular than ever' (Dowling, Beavis, Underwood, Sadeghi, & O'Malley, 2009, p. 6) with upwardly socially mobile parents regardless of their religion. Dowling et al. (2009) reported that parents enrol their children in Catholic secondary schools 'for predominantly pragmatic rather than religious reasons [with a resulting] marked decline in religious commitment' (p. 38). It appears that parents are more influenced by the quality of general education, while 'the desire for a specifically religious education does not appear to be dominant, even amongst Catholic schools' (Dowling et al., 2009, p. 20).

Meanwhile, McLaughlin and Standen (2013) reported that only one in three low-income Catholic Australian children attends Catholic schools, while the Catholic Bishops of New South Wales (NSW) and the Australian Capital Territory (ACT) (2007) noted that 'poorer Catholic children are increasingly attending State schools [and that] increasing accessibility for all students remains a significant challenge in some places' (p. 8). This led Croke (2007) to express concerns regarding the 'authenticity' of 'the Australian Catholic school of the early 21st century [with its] annually increasing proportion of non-Catholic students, along with students from mainly middle class Catholic families whose adhesion to their Faith is weak' (p. 823). As noted by Chambers (2012):

> One issue that confronts contemporary Catholic schools is their increasing enrolment of students who are not Catholics ... [which] brings into question traditional assumptions about the clientele of Catholic schools (Who belongs in the school?), the religious activity in Catholic schools (What is possible in catechesis?) and the ecclesial nature of Catholic schools (Is the school a faith community?). In short, this issue challenges the very nature and purpose of Catholic schools. (p. 186)

Meanwhile, Pascoe (2007) portrayed Australian Catholic Education as Janus-like:

> In describing the nature and purpose of Catholic schools to potential students and parents, emphases are likely to be on the education of the whole person, on faith and religious education and on pastoral care and learning outcomes. In liaising with government, emphases are likely to be on core purpose, support of democratic principles and institutions, parent choice, legislative compliance, good governance, sound educational practice, commitments to accountability, and fulfilment of elements of formal agreements. (p. 793)

Catholic Education in the United States

Just like Australia, the American Catholic Church has been shaped by immigration and a similar proportion (22%) of the US population was classified as Catholic in 2015. A higher proportion of US Catholics, approximately one-quarter, attend Mass on a regular basis (NCEA, 2017). Catholic schools have existed in the United States for over 200 years, reaching their peak in the mid-1960s with 13,000 schools educating 5.6 million students, representing 12% of all American schoolchildren and almost 89% of all private school attendees (Cattaro & Cooper, 2007). The vast majority (95%) of the teaching staff at that time were priests or religious. By the 1990s, Catholic school enrolments had reduced by 50% and they have continued to decline. Meanwhile, conservative Christian school enrolments increased by 4% and unaffiliated/independent and non-sectarian private school enrolments increased by 1% and 5%, respectively. While some new Catholic elementary and secondary schools have opened, closures have been common in urban areas (Newman, 2005; Miserandino, 2019). McLellan (2000) identified the main reasons for the decline in Catholic school enrolments between 1970 and 1995 in terms of 'the suburbanization of the Catholic population, racial population shifts in the central cities and the virtual disappearance of women religious teachers' (p. 30).

The religious affiliation of students enrolled in Catholic schools in the United States has also changed. In response to changing economic, social and political conditions, Catholic schools during the 1970s transformed themselves from closed institutions focused on maintaining the *status quo* to pluralistic institutions that mirrored the religious plurality of society in general. While the Church continues to respond to the needs of the poor in urban city communities, a survey of 631 urban Catholic schools, conducted in 2000, indicated that 27% of students were non-Catholic, up from 2% in 1972 (O'Keefe & Scheopner, 2000). As a result of this changing student profile,

> Catholic schools have drifted far from their origins as common schools for all Catholic children, with the mission of indoctrination and low-cost basic education … [A family that enrols children in a Catholic school] is significantly more likely to be wealthy is more likely to be non-white, and is more likely to pay a considerable tuition to attend the school [with the result that] almost one-half (45%) of all students in Catholic secondary schools in the nation are living in households in the top quarter of the income distribution. (Baker & Riordan, 1998, pp. 17–19)

These authors characterised such families as 'more demanding customers' with the result that 'Catholic school leadership is compromising its older religious mission in favor of intensive academics' (Baker & Riordan, 1998, p. 19). Taking account of the 57% decline in the population of Catholic elementary schools and the 44% decline in Catholic secondary schools since the late 1960s and acknowledging that such declines would be far larger 'were it not for the fact that a significant proportion of students attending Catholic schools are non-Catholics who are fleeing the public schools' (p. 22), Baker and Riordan (1998) posed the stark question: 'what does it mean to run a school system ostensibly for religious socialization if only about two of every 10 Catholic children attend?' (p. 22).

As in Australia, no tuition fees were charged in US Catholic schools for members of the parish between 1930 and 1960 when most teachers, being members of religious orders, were not in receipt of salaries – 'most children in the 1940s and 1950s attended their parish school free of charge, with tuition being collected in the Sunday collection, plus help from wealthier families' (Cattaro & Cooper, 2007, p. 64).

The number of religious teachers declined dramatically post-1970, resulting in an increase in the numbers of lay teachers[3] so that Catholic schools are now 'reliant on tuition fees and subsidies from faith-based agencies' (Cattaro & Cooper, 2007, p. 63). The National Catholic Educational Association (NCEA) website reports mean costs of $5,847 per elementary pupil and $11,790 per secondary pupil in 2016.[4] As in the case of Australia, these schools 'have priced poor and working-class families out of their markets and have become viable only for middle- and upper-middle-class families seeking top-flight academic schooling' (Baker & Riordan, 1998, p. 22). According to Miserandino (2019) the Catholic school system, since

> ... its peak in enrolment in the mid-60s has experienced a decrease to approximately 2 million students. The loss has been most dramatic in the inner cities of America. Ironically, this is precisely where American Catholic schools first got their start in the late nineteenth century ... The decrease is primarily due to school closings resulting from demographic change and the economic reality that Catholic schools are more costly to run today than in the 60s. (p. 105)

Dependence on tuition fees inevitably has serious financial implications for teachers who 'clearly make significant financial sacrifices to teach in these schools' (Schaub, 2000, p. 77). Bryk (1996) reported that 'Catholic high school teachers in our [seven purposefully selected] field sites were [on average] paid about 75% of prevailing local public school wages' (p. 27) and Przygocki (2004) concluded that

> Teachers in Catholic schools may start off earning 20% less than their public school counterparts. This trend continues over the course of a career with an eventual disparity approaching 60%. Differences in salary between Catholic and public school teachers are greater at the elementary level than the secondary level. (p. 539)

Schuttloffel (2007) notes that, in most areas,

> ... salaries and benefits continue to lag behind suburban school districts that are often perceived to be more attractive teaching locations ... in a typical metropolitan area, suburban public school districts may offer as much as 50% more salary and benefits to their principals. Catholic school teachers and principals in suburban or large metropolitan urban areas have both lower wages and a higher cost of living. (p. 91)

Inevitably then, public schools lure away many Catholic school teachers with their higher salaries and better benefits, and it is estimated that 50% of those hired by Catholic schools have left these positions within

5 years (Przygocki, 2004). According to Provasnik and Dorfman (2005), the Catholic education sector has turned over 21% of its teachers since 2000 against 15% in the case of public schools.

While there are many interesting similarities between Catholic Education in the two countries, the one glaring difference is that, unlike Australian Catholic schools, Catholic schools in the United States do not receive funding from either the federal or state governments. Against that background, the authors set out to compare the perceptions of teachers in Catholic schools in both countries of the importance of given characteristics of Catholic schools, a comparison not previously undertaken.

Method

This chapter reports on a secondary analysis of two data sets, one collected as part of a study of Catholic teachers in the United States (Convey, 2012) and congruent data collected in Queensland, Australia (Gleeson et al., 2018). School leaders and teachers in Catholic schools in both jurisdictions were asked to rate the importance of given characteristics of the Catholic school on a 4-point Likert scale of *essential, very important, important* and *unimportant*. Since Convey (2012) simply reports the proportions of US respondents rating each characteristic as 'essential', the focus of the current comparison is on that particular rating only.

The focus of Convey's (2012) study, conducted in 2010, was on 'what the teachers understood by the term Catholic identity' (p. 196). The Queensland study, which was concerned with various aspects of the faith-based identity of Catholic schools, used Convey's instrument as its reference point for the characteristics of Catholic schools. The Queensland instrument, developed with input from representatives of the main partners, was disseminated in 2013. It used 11 items that were either identical or very similar to Convey's items as shown in Table 8.1, where the third column shows the 'common' wording of each characteristic used in this chapter.

US study

Convey requested superintendents of Catholic schools in 47 dioceses to disseminate the online survey link to school principals, inviting them and their teachers to participate. Convey (2012) reports that 3,389 surveys were completed by teachers and administrators in US Catholic schools in 36 states. Fourteen per cent of his respondents were classified as administrators with the remainder being teachers who were evenly distributed across grade levels. The vast majority of respondents were Catholic and over half of them had worked in Catholic schools for at least 10 years. These respondents are not 'statistically representative of all Catholic schools administrators and teachers since a statistical probability sampling procedure was not employed that would assure a representative sample' (p. 196).

Table 8.1 Characteristics of Catholic schools: Survey items used in each jurisdiction

Category	The United States	Queensland	Common
Culture	The school has a strong community of faith	The school is a community of faith	Community of faith
Culture	The school's day/each class begins with a prayer*	Prayer is integral to the school's daily life for staff and students	Prayer in daily life of the school
Culture	School-wide liturgies occur periodically	The school community celebrated liturgies frequently	Celebration of school liturgies
Culture	Students participate in Christian service	The school engages in outreach and social justice programmes	Outreach and Christian service
Culture	A crucifix is present in every classroom	Christian symbols throughout the school	Display of Christian symbols
People	The principal is Catholic	The principal is Catholic	The principal is Catholic
People	The teacher of religion is Catholic	Teachers of religion are Catholic	Teachers of religion are Catholic
People	The vast majority of students are Catholic	The vast majority of students are Catholic	Vast majority of students are Catholic
People	The vast majority of teachers are Catholic	The vast majority of teachers are Catholic	Vast majority of teachers are Catholic
Curriculum	The Religion course presents the teachings of the Church	Religious Education (RE) programmes present the teachings of the Catholic Church	RE programmes present the teachings of the Church
Curriculum	Catholic teachings are integrated into academic subjects other than the religion course	The integration of Catholic teachings across ALL learning areas is intentionally planned	Integration of Catholic teachings across the formal curriculum

* Convey included two items dealing with the prayer life of the school, whereas the Queensland survey contained one such item. His item, *school day begins with a prayer*, is used in the current comparison because it had the higher mean score.

Building on Figure 8.1 (p. 163), his survey items dealt with culture (faith, prayer, liturgies, symbols and service), people (principal, students and teachers) and content (whole curriculum and RE) as shown in Table 8.1. Convey's (2012) overall conclusion was that

> The vast majority of respondents viewed the school's culture or faith community as the most important component of its Catholic identity .... Other aspects of Catholic identity that received high ratings were prayer, the content of the religion course, who taught religion, liturgical

celebrations, and participation in service. The respondents viewed the percentage of Catholic students as the least important aspect of Catholic identity. (p. 187)

Queensland study

With the assistance of the five Queensland Catholic Education Offices, the Queensland survey (Appendix 3) was sent to 6,832 teachers in March 2014 using Qualtrics software. Respondents were asked to rate the importance of 11 given characteristics of Catholic schools as outlined in Table 8.1. Two thousand two hundred and seventy-eight complete responses were received of which two-thirds were submitted electronically. The remaining responses were collected at school staff meetings in some 20 Archdiocese of Brisbane schools from teachers who had not submitted electronic responses. Although one might expect that the attitudes of teachers who had volunteered to respond electronically would be more positive, statistical tests found that this was not the case.

The overall response rate was 33.5% of whom 73% were female and 58% were primary teachers. They included a broad range of teaching experience and half of them had taught for more than 10 years in Catholic schools. Over 80% identified as Catholic with one-third saying that religion is very important to how they live their lives (subsequently referred to as religiosity), while one-third had added professional responsibilities ranging from principal to 'position of added responsibility'. Almost two-thirds had present or past experience of teaching RE and/or Study of Religion. While these proportions correspond closely with the profile of Catholic education teachers in Queensland by gender and level of school (QCEC, 2013), this sample cannot be regarded as strictly representative due to difficulties associated with access.

The vast majority of Queensland respondents believe that the faith-based identity of Catholic schools is important or very important. More than half of them gave the 'environment of Catholic schools' as their main reason for working in Catholic schools, followed by 'commitment to the Catholic faith'. Providing a 'safe and nurturing environment' was also the most popular choice for the purpose of Catholic schools, ahead of more explicitly faith-based options, while 'caring community' (not included in the US survey) was by far the most popular characteristic of Catholic schools (Gleeson et al., 2018).

Data analysis

The Pearson chi square was used to examine the statistical significance of differences in endorsement frequency between samples. A 2×2 contingency table was formed for each comparison of interest by tabulating frequency of endorsement of the *essential* category versus endorsement of any other category for a particular characteristic (e.g. all members of the US sample vs. all members of the Australian sample). Because there were 77 such contingency tables, a Bonferroni adjustment (Shaffer, 1995) was used to maintain the family-wise error rate at .05. This meant each individual test of a chi-square value was made at $p < .0006$ (.05/77).

To estimate effect size, we used the odds ratio (OR) which indexes by how much the probability of an event (in the present case, endorsing the *essential* category on the scale rather than not endorsing that category) differs between the US and Australian samples. OR computes the odds of an event occurring in one group (say, the US sample) divided by the odds of an event occurring in the other group (the Australian sample), where odds are the probability of the event divided by 1 minus the probability of the event. The OR varies from 1 (when there is no difference in odds between the two groups) to infinity, with increasing (or decreasing) values indicating larger effect sizes. For example, an OR of 2 means that the event is twice as likely for one group as it is for the other. Put another way, for every one respondent endorsing the essential category in one group there are two endorsing it in the other. These comparisons are presented for all respondents, administrators, teachers, non–Catholic respondents and religion teachers (Tables 8.2–8.5), for primary and secondary teachers (Table 8.6) and for non–Catholic (Table 8.7).

Limitations

Convey's (2012) survey was disseminated nationally in the United States, while the Queensland study was confined to one state. Although 2,287 responses were received from Queensland, representing one-third of all teachers in Catholic schools there, Convey's larger number of respondents (3,389) amounts to some 2% of teachers in Catholic schools in the United States. Forty-two per cent of US respondents had worked in Catholic schools for less than 10 years. When the authors invited professor Convey to comment on the representativeness of his US sample, he responded that he 'would presume that teachers [who were] more favourable toward Catholic identity would have responded to the survey' a point that might be reasonably made regarding the Queensland respondents as well. Convey also went on to explain that 'it would be a mistake to think that those who did not respond did not have a favourable view of Catholic identity [due to the] very heavy emphasis on the spiritual leadership of the principal and the development of the faith community in Catholic schools [over the past 25 years]' (Personal communication, September 21, 2016).

It should also be noted that there was a gap of 3 years between data collection in the United States and Queensland and that minor changes were made to the wording of some of the Queensland items in response to feedback from key stakeholders.

Results

The percentages of US and Queensland respondents who rated each given characteristic as essential are presented in Table 8.2, together with associated chi square (χ^2) and OR values for each correlation.

US respondents were far more likely to rate each of these items as essential, and some of the ORs were particularly large: teachers of religion are Catholic (25.81), celebration of school liturgies (11.64), RE programmes present the teachings of the Church (11.00), integration of Catholic teachings across the formal curriculum (8.86) and prayer in the daily life of school (8.68).

While a similar pattern emerged when administrators' ratings were compared (Table 8.3, p. 176), the inter-jurisdictional differences were not as great. Administrators in both jurisdictions were very likely to regard community of faith, the principal is Catholic and display of Catholic symbols as essential. Higher proportions of US administrators rated other characteristics as essential, and the ORs are particularly large in the following cases: teachers of religion are Catholic (28.69), RE programmes present the teachings of the Church (5.17), celebration of school liturgies (4.91), integration of Catholic teachings across the formal curriculum (4.53) and Christian service and outreach (3.68).

The majority of respondents in both jurisdictions identified as being Catholic and the percentages of Catholic respondents who rated each characteristic as essential are presented in Table 8.4 (p. 176).

In line with the overall ratings (Table 8.2), US teachers (excluding administrators) consistently rated the importance of each item higher than their Queensland counterparts. The OR values were particularly large in the following cases: teachers of religion are Catholic (25.63), the school is a community of faith (17.01), RE programmes present the Teachings of the Church

Table 8.2 Overall ratings of given characteristics as 'essential' by jurisdiction

Characteristic	% US (n = 3,389)	% Qld (n = 2,287)	χ^2	OR
Community of faith	91	58	878.88	7.32
Prayer in daily life of the school	92	57	1,033.47	8.68
Celebration of school liturgies	89	41	1,471.78	11.64
Outreach and Christian service	87	52	853.35	6.18
Display of Christian symbols	77	39	831.27	5.24
The principal is Catholic	74	46	464.79	3.34
Teachers of religion are Catholic	82	15	2,492.17	25.81
Vast majority of students are Catholic	15	5	140.12	3.35
Vast majority of teachers are Catholic	39	11	517.11	5.17
RE programmes present the teachings of the Church	90	45	1,387.11	11.00
Integration of Catholic teaching across the formal curriculum	61	15	1,170.47	8.86

Note: All of these differences were statistically significant at $p < .0006$.

176   Jim Gleeson, John O'Gorman, et al.

Table 8.3 School administrators' ratings of given characteristics as 'essential' by jurisdiction

Characteristic	% US (n = 457)	% Qld (n = 130)	χ^2	OR
Community of faith	91	87	1.92	1.51
Prayer in daily life of the school	94	88	6.11	2.14
Celebration of school liturgies*	93	73	39.72	4.91
Outreach and Christian service*	90	71	30.32	3.68
Display of Christian symbols	72	67	1.25	1.27
The principal is Catholic	84	82	0.45	1.15
Teachers of religion are Catholic*	89	22	240.46	28.69
Vast majority of students are Catholic	17	09	5.83	2.07
Vast majority of teachers are Catholic*	41	24	12.64	2.20
RE programmes present the teachings of the Church*	93	72	42.27	5.17
Integration of Catholic teaching across the formal curriculum*	70	34	56.22	4.53

* These differences were statistically significant at $p < .0006$.

(12.46), celebration of liturgies (11.00) and integration of Catholic teachings across the formal curriculum (8.68).

The proportions of religion teachers who rated the importance of each given characteristic as essential are presented in Table 8.5. Consistently higher proportions of US teachers of religion rated each of the given characteristics as essential. The ORs were particularly large in the following cases: teachers of religion are Catholic (32.11), celebration of school liturgies (15.67), RE

Table 8.4 Teachers' ratings of given characteristics as 'essential' by jurisdiction

Characteristic	% US (n = 2,895)	% Qld (n = 1,858)	χ^2	OR
Community of faith	93	43	1,454.57	17.01
Prayer in daily life of the school	92	59	730.12	7.99
Celebration of school liturgies	90	45	1,141.77	11.00
Outreach and Christian service	88	53	739.46	6.50
Display of Christian symbols	79	43	647.37	4.99
The principal is Catholic	77	51	349.67	3.22
Teachers of religion are Catholic	84	17	2,104.37	25.63
Vast majority of students are Catholic	14	06	75.11	2.55
Vast majority of teachers are Catholic	43	14	445.57	4.63
RE programmes present the teachings of the Church	92	48	1,161.01	12.46
Integration of Catholic teaching across the formal curriculum	64	17	1,017.21	8.68

Note: All of these differences were statistically significant at $p < .0006$.

The characteristics of Catholic schools   177

Table 8.5 Religion teachers' ratings for particular characteristics as 'essential' by jurisdiction

Characteristic	% US (n = 1,481)	% Qld (n = 1,448)	χ^2	OR
Community of faith	93	62	412.89	8.14
Prayer in daily life of the school	94	63	427.21	9.20
Celebration of school liturgies	94	50	814.36	15.67
Outreach and Christian service	89	52	489.56	7.47
Display of Christian symbols	84	45	484.01	6.42
The principal is Catholic	79	48	310.46	4.08
Teachers of religion are Catholic	85	15	1,422.10	32.11
Vast majority of students are Catholic	16	06	71.89	2.98
Vast majority of teachers are Catholic	48	14	401.36	5.67
RE programmes present the teachings of the Church	93	51	648.78	12.76
Integration of Catholic teaching across the formal curriculum	68	17	778.10	10.38

Note: All of these differences were statistically significant at $p < .0006$.

programmes present the teaching of the Church (12.76), integration of Catholic teachings across the formal curriculum (10.38), prayer in the daily life of the school (9.20) and community of faith (8.14). It should be noted that teachers of religion were more likely than other teachers to rate these characteristics as essential in both jurisdictions (Convey, 2012; Gleeson et al., 2018).

It is hardly surprising that, as may be seen from Table 8.6, similar inter-jurisdictional differences emerged when the ratings of primary/elementary and secondary teachers were compared.

Table 8.6 Comparison of US and Queensland Primary/Elementary and Secondary teachers on characteristics endorsed as essential for Catholic identity of a school

Primary teachers	% US (n = 2,049)	% Qld (n = 1,318)	χ^2	OR
Community of faith	93	64	455.32	7.53
Prayer in daily life of the school	94	67	431.78	7.85
Celebration of school liturgies	91	48	784.89	11.10
Outreach and Christian service	88	50	585.31	7.27
Display of Christian symbols	83	46	502.56	5.68
The principal is Catholic	77	48	283.78	3.5
Teachers of religion are Catholic	83	16	1,464.01	25.67
Vast majority of students are Catholic	16	06	80.46	3.10
Vast majority of teachers are Catholic	45	15	317.46	4.53
RE programmes present the teachings of the Church	92	52	710.78	10.58
Integration of Catholic teaching across the formal curriculum	64	18	684.26	8.13

(Continued)

178   Jim Gleeson, John O'Gorman, et al.

Table 8.6 Comparison of US and Queensland Primary/Elementary and Secondary teachers on characteristics endorsed as essential for Catholic identity of a school (*Continued*)

Secondary teachers	% US (n = 708)	% Qld (n = 969)	χ^2	OR
Community of faith	85	49	230.89	5.91
Prayer in daily life of the school	84	41	319.56	7.72
Celebration of school liturgies	82	33	400.46	9.41
Outreach and Christian service	82	54	141.56	3.87
Display of Christian symbols	62	29	178.26	3.94
The principal is Catholic	63	43	68.67	2.30
Teachers of religion are Catholic	76	14	660.67	19.89
Vast majority of students are Catholic	12	3	42.01	3.54
Vast majority of teachers are Catholic	22	6	93.10	4.36
RE programmes present the teachings of the Church	85	35	422.36	10.75
Integration of Catholic teaching across the formal curriculum	48	12	276.27	7.07

Note: All of these differences were statistically significant at $p < .0006$.

The OR values were particularly large for both primary/elementary and secondary respondents in the following cases: teachers of religion are Catholic (25.67 primary; 19.89 secondary), RE programmes present the teachings of the Church (10.58 primary; 19.89 secondary), celebration of liturgies (11.10 primary; 9.41 secondary), prayer in the daily life of the school (7.85 primary; 7.72 secondary), integration of Catholic teaching across

Table 8.7 Comparison of non-Catholic teachers in US and Queensland samples who endorsed given characteristics as essential

Characteristic	% US (n = 319)	% Qld (n = 335)	χ^2	OR
Community of faith	87	24	263.99	21.19
Prayer in daily life of the school	85	44	119.52	7.21
Celebration of school liturgies	79	27	178.00	10.17
Outreach and Christian service	82	48	83.03	4.94
Display of Christian symbols	57	24	74.88	4.20
The principal is Catholic	54	26	53.36	3.34
Teachers of religion are Catholic	64	06	243.92	27.85
Vast majority of students are Catholic	18	01	56.49	21.73
Vast majority of teachers are Catholic	10	01	26.92	11.00
RE programmes present the teachings of the Church	79	33	139.16	7.64
Integration of Catholic teaching across the formal curriculum	35	01	59.00	4.85

Note: All of these differences were statistically significant at $p < .0006$.

formal curriculum (8.13 primary; 7.07 secondary) and community of faith (7.53 primary; 5.91 secondary).

With 94% of US respondents and 85% of Queensland respondents identifying as Catholic, the comparative ratings for Catholic teachers corresponded closely with the overall ratings already reported in Table 8.2. The 'essential' ratings for teachers who did not identify as Catholic are reported in Table 8.7.

Five of the same characteristics that returned large inter-jurisdictional differences when the overall ratings were compared (Table 8.2) also produced large differences here: teachers of religion are Catholic (27.5), celebration of school liturgies (10.17), RE programmes present the teachings of the Church (7.64), prayer in the daily life of the school (7.21) and integration of Catholic teaching across formal curriculum (4.85). It is noteworthy that large differences also emerged in the case of three other characteristics: community of faith (21.19), vast majority of students are Catholic (21.73) and vast majority of teachers are Catholic (11.00).

Discussion

Compared with Queensland respondents, US teachers were consistently more likely to rate the given characteristics of Catholic schools as essential. The comparisons were statistically significant in almost all cases, and such differences are summarised below (Table 8.8) in terms of the OR index where the effect sizes for particular characteristics were especially large.

The first two characteristics in Table 8.8 are clearly concerned with transmission of the Catholic faith in classrooms with 'teachers of religion are Catholic' consistently emerging with very large OR values. There were also significant inter-jurisdictional differences with respect to the perceived

Table 8.8 US and Queensland ORs for ratings of given characteristics as "essential"

Characteristic	All	Admins	Teachers	Non-Catholics	RE teachers
Teachers of religion are Catholic	25.81	28.69	25.63	27.85	32.11
RE programmes present the teaching of the Church	11.00	5.17	4.63	7.64	12.76
Integration of Catholic teachings across the formal curriculum	8.86	4.53	8.68	4.85	10.38
Celebration of school liturgies	11.64	4.91	11.00	10.17	15.67
Community of faith	7.32	1.51	17.61	21.19	8.14
Prayer in daily life of the school	8.68	2.14	7.99	7.21	9.20
Christian service/outreach	6.18	3.68	6.50	4.94	7.47

importance of the celebration of school liturgies, school as a community of faith and the importance of prayer, as well as the curriculum integration of Catholic teachings (Gleeson & O'Neill, 2017) and Christian service/outreach.

Inter-jurisdictional differences between administrators' ratings were generally smaller than the differences for teachers. Both sets of administrators rated 'the principal is Catholic' item more highly than their teachers, while US administrators also gave higher ratings than their teachers to 'the religion teacher is Catholic' and to the integration of Catholic teaching (Convey, 2012). Queensland administrators rated all given characteristics more highly than their teachers, particularly 'community of faith' and 'prayer in the daily life of the school.' It is worth noting that length of service in Catholic education was positively associated with 'essential' ratings in both jurisdictions (Convey, 2012; Gleeson et al., 2018).

There are, as noted earlier, many similarities between these two education systems which are heavily influenced by globalisation and by neoliberal, market values. The proportion of Catholics in both countries is similar, and Catholic schools are enrolling greater numbers of students from diverse religious traditions and becoming increasingly elitist. Such similarities make it all the more difficult to come up with plausible explanations for the differences that have emerged, differences both in the case of Catholic and non-Catholic. Notwithstanding the limitations noted earlier, it is incumbent on the authors to suggest some possible explanations for these very large inter-jurisdictional differences. Two factors that may shed some light on this matter are now discussed – school funding policy differences and professional development structures.

Catholics, often immigrants from poor countries, were historically subservient to both countries. However, Catholic schools in Australia receive strong federal and state support, while Catholic schools in the United States do not, with the First Amendment of the Constitution stating that 'the government may neither establish an official state religion nor act to prohibit on the contrary practices thereof'. As Schuttloffel (2007) remarks '[US] Catholic education runs parallel to American public education and in tandem with the history of the American Catholic Church' (p. 85), while Earl (2007) observes that 'debates over "Church vs State" occupy much of the political realm, especially during campaigns for election and recent hearings of Supreme Court Justices' qualifications and ability to take the bench' (p. 39). In the context of this judicial policy, US Catholic schools 'fought for the right to exist and won some public support, and won under federal programming, but lost access to full or even partial tuition support, until recently when vouchers were made available [in some states] to private and Catholic school families' (Cattaro & Cooper, 2007, p. 63).

It seems reasonable to suggest that teachers who work in a self-funding system for significantly lower pay than their professional colleagues are likely to have a stronger sense of faith-based identity than teachers working in a system that has strong state support with teachers receiving the same levels of remuneration as their public sector colleagues. The teacher salary differential between US public and Catholic schools has been outlined earlier, and Convey (2014) found that slightly more than one-fifth of the teachers in his survey 'identified salary as a serious threat, with elementary school teachers indicating salary more frequently than high school teachers' (p. 14). He also notes however that religious factors play an important role in teachers' levels of job satisfaction insofar as

> … the school's environment and the teachers' love of teaching were high motivators for continuing to teach in a Catholic school for both Catholic and non-Catholic teachers. The results also show that teachers' comfort with their schools' academic philosophy and its environment contributes to their higher levels of job satisfaction. (p. 22)

Conscious that Convey's (2012) respondents represent a relatively small proportion of all teachers in US Catholic schools, the authors invited him to suggest some possible explanation for the emerging differences between the responses of Queensland and US teachers' ratings. Professor Convey responded as follows:

> For the past 25 years or so in the US, there has been a very heavy emphasis on the spiritual leadership of the principal and the development of the faith community in Catholic schools. The steep decline of teachers from religious congregations prompted this. The bishops have been strong in promoting this emphasis and so have the superintendents, so it is not surprising that the results overall were positive. (Personal communication, September 21, 2016)

It appears then that support structures for the spiritual and faith formation of teachers in Catholic schools provide a second possible explanation for the stark inter-jurisdictional differences reported above. The declining numbers of vowed religious in schools impacted significantly on the spiritual leadership of US Catholic schools (Earl, 2007) with concerns being expressed regarding teacher education opportunities because of the 'minimal encouragement to serve in Catholic schools by Catholic teacher preparation institutions … [while the] high tuition rates at Catholic colleges and universities preclude these students from taking a position in a Catholic school at a lower salary' (Schuttloffel, 2007, p. 90).

Krebbs (2000) recalls that the Catholic Archdiocese of New York established the Educational Community Opportunity for Stewardship initiative as early as 1972 'to prepare Catholic school educators in infusing Catholic values throughout the curriculum' (p. 309). The University Consortium for

Catholic Education (UCCE) and the Association for Catholic Leadership Programs (ACLP) have been

> ... major contributors to the renewal of Catholic education by providing a steady supply of valuable, well-prepared professionals to serve as teachers and administrators' .... [They] have positioned themselves to respond to the dramatic transition in the staffing of K–12 Catholic schools that has taken place over the last 50 years. (Smith & Nuzzi, 2007, pp. 103–104)

The ACLP, which now serves over 50 dioceses through more than 30 Catholic universities, was established as far back as 1983 to promote postgraduate programmes for Catholic school principals. ACLP provides

> ... free-standing graduate formation programs for experienced teachers interested in leadership that ... offer the requisite academic background for the principalship [and] replicate in some way the spiritual and religious formation that the previous generations of vowed and ordained men and women experienced within their respective communities. (Smith & Nuzzi, 2007, p. 110)

Notre Dame University recommitted itself in the early 1990s to 'the revitalization of America's Catholic schools through the Alliance for Catholic Education' (Smith & Nuzzi, 2007, p. 111) and this Alliance 'forged the path for the UCCE' (p. 112) which is 'taking seriously the mission to integrate what it means to be a Catholic educator into its pedagogical programs' (p. 117). The Alliance supports Catholic colleges and universities in the design and implementation of teacher formation programmes that are both professional and spiritual in nature and are aimed at 'energetic college graduates who are poised for vocation and ministry' (Smith & Nuzzi, 2007, p. 109). UCCE teachers live in faith communities where they are

> ... released from financial preoccupations that often burden lay teachers who must support a family [and] are able to offer monetary sacrifices with greater freedom .... [They] are often elevated by their youth, enthusiasm, and an initial otherness as strangers in a new community. (Smith & Nuzzi, 2007, p. 109)

From an Australian perspective, Croke (2007) highlights the importance of faith-based professional development while noting widespread concerns about the capacity of many young teachers and student teachers to contribute meaningfully to the goals of a Catholic school and concluding that 'ensuring quality of teachers, and eventually leaders, may well turn out to be the most difficult and threatening challenge to the future of Catholic schools in Australia' (p. 823).

Hansen (2001) argues that the Australian Church neglected the importance of the role of the lay Catholic school principal in a context where the Catholic school is the only experience of religiosity and Church for many young people (Engebretson, 2003; Rymarz & Graham, 2005). He remarks that, while the transition from religious to lay staffing and governance in Australian Catholic schools that began soon after the close of the Second Vatican Council was 'almost complete by 1985, 3 years before Rome formally acknowledged that it was occurring', diocesan literature continued to regard the role of the Catholic school principal as being 'pre-eminently the preserve of religious sisters, brothers, and priests' (Hansen, 2001, p. 37).

Dorman and D'Arbon's (2003) study of school leadership succession in Australia reported that the added challenges of leading a Catholic school community 'are a deterrent to persons applying to become principals' (p. 483). More recently, Belmonte and Cranston (2009) found that

> ... principals [of Australian Catholic schools] had had only a minor exposure to formal development programs, even though principals themselves viewed it as a priority for the promotion and maintenance of the Catholic identity in their schools. There is a major conflict in a system of schooling that exists to nurture the faith of young people, yet fails to realize and address the traditional spiritual capital of its leadership. (pp. 303–304)

Neidhart and Lamb (2016) remark that, due to the diminution of commitment to religious beliefs, Catholic schools are shifting their attention 'to faith leadership ... and there are new expectations being placed on the principal to preserve the Catholic identity and culture of the school and thus ensure the success of its evangelizing mission' (p. 59).

It would appear however that, operating in a less friendly environment, the US Church was quicker 'off the mark' than its Australian counterpart with respect to maintaining Catholic school identity.

Conclusion

Remarkably large differences have emerged between the two jurisdictions with respect to the people, cultural and curriculum characteristics of Catholic schools included in this study. It is important to acknowledge that neither sample is statistically representative and that the proportion of Queensland respondents was much greater than the case of the United States. And, of course, there is no guarantee that sentiments expressed in survey responses translate into behaviour in schools. That being said, these results are encouraging for Catholic authorities in the United States, while posing some challenging questions for Catholic school authorities in Queensland, particularly with respect to faith formation and development.

It seems reasonable to suggest that such differences are reflective of government policies on faith-based schooling as well as teachers' conditions of employment and approaches to professional development for school leaders and teachers in Catholic schools in each jurisdiction.

Looking ahead, school leadership succession is a growing problem in Catholic schools internationally. Drawing on data from 60 Catholic secondary head teachers in England and Wales, Grace (2002) expressed concern regarding the religious formation of principals, and notes that, while 'current principals drew on experiences gained from members of religious congregations ... the new generation of teachers and leaders have had no affiliation with living out the norms of religious orders' (p. 237). According to Smith and Nuzzi (2007), 'the most recent study of Catholic school leadership needs [in the US] found several alarming trends' (p. 118), with over half of new principals and 95% of those hired from the public school system lacking theological and spiritual formation. Meanwhile, the religious dimension of Catholic schools in Australia is being marginalised by the pressure for academic success (Flynn & Mok, 2002) and by media influences, people's disengagement from the Church (Rymarz & Graham, 2005) and the secular culture of Australian society (Croke, 2007; McLaughlin, 2000). The challenges for Catholic education leadership in both systems under consideration in this chapter are indeed considerable!

Notes

1. This paper was originally published in Journal of Catholic Education, 21(2), 76–106.
2. http://www.abs.gov.au/ausstats/abs@.nsf/mf/2024.0.
3. In 1965, there were 12,271 teaching brothers, while in 2005 there were 5,451, a 55% decline. An even more significant drop occurred for religious sisters with 179, 954 teaching sisters in 1965 dropping to 68,834 sisters in 2005 – a 62 % reduction (Cattaro & Cooper, 2007, p. 76).
4. http://www.ncea.org/NCEA/Proclaim/Catholic_School_Data/Schools _and_Tuition/NCEA/Proclaim/Catholic_School_Data/Schools_and_Tuition .aspx?hkey=e8a681a5-8d00-4d73-997b-4de7c6be68c1

References

Abbott, W. M. (Ed.). (1966). *The documents of Vatican II*. New York, NY: Guild Press.

Arthur, J. (2013). The de-Catholicising of the curriculum in English Catholic schools. *International Studies in Catholic Education, 5*(1), 83–98.

Australian Catholic Bishops Conference. (2013). *A profile of the Catholic community in Australia March 2013*. Melbourne: Australian Catholic Bishops Conference Pastoral Research Office, Australian Catholic University. Retrieved from www.catholic.org.au

Baker, D. P., & Riordan, C. (1998). The 'eliting' of the common American Catholic school and the national education crisis. *Phi Delta Kappan, 80*(1), 16–23.

Ball, S. J. (2012). *Global Education Inc.: New policy networks and the neo-liberal imaginary*. London: Routledge.

Belmonte, A., & Cranston, N. (2009). The religious dimension of lay leadership in Catholic schools: Preserving Catholic culture in an era of change. *Catholic Education: A Journal of Inquiry and Practice, 12*(3), 294–319.

Boeve, L. (2005). Religion after detraditionalization: Christian faith in a post-secular Europe. *Irish Theological Quarterly, 70*(2), 99–122.

Bryk, A. S. (1996). Lessons from Catholic high schools. In T. H. McLaughlin, J. O'Keefe, & B. O'Keeffe (Eds.), *The contemporary Catholic school: Context, identity and diversity* (pp. 25–41). London: Falmer Press.

Catholic Bishops of New South Wales (NSW) and the Australian Capital Territory (ACT). (2007). *Catholic schools at a crossroads: Pastoral letter.* Sydney: Author.

Cattaro, G. M., & Cooper, B. S. (2007). Developments in Catholic schools in the USA: Politics, policy and prophesy. In G. Grace & J. O'Keefe (Eds.), *International handbook of Catholic education: Challenges for school systems in the 21st century* (pp. 61–83). Dordrecht: Springer.

Chambers, M. (2012). Students who are not Catholics in Catholic schools: Lessons from the Second Vatican Council about the Catholicity of schools. *International Studies in Catholic Education, 4*(2), 186–199. doi: 10.1080/19422539.2012.708174.

Coleman, J. S., Hoffer, T., & Kilgore, S. (1982). *High school achievement: Public, Catholic, & private schools compared.* New York: Basic Books.

Congregation for Catholic Education (CCE). (1977). The Catholic school. Retrieved from http://www.vatican.va/roman_curia/congregations/ccatheduc/documents/rc_con_ccatheduc_doc_19770319_catholic-school_en.html

Congregation for Catholic Education (CCE). (1997). *The Catholic school on the threshold of the third millennium.* London: Catholic Truth Society.

Congregation for Catholic Education (CCE). (2013). *Educating to intercultural dialogue in Catholic schools: Living in harmony for a civilization of love.* London: Catholic Truth Society.

Congregation for Catholic Education (CCE). (2014). *Educating today and tomorrow: A renewing passion – Instrumentum laboris.* London: Catholic Truth Society.

Convey, J. J. (2012). Perceptions of Catholic identity: Views of Catholic school administrators and teachers. *Catholic Education: A Journal of Inquiry and Practice, 16*(1), 187–214.

Convey, J. J. (2014). Motivation and job satisfaction of Catholic school teachers. *Journal of Catholic Education, 1*(1). Retrieved from http://dx.doi.org/10.15365/joce.1801022014

Croke, B. (2007). Australian Catholic schools in a changing political and religious landscape. In G. Grace & J. O'Keefe (Eds.), *International handbook of Catholic education: Challenges for school systems in the 21st century* (pp. 811–834). Dordrecht: Springer.

Davis, R. A., & Franchi, L. (2013). A Catholic curriculum for the twenty-first century? *International Studies in Catholic Education, 5*(1), 36–52.

Dorman, J. P., & D'Arbon, T. (2003). Assessing impediments to leadership succession in Australian Catholic schools. *School Leadership & Management, 23*(1), 25–40. doi: 10.1080/1363243032000080014.

Dowling, A., Beavis, A., Underwood, C., Sadeghi, R., & O'Malley, K. (2009). *Who's coming to school today? Final report.* Brisbane: ACER, Brisbane Catholic Education.

Earl, P. H. (2007). Catholic schooling in the USA: Problem and response. In G. Grace & J. O'Keefe (Eds.), *International handbook of Catholic education: Challenges for school systems in the 21st century* (pp. 37–60). Dordrecht: Springer.

Engebretson, K. (2003). Young people, culture and spirituality: Some implications for ministry. *Religious Education, 98*(1), 5–24.

Flynn, M. (1993). *The culture of Catholic schools: A study of Catholic schools: 1972–1993.* Homebush: St Pauls.

Flynn, M., & Mok, M. M. C. (2002). *Catholic schools 2000: A longitudinal study of Year 12 students in Catholic schools, 1972–1982–1990–1998*. Sydney: Catholic Education Commission.

Francis. (2015). *Laudato 'Si. On care for our common home*. Strathfield: St. Pauls.

Francis, L. J., & Egan, J. (1990). The Catholic schools as 'faith community': An empirical inquiry. *Religious Education, 85*(4), 588–603.

Gleeson, J. (2015). Critical challenges and dilemmas for Catholic education leadership internationally. *International Studies in Catholic Education, 7*(2), 145–161.

Gleeson, J., O'Gorman, J., & O'Neill, M. (2018). The identity of Catholic schools as seen by teachers in Catholic schools in Queensland. *International Studies in Catholic Education, 10*(1).

Gleeson, J., & O'Neill, M. (2017). Curriculum, culture, and Catholic education: A Queensland perspective. *Curriculum Perspectives, 37*(2), 121–133.

Grace, G. (2002) *Catholic schools: Mission, markets and morality*. London: Routledge, Falmer.

Grace, G. (2010). Renewing spiritual capital: An urgent priority for the future of Catholic education internationally. *International Studies in Catholic Education, 2*(2), 117–128.

Grace, G. (2013). Catholic social teaching should permeate the Catholic secondary school curriculum: An agenda for reform. *International Studies in Catholic Education, 5*(1), 99–109.

Groome, T. H. (1996). What makes a school Catholic? In T. H. McLaughlin, J. O'Keefe, & B. O'Keeffe (Eds.), *The contemporary Catholic school: Context, identity and diversity* (pp. 107–125). London: Falmer.

Hansen, P. J. (2001). Catholic school lay principalship: The neglected ministry in Church documents on Catholic education: An Australian perspective. *Journal of Catholic Education, 5*(1), 28–38.

Institute for Catholic Education. (1996). *Curriculum matters: A resource for Catholic educators*. Toronto: Author.

Krebbs, M. J. (2000). Values infusion: A systematic response to Catholic identity. *Journal of Catholic Education, 3*(3), 306–314.

Lane, D. A. (1991). *Catholic education and the school: Some theological reflections*. Dublin: Veritas.

Lane, D. A. (2015). *Catholic education in the light of Laudato'Si*. Dublin: Veritas.

Lawton, D. (1975). *Class, culture and the curriculum*. London: Routledge and Kegan Paul.

Lingard, B. (2010). Policy borrowing, policy learning: Testing times in Australian schooling. *Critical Studies in Education, 51*(2), 129–147. doi: 10.1080/17508481003731026.

Maddox, M. (2014). *Taking god to school: The end of Australia's egalitarian education?* Sydney: Allen and Unwin.

McLaughlin, D. (2000). *The Catholic school: Paradoxes and challenges*. Strathfield: St Pauls.

McLaughlin, D., & Standen, P. (2013, August 12). *The rise and demise of Australian Catholic education?* Unpublished paper read at Australian Catholic School Leadership Conference, Sydney.

McLellan, J. (2000). Rise, fall, and reasons why: U.S. Catholic elementary education, 1940–1995. In J. E. Youniss & J. J. Convey (Eds.), *Catholic schools at the crossroads: Survival and transformation* (pp. 17–32). New York: Teachers College Press.

Miserandino, A. (2019). The funding and future of Catholic education in the United States. *British Journal of Religious Education, 41*(1), 105–114. doi:10.1080/01416200.2017.1352484.

Murray, D. (1991). *A special concern*. Dublin: Veritas.

NCEA. (2017). *United States Catholic elementary and secondary schools 2016–2017: The annual statistical report on schools, enrolment, and staffing*. Arlington, Virginia: Author.

Neidhart, H., & Lamb, J. T. (2016). Australian Catholic schools today: School identity and leadership formation. *Journal of Catholic Education, 19*(3), 49–65. doi: 10.15365/joce.1903042016.

Newman, A. (2005, February 10). Diocese to close 22 schools in Brooklyn and Queens. *New York Times*, A23.

O'Donoghue, T. A., & Burley, S. (2008). God's antipodean teaching force: An historical exposition on Catholic teaching religious in Australia. *Teaching and Teacher Education, 24*, 180–189.

O'Keefe, J., & Scheopner, A. (2000). No margin, no mission: Challenges for Catholic urban schools in the USA. In G. Grace & J. O'Keefe (Eds.), *International handbook of Catholic education: Challenges for school systems in the 21st century* (pp. 15–35). Dordrecht: Springer.

Pascoe, S. (2007). Challenges for Catholic education in Australia. In G. Grace & J. O'Keefe (Eds.), *International handbook of Catholic education: Challenges for school systems in the 21st century.* (pp. 787–810).

Pollefeyt, D., & Bouwens, J. (2010). Framing the identity of Catholic schools: Empirical methodology for quantitative research on the Catholic identity of an education institute. *International Studies in Catholic Education, 2*(2), 193–211.

Provasnik, S., & Dorfman, S. (2005). *Mobility in the teacher workforce: Findings from the condition of education.* Washington, DC: National Center for Education Statistics, U.S. Department of Education Institute of Education Sciences.

Przygocki, W. F. (2004). Teacher retention in Catholic schools. *Journal of Catholic Education, 7*(4). Retrieved from http://digitalcommons.lmu.edu/ce/vol7/iss4/8

QCEC. (2013). *Queensland Catholic schools 2012.* Brisbane: Author.

Rossiter, G. (2013). Perspective on the use of the construct 'Catholic identity' for Australian Catholic schooling: Part 1: The sociological background and the literature. *Journal of Religious Education, 61*(2), 1–12.

Rymarz, R., & Graham, J. (2005). Going to church: Attitudes to church attendance amongst Australian core Catholic youth. *Journal of Beliefs and Values, 26*(1), 55–64.

Scanlan, M. (2011). How principals cultivate a culture of critical spirituality. *International Journal of Leadership in Education: Theory and Practice, 14*(3), 293–315. doi: 10.1080/13603124.2011.560283.

Schaub, M. (2000). A faculty at a crossroads: A profile of American Catholic school teachers. In *Catholic schools at the crossroads: Survival and transformation* (pp. 72–86). New York, NY: Teachers College Press.

Schuttloffel, M. J. (2007). Contemporary challenges to the recruitment, formation, and retention of Catholic school leadership in the USA. In G. Grace & J. O'Keefe (Eds.), *International handbook of Catholic education: Challenges for school systems in the 21st century* (pp. 85–102). Dordrecht: Springer.

Shaffer, J. P. (1995). Multiple hypothesis testing. *Annual Review of Psychology, 46*, 561–584.

Smith, P. A., & Nuzzi, R. J. (2007). Beyond religious congregations: Responding to new challenges in Catholic education. In G. Grace, J. O'Keefe & B. O'Keefe (Eds.), *International handbook of Catholic education: Challenges for school systems in the 21st century* (pp. 103–124). Dordrecht: Springer.

Trant, A. (2007). *Curriculum matters in Ireland.* Dublin: Blackhall Press.

Treston, K. (2001). *Emergence for life, not fall from grace.* Brisbane: Morning Star Publishing.

Wilkinson, P. (2013). Latest Australian mass participation stats. Retrieved from http://www.catholica.com.au/gc4/pw/005_pw_print.php

Youniss, J. (2000). Introduction. In J. Youniss & J. Convey (Eds.), *Catholic schools at the crossroads: Survival and transformation* (pp. 1–12). New York: Teachers College Press.

Chapter 9

Longitudinal study of the attitudes of pre-service teachers at an Australian Catholic University to key aspects of faith-based education: Some conundrums to ponder

Jim Gleeson and Maureen O'Neill

Introduction

Faith-based schooling in Australia, as elsewhere, is increasingly challenged by accelerating rates of secularisation (Boeve, 2005) and market-driven educational ideologies (Ball, 1994, 2012; Gleeson, 2015; Lingard, 2010). Meanwhile, in conjunction with these developments, the profile of teachers and students in Catholic schools is changing rapidly (Dowling, Beavis, Underwood, Sadeghi, & O'Malley, 2009). The student teachers of today are tomorrow's teachers and the authors felt it was important to conduct a longitudinal study of the opinions, beliefs and attitudes of pre-service teachers at one of the main provider universities for teachers in the Australian Catholic Education system. The study set out was to track pre-service teachers' beliefs regarding the aims of education, approaches to teaching and learning, the purposes of schooling and the identifying characteristics of Catholic schools.

Survey data were collected from 168 first-year students in 2014 and these findings have already been published (Gleeson & O'Neill, 2017). When the authors administered the same survey[1] (see Appendix 4) to fourth-year pre-service teachers in 2017, towards the end of their programme, 103 responses were received. This chapter is based on data from the 60 students who responded on both occasions.

The chapter begins by locating Catholic Education in the broader contexts of education in modern-day Australia and the culture of Australian youth. The methodology and findings of the longitudinal study are then outlined and the implications for Catholic Education are considered.

Current trends in Australian education

The National Framework for Values Education in Australian Schools (Department of Education, Science and Training, 2005) represents an important reference point for Australian schools. This Framework advocates explicit teaching about, through, and for values education using enquiry-based learning. Given the influence of the Judeo-Christian tradition on Australian culture and values, it is hardly surprising to find Christian values reflected in the Framework: care and compassion; pursuit and protection of the common good in a just society; honesty, sincerity and truth; moral integrity; respect for others; accountability for one's actions and tolerance and inclusion in a democratic society.

The prioritisation and realisation of these values are however increasingly difficult in an environment where market ideology is portrayed 'as a natural way of doing things' (Gandin, 2006, p. 192), one where social and education policy decisions are increasingly defined by powerful intergovernmental organisations such as the Organization for Economic Cooperation and Development (OECD), the World Bank and the International Monetary Fund (Ball, 2008; Ditchburn, 2012; Spring, 2009). This is an environment where education policy is increasingly concerned with performativity and league tables in the interests of economic growth, where the focus is on consumer choice, 'deliverable' products, measurable outputs, employment-related skills and competences and standardised testing. It is an environment where the OECD's Programme for International Student Assessment (PISA) exerts disproportionate influence on education policy (Lingard, 2010; Polesel, Rice, & Dulfer, 2014), one where the proliferation of standardised testing programmes such as Australia's National Assessment Plan – Literacy and Numeracy (NAPLAN) have resulted in tensions between educational quality and [e]quality, education as public good and competitive private commodity and 'having an education' and 'being an educated person'.

The underlying principles of the 2008 Melbourne Declaration on Educational Goals for Young Australians included equity, excellence, successful learners, confident and creative individuals and active and informed citizens. However, some of these principles, for example equity and excellence, quality and (e)quality, are notoriously difficult to reconcile and the associated quest for balance continues to be a major issue of concern at all levels of education (Ball, 1994; Brown & Lauder, 1996; Cuban, 1988; Van den Branden, Van Avermaet, & Van Houtte, 2010).

Various commentators including the independent reviewers of the Australian Curriculum (Australian Government, 2014) and Lingard and McGregor (2014) see the Melbourne Declaration as the foundational document for the national curriculum. The independent reviewers concluded however that the Australian Curriculum fails to reflect the Declaration's emphasis on 'moral and spiritual values' (Australian Government, 2014, p. 237). Meanwhile, Lingard (2010) sees the primary purpose of the national curriculum in terms of a nation-building exercise involving the alignment of curriculum with global economic imperatives:

> ... the global policy convergence in schooling has seen the economization of schooling policy, the emergence of human capital and productivity rationales as meta-policy in education, and new accountabilities,

including high-stakes testing and policy, as numbers, with both global and national features. (p. 136)

As former Australian Prime Minister Gillard stated,

Put simply, we cannot have the strong economy we want tomorrow, unless we have the best of education in our schools today. That is why the plan that I am announcing today is a plan for our schools to be in the world's top five by 2025. (*The Australian*, 14 April 2013)

The independent reviewers (Australian Government, 2014) suggest that the purpose of the Australian Curriculum is to

... make the Australian economy more efficient and productive by teaching work-related skills and competencies. So-called 21st century capabilities and skills are especially important, according to this argument, as the future is impossible to predict. (p. 28)

The reviewers are particularly critical of the failure of the Australian Curriculum, Assessment and Reporting Authority (ACARA, 2012) to provide 'an educational foundation for the curriculum' (Australian Government, 2014, p. 111) and they argue that the purpose of education should, 'by its very nature, deal with the transcendent, including morality and spirituality' (p. 155). It is becoming clear that Australia has seen a shift in the perceived purposes of education in recent years, as reflected in the 'privileging of ... the private purposes of schooling like social mobility at the expense of the public purposes of schooling ... [including] democratic equality, citizenship, equity and social justice' (Cranston, Kimber, Mulford, Reid, & Keating, 2010, p. 183). Having considered the dominant influences on the Australian education system, it is important to locate the study participants in the broad context of youth culture in Australia.

Religious affiliation, religiosity and culture of young Australians

The Gallup World Poll on the Religiosity of Nations places Australia at 143rd of 154 nations on religiosity (Diener, Tay, & Myers, 2011) with just one-third of the population seeing themselves as religious. According to the 2011 Australian census of population, 25% of the Australian population are Catholic with 22% falling into the 'no religion' category. Noting that the percentage of Catholics attending Mass in Australia 'has been falling more or less steadily since it peaked in the mid-1950s', the Australian Catholic Bishops Conference (2013) reported that 'the total number of people at Mass in Australia on a typical weekend [in 2011] was only about one-eighth of the total number of Catholics' (p. 2), while Wilkinson (2013) estimates that proportion to be 10.6%.

Australia has a tripartite education system with a very heavy emphasis on school choice. Catholic schools fall between Independent and state schools in terms of cost and prestige. While 22% of Australian secondary school pupils are educated in Catholic schools, some 30% of Catholic school students are not Catholic. Meanwhile, some 60% of students in Catholic schools come from middle and upper middle class backgrounds, while only one-third of Catholics from disadvantaged backgrounds attend Catholic schools (McLaughlin & Standen, 2013).

'Believing without belonging' (Inglis, 2007; Voas & Crockett, 2005) has become the catchphrase of much European research on religion. Mason, Singleton, and Webber (2007, p. 94) found that Australian young people (Generation Y) had rather low levels of interest in and involvement with religion or spirituality with only 'one-quarter of [13–24 year olds] consider[ing] religious faith important or very important in shaping the way they live their daily lives', while 14% rated it as being of some importance. Mason et al. (2007) also reported that only 13% of Australian young people believe that only one religion is true. Drawing on data from some 10,000 Dutch secondary school students, Dijkstra and Veenstra (2001) came up with broadly similar conclusions. They reported that scores for the importance of religion in students' lives across public, Catholic, Protestant and other religious schools were 'very similar on the whole' (Dijkstra & Veenstra, 2001, p. 197) with 'the lowest scores for the public sector and increasing from the Catholic to the Protestant schools to the Orthodox-Protestant denomination' (Dijkstra & Veenstra, 2001, p. 195).

Hughes (2007) suggest that Australian young people are influenced by existential experiences and feelings rather than *a priori* arguments with the result that they eschew universal judgements about moral values, while Mason et al. (2007, p. 324) reported a 'strong and widespread consensus' regarding the subjective and individualistic nature of values and morals.

Catholic school identity

The Congregation for Catholic Education (CCE, 2014, p. 13) highlights the evangelical function of Catholic schools in an environment where 'the population of Catholic schools is characterized by a multiplicity of cultures and beliefs, religious formation in schools must be based on the awareness of the existing pluralism and constantly be able to be meaningful in contemporary society'. The Congregation defines its educational project as a 'synthesis between culture and faith' (CCE, 1997, para 14), one where 'faith, culture and life are brought into harmony' (CCE, 1997, para 11). Coming out of that tradition Grace (2002, p. 7) reminds us that 'Catholic schools in England, USA and Australia were, in their origins, constructed and constituted as citadels and fortresses for the preservation of faith in a hostile external environment'. As Groome (2003, p. 122) puts it, the Catholic school educates 'the very 'being' of its students to inform, form, and transform their identity and agency [to become] just and compassionate disciples of Jesus [who are] personally influenced and enriched by Catholic faith'.

Secularisation however is challenging the faith-based identities of Catholic parents and students and posing serious questions for Catholic school identity (Pollefeyt & Bouwens, 2010). As Rymarz (2011) puts it,

> ... the days of uncritical, almost passive, enculturation appear to be over. For Catholic schools, strong identity is not an option as much as a necessity in a culture where options abound... Catholic schools face the challenge of having to articulate a message and a rationale to a more demanding and discerning audience. (pp. 7–8)

The first-year pre-service teachers surveyed for this longitudinal study in 2017, regardless of their religious affiliation, religiosity or type of secondary school attended, gave 'safe and caring environment' as the most influential reason for their choice of secondary school and chose 'caring community' as the most important characteristic of the Catholic school. Meanwhile, faith-based reasons for school choice and for school purposes received particularly low ratings.

The Western Australia teachers in Byrne's (2005, p. 150) study identified a 'gap between the reality and rhetoric of Catholic schooling', while Belmonte and Cranston (2009) noted that Catholic schools in Australia are being increasingly challenged to

> ... maintain their overall character and ethos in a changing religious and social reality [and to] prove their validity as viable educational institutions, as well as satisfy the requirements of the Church, while simultaneously responding to government accountability and Church expectations. Their identity as Catholic schools is fundamental to their existence, and, when they cease to be Catholic ... they cease to exist. (p. 296)

Muller and Associates (2008) found that parents are 'more likely to put the right balance between academic achievement and personal development at the top of the list' when choosing a secondary school for their child and that 'the school's religious or cultural affiliation are second-order factors ... followed by the feel or atmosphere of the school' (p. 5). Along similar lines Dowling et al. (2009) concluded from their Brisbane-based study that the parents 'have a pragmatic view of Catholic Education and are most concerned about quality instruction and training for employment' (p. 114).

Chambers (2012) draws attention to increasing enrolments in Catholic schools of non-Catholic students and suggests that this 'brings into question traditional assumptions about the clientele of Catholic schools, the religious activity in Catholic schools and the ecclesial nature of Catholic schools' (p. 186). Croke (2007) too expresses concern regarding the 'authenticity' of the modern Catholic school insofar as it 'has an annually increasing proportion of non-Catholic students, along with students from mainly middle class Catholic families whose adhesion to their Faith is weak' (p. 823).

Croke (2007) also notes the widespread concerns about the capacity of many young teachers and student teachers to contribute meaningfully to the goals of a Catholic school in an increasingly secularised Australia and he concludes that 'ensuring quality of teachers, and eventually leaders, may well turn out to be the most difficult and threatening challenge to the future of Catholic schools in Australia' (p. 823).

Against that background the authors sought the views of first- and fourth-year pre-service teachers regarding the aims of education, approaches to teaching and learning, school purposes and the characteristics of faith-based Catholic Education.

Research methods

The overall aim of this longitudinal study is to establish and track the opinions, beliefs and attitudes of pre-service teachers at a Catholic university with regard to the aims of education, approaches to teaching and learning, the purpose of schools and their perceptions of the characteristics of Catholic schools.

Since access to students was limited, it was decided to adopt a mixed methods approach. The first stage involved the design of a survey that included closed and open questions. Pre-service teachers were requested to complete the survey during the first term of their first year and again during the final term of their fourth year, with slight amendments to the Year 4 version of the survey where appropriate. This survey was informed by discussions with teachers in Catholic schools in Queensland. Twelve of the 15 named characteristics of Catholic schools used in the survey (Appendix 4, Question 15) had been used by Convey (2012) in his research with teachers in Catholic schools in the United States. The Cronbach's α value for the 15 given characteristics is .71.

The survey took students approximately 20 minutes to complete and it included items regarding reasons for students' choice of secondary school, the type of school they would like to teach in and their opinions regarding the aims of education, teaching and learning and the characteristics of Catholic schools. As previously mentioned, Catholic schools had originally been established by religious orders and Catholic diocesan authorities for faith-based reasons. The authors felt it was important to include an item regarding school purposes. However, they thought it was more appropriate to ask this diverse range of students, of whom less than 50% were Catholic, about the purpose of schools in general rather than Catholic schools in particular and to use the independent variables of religion and school attended in order to differentiate students' responses. Participating students were invited to volunteer for follow-up interviews in order to illuminate and explicate trends and themes emerging from the survey. However, no responses were received to this invitation.

In conjunction with the survey of their attitudes and opinions, pre-service teachers also took the Defining Issues Test (DIT2) of moral reasoning in Years 1 and 4. The DIT2 (Bebeau & Thoma, 2003) is an internationally validated paper-based test of levels of moral reasoning that was developed by James Rest (Rest, Narvaez, Bebeau, & Thoma, 1999) at the University of Minnesota drawing on the pioneering work of Lawrence Kohlberg. Participants are asked to rank and rate the importance of each of 12 statements of associated issues when deciding on the appropriate course of action in response to five hypothetical moral dilemmas. Weighted points are allocated to the four most important issues identified by the respondent with respect to each scenario.

Factor analysis of a mega-sample of over 44,000 subjects (Rest, Thoma, & Edwards, 1997) indicated that DIT items cluster around three general moral schemas: Personal Interest, Maintaining Norms and Post-conventional. The Maintaining Norms and Post-Conventional schemata are more advanced in attaining a socio-centric perspective than the egocentric perspective of the Personal Interest schema. The Maintaining Norms schema means that moral decisions are primarily influenced by adhering to the established social order and maintaining the status quo. Those who fit the Post-Conventional schema arrive at moral decisions on the basis of shared ideals that are fully reciprocal and open to scrutiny (Rest, Thoma, & Bebeau, 1999a, 1999b) and they are prepared to question and suggest changes to the status quo (Narvaez & Bock, 2002).

The points corresponding to Post-Conventional moral reasoning – Stages 5 and 6 – are used to construct a single measure known as the individual 'P' score (standing for 'principled moral thinking') (Rest, 1994). P score is regarded as a direct indicator of the development of moral reasoning from adolescence to adulthood (Thoma, 2002). The N2 score represents a modified version of the P score adjusted by the degree to which an individual respondent discriminates clearly between lower and higher staged DIT items (Bebeau & Thoma, 2003).

The DIT2 was administered to first-year students in lecture settings and approximately 50% of these responses had to be purged because they failed internal reliability checks. This high rate of invalid responses may be due to factors such as: (a) random box ticking, (b) incomplete responses, (c) choice of meaningless or nonsense items which are deliberately included on the DIT and (d) failure to discriminate by giving same rating to all items. The DIT2 was administered electronically to fourth-year students in 2017. The number of individuals who submitted valid responses in *both* years was 33 (28 of whom were female).

The study received ethical approval from the host institution and respondents were assured of confidentiality and anonymity. Survey data were analysed using SPSS and the longitudinal comparisons used paired samples *t* tests for analysis purposes.

Profiles of longitudinal subjects

Australian Catholic University (ACU), a state-funded university, is one of two Catholic universities in Australia. Entry to pre-service teacher education programmes is open to all eligible applicants regardless of religious affiliation. In order to be eligible to teach in Catholic or Independent schools students must take two Religious Education (RE) units and two Theology units as well as 36 mandatory units. These RE units were taken by almost 90% of the study cohort and employers know from a student's transcript whether he/she has taken them. Five of the eight students who did not take them selected the 'No Religion' option for Question 6 in the survey (Appendix 4).

Religious Education programme learning outcomes that are of relevance to the faith-based identity of Catholic schools include

- the analysis and application of Catholic social teaching and moral/values education to the primary classroom religion programme and
- the exploration of the Catholic school identity in light of relevant Vatican documents and the nature of its relationship with the wider Church.

Meanwhile the ACU graduate attributes include the ability to: demonstrate respect for the dignity of each individual and for human diversity and recognise their responsibility to the common good, the environment and society.

Over two-thirds (68%) of the 195 first-year pre-service teachers completed the survey in 2014 (Gleeson & O'Neill, 2017). While some 95 fourth-year students took the survey in 2017, only 60 of these had also responded in 2014 – others had either been absent on the day the survey was administered or had come from a different year cohort. This chapter compares the responses of the 60 participants who took the survey as first years and again as fourth years.

The vast majority of the students who make up this longitudinal study cohort were female. When the survey was administered in 2014, more than a third (37%) of the respondents were under 18 years of age, with 47% being aged 18–21 and the remainder being above 21. Almost 70% had entered university by the OP route[2] with the remainder qualifying on the basis of rank entry scores or mature age regulations. Two-thirds were taking the Early Childhood/Primary BEd with the remainder taking the Primary BEd. Since the curricula for both programmes are very similar and the student responses from both groups were very similar in 2014, the authors decided to ignore this variable in their analysis.

Religious affiliation and reasons for choice of secondary school

Two-thirds of the longitudinal cohort gave their religion as Catholic with 15% belonging to 'Other Christian' denominations and 18% identifying as atheist or having no religion. Seventy-two per cent had attended Catholic schools and 26% had attended state schools with the remainder attending Independent schools. Students were asked to rank their reasons for choice of secondary school in order of importance from a given list of possible reasons (Appendix 4, Question 10). Their chosen reasons were given weighted scores (3 for first, 2 for second, 1 for third) and mean scores were calculated for each reason as set out in Figure 9.1.

The two most influential factors in school choice were 'safe and caring environment' and 'convenient location', while the mean score for choice of school on 'religious grounds' was relatively low. The means for Catholic respondents were very similar to the overall means although they were less concerned about academic reputation ($\mu = .57$), while Catholic school attendees were somewhat less concerned about convenience of location ($\mu = 1.02$).

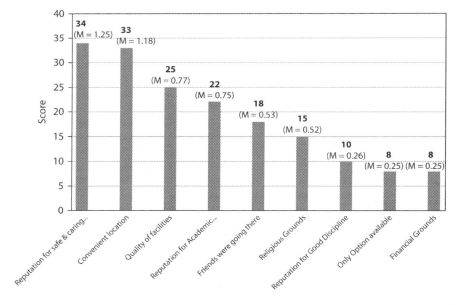

Figure 9.1 Reasons for choice of secondary school (N = 60)

Table 9.1 Type of school that respondents would like to teach in after graduation (*N* = 60)

Type of school	2014 (%) preference	2017 (%) preference
Catholic	70	55
State	10	25
Independent/other	20	20

Preferred workplace

Students were also asked to indicate the type of school they would ideally like to teach in after graduation (Table 9.1). While the proportion of students wishing to teach in the Independent sector was unchanged, the proportion opting for Catholic schools decreased. All final year students wishing to teach in Catholic schools were both female and Catholic with two-thirds of them regarding religion as either 'very important' or 'important' to how they live their lives. The nine students who changed their preference from Catholic schools (2014) to state schools (2017) were non-Catholic and saw religion as somewhat important to how they live their lives. In responding to an open-ended follow-up question, many students recalled their positive experiences of Catholic Education, for example

> I love Catholic schools, spirit and faith. They teach and guide students to be good citizens.

> I went to Catholic schools for all my schooling life and want to follow that on and teach students about God, their faith and, with the support of the Catholic values, create active and informed citizens in society and in their personal identities.

> Because I wish to teach Religion and continue to learn about my faith.

> I would love to pass on my beliefs as part of a community that shares my religious identity.

> I believe in the holistic way of teaching and learning.

Almost half the study cohort would prefer to work in either the Independent or state school sectors for reasons such as:

> I attended a state school throughout my education.

> I've always wanted to work in state schools.

> I've had placement at Catholic schools but still prefer State schools.

> I love the State system and believe it needs great teachers.

Some respondents felt they were ineligible to teach in Catholic school while others had principled reasons for not wanting to work in the Catholic sector:

> I wish to show students there are many different religions …. I don't agree with only ONE religion, therefore I can't teach only one.

> I prefer state schools due to my religious preferences.

> I personally don't practise any one religion and feel it would be hypocritical of me to 'pretend' in a Catholic school.

Five respondents were open to teaching in any sector, for example 'I just want to make an impact in any school I go to'.

Religiosity

Students were asked to rate the importance of their religion to how they live their lives (Appendix 4, Question 7).

The proportion of respondents for whom religion is important or very important doubled over the duration of the programme with resulting decreases in the proportions that saw religion as unimportant/not applicable. When levels of importance were 'collapsed' into three categories – high (3 points), medium, (2 points) and low (1 point) – the overall religiosity mean for first-year students was 1.77 while the fourth-year mean was 2.05 and these differences were statistically significant ($p = .03$). It is clear from the below Table 9.2 that similar patterns emerged in the case of Catholic students and in the case of students who had attended Catholic secondary schools. Although these students would appear to value religion more highly than Generation Y (Mason et al., 2007) subjects, it should also be noted that two-thirds of fourth-year respondents regard religion as being either 'somewhat important', unimportant or irrelevant to how they live their lives.

Table 9.2 Importance of religion to how students live their lives

Level of importance	All respondents (N = 60)		Catholics (n = 40)		Catholic school attendees (n = 43)	
	2014 (%)	2017 (%)	2014 (%)	2017 (%)	2014 (%)	2017 (%)
Very important	03	12	03	15	05	09
Important	13	22	15	28	16	26
Somewhat important	43	38	58	38	49	39
Unimportant	15	13	18	08	.16	14
Very unimportant	10	07	03	08	07	07
Not applicable	15	08	03	05	07	05

Longitudinal study and pre-service teachers 199

Table 9.3 Catholic students' knowledge of Catholic Teaching ($n = 40$)

Teaching	2014 (%)			2017 (%)		
	Good	Fair	Poor	Good	Fair	Poor
Catholic teaching	80	17.5	2.5	70	30	-
Catholic social teaching	57.5	40	2.5	67.5	27.5	5
Catholic moral teaching	72.5	25	2.5	65	35	-
Scripture	20	55	25	17.5	65	17.5

Heinz, Davison, and Keane (2018) recently studied the attitudes of Irish applicants for entry to teacher education programmes towards teaching religion. They concluded that 'a significant proportion … rarely or never attend religious services and/or practice their religion (32–35%). Indeed, just 58% of our respondents considered themselves "a religious person"' (p. 242).

Knowledge of Catholic teaching

Catholic respondents were asked to rate their knowledge of Catholic teaching (general), Catholic social teaching, Catholic moral teaching and Sacred Scripture on a 5-point scale (Appendix 4, Question 8). These ratings were collapsed into three categories (good, fair, poor) for purposes of comparing the responses of first- and fourth-year students (Table 9.3).

The proportions of Catholic respondents who rated their knowledge of Catholic teaching as good/very good are remarkably high. Some interesting trends to emerge from the above data include the following:

- Students rated their general knowledge of 'Catholic teaching' more highly than their knowledge of its more specific categories.
- With the exception of Catholic social teaching, students' self-reported knowledge levels were somewhat lower in fourth year than in first year.
- The proportion of students who regarded their knowledge of Scripture as good was considerably less than in other areas.

Summary profile of longitudinal study participants

The participants, who were mainly female, represented a wide spread of ages and academic achievement. More than two-thirds of them had attended Catholic schools and over 50% intended to work in Catholic schools after graduation. The most influential factors in their choice of secondary school were 'safe and caring environment' and 'convenient location' rather than 'religious grounds'. Mean ratings for religiosity were higher in the case of fourth years and these differences were statistically significant. Catholic students' self-ratings of their knowledge of Catholic teaching were high, particularly in fourth year (with the exception of Scripture). While these increases in religiosity and knowledge are noteworthy, it should also be recognised that they are based on self-ratings and that two-thirds of final year students regard religion as 'somewhat important', unimportant or irrelevant to how they live their lives.

Findings

The focus in this section is on comparing the responses of our longitudinal study cohort of 60 pre-service teachers to the same survey questions at the beginning and end of their teacher education programme. These comparisons are reported under the following headings: perceived purposes of schools; levels of moral reasoning; aims of education and beliefs regarding teaching and learning; characteristics of Catholic schools.

Purpose of schools

Respondents were invited to rank five given purposes of school in order of importance (Appendix 4, Question 11). Weighted pre- and post-mean scores were calculated on the basis of 3 points for their first purpose chosen, 2 points for the second purpose chosen and 1 point for the third choice purpose. The results are outlined in Figure 9.2.

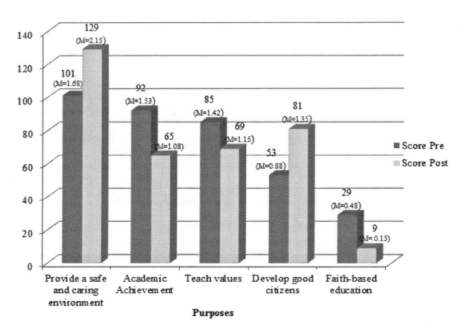

Figure 9.2 Mean school purposes scores for first year (pre) and final year (post) students (N = 60)

Table 9.4 Mean scores for importance of given school purposes for whole cohort, Catholics and Catholic school attendees

Purposes	All respondents (N = 60)		Catholics (n = 40)		Catholic school attendees (n = 43)	
	2014	2017	2014	2017	2014	2017
Provide safe and caring environment	1.68	2.25	1.58	2.08	1.63	2.23
Academic achievement	1.53	1.08	1.53	1.13	1.40	1.00
Teach values	1.42	1.15	1.35	1.05	1.47	1.21
Develop good citizens	0.88	1.35	0.93	1.45	0.84	1.35
Faith-based education	0.48	0.15	0.63	0.15	0.67	0.09

The mean scores for 'provide a safe and caring environment' and 'develop good citizens' increased over the duration of the programme, while the means for the other purposes decreased accordingly. Notwithstanding a very low score in 2014, the mean score for 'provide faith-based education' had dropped even further by 2017.

Pre- and post-mean scores were compared in respect of each school purpose for all respondents, Catholic respondents and Catholic school attendees and the results are reported in Table 9.4.

Mean scores for 'safe and caring environment' and 'develop good citizens' increased for all three categories of students while they decreased accordingly for 'teach values', 'academic achievement', and, most notably, 'faith-based education'. Analysis of variance between the mean first- and fourth-year scores for all three categories was calculated using paired samples t tests and the outcomes are presented in Table 9.5.

The increase in mean scores for the importance of 'develop good citizens' and the decrease in the mean scores for the importance of 'faith-based education' are statistically significant at the $p < .05$ level for all three categories. The p-value for 'faith-based education' is particularly significant in the case of Catholics and Catholic school attendees. The increased means for 'safe and

Table 9.5 Paired samples *t*-test *p* values for mean scores for importance of given purposes of schools

School purpose	All respondents (N = 60)	Catholics (n = 40)	Catholic school attendees (n = 43)
Provide a safe and caring environment	.01	.06	.01
Develop good citizens	.01	.03	.02
Academic achievement	.01	.07	.07
Teach values	.15	.18	.22
Faith-based education	.02	.01	.00

caring environment' generated a p-value of .01 in the case of all respondents and Catholic school attendees and .06 in the case of Catholic respondents. Further analysis showed that final year students' levels of religiosity did not have any statistically significant effect on the perceived importance of faith-based education for the full cohort, Catholic students or Catholic school attendees.

In summary, the mean scores for the importance of 'safe and caring environment' and 'develop good citizens' increased at statistically significant levels over the four years. The corollary was that the mean scores of 'academic achievement', 'teach values' and 'faith-based education' declined. While the mean for faith-based education was very low to begin with, it had almost dropped to zero in 2017, particularly in the case of those who were Catholic and Catholic school attendees.

Levels of moral reasoning

The mean P and N2 scores of the 33 longitudinal study cohort members and the results of the associated analysis of variance are presented in Table 9.6. As one might reasonably expect, pre-service teachers' Post-Conventional (P and N2) scores on the DIT2 were higher in final year than in first year and these differences were statistically very significant. Freshmen with the highest P scores were female, Catholic, had high levels of academic achievement, had attended Independent or Catholic schools and had high levels of religiosity. Final year students' Personal Interest (PI), Maintaining Norms (MN) and Post-Conventional (P) scores for were broadly similar. This indicates that some two-thirds of them were not exhibiting post-conventional levels of moral reasoning.

Dong's (2009) meta-analysis of the entire data set held by the Centre for the Study of Ethical Development, University of Alabama, found that college freshmen achieve an average P score of 34.1, sophomores had an average score of 35.2, Senior College students had an average of 36 and graduates with a professional degree exhibit an average P score of 41. The mean P score of final year students in this study was almost 3 points below the international average for freshmen and almost 10 points below the international average for graduates. However, their scores are on a par with those of pre-service teachers at an Irish University ($n = 102$), where the average P scores were 25.4 in the case of freshmen and 33.6 in the case of final year students (O'Flaherty & Gleeson, 2014).

Table 9.6 DIT2 scores for Year 1 (2014) and Year 4 (2017) students and associated ANOVA values

DIT2 scores	Year 1 (N = 33)	Year 4 (N = 33)	t-test p values
P score (SD)	25.72 (14.51)	31.35 (16.23)	.003
N2 score (SD)	21.61 (13.76)	29.35 (15.75)	.001

Longitudinal study and pre-service teachers 203

Table 9.7 Perceived importance of given aims of education (pre/post)

	All respondents (%) (N = 60)				Catholic respondents (%) (N = 40)			
	Educate whole child (%)		Facilitate well-being and promote active citizenship (%)		Educate whole child (%)		Facilitate well-being and promote active citizenship (%)	
Beliefs	Pre	Post	Pre	Post	Pre	Post	Pre	Post
Holistic	67	82	67	85	62.5	85	62.5	90
Instrumental	02	02	02			2.5		
Equally important	32	17	32	15	37.5	12.5	37.5	10

Aims of education and beliefs about teaching and learning

Students were presented with the following bipolar statements regarding the aims of education (Appendix 4, Question 19):

Holistic	Instrumental
The primary purpose of schools is to educate the whole child	The primary purpose of schools is to help students get high grades and good jobs
The primary purpose of education is to facilitate personal well-being and promote active citizenship	The primary purpose of education is to promote economic growth

Students were also asked to locate themselves on a continuum ranging from holistic to instrumental and their responses (all students and Catholic students) are shown in Table 9.7.

Two-thirds of first-year respondents and 80% of fourth-year respondents (both full cohort and Catholic) saw the primary purpose of schooling in holistic rather than instrumental terms and most of the others felt that both options were equally important.

Drawing on the work of Sergiovanni (2000, pp. 64–65), respondents were also invited to locate their beliefs around teaching and learning on the following continuum ranging from 'life liberating' to 'life limiting' beliefs (Appendix 4, Question 20)

Life-liberating	Life-limiting
Students learn best by collaborating with each other	Competition is necessary to bring out the best in students
All students are capable of high academic achievement	Only a few students are capable of high academic achievement
Students are best served by mixed ability grouping	Students are best served by Streaming according to ability

First- and fourth-year students' preferences for life-liberating and life-limiting beliefs are shown in Table 9.8.

204 Jim Gleeson and Maureen O'Neill

Table 9.8 Students' beliefs about teaching and learning (*n* = 60).

Beliefs about teaching and learning	Liberating beliefs (%)		Limiting beliefs (%)		Equally important (%)	
	2014	*2017*	*2014*	*2017*	*2014*	*2017*
Collaboration vs. competition	57	73	05	03	38	23
All students capable of high academic achievement	75	87	05	07	20	07
Mixed ability grouping	52	63	03	08	45	28

Levels of support for life-limiting beliefs were minimal, with final year respondents more likely than first years to endorse life-liberating beliefs. While first-year students were particularly supportive of 'all students are capable of high academic achievement' this support had increased by 12% ($p < .05$) in 2017. Support for collaboration over competition increased by 16% ($p < .05$), while support for mixed ability grouping also increased.

Characteristics of Catholic schools

Respondents were invited to rate the importance of 15 given characteristics of Catholic schools as 'essential', 'very important', 'important' or 'unimportant' (Appendix 4, Question 15). Weighted scores were allocated for the ratings of each characteristic (3 for essential, 2 for very important, 1 for important) and mean scores for the perceived importance of each characteristic. The mean values for all/Catholic first-/fourth-year respondents are set out in Table 9.9.

'Caring community' clearly had the highest rating followed by 'teachers of RE are accredited to teach RE' and engagement in outreach and social justice programmes. Other highly rated characteristics included 'school is a community of faith', strong links to wider Church and 'RE programmes present the teachings of the Catholic Church'. At the other end of the scale, limited importance was afforded to 'principal is Catholic', 'teachers of RE Catholic', 'annual religious retreats' and 'the vast majority of teachers/students are Catholic'.

Paired sample *t* tests for differences between pre- and post-ratings of given characteristics found statistically significant differences ($p < .03$) in the case of the two lowest rated items, 'vast majority of students/teachers are Catholic', where means had reduced dramatically by 2017. Although the perceived importance of religious retreats had declined somewhat by fourth year, the perceived importance of prayer increased.

It is noteworthy that, with the exception of 'prayer is integral to the school's daily life' (which remains the same), the mean ratings for final year Catholic students are lower than their means in 2014. Catholic students' means are also

Table 9.9 All respondents' and Catholic respondents' mean ratings of each given characteristic*

Characteristics	All respondents		Catholic respondents	
	2014	2017	2014	2017
Caring community	2.57	2.72	2.75	2.65
Teachers of RE are accredited to teach RE	2.13	2.12	2.38	2.08
School engages in outreach and social justice programmes	1.92	1.92	2.05	1.70
The school is a community of faith	1.67	1.88	1.85	1.75
RE programmes present the teachings of the Catholic Church	1.52	1.72	1.78	1.63
Strong links to wider Church	1.55	1.57	1.88	1.40
Prayer is integral to the school's daily life	1.25	1.52	1.50	1.50
Celebration of school liturgies frequently	1.30	1.50	1.55	1.48
Catholic symbols throughout school	1.33	1.28	1.50	1.33
Principal is Catholic	1.10	1.12	1.28	1.08
Integration of Catholic teachings across ALL curriculum areas	0.88	1.02	0.98	1.03
Teachers of RE are Catholic	1.08	0.95	1.40	0.98
Annual religious retreats	1.18	0.93	1.35	0.80
Vast majority of teachers are Catholic	0.93	0.58	1.07	0.53
Vast majority of students are Catholic	0.60	0.32	0.78	0.33

* Characteristics are listed in order of 2017 respondents' mean ratings.

lower than the means for the full cohort and these differences are statistically significant in case of 'links to wider church' ($p < .04$) and 'vast majority of teachers/students are Catholic' ($p < .005$).

Students were also invited to use their ratings to rank these same characteristics in order of importance (Appendix 4, Question 16). Weighted scores were allocated to the six characteristics with the highest rankings (6 points for item ranked 1, 5 points for item ranked 2, etc., with the maximum possible score being 360) and the outcomes are presented in Table 9.10 (p. 206).

Caring community received twice as many points as the second ranked item, engagement in outreach and social justice programmes. 'The school is a community of faith' and 'prayer is integral to the school's daily life' were ranked joint third by final year respondents, followed by two RE-related items, 'teachers of RE are accredited to teach RE' and 'RE programmes present the teaching of the Catholic Church'. As with the ratings reported above, the characteristics that received the lowest rankings both from all and Catholic 2017 respondents were 'teachers of RE are Catholic', 'the principal is Catholic', 'vast majority of teachers are Catholic' and 'vast majority of students are Catholic'.

The pattern emerging then is that generic characteristics are rated and ranked as being more important than explicitly faith-based items, with the

206 Jim Gleeson and Maureen O'Neill

Table 9.10 All students' and Catholic students' pre- and post-rankings of the characteristics of Catholic schools*

Characteristics	All (N = 60)		Catholic (n = 40)	
	Pre (2014)	Post (2017)	Pre (2014)	Post (2017)
Caring community	279(1)	291(1)	191(1)	200(1)
School engages in outreach and social justice programmes	138(2)	145(2)	99(2)	103(2)
The school is a community of faith	98(4)	126(3)	68(4)	80(4)
Prayer is integral to the school's daily life	63(9)	126(3)	43(9)	70(5)
The teachers of RE are accredited to teach RE	102(3)	117(5)	72(3)	86(3)
RE programmes present the teachings of the Catholic Church	88(5)	82(6)	62(5)	62(6)
School community celebrates school liturgies frequently	76(6)	66(7)	56(7)	30(10)
Catholic symbols throughout the school	66(8)	63(8)	44(8)	35(11)
Planned integration of Catholic teachings across ALL learning areas	29(13)	56(9)	19(13)	41(7)
Annual age appropriate religious retreats are available to students	75(7)	53(10)	58(6)	36(9)
The school has strong links to wider Church	48(11)	53(10)	36(11)	41(7)
Teachers of RE are Catholic	50(10)	41(12)	37(10)	26(12)
The principal is Catholic	41(12)	24(13)	30(12)	14(13)
Vast majority of teachers are Catholic	26(14)	9(14)	15(14)	9(14)
Vast majority of students are Catholic	15(15)	2(15)	12(15)	2(15)

* Characteristics listed according to order of 2017 rankings for all respondents.

religious affiliations of school principals, teachers and students being regarded as relatively unimportant. It is also noteworthy that Catholic students' ratings for the importance of all given characteristics (with the exception of prayer) had declined at the end of 4 years and that their mean ratings were generally lower than the means for the overall study cohort.

Discussion of findings

The main positives to be taken from the above data include the strong commitment of pre-service teachers to safe and caring school environments, holistic educational aims and 'life-liberating' (Sergiovanni, 2000) educational beliefs. It is however a matter of some concern that pre-service teacher gave low ratings to 'faith-based education' as a reason for choice of secondary school and as a school purpose. When students were invited to rank given school characteristics in order of importance, generic items were deemed more important than faith-based items while pre-service teachers' levels of moral reasoning as measured by the DIT2 were primarily conventional and instrumental.

These emerging trends throw up three conundrums for discussion here:

1 While pre-service teachers' commitment to safe and caring school environments and to holistic education are very much in line with Catholic beliefs and values, these generic values are not unique to faith-based schooling.
2 Pre-service teachers' preference for generic over faith-based characteristics of schools and their low ratings for the importance of faith-based education pose serious challenges for the faith-based identity of Catholic schools.
3 While pre-service teachers' commitment to holistic education values fits very well with the traditions and values of Catholic Education, they will find themselves working in a neo-liberal educational environment where such traditions are not valued.

These conundrums are now briefly discussed with reference to Sockett's (2008, p. 47) four ideal types or models for 'the professional teacher's moral and epistemological stances' which are critical 'in enhancing the quality of practitioners in teaching [and] contributing to the ... public status of the occupation of teaching' (2008, p. 45). His types of professional are as follows:

- The scholar is 'dedicated to imparting wisdom and fostering the life of the mind' (2008, p. 48).
- The nurturer is 'primarily focused on the development of the individual ... on relationships with children' (2008, p. 48).
- The clinician focuses primarily on 'social purposes such as social justice with socialization as the educational aim' (2008, p. 49).
- The moral agent 'is primarily focused on the child's comprehensive development and growth ... to integrate academic content with intellectual and moral virtues' (2008, p. 49).

Conundrum I: Commitment to caring and holistic values is not unique to faith-based schooling

The commitment of pre-service teachers to 'caring community' and 'safe and nurturing environment' certainly satisfies the expectation of the Australian Institute for Teaching and School Leadership (AITSL, 2014, p. 14) of teachers 'creating and maintaining supportive and safe learning environments', while their strong nurturing tendencies resonate with the increasing focus on student well-being in curriculum reforms across countries (Clement, 2010; Lovat, 2010).

Meanwhile their commitment to the values of holistic education is consistent with the philosophy of Catholic Education espoused by the CCE and authors such as Maritain (1943) and Murray (1991). For example, in its *Lay Catholics in Schools* (CCE, 1982), the Congregation calls for 'the integral formation of the human person which is the purpose of education, includ[ing] the development of all the human faculties of the students, together with preparation for the professional life ...' (para 17). Ever cognisant of the need to achieve balance between the development of the human person and the demands of employment, Murray (1991) articulates the holistic aims of education as follows:

> Education should address the whole person and every aspect which concerns the integral development of the person: aesthetic, creative, critical, cultural, emotional, intellectual, moral, physical, political, social and spiritual. (pp. 19–20)

Students' endorsement of holistic rather than instrumental[3] educational aims was consistent with their relatively low ratings for academic outcomes as school purposes. This attitude was also reflected in their positive levels of support for life-liberating (Sergiovanni, 2000) teaching and learning beliefs such as 'all students are capable of high academic achievement'. Sergiovanni (2000) champions such beliefs not only because they make good sense, but because they are appropriate for 'a covenantal community, a group of people who share certain purposes, values and beliefs' (p. 65).

Pre-service teachers' strong endorsement of caring, safe and nurturing school environments and holistic educational values strongly suggests that they fit Sockett's (2008) nurturer-professional type whose 'epistemic purpose ... is embedded in its moral purpose [suggesting] a still more extensive view of relationships and caring' (p. 53). While the nurturer-professional type has 'its ancestry in child-centered education' (p. 52), Sockett argues that it is 'firmly rooted in the feminism of the second half of the twentieth century [with its] moral focus ... on motherliness' (p. 52) as well as in Buber's (1996) 'I-Thou' philosophy and Noddings' (1984, 1988) focus on relationships and caring. Sockett's characterisation of his nurturing type is particularly interesting in view of the increasing feminisation of the teaching profession (Drudy, 2008) and the fact that almost 90% of the pre-service teachers in this study were female.

The emerging irony however is that, while the participating students have expressed a clear preference for the importance of nurturing educational environments and holistic educational aims and beliefs, these generic values are by no means unique to Catholic schools. Meanwhile, fourth students' levels of support for faith-based education have decreased from an already low base. This begs the fundamental question: where is the value-added dimension in Catholic teacher education?

Conundrum 2: What are the implications of participating students' predilection for generic characteristics for the faith-based identity of Catholic schools?

The Second Vatican Council's Declaration on Christian Education (Pope Paul VI, 1965) declares that 'education ... has the duty of proclaiming the way of salvation to all, of communicating the life of Christ to those who believe' (para 3) and the evangelical role of the Catholic school has been emphasised by the CCE:

> ... the Catholic school forms part of the saving mission of the Church, especially for education in the faith ... It is precisely in the Gospel of Christ... that the Catholic school finds its definition as it comes to terms with the cultural conditions of the times. (1977, para 9)

> ... teachers and educators fulfil a specific Christian vocation and share an equally specific participation in the mission of the Church, to the extent that it depends chiefly on them whether the Catholic school achieves its purpose. (1997, para 19)

The Congregation presents Catholic Education in terms of a synthesis of faith, culture and life (CCE, 1997; Lane, 1991). Increasing secularisation however is raising critical questions for Catholic Education. According to Lovat and Clement (2014, p. 567), new research insights are 'challenging some of the assumptions held by faith-based schools in earlier times that part of their system's distinctiveness was to be found around the values agenda ... [with the result that] values education is being seen increasingly to have outgrown any earlier conceptions of being exclusively germane to, much less dependent on, the faith-based setting'. Pollefeyt and Bouwens (2014, p. 290) in their study of Catholic schools in Victoria, Australia, have identified the 'rising level of *Institutionalized Secularization* among the student groups'. This reflects what Rymarz and Graham (2006, p. 80) call 'the disassociation of most students with the faith tradition' and resonates with Flynn and Mok (2002) findings that students in Catholic schools and their parents afford a higher priority to personal and social development, academic achievement and preparation for employment than to religious goals. Our pre-service teachers' mean scores for 'values education' as a school purpose and the relatively low ratings for faith-related purposes and characteristics are consistent with the findings of other studies:

> Many young people in Australia are following an avowedly secular path. (Mason et al., 2007, p. 227)

> Approximately half of Year 9 and Year 12 students [in Brisbane Catholic schools] never attend a religious service outside of school .... [There is] a progressive decline in the importance of faith as students grow older .... BCE Year 12 students display less religious faith and observance than 1998 Year 12 students. (Dowling et al., 2009, p. 2)

> For many students [in Catholic schools in New South Wales], the Church as an institution has simply lost its relevance [and students are] profoundly concerned about social justice issues [while] not disposed favourably towards traditional Catholic practice. (Dorman, 1999, p. 38)

The emerging profile of our pre-service teachers is one of 'nurturing' professionals who are committed to the provision of safe and caring environments and holistic educational values. It is only reasonable however to expect that all educational institutions, faith-based or not, should provide safe and caring environments and contribute to the formation of caring communities.

While recognising that the open-ended responses of students intending to work in Catholic schools are somewhat encouraging, the commitment of members of the study cohort to evangelisation in situations 'where the Gospel has been forgotten or meets with indifference as a result of widespread secularism' (Pope Benedict XVI, 2010, para 122) might be described as uncertain. Two-thirds of the graduating students did not regard religion as important to how live their lives, their self-rated knowledge of Scripture is quite low and their views on the characteristics of Catholic schools are more 'secular' than those of serving teachers in Catholic schools in Queensland (Chapter 7). Such uncertainty poses critical questions for the faith-based identity of Catholic schools and the formation of their teachers.

Respondents ranked 'engagement in outreach and social justice programmes' as the second most important characteristic of Catholic schools. This is indicative of Sockett's (2008) 'clinician-professional' type which he associates primarily with Darling-Hammond and Bransford (2005) who are concerned with the promotion of many goals that are also included in the aforementioned Australian Framework for Values Education. These include social morality, distributive justice, equality of treatment, local community needs and the development of *all* children so that they can take their place in adult, democratic society. Social justice programmes have additional relevance for Catholic schools whose various founding charisms constitute an important dimension of the identity of Catholic schools in Australia (Gleeson & O'Flaherty, 2016). The pursuit of social justice also opens the door for young teachers to embrace key aspects of Catholic social teaching (see Chapter 10), thus enabling the 'principles of the gospel become the educational norms, since the school has them as its internal motivation and final goal' (CCE 1997, para 34).

As with the provision of safe and nurturing school environments however, the conundrum remains that the pursuit of social justice is a valid aspiration for and expectation of all educational institutions, not just faith-based ones.

Conundrum 3: Notwithstanding their commitment to holistic education values these teachers will find employment in a system dominated by market values

While pre-service teachers in this study fall primarily into Sockett's 'nurturer' and 'clinician' types, they will find themselves working within the 'bureaucratic and technical framework of modern schooling ... [which] makes it difficult to imagine such a concept of the nurturer-professional gaining any credibility in public schooling' (Sockett, 2008, p. 53). Such an environment does not offer a hospitable environment for holistic educational beliefs and values:

> Education is at the service of the integral development of the human person ... it will not be satisfied to act as though the young person were merely a potential worker. (Murray, 1991, p. 9)

> [The competitive global economy] is neither the be-all and end-all of education, nor the be-all and end-all of life'. (Biesta, 2013, p. 739)

As noted in earlier chapters, the CCE (2014, p. 12) is critical of the hegemony of market values in education, and the associated temptation for governments to simply respond to the demands of 'the ever-changing economic situation' (CCE, 2014, p. 64) and the edits of agencies such as the European Union, OECD and World Bank. Pope Francis (2015) has called for a 'distinctive way of looking at things [including] an educational programme, a lifestyle and a spirituality which together generate resistance to the assault of the techno-cratic paradigm' (para 111).

The independent review of the Australian Curriculum characterises the prevailing environment of Australian schools in terms of a 'utilitarian and technocratic approach to the purpose of education' (Australian Government, 2014, p. 27), one where the high-stakes NAPLAN testing regime 'distorts teaching practices, constrains the curriculum and narrows students' educational experiences' (Polesel et al., 2014, p. 640). The Catholic Education Commission of New South Wales (2014, p. 6) sees the Australian Curriculum in terms of 'an essentially instrumental view [of education that] does not describe the benefits of schooling in terms of the holistic growth of each individual student ... does not articulate a view of Australian students in terms of their overall development'. Meanwhile, the independent reviewers concluded that for Catholic educators, the instrumental view of curriculum found in the Melbourne Declaration, the foundation of the Australian Curriculum 'has always been seen, at best, as a partial description of the desirable outcomes of schooling and, at worst, as a depiction of a lack of understanding of human dignity' (Australian Government, 2014, p. 95).

When the subjects of the study reported here find employment as newly qualified teachers, their natural tendency will be to accommodate to the prevailing educational environment. The point of this third conundrum is that such accommodation will pose serious challenges for these young teachers' holistic educational philosophies. As argued in Chapter 1, this is ultimately an issue for Catholic Education leadership rather than individual teachers.

In concluding this discussion, it is interesting to compare the findings of this study with the outcomes of Coll's (2007) qualitative study of Scottish pre-service teachers, which revealed two related aspects to the role of the Catholic teacher, one involving 'the imparting of information and knowledge [including] RE lessons', and a second which involves the 'pastoral role of the teacher [in] day-to-day interaction with the children and staff and the promotion of the Catholic faith throughout' (2007, p. 462). This suggests that both Queensland and Scottish pre-service teachers fit Sockett's nurturer-professional type with the former also fitting his clinician-professional type and the latter leaning more towards his scholar-professional type.

Conclusion

These conundrums present serious challenges for Catholic schools whose 'religious character and mission are the unique characteristics that distinguish them both as educational institutions and as agencies that help to hand on Catholic religious traditions' (Belmonte & Cranston, 2009, p. 295). The future of Catholic Education in Queensland is in the hands of young teachers such as those included in this study. These students' commitment to holistic and liberating educational values provides a valuable foundation for this task and those who find employment in Catholic schools will be able to draw on their founding charisms. For example, the four touchstones of Catholic Schools in the Edmund Rice Tradition are Gospel spirituality, liberating education, justice and solidarity and inclusive community.

The changing profile of teachers in Catholic schools has obvious implications both for faith-based school identity (Pollefeyt & Bouwens, 2010) and for the preservation of school charisms. Although the Catholic school teachers of the past were educated in faith-based institutions, the Catholic Education sector of today must draw its teachers from state-funded universities using common entry systems such as the Queensland Tertiary Admissions Centre where religious affiliation is not a consideration in the allocation of places.

For Catholic schools in Australia to retain their faith-based identity, their teachers should have knowledge and understanding of the Catholic tradition along with commitment to Gospel values. While this obviously requires the on-going faith-related professional development of teachers, it also has implications for the criteria used when appointing teachers to Catholic schools and for system leadership. Given the important role of senior leadership, it is a cause of some concern that

> ... principals [of Australian Catholic schools] had had only a minor exposure to formal development programs, even though principals themselves viewed it as a priority for the promotion and maintenance of the Catholic identity in their schools. There is a major conflict in a system of schooling that exists to nurture the faith of young people, yet fails to realize and address the traditional spiritual capital of its leadership. (Belmonte & Cranston, 2009, pp. 303–304)

While Catholic schools in the United States do not receive state support, Convey's (2012) findings indicate that their teachers were far more likely to rate the faith-based characteristics of Catholic schools used in this study as essential than either the pre-service teachers in this study or existing teachers in Catholic schools in Queensland (Chapter 8). When asked to comment on this finding, Convey highlighted the importance of faith formation:

> For the past 25 years or so in the US, there has been a very heavy emphasis on the spiritual leadership of the principal and the development of the faith community in Catholic schools. The steep decline of teachers from religious congregations prompted this. The Bishops have been strong in promoting this emphasis and so have the superintendents, so it is not surprising that the results [of my survey] overall were positive. (Personal communication, September 21, 2016)

Of course, it must also be also recognised that Catholic schools internationally exist in environments dominated by market values and performativity (Ball, 2012; Lingard, 2010). Some 30 years ago, the Congregation acknowledged the challenge of reconciling the 'Catholic school [as] a "civic institution" [whose] aim, methods and characteristics are the same as those of every other school [with its being a] "Christian community", whose educational goals are rooted in Christ and his Gospel' (CCE, 1988, para 67). This 'wicked problem' is getting more difficult all the time.

Sockett's (2008) moral agent-professional model may offer some guidance insofar as it 'accepts the legitimacy of the three conflicting educational purposes [scholar, nurturer, clinician] ... [and] regards none as having priority since its focus is on teaching as ... a moral activity' (p. 49). This 'moral agent' model includes individual virtues such as care and empathy, social virtues such as justice and tolerance and knowledge virtues. Suggesting that this overarching model might be realised in 'some parochial schools' (p. 60), Sockett (2008) believes that it enables both the school curriculum and the teacher education curriculum to 'be conceptualised through the development of ... virtues [or] qualities [that] range over intellectual, social, personal life and life in the workplace' (p. 61). This call for a holistic educational experience is consistent with the integration of Catholic social teaching principles as outlined earlier in Part 1 of this book.

Notes

1. Amended appropriately to exclude items where the response would not have changed since first year and to include items of relevance to final rather than first year students. The version in Appendix 4 was administered to first years.
2. An OP (overall position) score is a student's position in a state-wide rank order based on overall achievement in Queensland Curriculum and Assessment Authority (QCAA) subjects. It indicates how well a student has done in comparison to all other OP-eligible students in Queensland. Students are placed in 1 of 25 OP bands from 1 (highest) to 25 (lowest).
3. For example, high grades, good jobs and education for economic growth.

References

Australian Catholic Bishops Conference. (2013). *A profile of the Catholic community in Australia March 2013.* Australian Catholic Bishops Conference Pastoral Research Office, Australian Catholic University, Melbourne. Retrieved from www.catholic.org.au

Australian Curriculum, Assessment and Reporting Authority (ACARA). (2012). *Curriculum development process: Version 6.* Retrieved from http://docs.acara.edu.au/resources/ACARA_Curriculum_Development_Process_Version_6.0_-_04_April_2012_-_FINAL_COPY.pdf

Australian Government. (2014). *Review of the Australian curriculum: Final report.* Canberra: Author.

Australian Institute for Teaching and School Leadership (AITSL). (2014). Victoria: Australian Professional Standards for Teachers. Education Council. Retrieved from https://www.vit.vic.edu.au/registered-teacher/standards

Ball, S. J. (1994). *Education reform: A critical and post-structural approach.* Buckingham: Open University Press.

Ball, S. J. (2008). *The education debate.* Bristol: The Policy Press.

Ball, S. J. (2012). *Global Education, Inc. New policy networks and the neo-liberal imaginary.* London: Routledge.

Bebeau, M., & Thoma, S. J. (2003). *Draft guide for DIT-2, version 3.0.* Minneapolis, MN: University of Minnesota, Centre for the Study of Ethical Development.

Belmonte, A., & Cranston, N. (2009). The religious dimension of Lay leadership in Catholic schools: Preserving Catholic culture in an era of change. *Journal of Catholic Education, 12*(3), 294–319.

Biesta, G. J. J. (2013). Responsive or responsible? Democratic education for the global networked society. *Policy Futures in Education, 11*(6), 733–744.

Boeve, L. (2005). Religion after detraditionalization: Christian faith in a post-secular Europe. *Irish Theological Quarterly, 70*(2), 99–122. doi: 10.1177/002114000507000201.

Brown, P., & Lauder, H. (1996). Education, globalisation and economic development. *Journal of Education Policy, 11*(1), 1–25.

Buber, M. (1996). *I and Thou* (M. Kaufmann, Trans.). New York: Touchstone.

Byrne, D. (2005). *The understandings of Catholic lay secondary teachers on the nature and purpose of Catholic schooling* (Unpublished thesis, Master of Educational Management Degree), University of Western Australia, Perth, WA, Australia.

Catholic Education Commission New South Wales. (2014). *Submission to the review of the Australian curriculum*. Sydney: Author.

Chambers, M. (2012). Students who are not Catholics in Catholic schools: Lessons from the Second Vatican Council about the Catholicity of schools. *International Studies in Catholic Education, 4*(2), 186–199. doi: 10.1080/19422539.2012.708174.

Clement, N. (2010). Student well-being at school: The actualization of values in education. In T. Lovat, R. Toomey, & N. Clement (Eds.), *International research handbook on values education and student well-being* (pp. 37–62). Dordrecht: Springer.

Coll, R. (2007). Student teachers' perception of their role and responsibilities as Catholic educators. *European Journal of Teacher Education, 30*(4), 445–465.

Congregation for Catholic Education (CCE). (1977). *The Catholic school*. Vatican City: Author.

Congregation for Catholic Education (CCE). (1982). *Lay Catholics in schools*. Vatican City: Author.

Congregation for Catholic Education (CCE). (1988). *The religious dimension of education in a Catholic school. Guidelines for reflection and renewal*. Vatican City: Author.

Congregation for Catholic Education (CCE). (1997). *The Catholic school on the threshold of the third millennium*. Vatican City: Author.

Congregation for Catholic Education (CCE). (2014). *Educating today and tomorrow: A renewing passion, instrumentum laboris*. Vatican City: Author.

Convey, J. J. (2012). Perceptions of Catholic identity: Views of Catholic school administrators and teachers. *Catholic Education: A Journal of Inquiry and Practice, 16*(1), 187–214.

Cranston, N., Kimber, M., Mulford, B., Reid, A., & Keating, J. (2010). Politics and school education in Australia: A case of shifting purposes. *Journal of Educational Administration, 48*(2), 182–195.

Croke, B. (2007). Australian Catholic schools in a changing political and religious landscape. In T. H. McLaughlin, J. O'Keefe, & B. O'Keefe (Eds.), *International handbook of Catholic education* (pp. 811–833). Dordrecht: Springer.

Cuban L. (1988). Why do some reforms persist? *Educational Administration Quarterly, 24*(3), 329–335.

Darling-Hammond, L., & Bransford, J. (2005). *Preparing teachers for a changing world: What teachers should learn and be able to do*. Hoboken, NJ: John Wiley & Sons.

Department of Education, Science and Training. (2005). *National framework for values education in Australian schools*. Retrieved from www.curriculum.edu.au/values/val_national_framework_for_values_education,8757.html

Diener, E., Tay, L., & Myers, D. (2011). The religion paradox: If religion makes people happy, why are so many dropping out? *Journal of Personality and Social Psychology, 101*(6), 1278–1290.

Dijkstra, A., & Veenstra, R. (2001). Do religious schools matter? Beliefs and lifestyles of students in faith-based secondary schools. *International Journal of Education and Religion, 2*(1), 182–206.

Ditchburn, G. M. (2012). The Australian curriculum: Finding the hidden narrative? *Critical Studies in Education, 53*(3), 347–360. doi: 10.1080/17508487.2012.703137.

Dong, Y. (2009). *Norms for DIT2: From 2005–2009* (pp. 1–19). Tuscaloosa, AL: Center for the Student of Ethical Development, University of Alabama. *Retrieved from* http://www.ethicaldevelopment.ua.edu/wp-content/uploads/2010/11/Norms-for-DIT2-05-09.pdf

Dorman, J. (1999). Assessment of students' attitudes to Christianity in Catholic secondary schools. *Journal of Religious Education, 47*(4), 33–39.

Dowling, A., Beavis, A., Underwood, C., Sadeghi, R., & O'Malley, K. (2009). *Who's coming to school today? Final report*. Brisbane: ACER, Brisbane Catholic Education.

Drudy, S. (2008). Gender balance/gender bias: The teaching profession and the impact of feminisation. *Gender and Education, 20*(4), 309–323. doi: 10.1080/09540250802190156.

Flynn, M., & Mok, M. M. C. (2002). *Catholic schools 2000: A longitudinal study of year 12 students in Catholic schools, 1972–1982–1990–1998.* Sydney: Catholic Education Commission.

Gandin, L. A. (2006). Creating real alternatives to neoliberal policies in education. In M. W. Apple & K. L. Buras (Eds.), *The subaltern speak: Curriculum, power and educational struggles* (pp. 217–241). New York: Routledge.

Gleeson, J. (2015). Critical challenges and dilemmas for Catholic education leadership internationally. *International Studies in Catholic Education, 7*(2), 145–161.

Gleeson, J., & O'Flaherty, J. (2016). The teacher as moral educator: Comparative study of secondary teachers in Catholic schools in Australia and Ireland. *Teaching and Teacher Education, 55*, 45–56.

Gleeson, J., & O'Neill, M. (2017). Student-teachers' perspectives on the purposes and characteristics of faith-based schools: An Australian view. *British Journal of Religious Education, 40*(1), 55–69. doi: 10.1080/01416200.2016.1256266.

Grace, G. (2002). *Catholic schools: Mission, markets and morality.* Abingdon, London: Routledge.

Groome, T. H. (2003). What makes a school Catholic? In T. H. McLaughlin, J. O'Keefe, & B. O'Keefe (Eds.), *The contemporary Catholic school* (pp. 111–129). Routledge.

Heinz, M., Davison, K., & Keane, E. (2018) 'I will do it but religion is a very personal thing': Teacher education applicants' attitudes towards teaching religion in Ireland, *European Journal of Teacher Education, 41*(2), 232–245. doi: 10.1080/02619768.2018.1426566.

Hughes, P. J. (2007). *Putting life together: Findings from Australian youth spirituality research.* Victoria: Fairfield Press.

Inglis, T. (2007). Catholic identify in contemporary Ireland: Belief and belonging to tradition. *Journal of Contemporary Religion, 22*(2), 205–220.

Lane, D. A. (1991). Catholic education and the school. *Some theological reflections.* Dublin: Veritas.

Lingard, B. (2010). Policy borrowing, policy learning: Testing times in Australian schooling. *Critical Studies in Education, 51*(2), 129–147. doi: 10.1080/17508481003731026.

Lingard, B., & McGregor, G. (2014). Two contrasting Australian curriculum responses to globalisation: What students should learn or become. *Curriculum Journal, 25*(1), 90–110. doi: 10.1080/09585176.2013.872048.

Lovat, T. (2010). The new values education: A pedagogical imperative for student wellbeing. In *International research handbook on values education and student wellbeing* (pp. 3–18). Dordrecht: Springer.

Lovat, T., & Clement, N. (2014). So who has the values? Challenges for faith-based schools in an era of values pedagogy. In *International handbook of learning, teaching and leading in faith-based schools* (pp. 567–582). Dordrecht: Springer.

Maritain, J. (1943). *Education at the crossroads.* New Haven, CT: Yale University Press.

Mason, M., Singleton, A., & Webber, R. (2007). *The spirit of generation Y. Young people's spirituality in a changing Australia.* Melbourne: John Garratt Publishing.

McLaughlin, D., & Standen, P. (2013). The rise and demise of Australian Catholic education? Unpublished paper read at Australian Catholic School Leadership Conference, Sydney.

Murray, D. 1991. *A special concern.* Dublin: Veritas.

Muller, D., & Associates. (2008). *Values and other issues in the education of young Australians.* Carlton: The Australian Parents Council and the Department of Education, Science and Training.

Narvaez, D., & Bock, T. (2002). Moral schemas and tacit judgement or how the Defining Issues Test is supported by cognitive science. *Journal of Moral Education, 31*(3), 297–314.

Noddings, N. (1984). *Caring: A feminine approach to ethics and moral education*. Berkeley, CA: University of California Press.

Noddings, N. (1988). An ethic of caring and its implications for instructional arrangements. *American Journal of Education, 96*(2), 215–230.

O'Flaherty, J., & Gleeson, J. (2014). Longitudinal study of levels of moral reasoning of undergraduate students in an Irish university: The influence of contextual factors. *Irish Educational Studies, 33*(1), 57–74.

Polesel, J., Rice, S., & Dulfer, N. (2014). The impact of high-stakes testing on curriculum and pedagogy: A teacher perspective from Australia. *Journal of Education Policy, 29*(5), 640–657. doi: 10.1080/02680939.2013.865082.

Pollefeyt, D., & Bouwens, J. (2010). Framing the identity of Catholic schools: Empirical methodology for quantitative research on the Catholic identity of an education institute. *International Studies in Catholic Education, 2*(2), 193–211.

Pollefeyt, D., & Bouwens, J. (2014). *Identity in dialogue. Assessing and enhancing Catholic school identity. Research methodology and research results in Catholic schools in Victoria, Australia* (Vol. 1). Münster: LIT Verlag.

Pope Benedict XVI. (2010). *Post-Synodal Apostolic Exhortation: Verbum Domini*. Vatican City. Retrieved from https://en.wikipedia.org/wiki/Verbum_Domini

Pope Francis. (2015). *Laudato Si'*. Vatican City

Pope Paul VI. (1965). *Declaration on Christian education: Gravissimum educationis*. Vatican City. Retrieved from https://en.wikipedia.org/wiki/Gravissimum_educationis

Rest, J. (1994). Background: Theory and research. In J. R. Rest & D. Narvaez (Eds.), *Moral development in the professions: Psychology and applied ethics* (pp. 1–26). Hillsdale, NJ: Lawrence Erlbaum.

Rest, J., Narvaez, D., Bebeau, M., & Thoma, S. (1999). A Neo-Kohlbergian approach: The DIT and schema theory. *Educational Psychology Review, 11*(4), 291–324.

Rest, J., Thoma, S., & Bebeau, M. J. (1999a). *Postconventional moral thinking: A neo-Kohlbergian approach*. Mahwah, NJ: Lawrence Erlbaum.

Rest, J., Thoma, S., & Edwards, L. (1997). Designing and validating a measure of moral judgement: Stage preference and stage consistency approaches. *Journal of Educational Psychology, 89*(1), 5–28.

Rymarz, R., & Graham, J. (2006). Australian core Catholic youth, Catholic schools and religious education. *British Journal of Religious Education, 28*(1), 79–89. doi: 10.1080/01416200500273745.

Rymarz, R. M. (2011). The future of Catholic schools in a secular culture of religious choice. *Journal of Religion and Society, 13*, 1–12.

Sergiovanni, T. J. (2000). *Leadership for the schoolhouse*. San Francisco: Jossey-Bass.

Sockett, H. (2008). The moral and epistemic purposes of teacher education. *Handbook of research on teacher education. Enduring questions in changing contexts* (pp. 45–65). Abingdon, London: Routledge.

Spring, J. (2009). *Globalisation and education: An Introduction*. Abingdon, London: Routledge.

Thoma, S. J. (2002). An overview of the Minnesota approach to research in moral development. *Journal of Moral Education, 31*(3), 225–245. doi: 10.1080/0305724022000008098.

Van den Branden, K., Van Avermaet, P., & Van Houtte, M. (Eds.). (2010). *Equity and excellence in education: Towards maximal learning opportunities for all students*. Abingdon, London: Routledge.

Voas, D., & Crockett, A. (2005). Religion in Britain: Neither believing nor belonging. *Sociology, 39*(1), 11–28.

Wilkinson, P. (2013). *Latest Australian Mass participation stats. Catholica*, September 6.

Chapter 10

Curriculum, culture and Catholic Education: A Queensland perspective[1]

Jim Gleeson, John O'Gorman and Maureen O'Neill

Introduction

Familiar descriptions of curriculum as a 'selection from the culture made on the basis of ideology' (Lawton, 1975) and 'the story we tell our children about the good life' (Trant, 2007) are indicative of the reality that curricula are never value-free (Cornbleth, 1990; Grundy, 1987). Various faith communities understandably wish to see their particular worldviews reflected in their curricula (Hewer, 2001; Walford, 2002). For example, the Congregation for Catholic Education (CCE, 1977) portrays the Catholic school as a 'synthesis of culture and faith and a synthesis of faith and life' (p. 37), while Groome (1996) argues that the 'distinctive characteristics of Catholicism should be reflected in the whole curriculum of Catholic schools' (p. 107). Arthur (2013) suggests that

> ... religion cannot be separated or divorced from the rest of the curriculum ... The idea that the school subjects that make up the curriculum (excluding religious education) are value-free and therefore somehow separate from the Catholic faith is clearly contrary to the Catholic worldview. (p. 86)

There is, however, a paucity of research in relation to curriculum implementation in Catholic schools (Dorman, Fraser, & McRobbie, 1994):

> The rhetoric of the Catholic Church and its schools supports the view that the Catholic school and its classrooms are permeated by a Catholic ethos which manifests itself in distinctive classroom environments. This assertion has not been substantiated by empirical evidence. (p. 7)

The authors have not been able to locate evidence to suggest that this lacuna has subsequently been filled. Drawing on survey and interview data from teachers in Catholic schools in Queensland, the current chapter examines the relationship between curriculum and the faith-based identity of Catholic schools from the perspectives of curriculum planning and classroom practice.

Curriculum integration and faith-based identity

Integrative approaches to curriculum design (Beane, 1995; Dewey, 1938; Kliebard, 1995) are essentially student-centred, whereas teacher-centred, discipline-based approaches, which have their origins in Herbart, are concerned with the correlation of disparate subjects and the avoidance of overlap. As noted by Garcia-Huidobro (2018), 'decades of research on curriculum integration show that its implementation is very difficult because it challenges key assumptions of traditional schooling and requires a considerable amount of time for negotiation and management [and] the hardest challenge is socio-cultural [insofar as] parents who are concerned for the cultural capital of their children usually resist it' (p. 33). Drawing on Bourdieu (1990), Garcia-Huidobro (2018) favours interdisciplinary 'curriculum integration without erasing the boundaries between areas that have different criteria and processes for constructing knowledge curriculum [known as] interstitial' (p. 34). Beane (1995) recognises the importance and complexity of curriculum integration as 'a way of thinking about what schools are for, about the sources of curriculum, and about the uses of knowledge' (p. 1).

Drake (2012, pp. 14–26) identifies four main forms of curriculum integration:

- Intra-disciplinary where a particular theme or topic is fused with an existing subject-based curriculum, for example environmental sustainability in one or more discrete learning areas (Krebbs, 2000).
- Multidisciplinary integration where deliberate connections are made, when appropriate, between distinct subject disciplines, for example Study of Society and Environment in Australia (Dowden, 2007).
- Interdisciplinary integration where common themes are identified, prioritised and explicated across existing learning areas, for example the Humanities Curriculum Project (Stenhouse, 1968). The general capabilities in the Australian Curriculum (ACARA, 2012) have the (unrealised) capacity to play such a role.
- Transdisciplinary integration, starting from students' authentic interests and questions, corresponding with Beane's (1995) assertion, reminiscent of Dewey, that 'the sources of curriculum ought to be problems, issues, and concerns posed by life itself' (p. 1).

While such categories do not formally feature in Catholic Education discourse, the CCE and various Catholic commentators would appear to favour an interdisciplinary approach to knowledge:

> Each discipline is not an island inhabited by a form of knowledge that is distinct and ring fenced; rather, it is in a dynamic relationship with all other forms of knowledge, each of which expresses something about the human person and touches upon some truth. (CCE, 2014, p. 67)

Education should lead to the integration of what is learned, breaking down traditional subject demarcations, overcoming fragmentation and encouraging dialogue between disciplines ... address[ing] the integral development of the person: aesthetic, creative, critical, cultural, emotional, intellectual, moral, physical, political, social and spiritual. (Murray, 1991, p. 20)

RE alone does not make the Catholic school ... The Catholic school seeks to integrate the curriculum, to unify faith and culture, and to bring together the different pieces of the school programme into a higher synthesis that influences the social and spiritual formation of pupils. (Lane, 1991, p. 12)

In similar vein, Grace (2010, 2013; see Chapter 4 in this book) argues that Catholic social teaching (CST) should permeate the Catholic secondary school curriculum across the following areas:

- Religious, moral and cultural.
- Economic, business and enterprise.
- Social, environmental and political.

CST emerged in the late 19th century out of concern for the rights of workers and societal inequalities and injustices associated with the excesses of capitalism. Grounded in a theological and philosophical anthropology of the human person, it draws on the rich justice teachings of the Hebrew and Christian scriptures. The 1963 papal encyclical, *Pacem in Terris* (Pope John XXIII), affirmed that every human being has universal and inviolable rights and duties. Most recently, Pope Francis has promulgated his broad-ranging and celebrated encyclical *Laudato Si'* (Pope Francis, 2015) focusing on care for our common home, the ecological crisis and ecological education.

The Ontario Institute for Catholic Education (1996) views curriculum as holistic and transformative and draws a useful distinction between curriculum *separation* (Religious Education), curriculum *permeation* (school ethos/culture) and curriculum *integration* (see Chapter 6 in the current volume):

[Curriculum is a] vehicle for personal and social change based on principles of justice and the view of the learner as agent-of-change ... an interdisciplinary or transdisciplinary experience ... [that] demonstrates the Catholic character of learning [and] bring[s] about a critical perspective on social and global issues. (p. 26)

The Institute wisely warns against superficial and trivial links where religious concepts and ideas are forcefully imposed on learning areas in the name of integration. Their initial approach involved the fusion of their Graduate Expectations[2] (Institute for Catholic Education, 1998) with the Ontario

Ministry of Education's expected learning outcomes for specific subjects. More recently, their focus has shifted to the integration of CST and critical literacy across the curriculum. Arthur (2013) describes the work of the Institute as 'impressive insofar as it seeks no less than the integration of the Catholic faith into all aspects of the curriculum' (p. 94). The Ontario approach, involving key themes and essential questions, represents a combination of Drake's (2012) transformative and interdisciplinary models in a manner consistent with State requirements.

The Australian Curriculum (ACARA, 2012) attempts 'to integrate a range of often conflicting approaches embodied in previous curriculum models' (Australian Government, 2014, p. 76), namely subject disciplines, general capabilities and cross-curriculum priorities. The student-centred outcomes based education (Donnelly, 2007) approach has been replaced by a standards based curriculum where 'explicit content and assessment' (p. 17) are delineated for academic subjects. While the recent curriculum review (Donnelly, 2007) recognises that 'the lack of integration of the curriculum in the primary years ... has exacerbated the issue of an overcrowded curriculum' (p. 3), it expresses a clear preference for a subject-centred curriculum: 'Basing the curriculum on the world of the child ... faces the risk of narrowly defining what students learn and what they experience' (Donnelly, 2007, p. 29).

This is the background against which the Catholic Education authorities in Queensland, judiciously avoiding the problematic concept of 'Catholic curriculum' (D'Orsa, 2013; Davis & Franchi, 2013), established a Chair of Identity and Curriculum in Catholic Education at the Australian Catholic University, Brisbane. The ensuing research began with a reconnaissance of the attitudes and professional practices of teachers in Catholic schools that focused on their perceptions of the relationship between curriculum and identity.

Methodology

The authors adopted a mixed methods approach, involving a survey of the professional beliefs and practices of teachers in Queensland Catholic primary and secondary schools and some follow-up interviews, focusing on two related questions:

- What importance do teachers attach to the planned integration of a Catholic perspective across the whole curriculum of Catholic schools and why?
- To what extent do teachers in Catholic schools integrate a Catholic perspective when teaching of their subjects?

Representatives of the main stakeholders were consulted about the design of the survey which also drew on a cognate USA-based study of Catholic School administrators and teachers (Convey, 2012). The survey (see Appendix 3) included items about the faith-based identity and purposes of Catholic schools (Gleeson, O'Gorman, & O'Neill, 2018) as well as specific closed and open-ended items regarding faith-based aspects of curriculum planning and practice. Ethical approval was granted by the University Research Ethics Committee and the informed consent of the relevant school authorities and participating teachers was secured.

The survey was set up in Qualtrics software and piloted with 88 teachers in four Rockhampton Catholic schools. It was distributed electronically to all 6,832 teachers in Queensland Catholic schools in March 2014 and subsequently administered at school staff meetings in 20 Brisbane schools. In accordance with the normal requirements of research ethics, the associated information letter explained that the purpose of the study was to establish teachers' views in relation to the integration of a Catholic perspective across the formal curriculum as an expression of the faith-based identity of the school. Two thousand two hundred and eighty-seven completed surveys were received by January 2015, representing an overall response rate of 33.5%.

These respondents were representative of the population of teachers in Queensland Catholic schools by gender and school type and included a broad range of ages (mode 40–49) and teaching experience (mode 11–20). Half the respondents had taught for more than 10 years in Catholic schools, while over 80% identified as Catholic and one-third said that religion is very important to how they live their lives (subsequently referred to as religiosity). One-third had added professional responsibilities ranging from Principal to 'Position of Added Responsibility'. Almost two-thirds had current or past experience of teaching Religious Education and/or Study of Religion (RE/SoR) and three-quarters rated their knowledge of Catholic teaching as either very good (24%) or good (53%).

Survey data were analysed using SPSS and multiple sequential regression analysis was used for deeper analysis (Gleeson, O'Gorman, & O'Neill, 2018). Given the size of the sample, statistical significance was defined in terms of very large degrees of freedom at the very conservative level of .003.[3] In view of the large number of independent and outcome variables it was decided to combine them into composite sets in the interests of increased reliability and reducing the problem of multiple tests. These composites are set out in Table 10.1.

Sets 1–5 variables have to do with teacher-related variables while Set 6 variables (faith-based identity and school characteristics) relate to the schools in which they teach while Sets 7 (curriculum integration) and 8 (confidence and willingness to integrate) are the output variables of particular relevance to this chapter. The order of entry to the regression was determined by the causal priority of variables (Cohen & Cohen, 1975) with sets involving teacher 'demographic' variables being entered first followed by school-related variables. Where beta weights are reported, it should be noted that, according to Cohen and Cohen (1975), social scientists consider correlations of .1 to .3 as small to medium.

Table 10.1 Variables used in regression analysis

Set 1	Demographics	Gender, age, level, length of service, level of appointment (APPOINT)
Set 2	Role in Catholic school	Teacher of Religion/Studies of Religion (RELTEACH); responsibility for curriculum leadership, length of service in Catholic Education (LOSCATH)
Set 3	Religion and religiosity	Nominated religion; importance of 'religion to how I live my life' (RELGIMP)
Set 4	Self-reported levels of knowledge	Self-reported levels of knowledge of Catholic teaching/social teaching/moral teaching combined to form a single variable (KNOWTOT).
Set 5	Reasons for working in Catholic schools	School environment (ENVIRO) Commitment to Catholic faith (COMIT)
Set 6	Purpose and Identity of Catholic schools	Faith-based purpose (PURPCATH); Catholic school are different (CATSCHDF); importance of Catholic identity of schools (CATIDIMP); importance of religious practices to the identity of the Catholic school (PRACTICES); importance of school community members to the identity of the Catholic school (PEOPLE)
Set 7	Planned integration of Catholic teaching across the curriculum	As a characteristic of Catholic schools (INTEGR1) Its importance for faith-based identity (INTEGR2) Classroom practice (INTEGR3)
Set 8	Confidence and willingness	Confidence to integrate a Catholic perspective Willingness to integrate a Catholic perspective

Principal component analysis (PCA) of the 14 individual Set 6 characteristics, followed by Varimax rotation, indicated that two components – PRACTICES and PEOPLE – accounted for 49% of the variance. The former component links the Catholic identity of the school to expressions of religious faith such as prayer, liturgies, retreats, symbols, the orthodoxy of RE and caring community. The PEOPLE component links the identity of the school to the Catholicity of the members of the school community, that is principal, students and teachers.

Some 43 survey respondents, representing a wide range of teaching experience, volunteered for follow-up individual interviews. Following analysis of the survey data, semi-structured interviews were conducted with 20 of these volunteers (13 female, 7 male, equally divided between primary and secondary) to explore and illuminate the main survey findings. Given the particular focus of the study on the wider curriculum, secondary teachers of RE were not included in this first state of interviews. The main purpose of the interviews, which took approximately 35 minutes and were digitally recorded, was to explore teachers' understandings of the relationship between the identity of Catholic schools and the formal curriculum.

Analysis of interview responses as well as open-ended survey questions involved an interpretivist paradigm going beyond statistics, measurements and numbers and allowing for thick descriptions (Dumas & Anderson, 2014).

224 Jim Gleeson, John O'Gorman, et al.

Using a thematic coding approach (Miles & Huberman, 1994), responses were categorised according to emergent themes (Lewis, 2009). Transcripts were studied, themes were identified and responses were indexed, organised and classified in line with the emerging themes (Creswell, 2012). Use of *NVivo* Version 11 supported the process of coding. This bottom–up approach to coding enabled the emergence of new codes, while having two independent coders with inter-rater reliability ranging in the ninetieth percentile, allowed for the reliable application of the coding scheme.

Findings

Survey and interview findings are presented in separate sections.

Survey findings

When teachers were invited to rate the importance of each one of 15 given characteristics of Catholic schools (Question 17, Appendix 3), 40% of respondents regarded the planned integration of Catholic teachings across all learning areas as a very important characteristic of Catholic schools with 39% rating it as important and 21% as unimportant. However, when weighted points were allocated to the ratings and rankings for this item, it came 11th of the 15 given characteristics for both ratings and rankings.

Regression analysis found that Sets 1–5 variables accounted for 12% of the variance in these ratings ($p < .001$) and religiosity (RELGIMP), with a beta value greater than .1, was the only statistically significant predictor variable ($p < .003$) (see Appendix 2, Table B9).

When Set 6 variables were added to the regression, an additional 13% of the variance was accounted for. The overall regression remained significant ($p < .001$) and the strongest predictors ($p < .001$) were, in order of importance, the perceived importance of community characteristics (PEOPLE), of faith-based school practice characteristics (PRACTICES) (both with beta weights greater than .1) and religiosity (see Appendix 2, Table B9).

In order to address the two explicit research questions introduced earlier, the survey sought responses to the following items (Set 7) on a scale of strongly agree, agree, unsure, disagree, strongly disagree:

A. The planned integration of a Catholic perspective across the whole curriculum should be a key characteristic/feature of the Catholic school.
B. When teaching my subjects I integrate a Catholic perspective.

Statement A

Some 58% of teachers agreed or strongly agreed with Statement A while almost 25% were 'unsure', an option that was not provided for in the case of Question 17. Predictor Sets 1–5 accounted for approximately 16% of the variance with respect to Statement A and this was statistically significant ($p < .001$). Inspection of Table B10 (Appendix 2) indicates that three predictors had statistically significant beta weights ($p < .003$), all greater than .1, namely RELGIMP, KNOWTOT and COMIT. The planned integration of a Catholic perspective across the whole curriculum is seen as most important by those who consider their religion important to how they live their lives, who consider they have a better knowledge of the Catholic faith and who have chosen to teach in Catholic schools because of their faith commitment.

When Set 6 variables are added to the regression (Table B10, Appendix 2) the overall regression remains significant ($p < .001$) and an additional 5% of the variance is accounted for. The strongest predictor of the perceived importance ($p < .003$) of Statement A was the perceived importance of PEOPLE characteristics of Catholic schools, followed by RELGIMP, the perceived importance of PRACTICES characteristics of Catholic schools and the perceived importance of the faith-based identity of a Catholic school (CATIDIMP). Beta weights were greater than .1 in the case of all four variables.

The survey also included an open-ended question inviting teachers to justify their ratings for the importance of the planned integration of a Catholic perspective across the whole curriculum. While very few indicated unqualified agreement with this idea, more than a quarter said that the integration of a Catholic perspective reinforces or expresses the identity of their school, for example

> A Catholic perspective is one of the things that sets a Catholic school apart from independent and state schools [and] should be integrated across the whole curriculum.

> Integrating Gospel values is what makes us different from other schools.

> Because it is at the heart of what we do and who we are.

> It is our core business and the main reason for our school's existence.

Others responded in terms of Catholic school ethos and the importance of teaching values such as social justice and giving personal witness, for example

> What makes us unique as a Catholic School [is that] issues are discussed in terms of the Christian values of social justice, stewardship and equity.

> It should be part of who we are as teachers in a Catholic school.

Approximately 15% saw curriculum integration in terms of the unplanned use of 'teachable moments'.

> Integration should not be manufactured ... we do it incidentally as often as we can.

> Whenever the opportunity to teach gospel values arises we should take it.

One-third of the teacher responses were vague or unhelpful, while 10% clearly disagreed with the idea of integrating a Catholic perspective and a similar proportion identified particular subjects where they felt this was not feasible (particularly mathematics teachers).

Respondents were also asked to rate their confidence and willingness with respect to planning for the integration of Catholic teaching across the curriculum (Set 8). Three-quarters indicated willingness to do so (particularly social and moral teaching) and two-thirds expressed confidence in their ability to do so. Regression analysis (see Table 10.3) found that the strongest predictors of both willingness and confidence were high levels of KNOWTOT, being a teacher of RE/SoR, having added professional responsibilities and higher levels of religiosity – all of which were also highly predictive of positive responses to Statement A above. When Sets 5–6 variables are included in the regression, the three faith-based school identity-related variables (CATIDIMP, PRACTICES and PEOPLE) as well as KNOWTOT and being Catholic were the strongest predictor of willingness while the strongest predictors of teachers' confidence were KNOWTOT, PRACTICES and CATIDIMP in that order.

Statement B

While Statement A sought respondents' views regarding the whole idea of integrating Catholic perspectives across the curriculum, the focus of Statement B was on classroom practice. Over half the respondents said they integrated a Catholic perspective in their teaching often or very often while 40% said they 'sometimes' did so. Sets 1–5 variables accounted for 29% of the variance and this was statistically significant ($p < .001$). Inspection of Table B11 (Appendix 2) indicates that four predictors had statistically significant beta weights ($p < .003$): KNOWTOT, RELTEACH, COMIT and RELGIMP with all four variables having beta weights greater than .1. Those who considered their knowledge of the Catholic faith to be good, teachers of religion, those who chose to teach in a Catholic school because of their faith commitment and those who considered their religion as important to how they lived their lives were most likely to report that they integrated Catholic teaching across the curriculum as part of their classroom practice. The addition of Set 6 to the predictive model (Table B11, Appendix 2) increased the variance accounted for to 30% and this was statistically significant ($p < .001$). KNOWTOT, RELGIMP, and RELTEACH remained statistically significant ($p < .003$) while two Set 6 predictors were also statistically significant: CATIDIMP and PRACTICES. The beta weight for KNOWTOT indicates that it remained the most important predictor and this was confirmed by the part correlation. Those who considered that their knowledge of Catholic teaching was good, who saw the faith-based identity of Catholic schools as important and who considered the PRACTICES characteristics of the school as important were most likely to report that the curriculum integration of Catholic teaching was part of their practice.

Respondents were also asked to rate their confidence and willingness with respect to implementing the integration of Catholic teaching across the curriculum. More than two-thirds of them indicated confidence in their capacity to do so (particularly Catholic social and moral teaching) and three-quarters expressed willingness to do so. Regression analysis revealed a very clear pattern insofar as KNOWTOT and RELGIMP were the strongest predictors of confidence from both Sets 1–5 and 1–6 ($p < .003$) (Table B12, Appendix 2). While these variables were also the strongest Sets 1–5 predictors of willingness, KNOWTOT was the strongest Sets 1–6 predictor of willingness followed by PRACTICES, being Catholic, RELGIMP, PEOPLE and CATIDIMP (Table B13, Appendix 2). What emerges then is that those who were most willing to integrate Catholic perspectives across the curriculum rated their knowledge of Catholic teaching highly, considered PRACTICES characteristics important for Catholic school identity, were Catholic, scored highly on religiosity, considered PEOPLE characteristics important for Catholic school identity and considered the Catholic identity of the school as important. One of the many implications is that non-Catholics were less willing than Catholics to integrate Catholic teachings across the curriculum.

Interview findings

It is reasonable to assume that teachers who were happy to volunteer for interview were likely to have a relatively strong commitment to faith-based school identity. Consistent with survey respondents' ratings and rankings for this item, interviewees did not see the integration of a Catholic perspective across the curriculum as a priority for Catholic schools. A male teacher working in middle management at secondary level suggested that 'threading that [Christian] philosophy and understanding through the broader curriculum is, to be honest, a bit hit and miss'. Asked about their curriculum planning and implementation, interviewees expressed a range of views, ranging from positive responses to saying that the planned integration of Catholic identity across the formal curriculum was either not desirable or not feasible. A fuller account of the interview data is available on the project website at http://www.acu.edu.au/775158. For purposes in this chapter, their responses are categorised under three main headings:

- Availing of 'teachable moments' that may spontaneously arise.
- Teacher-student relationships as reflected in the axiom, 'I teach who I am'.
- Intra-disciplinary integration in some individual subjects.

Teachable moments

When asked whether they integrated a Catholic perspective in a planned way, many interviewees made reference to 'teachable moments' or 'incidental opportunities'. The general understanding of 'teachable moments' was that they arise spontaneously and require opportunism on the teacher's part. Primary teachers were at pains to emphasise the importance of an organic rather than a planned approach to curriculum integration, for example 'we try not to force it too much ... there are opportunities without making it artificially forced'; 'if you try to force, it's too false'. An experienced primary teacher, who regards teachable moments as 'precious', felt that they are 'difficult to plan for' and that you need to be 'sincere to get the most out of it', while a secondary school principal referred to them as 'a great gift'. A secondary teacher suggested that one had to 'avail of the opportunity when it arises naturally [when] a Catholic perspective is there accidentally or coincidentally'. Another secondary teacher remarked that 'if things come up regarding something theological – for example HPE and sex education – you run with that'.

There was a definite sense that the usefulness of 'teachable moments' depends on the teacher. A secondary teacher with a background in theology remarked that 'it's not something that's pre-planned but the knowledge that I have has allowed me to encourage those discussions'. A Health and Physical Education (HPE) teacher opined that 'it depends on the teacher's familiarity with the RE curriculum'. An experienced secondary teacher gave an example of a relevant, unplanned, teachable moment that arose in a Pre-Vocational Maths lesson:

> I was doing a unit on investing your money, stock exchange, whatever …. This generated into a discussion on the good and bad of gambling. So I said, let's jump on Google and find out what Jesus says about gambling instead of giving to your family and the selfishness of that … I don't specifically plan to bring those things in. But they just happen. I don't specifically write in my plan for the day …

Some interviewees were particularly conscious of the value of building on students' questions:

> … the most valuable time to teach Catholic spirituality is when children have questions [leading to] discussions about God stuff …. these kids are just itching to ask such questions …. but no one really discusses it with them because they don't talk religion at home. (Primary teacher)

'I teach who I am'

A number of interviewees saw the transmission of Catholic identity in terms of giving witness to the faith, for example

> Catholic identity for me is in the whole curriculum because it's who I am. That just comes naturally to me. When you're teaching history and

teaching about the treatment of the Indigenous people ... That again is who I am. (Primary teacher)

Two main sub-themes emerged here – relationship and role modelling. Those who emphasised relationship referred to Gospel values and pastoral care aspects of curriculum. For example

> It would come out through your relationship with the students within the subject class, for example through behaviour management ... [I say] I'm never going to judge you, I'm just going to manage your behaviour and the kids really respect that .... (Secondary)

A number of interviewees made reference to the teacher as role model:

> Teaching in a Catholic school isn't just a job ... it's actually an invitation to these kids to be part of something bigger ... and they will best model that from the behaviour of the teacher. (Secondary)

> Teachers in a Catholic school ... are modelling to our kids and to the parents what it is to be a Catholic and what it is to live the life in a Catholic school in general in society. (Secondary)

> They know you are a Catholic, a Christian and you have those standards and it sort of emanates from you and the students understand that. (Secondary)

> You teach what you are by default, unless you're a very, very good actor. (Primary)

Intra-disciplinary integration

Some teachers offered practical examples of curriculum integration within their own individual subjects. English was the most commonly mentioned subject in this regard, for example

> We select texts knowing that we talk about them from a Catholic perspective ... for example, social justice perspectives come through as a common theme [in] Nineteen Eighty-Four. (Secondary teacher)

> When doing narratives in English literacy groups I might deconstruct the text of Bible stories for spelling. (Primary teacher)

Three primary teachers and a secondary teacher found Science to be a good vehicle for integrating a Catholic perspective. One primary teacher felt 'that Science allows awe and wonder to be raised ... that a creator that did this knows us intimately'. A secondary teacher of physics saw opportunities in 'the Big Bang theory and what actually happened prior to that' while another primary teacher remarked that 'the science debate would be interesting [especially] with the Pope making his Big Bang proclamation'. She also identified the potential of sustainability as a topic:

> I like to get into the theological questions with them, so is it our duty as people of the world to look after our Earth so that our children have somewhere to live, or is it our duty as Catholics, or good Christians to take care of the Earth that God has given us?

A secondary teacher instanced 'business concentration' as an example of the opportunities to introduce CST afforded in Economics. A primary teacher gave an example from History:

> When we talked about the effects of colonisation we were able to link in religion and challenge it …. We've been looking at explorers and the Columbian Exchange, with the bringing of Christianity and asking was that a right or wrong thing to do as well.

Working with teachers of Art, English, Geography, HPE and Science at different year levels on a subject-by-subject basis, the social justice coordinator in a secondary school remarked that, due to a lack of relevant knowledge, most teachers had not 'made an explicit link back to Catholic social teaching, gospel values' when dealing with sustainability.

A number of interviewees expressed reservations about the ability of their colleagues to integrate a Catholic perspective across the curriculum due to certain knowledge deficits. For example, a secondary Science teacher felt strongly that

> Integration is not always possible. Say I'm teaching evolution, I'll only ever take the view of biological theories. I won't actually include religious views in terms of say evolution versus creation … that should be left with people who have got much more formal training than myself to talk about evolution versus creation.

Meanwhile, some experienced teachers expressed concerns regarding the declining levels of teachers' knowledge of the faith on the part of younger, less experienced, colleagues, for example

> One of the biggest challenges that we have in Catholic schools at the moment is that so many teachers are not practising Catholics themselves … a lot of people whose knowledge of the Catholic faith has stopped in Grade 7 are now teaching kids … You have to have that knowledge base. (Secondary)

> The new generation of teachers coming through don't have their own faith themselves. (Primary)

> Younger people at this campus are not as familiar with Catholic traditions or the teachings. (Primary)

Summary

When interviewees were asked about their classroom practice, most saw the integration of a Catholic perspective in terms of using spontaneous 'teachable moments' and/or personal witness ('I teach who I am'). Interviewees also expressed concern regarding teachers' levels of theological literacy, feeling they were not sufficient to allow them engage with curriculum topics from a faith perspective with more experienced teachers suggesting that this was particularly problematic in the case of younger teachers. More than half the survey respondents were positively disposed towards the planned integration of a Catholic perspective in their curriculum planning and a similar proportion indicated that they integrated a Catholic perspective in their classroom practice. However, their mean ranking for the importance of this characteristic of Catholic schools was 11th of the 15 given items.

An overview of the most statistically significant predictors emerging from the survey data is presented in Table 10.2.

RELGIMP emerges as a consistently strong predictor (Sets 1–5 *and* Sets 1–6) of both integration statements, while KNOWTOT is also a strong Sets 1–5 predictor of both statements and of curriculum practice in the case of Sets 1–6. COMIT is a strong Sets 1–5 predictor of both statements while being a teacher of religion is a strong predictor of curriculum practice. When the school identity and characteristics variables (Set 6) are included, PRACTICES characteristics and CATIDIMP are consistently strong predictors along with while PEOPLE characteristics remain statistically significant in the case of Statement A.

A summary of statistically significant predictor variables for respondents' confidence and willingness with regard to the integration of Catholic perspectives across the curriculum is presented in Table 10.3.

KNOWTOT and RELGIMP are clearly the strongest and most consistent predictors (Sets 1–5 *and* Sets 1–6) while PRACTICES, PEOPLE,

Table 10.2 Statistically significant predictors of Statements A and B

Predictor variables	Statement A Curriculum planning		Statement B Curriculum practice	
	Sets 1–5	Sets 1–6	Sets 1–5	Sets 1–6
KNOWTOT	√		√	√
RELGIMP	√	√	√	√
RELTEACH			√	√
COMIT	√		√	
PEOPLE	-	√	-	
PRACTICES	-	√	-	√
CATIDIMP	-	√	-	√

232 Jim Gleeson, John O'Gorman, et al.

Table 10.3 Statistically significant predictors of teachers' confidence and willingness to plan for/implement the integration of Catholic perspectives across the curriculum

Predictor variables	Confidence		Willingness	
	Sets 1–5	Sets 1–6	Sets 1–5	Sets 1–6
KNOWTOT	√	√	√	√
RELTEACH	√			
RELGIMP	√	√	√	√
CATHOLIC				√
PRACTICES		√		√
PEOPLE				√
CATIDIMP				√

CATIDIMP and being Catholic are strong Sets 1–6 predictors of willingness to integrate Catholic perspectives across the curriculum.

Overall then, the survey data reveals a consistent and not unexpected picture insofar as the strongest Sets 1–6 predictors of the perceived importance of integrating Catholic perspectives across the curriculum and of the reported integration of Catholic perspectives – KNOWTOT, RELGIMP, PRACTICES, PEOPLE and CATIDIMP – are faith-related while COMIT is a strong Set 1–5 predictor of Statement A and being a teacher of religion is a strong predictor of Statement B.

Discussion

Some of the more interesting themes arising from the above findings are now considered from both empirical and theoretical perspectives. Discussion of the empirical findings focuses on the stark contrast between survey and interview responses and on the variables that are consistently associated with the integration of Catholic perspectives across the curriculum at levels that are very statistically significant. The theoretical aspects of the discussion focus on the relationship between curriculum and culture in Catholic schools, the potential of CST to give meaning to the integration of Catholic perspectives across the curriculum, and, given the countercultural nature of those teachings, the associated issue of the role of the teacher when dealing with controversial issues in the classroom.

The empirical evidence

The generally positive responses of survey respondents to planning for and implementing the integration of Catholic perspectives across the curriculum are at variance with interviewees' accounts of their classroom practice. Whereas over half the survey respondents said they integrated a Catholic perspective in their teaching often or very often, interviewees saw such integration in terms of using spontaneous 'teachable moments' and/or personal witness ('I teach who I am'). This may suggest that the former interpreted the relevant survey item (Statement B above) rather liberally or it may simply indicate a sharp divide between rhetoric and reality.

Notwithstanding the importance of personal witness, such teacher-student relationships are a fundamental aspect of all classroom interactions regardless of the denomination of the school. The use of teachable moments is a characteristic of good teaching. For example, Hess and Stoddard (2007) remark that 'the attacks of 9/11 are just too important to ignore. They present the ultimate teachable moment' (p. 231). While the spontaneous organic nature of such moments is an obvious strength, it is also a weakness insofar as such moments may be infrequent and the teacher may be ill prepared to avail of them when they do arise. Although systematic curriculum planning and teachable moments may appear to be polar opposites, the adoption of a nuanced approach to their relationship is worth considering. As discussed in the next chapter, some participating teachers in our classroom-based action research (see Chapter 11) as well as some participants in the associated dissemination workshop had reservations about a systematic curriculum planning strategy. The compromise solution here is the 'planned teachable moment' where the teacher introduces her/his pre-prepared curriculum response when the opportunity, either natural or contrived, presents itself. In other words, a 'process' approach to curriculum design may be more appropriate than a 'product' approach (Stenhouse, 1975), particularly in the context of a system that is already obsessed with pre-defined learning outcomes.

With respect to the survey findings for the integration of Catholic perspectives across the curriculum, regression analysis consistently identifies certain faith-based variables as the most statistically significant predictors of Statements A and B above and of teachers' associated confidence and willingness. As in the case of the faith-based identity and characteristics of Catholic schools (Chapter 7), high levels of teacher religiosity and knowledge of Catholic teaching emerged as consistently strong predictors of positive attitudes towards the integration of Catholic perspectives across the curriculum (Table 10.2). It is also noteworthy that it is faith-based rather than demographic variables such as gender, age, religion and position that emerged as the strongest predictors. While teachers of religion are also well disposed towards the integration of Catholic perspectives, the focus of the current research was on the curriculum beyond Religious Education.

These findings provide valuable guidance and criteria for any future attempts at the integration of Catholic perspectives across the curriculum. They clearly indicate that leadership of any such initiative should be entrusted to teachers for whom is important to how they live their lives, who believe that their own knowledge of Catholic teaching is high, who have chosen to work in Catholic schools because of their faith commitment and whose ratings of the importance of faith-based characteristics of Catholic schools are high. This leaves us with the big question of the availability of sufficient teachers meeting these criteria.

The predictive strength of these faith-based variables is particularly noteworthy in a post-secular age, characterised by de-traditionalisation (Boeve, 2005; Pollefeyt & Bouwens, 2010) and pluralisation (Arbuckle, 2013). Croke (2007) suggests that the authenticity of Catholic schools in Australia has become problematic in an environment where their growth 'is being entirely sustained by middle class families of other Christian denominations, and non-Christian faiths (Muslim, Buddhist, Hindu)' (p. 805). Dowling, Beavis, Underwood, Sadeghi, and O'Malley (2009, p. 28) report on the 'remarkable greening' of Brisbane Catholic schools where the age profile of teachers is lowering and the proportion of non-Catholic teachers is growing. Croke (2007) reminds us of the imminent retirement of 'qualified teachers, many former religious or religiously formed to some extent, whose careers have developed with the system' and notes that available studies of those already teaching in Catholic schools have 'raised alarm bells in some quarters' (pp. 815–816).

The profile of students attending Catholic schools is also changing. Dowling et al. (2009) found that upwardly mobile parents, regardless of their religion, are enrolling their children in Catholic secondary schools 'for predominantly pragmatic rather than religious reasons [at a time when there is a] marked decline in religious commitment' (p. 38). The faith commitment of students in Catholic schools is tenuous (Croke, 2007; Mason, Singleton, & Webber, 2007; Pollefeyt & Bouwens, 2014) and the 'authenticity of the Catholic school [is being challenged by the] annually increasing proportion of non-Catholic students, along with students from mainly middle class Catholic families whose adhesion to their Faith is weak' (Croke, 2007, p. 823).

Curriculum and culture in Catholic Education

If teachers and school leaders are to address these emerging challenges and dilemmas and to apply the lessons of the research reported above they would do well to revisit the relationship between curriculum and culture. Curriculum is best seen as contextualised social process (Cornbleth, 1990) and any attempts on the part of Catholic schools to integrate faith-based perspectives must take cognisance of the rapidly changing environment in which these schools exist, one where their faith-based identity is increasingly challenged by secularisation on the one hand and by an educational environment characterised by neoliberal ideology (Gleeson, 2015) and the hegemony of subjects on the other.

The CCE is rightly critical of the growing popularity of a 'merely functional view of education' (CCE, 2014, p. 12) and concerned about the dominance of market values in education and the associated temptation for governments to simply respond to 'the demands deriving from the ever-changing economic situation' (p. 64). For example, it is some 30 years since Lynch (1985, p. 13) observed the disparity between 'the rhetoric' of Catholic teaching regarding the importance of educating the whole person and 'the realities of our institutions' in an Ireland where almost all primary schools and the majority of secondary schools were Catholic. More recently, Dunne (2002, p. 83) suggests that the 'colonization' of the Irish education system by economic considerations has resulted in 'the triumph of a managerialist ethos which reduces accountability to accountancy ... [with] the whole system so highly centralised and every content area reduced to a common currency ... [that there is] little freedom for teachers or schools to experiment with different approaches'.

There is widespread recognition of the growing influence of neoliberal market values on Australian education and curriculum policy (Ditchburn, 2012; Klenowski & Wyatt-Smith, 2012; Lingard, 2010; Polesel, Rice, & Dulfer, 2014). Similar concerns have been noted in Ontario Catholic schools where 'a demanding curriculum that focuses on results ... is another issue of concern for many school boards [and teachers] feel pressure from the Ministry of Education to improve EQAO[4] results and implement government initiatives' (Institute for Education, 2007, p. 10). Meanwhile Pascoe (2007) suggests that Australian Catholic Education is faced with the dilemma of having to serve two masters:

> In describing the nature and purpose of Catholic schools to potential students and parents, emphases are likely to be on the education of the whole person, on faith and religious education and on pastoral care and learning outcomes. In liaising with government, emphases are likely to be on core purpose, support of democratic principles and institutions, parent choice, legislative compliance, good governance, sound educational practice, commitments to accountability, and fulfilment of elements of formal agreements. (p. 797)

The support of the CCE for an interdisciplinary curriculum has been introduced earlier in this chapter. However, as noted by Goodson (1994), Stenhouse (1975) and others, the hegemony of subjects is difficult to break down. Stenhouse (1968) found that it militated heavily against his integrated Humanities Curriculum Project while Beane (1995) remarks that

> The separate-subject approach is a legacy of Western-style classical humanism, which views the world in divided compartments [or] territories carved out by academicians for their own interests and purposes ... [and] suggests that the 'good life' consists of intellectual activity within narrowly defined areas. (p. 4)

Australian curriculum discourse, at both State and Federal levels, has been also dominated by subject disciplines to such an extent that the title of Fraser and Bosanquet's (2006) paper, '[t]he curriculum? That's just a unit outline, isn't it?'

seems appropriate at primary and secondary level as well as higher education. In an environment with a strong tendency to see curriculum in terms of content, expected learning outcomes and attainment targets, attempts at curriculum integration are swimming against the tide. For example, the independent reviewers of the Australian Curriculum express regret at the failure to develop 'an overall curriculum framework document ... so as to capture ... potential for flexibility including for integration across learning areas' (Australian Government, 2014, p. 98). This resonates with Dowden's (2007) earlier cautionary words regarding curriculum integration in Australia:

> Powerful forces are allied with the traditional subject-centred single-subject curriculum, not the least being middle grade teachers' own conceptions and views of themselves as 'subject teachers'. As a result, stakeholders in the traditional curriculum may impede the development of student-centred approaches, thus stifling general acceptance of the integrative model. (p. 65)

The general capabilities[5] of the Australian Curriculum, which were developed independently of the learning areas, offer exciting opportunities for a more integrated approach to curriculum. The independent review however notes that, although welcomed and supported in principle, these capabilities 'produced much dissent from [state] jurisdictions – some of which are refusing to incorporate them' (Australian Government, 2014, p. 239). This highlights yet again the tenuous nature of the rhetoric/reality relationship (Apple, 2004; Tiwari, Das, & Sharma, 2015) as reflected in the recommendation of the reviewers that the general capabilities only be embedded in relevant areas of learning. Scanlan (2008, p. 30) believes that the prevailing 'grammar of Catholic schooling' in the United States, those regular structures and rules that have become 'legitimized to the point that they are unquestioned', inhibits many Catholic schools from adhering to CST principles.

The potential of Catholic social teaching

There are, however, beliefs and values that transcend market ideology and provide the basis for alternatives to neoliberalism and the Global Education Reform. As Spring (2009) reminds us, 'some religious and indigenous groups are major dissenters to the world culture and the materialism embodied in the human capital and progressive education models' (p. 144). The radical Catholic movement known as Liberation Theology (Boff, 1987; Smith, 1991), influenced by Paulo Freire among others, is one such movement that seeks to 'free humans from the spiritual vacuum caused by political and economic repression' (Spring, 2009, p. 161).

The interdisciplinary treatment of contemporary social justice issues from the perspective of CST, which is essentially counter-cultural (Scanlan, 2008), provides a realistic opportunity for the tangible expression of faith-based school

Curriculum, culture and Catholic Education   237

identity (Grace, 2010, 2013; Institute for Catholic Education, 1996). As considered in Chapter 2, the main principles of CST include the preferential option for the poor, stewardship of the earth, human solidarity and equality, and respect for human life. Grace (2013) argues that Catholic schools have the

> ... potential to be significant innovators in bringing together the study of Economics, Finance, Business Administration and Enterprise with an in-depth understanding of Catholic religious, moral and social teaching, so that a higher-order level of knowledge and understanding can be achieved in these crucial contemporary subjects. (p. 102)

Conscious of the prevailing influence of market values on education, Grace (2013) calls for the application of CST to real-life situations in response to the 'urgent need to strengthen the Catholic cultural content of the curriculum in general to prevent a process of incorporation into a secularised and technicist educational culture' (p. 104). In an American context Chubbuck (2007) argues that a combination of Ignatian pedagogy[6] with its strong commitment to CST and critical pedagogy supports the development of socially just teachers.

The Ontario Institute for Catholic Education (see Chapter 6 of this volume) allocates various CST principles across different year groups in conjunction with a common set of 'essential questions' that provide a focus for all school subjects. Their review of priorities and issues in Catholic Education (Institute for Catholic Education, 2007) reported that

> Gospel values are lived out in the school's approach to discipline and organization and are infused throughout all aspects of the school curriculum. (p. 3)

> Many school boards reported [that] the teaching of Catholic social justice values and service to others is a very distinctive component of Catholic education .... Community service is a Catholic tradition. There is a real commitment to serving others, especially those less fortunate. (p. 4)

The inclusion of general capabilities in the Australian Curriculum (ACARA, 2012, particularly 'ethical understanding', 'intercultural understanding' and 'critical and creative thinking', provides obvious opportunities for the introduction of some of the basic principles of CST (see Chapter 2). The same is true of cross-curriculum priorities such as 'Aboriginal and Torres Strait Islander histories and cultures' and 'Sustainability'.

Controversial issues in the classroom

The curriculum integration of CST principles inevitably brings to the forefront controversial social and moral issues such as environmental sustainability, war and peace, genocide, racism, migration and food security. Such issues are good examples of teachable moments. While Queensland teacher interviewees had less 'notorious' issues to address than what Hess and Stoddard (2007) had in mind, their attempts to integrate CST principles raised issues such as the treatment of those seeking refuge from persecution, the future of the coalmining industry in the state and the dangers of the pervasive gaming industry, as well as more overtly faith-based concerns such as euthanasia and abortion. The interdisciplinary nature of such issues affords teachers excellent opportunities to go beyond teachable moments by planning multi- or interdisciplinary integration and engaging in critical reflection on their professional roles (Kelly & Minnes Brandes, 2001). Indeed their treatment demands both preparatory research and careful advance planning.

Classroom treatment of controversial issues requires the adoption of critical pedagogy (Cowan & Maitles, 2012) with its focus on 'how domination manifests as both a symbolic and institutional force [in a context where] schools are often rightly criticized for becoming adjuncts of corporations or for modelling themselves on a culture of fear and security' (Giroux, 2011, p. 4). While the treatment of such controversial issues in an educationally appropriate manner poses significant challenges for all teachers, critical pedagogues in Catholic schools are faced with two additional dilemmas. Firstly, how to deal with a situation where the students' views are at variance with official Church teaching; secondly, the very institution that controls their schools is itself not run on democratic lines (Bordell, 2000, pp. 880–883; Kung, 2001).

Out of respect for the autonomy of students and the diversity of their backgrounds, it is incumbent on the teacher as educator to adopt the role of impartial facilitator or neutral chairperson when controversial issues are being considered in the classroom (Brookfield & Preskill, 2005; Cotton, 2006; Kyburz-Graber, 1999; Oulton, Day, Dillon, & Grace, 2004). The teacher's options include presenting all relevant viewpoints 'objectively'; presenting their personal views in a balanced manner; playing 'Devil's advocate' by adopting the most controversial position on the topic (Harwood, 1997). This does not preclude presenting the Church's position where necessary. It is noteworthy that, when English Catholic schools adopted the Humanities Curriculum Project (Stenhouse, 1968), a report commissioned by the Catholic Education Council found that the role of the teacher in dealing with controversial issues emerged as the main concern with 'most of the teachers aspir[ing] to neutrality' (Higgins, 1979, p. 64).

Concluding remarks

At a time when all Australian schools, including Catholic schools, are subject to market forces (Croke, 2007; Lingard, 2010; Rymarz, 2011), the prevalence of neoliberal educational values does not provide a hospitable environment for either curriculum integration or critical pedagogical practices. Meanwhile, the evidence from the Australian research community

(Croke, 2007; Dowling et al. 2009; Mason, Singleton, & Webber, 2007; Pascoe, 2007) suggests that the faith-based identity of Catholic schools is facing serious challenges. The current study found that the teachers who are most positively disposed towards the integration of Catholic perspectives across the curriculum give higher ratings than their peers to the faith-based identity and characteristics of schools, to the importance of religion to how they live their lives and to their own knowledge of Catholic teaching.

The profile of teachers in Catholic schools is changing and teachers' levels of faith commitment and theological literacy are diminishing. As Dorman, Fraser, and McRobbie (1994) remarked some 25 years ago, 'the distinctive nature of Catholic schooling [in Australia] does not extend to all classroom environment dimensions deemed important to Catholic education' (p. 3). Meanwhile, secularisation is challenging the faith-based identities of parents and students. Against all of this background, serious questions are being asked about the faith-based identity of Catholic schools (Pollefeyt & Bouwens, 2010, 2014; Rymarz, 2011). In order to address these challenges by attempting to integrate faith-based perspective across the curriculum, the focus of this chapter, Catholic schools will need to attract and retain teachers who subscribe to and understand Catholic beliefs and traditions. The findings of our longitudinal study of pre-service teachers at an Australian Catholic University clearly indicates that the teachers of the future are more committed to generic professional values rather than the underlying faith-based values of Catholic schooling (see Chapter 9 in this book).

The potential for synergy between CST and education for human rights and social justice provides a valuable platform on which Catholic Education leaders can develop the faith-based identity of their schools at a time when teachers in non-faith based schools are actively engaging with global citizenship issues – see for example *Curriculum Perspectives,* Volume 36, No. 2 (2016). The experience of those teachers who worked on our action research initiative (see Chapter 11) suggests that they were challenged to engage more deeply with their religious beliefs, values education, global citizenship, social justice and human rights when they were actively engaged in integrating CST across the curriculum.

Notes

1. Following further analysis of the empirical data and reconfiguration of the discussion of findings, this chapter is a revised version of our earlier paper in *Curriculum Perspectives, 2017,* 37(2), pp. 121–133.
2. See http://www3.dpcdsb.org/students/catholic-graduate-expectations. These expectations are based on Catholicism's core understanding of the human condition and a Christian vision of the human journey that is best understood within the context of relationship and accomplished in solidarity with community. The core expectation is of 'a discerning believer formed in the Catholic Faith community who celebrates the signs and sacred mystery of God's presence through word, sacrament, prayer, forgiveness, reflection and moral living'.

3. With multiple variables in the equation some adjustment of the conventional levels of significance was necessary. This took the form of a Bonferroni adjustment which reduces the nominated alpha level by dividing by the number of tests being made. This meant that our regression weights were judged statistically significant only where $p < .003$. Further information regarding data analysis is set out in Appendix 1.
4. Education Quality and Accountability Office.
5. The general capabilities proposed by ACARA, which are eminently compatible with Catholic Social Thought, include critical and creative thinking, ethical understanding, intercultural understanding, personal and social capability as well as literacy, numeracy and ICT capability.
6. Ignatian pedagogy derives from St. Ignatius Loyola's Spiritual Exercises. Taking a holistic view of the world, its three main elements are Experience, Reflection and Action. St. Ignatius founded the Society of Jesus (Jesuits).

References

Apple, M. (2004). *Ideology and curriculum*. New York: Routledge and Falmer.

Arbuckle, G. A. (2013). *Catholic identity or identities? Re-founding ministries in chaotic times.* Minnesota: Liturgical Press.

Arthur, J. (2013). The de-Catholicising of the curriculum in English Catholic schools. *International Studies in Catholic Education, 5*(1), 83–98.

Australian Curriculum and Reporting Authority (ACARA). (2012). *Curriculum Development Process, Version* Sydney: ACARA.

Australian Government. (2014). *Review of the Australian Curriculum: Final report.* Canberra: Department of Education.

Beane, J. A. (1995). Curriculum integration and the disciplines of knowledge. *Phi Delta Kappan, 76*(8), 1–13.

Boeve, L. (2005). Religion after detraditionalization: Christian faith in a post-secular Europe. *Irish Theological Quarterly, 70*(2), 99–122. doi: 10.1177/002114000507000201.

Boff, L. (1987). *Introducing liberation theology.* Maryknoll: Orbis Books.

Bordell, D. (2000). *Catechism of the Catholic Church.* Washington: United States Conference of Catholic Bishops.

Bourdieu, P. (1990). Principles for reflecting on the curriculum. *The Curriculum Journal, 1*(3), 307–314.

Brookfield, S. D., & Preskill, S. (2005). *Discussion as a way of teaching: Tools and techniques for democratic classrooms.* San Francisco: Jossey-Bass.

Chubbuck, S. M. (2007). Socially just teaching and the complementarity of Ignatian pedagogy and critical pedagogy. *Christian Higher Education, 6,* 239–265.

Cohen, J., & Cohen, P. (1975). *Applied multiple regression/correlation analysis for the behavioural sciences.* Hillsdale, NJ: Erlbaum.

Congregation for Catholic Education (CCE). (1977). *The Catholic school.* London: Catholic Truth Society.

Congregation for Catholic Education (CCE). (2014). *Educating today and tomorrow, a renewing passion, instrumentum laboris.* London: Catholic Truth Society.

Convey, J. J. (2012). Perceptions of catholic identity: Views of Catholic school administrators and teachers. *Catholic Education: A Journal of Inquiry and Practice, 16*(1), 187–214.

Cornbleth, C. (1990). *Curriculum in context.* London: Falmer.

Cotton, D. R. E. (2006). Implementing curriculum guidance on environmental education: The importance of teachers' beliefs. *Journal of Curriculum Studies, 38*(1), 67–83.

Cowan, P., & Maitles, H. (Eds.). (2012). *Teaching controversial issues in the classroom: Key issues and debates.* London: Continuum.

Creswell, J. (2012). *Planning, conducting, and evaluating quantitative and qualitative research* (4th ed.). Boston: Pearson.

Croke, B. (2007). Australian Catholic schools in a changing political and religious landscape. In G. Grace & J. O'Keefe (Eds.), *International handbook of Catholic Education – Challenges for school systems in the 21st century* (pp. 811–834). Dordrecht: Springer.

D'Orsa, T. (2013). Catholic curriculum: Re-framing the conversation. *International Studies in Catholic Education, 5*(1), 68–82. doi: 10.1080/19422539.2012.754589.

Davis, R. A., & Franchi, L. (2013). A Catholic curriculum for the twenty-first century? *International Studies in Catholic Education, 5*(1), 36–52.

Dewey, J. (1938). *Experience and Education.* New York: Macmillan.

Ditchburn, G. M. (2012). The Australian Curriculum: Finding the hidden narrative. *Critical Studies in Education, 53*(3), 347–360. doi: 10.1080/17508487.2012.703137.

Donnelly, K. (2007). Australia's adoption of outcomes based education: A critique. *Issues in Educational Research, 17*(2), 183–206.

Dorman, J., Fraser, B., & McRobbie, C. (1994). Rhetoric and reality: A study of classroom environments in Catholic and government secondary schools. Paper presented at Annual Meeting of American Educational Research Association (AERA), New Orleans.

Dowden, T. (2007). Relevant, challenging, integrative and exploratory curriculum design: Perspectives from theory and practice for middle level schooling in Australia. *The Australian Educational Researcher, 34*(2), 51–71.

Dowling, A., Beavis, A., Underwood, C., Sadeghi, R., & O'Malley, K. (2009). *Who's coming to school today? Final report.* Brisbane: ACER, Brisbane Catholic Education.

Drake, S. (2012). *Creating standards-based integrated curriculum.* Thousand Oaks, CA: Corwin Press.

Dumas, M., & Anderson, G. L. (2014). Qualitative research as policy knowledge: Framing policy problems and transforming education from the ground up. *Education Policy Analysis Archives, 22*(11), 1–20.

Dunne, J. (2002). Citizenship and education. In P. Kirby, L. Gibbons, & M. Cronin *(Eds.), Reinventing Ireland. Culture, society and the global economy* (pp. 68–88). London: Pluto Press.

Fraser, S. P., & Bosanquet, A. M. (2006). The curriculum? That's just a unit outline, isn't it? *Studies in Higher Education, 31*(3), 269–284. doi: 10.1080/03075070600680521.

Garcia-Huidobro, J. C. (2018) Addressing the crisis in curriculum studies: Curriculum integration that bridges issues of identity and knowledge. *The Curriculum Journal, 29*(1), 25–42. doi: 10.1080/09585176.2017.1369442.

Giroux, H. A. (2011). *On critical pedagogy.* New York: Continuum.

Gleeson, J. (2015). Critical challenges and dilemmas for Catholic Education leadership internationally. *International Studies in Catholic Education, 7*(2), 145–161. doi: 10.1080/19422539.2015.1072955.

Gleeson, J., O'Gorman, J., & O'Neill, M. (2018). The identity of Catholic schools as seen by teachers in Catholic schools in Queensland. *International Studies in Catholic Education, 10*(1), 44–65.

Goodson, I. F. (1994). *Studying curriculum.* London: Falmer.

Grace, G. (2010). Renewing spiritual capital: An urgent priority for the future of Catholic Education internationally. *International Studies in Catholic Education, 2*(2), 117–128.

Grace, G. (2013). Catholic social teaching should permeate the Catholic secondary school curriculum. An agenda for reform. *International Studies in Catholic Education, 5*(1), 99–109.

Groome, T. H. (1996). What makes a school Catholic? In T. H. McLaughlin, J. O'Keefe, & B. O'Keefe (Eds.), *The contemporary Catholic school*. (pp. 107–125). London: Falmer.

Grundy, S. (1987). *Curriculum: Product or praxis*. London: Falmer.

Harwood, D. (1997). *Global express: Tune in to the news*. Manchester: DEP.

Hess, D., & Stoddard, J. (2007). 9/11 and terrorism: 'The ultimate teachable moment' in textbooks and supplemental curricula. *Social Education, 71*(5), 231–240.

Hewer, C. (2001). Schools for Muslims. *Oxford Review of Education, 27*(4), 515–527. doi: 10.1080/03054980120086211.

Higgins, T. (1979). *Teaching about controversial issues in Catholic schools (No. 7)*. Norwich: University of East Anglia.

Institute for Catholic Education. (1996). *Curriculum matters: A resource for Catholic Educators*. Toronto: Institute for Catholic Education.

Institute for Catholic Education. (1998). *Graduate expectations*. Toronto: Institute for Catholic Education.

Institute for Catholic Education. (2007). *Our Catholic schools 2006–2007*. Toronto: Institute for Catholic Education.

Kelly, D. M., & Minnes Brandes, G. (2001). Shifting out of 'Neutral': Beginning teachers' struggles with teaching for social justice. *Canadian Journal of Education, 26*(4), 437–454.

Klenowski, V., & Wyatt-Smith, C. (2012). The impact of high stakes testing: The Australian story. *Assessment in Education: Principles, Policy & Practice, 19*(1), 65–79. doi: 10.1080/0969594X.2011.592972.

Kliebard, H. M. (1995). The Tyler rationale revisited. *Journal of Curriculum Studies, 27*(1), 81–88. doi: 10.1080/0022027950270107.

Krebbs, M. J. (2000). Values infusion: A systematic response to Catholic identity. *Catholic Education: A Journal of Inquiry and Practice, 3*(3), 306–314.

Kung, H. (2001). *The Catholic Church: A short history*. New York: Modern Library.

Kyburz-Graber, R. (1999). Environmental education as critical education: How teachers and students handle the challenge. *Cambridge Journal of Education, 29*(3), 415–432. doi: 10.1080/0305764990290310.

Lane, D. A. (1991). *Catholic Education and the school. Some theological reflections*. Dublin: Veritas.

Lawton, D. (1975). *Class, culture and the curriculum*. London: Routledge and Kegan Paul.

Lewis, J. (2009). Redefining qualitative methods: Believability in the fifth moment. *International Journal of Qualitative Methods, 8*(2), 1–15.

Lingard, B. (2010). Policy borrowing, policy learning: Testing times in Australian schooling. *Critical Studies in Education, 51*(2), 129–147. doi: 10.1080/17508481003731026.

Lynch, K. (1985). Ideology, interests and Irish education. *The Crane Bag, 9*(2), 77–96

Mason, M., Singleton, A., & Webber, R. (2007). *The spirit of generation Y. Young people's spirituality in a changing Australia*. Victoria: John Garratt Publishing.

Miles, M., & Huberman, M. (1994). *Qualitative data analysis: A source book of new methods*. London: Sage.

Murray, D. (1991). *A special concern*. Dublin: Veritas.

Oulton, C., Day, V., Dillon, J., & Grace, M. (2004). Controversial issues – teachers' attitudes and practices in the context of citizenship education. *Oxford Review of Education, 30*(4), 489–507. doi: 10.1080/0305498042000303973.

Pascoe, S. (2007). Challenges for Catholic Education in Australia. In G. Grace & J. O'Keefe (Eds.), *International handbook of Catholic Education – Challenges for school systems in the 21st Century* (pp. 787–810). Dordrecht: Springer.

Polesel, J., Rice, S., & Dulfer, N. (2014). The impact of high-stakes testing on curriculum and pedagogy: A teacher perspective from Australia. *Journal of Education Policy*, *29*(5), 640–657. doi: 10.1080/02680939.2013.865082.

Pollefeyt, D., & Bouwens, J. (2010). Framing the identity of Catholic schools: Empirical methodology for quantitative research on the Catholic identity of an education institute. *International Studies in Catholic Education*, *2*(2), 193–211.

Pollefeyt, D., & Bouwens, J. (2014). *Identity in dialogue. Assessing and enhancing Catholic school identity. Research methodology and research results in Catholic schools in Victoria, Australia* (Vol. 1). LIT Verlag: Zurich and Berlin.

Pope Francis. (2015). Encyclical letter *Laudato si'*. Retrieved from http://w2.vatican.va/content/francesco/en/encyclicals/documents/papa-francesco_20150524_enciclica-laudato-si.html.

Pope John XXIII. (1963). Encyclical letter *Pacem in terris*. Retrieved from http://w2.vatican.va/content/john-xxiii/en/encyclicals/documents/hf_j-xxiii_enc_11041963_pacem.html.

Rymarz, R. (2011). The future of Catholic schools in a secular culture of religious choice. *Journal of Religion and Society*, *13*, 1–12.

Scanlan, M. (2008). The grammar of Catholic schooling and radically 'Catholic' schools. *Catholic Education: A Journal of Inquiry and Practice*, *8*(1), 25–54.

Smith, C. (1991). *The emergence of liberation theology: Radical religion and social movement theory*. London: University of Chicago Press.

Spring, J. (2009). *Globalisation and education: An introduction*. New York: Routledge.

Stenhouse, L. (1968). The humanities curriculum project. *Journal of Curriculum Studies*, *1*(1), 26–33.

Stenhouse, L. (1975). *An introduction to curriculum research and development*. London: Heinemann.

Tiwari, A., Das, A., & Sharma, M. (2015). Inclusive education a 'rhetoric' or 'reality'? Teachers' perspectives and beliefs. *Teaching and Teacher Education*, *52*, 128–136.

Trant, A. (2007). *Curriculum matters in Ireland*. Dublin: Blackhall Press.

Walford, G. (2002). Classification and framing of the curriculum in Evangelical Christian and Muslim schools in England and the Netherlands. *Educational Studies*, *28*(4), 403–419.

Chapter 11

The integration of Catholic social teaching across the curriculum: A school-based action research approach

Jim Gleeson

Introduction

The purpose of this chapter is to report on the action research conducted by the Identity and Curriculum in Catholic Education project team in collaboration with teachers in Brisbane Catholic schools during 2015 and 2016. The broad context is provided in the treatment of Catholic social teaching (CST) in Chapters 2–4 and in the survey/interview findings for teachers in Queensland Catholic schools in Chapters 7 (faith-based school identity) and 10 (curriculum and identity focus).

In an environment characterised by secularisation, detraditionalisation and pluralisation (Boeve, 2005), as well as new anthropological and scientific insights and developments (Lane, 2015), the faith-based identity of Catholic schools is subject to considerable scrutiny (Arbuckle, 2013; Pollefeyt & Bouwens, 2010). The Congregation for Catholic Education (CCE) has consistently adopted a holistic, integrated approach to education and has expressed its concern regarding the 'noticeable tendency to reduce education to its purely technical and practical aspects' (CCE, 1997, p. 10). It defines its educational project (CCE, 1997) as a 'synthesis between culture and faith', (p. 14) one where the Catholic school is concerned with the 'integral education of the human person through a clear educational project of which Christ is the foundation' (p. 4). The CCE (1997) encourages the integration of a Catholic perspective across the curriculum:

> Each discipline is not an island inhabited by a form of knowledge that is distinct and ring fenced; rather, it is in a dynamic relationship with all other forms of knowledge, each of which expresses something about the human person and touches upon some truth. (p. 67)

Drawing on *Caritas in Veritate*, Grace (2010, 2013) argued that CST should permeate the curriculum of Catholic schools. Two Catholic educationalists in Ireland have strongly argued the case for curriculum integration:

> Education should break down traditional subject demarcations, encourage dialogue between disciplines [and] address the integral development

of the person: aesthetic, creative, critical, cultural, emotional, intellectual, moral, physical, political, social and spiritual. (Murray, 1991, p. 20)

RE alone does not make the Catholic school ... The Catholic school seeks to integrate the curriculum, to unify faith and culture, and to bring together the different pieces of the school programme into a higher synthesis that influences the social and spiritual formation of pupils. (Lane, 1991, p. 12)

When it comes to the implementation of these noble ideals, the Ontario Institute for Catholic Education and its District Boards have taken the lead (Chapter 6). The Institute advocates the integration of CST and critical literacy across the curriculum. It eschews trivial and superficial approaches to curriculum integration and sees curriculum as a transformative vehicle for 'personal and social change based on principles of justice and the view of the learner as agent-of-change [resulting in] an interdisciplinary or transdisciplinary experience [that] demonstrates the Catholic character of learning [and] a critical perspective on social and global issues' (Institute for Catholic Education, 1996, p. 26). Arthur (2013) describes the work of Ontario schools as 'impressive for it seeks no less than the integration of the Catholic faith into all aspects of the curriculum' (p. 94).

Some relevant Australian context

The Identity and Curriculum in Catholic Education initiative (see Introduction) was established at a time of increasing concern regarding the faith-based identity of Catholic schools in Australia. For example, Dowling, Beavis, Underwood, Sadeghi, and Malley (2009) noted the growing proportion of non-Catholic teachers and the lowering age profile of teachers in Brisbane Catholic schools and found that upwardly socially mobile parents, regardless of their religion, were enrolling their children in Catholic secondary schools 'for predominantly pragmatic rather than religious reasons [with a resulting] marked decline in religious commitment' (p. 38). Pascoe (2007) characterised Australian Catholic Education as Janus-like: 'while Catholic schools emphasise holistic education and faith-based values when addressing students and parents, they focus on core academic purpose, academic attainment, parental choice, legislative compliance, good governance and accountability in their dealings with government' (p. 793). With Catholic Education being caught on the horns of this dilemma, Croke (2007) believes that the Australian bishops are 'right to be concerned at the level of religious understanding and commitment of the next generation of Catholic school teachers [in a context where] Australian research on senior school students suggests that their commitment to their faith is tenuous' (p. 823).

Like many modern schooling systems, Australian education is characterised by an undue emphasis on the relationship between education and economic growth and a growing obsession with performativity, league tables and testing programmes such as the Programme for International Student Assessment (PISA; Ball, 1998, 2012; Lingard, 2010). The recently introduced Australian Curriculum involves the alignment of curriculum with such global economic imperatives (Gleeson, Klenowski, & Looney, forthcoming; Lingard, 2010) as evidenced by the National Assessment Plan – Literacy and Numeracy (NAPLAN). All of this results in growing tensions between educational quality and [e]quality, between education as a public good and competitive private commodity and between the teacher's role as technician or professional (Ditchburn, 2012; Luke, 2010).

Such market values are clearly at variance with Gospel values, and the CCE (2014) warns Catholic schools against simply responding to 'the demands deriving from the ever-changing economic situation', recommending that they 'place centre-stage both individuals and their search for meaning [because] what is taught is not neutral, and neither is the way of teaching it' (p. 64).

The action research initiative

The purpose of establishing the Chair of Identity and Curriculum in Catholic Education was to strengthen the faith-based identity of Catholic schools by integrating Catholic perspectives across the prescribed curriculum beyond Religious Education (RE). Realising that the notion of 'Catholic perspectives' needed to be more specifically defined, the project team decided to focus on CST. They were influenced here by the considerations set out in Chapters 2–4 and by the CCE's (2013) proposition that the curriculum of Catholic schools must address 'the unequal distribution of resources, poverty, injustice and human rights denied' (p. 66). They were also influenced by the obvious synergy between CST and Australian Curriculum general capabilities (e.g. ethical understanding, critical thinking, intercultural understanding) and cross-curricular themes such as sustainability and Aboriginal and Torres Strait Islander (ATSI) histories and cultures.

The direction of the project was informed in a special way by the aforementioned example of the Ontario Catholic Education system (see Chapter 6) whose Institute for Catholic Education (1996) developed the following framework of curriculum tasks:

- *Separation* of subjects where Catholic identity is the task of RE alone.
- *Permeation* where Catholic identity is promoted by the school culture, including the religious life of the school.
- *Integration* where Catholic perspectives are integrated across traditional subjects/learning areas.

Our attempts to establish the feasibility and effectiveness of the latter curriculum task are the focus of this chapter. Whereas traditional curriculum frameworks are premised on disparate disciplines and the avoidance of subject overlap (Hirst & Peters, 1970; Young, 7), integrated curricula are essentially student-centred (Beane, 1995; Dewey, 1938; Kliebard, 1995). Drake (2012, pp. 14–26) identifies four main forms of curriculum integration:

- Intradisciplinary where a particular theme or topic is fused with (an) existing subject(s).
- Multidisciplinary where deliberate connections are made between subject disciplines.
- Interdisciplinary integration where common themes rather than subjects are prioritised and integrated across existing subjects.
- Transdisciplinary integration, starting from students' authentic interests and questions.

Given the hegemony of discrete subjects (Goodson, 1993) and the prevalence of balkanisation in schools (Hargreaves, 1994), curriculum integration is always an ambitious undertaking whose success depends on the active engagement of school leaders and teachers. Bell (2003) reminds us that action research

> has proved particularly attractive to educators because of its practical, problem-solving emphasis, because practitioners (sometimes with researchers outside the institution) carry out the research and because the research is directed towards greater understanding and improvement of practice over a period of time. (p. 10)

The main stages of our action research initiative are now outlined.

Reconnaissance stage

The reconnaissance phase involved a survey of the attitudes and professional practices of teachers in Queensland Catholic schools, which included items regarding their perceptions of the faith-based identity of these schools (Chapter 7) and the relationship between curriculum and the faith-based identity of schools (Chapter 10). The vast majority of the 2,287 survey respondents rated the faith-based identity of Catholic schools as important or very important, and more than half were positively disposed towards the planned integration of a Catholic perspective in their curriculum planning with a similar proportion indicating that they actually practised such integration in their classrooms.

Although survey respondents ranked the importance of integrating Catholic teaching across the curriculum, 11th of 15 given characteristics of Catholic schools, four-fifths of them rated it as important or very important. As reported in Chapter 10, regression analysis found that support for integration was strongly associated with self-reported knowledge of Catholic teaching, religiosity, faith commitment and the perceived importance of the faith-based school identity and given characteristics of Catholic schools.

However, when asked about the integration of Catholic teaching in their own classrooms, teacher interviewees saw this either in terms of utilising spontaneous 'teachable moments' or giving personal witness ('I teach who I am'). Many interviewees suggested that teachers' levels of theological literacy were not sufficiently strong to allow them to engage with curriculum topics from a faith perspective, and more experienced teachers suggested that younger teachers' knowledge of the faith was particularly problematic.

It was a fundamental objective of the current project to move beyond the use of spontaneous, unplanned, teachable moments to the planned, intentional, integration of a Catholic perspective.

Implementation stage

Teachers in Queensland schools had previous experience of the objectives-based approach to curriculum design (Donnelly, 2007; Queensland Department of Education and the Arts, 2005) with its emphasis on outcomes and product. Given the exploratory nature of action research with its focus on process rather than product, and our uncertainty regarding the amount of time available for collaboration with teachers, the project team thought it best to take the following basic model as its starting point (Figure 11.1).

Schools were invited to enter a partnership with the university where the project team would undertake to

- provide professional learning/development (PD) opportunities in relation to CST and action research;

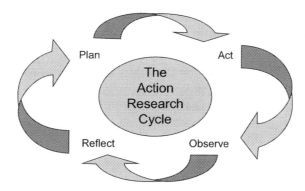

Figure 11.1 The action research cycle

The integration of Catholic social teaching 249

- support and facilitate participating teachers in curriculum planning and implementation, critical reflection and evaluation of student outcomes;
- pay for teacher release to enable participating teachers to attend PD and collaborate with the project team;
- assist teachers with locating relevant resources;
- provide opportunities for participating teachers to showcase their work and
- make it possible for participating teachers to gain academic credit at master's level by completing related assignments.

In return, school leaders were expected to support the action research by facilitating teacher collaboration with the project team and participation in associated professional development. In both secondary schools, the Assistant Principal for Religious Education (APRE) was the liaison person between the project and participating teachers, while some primary schools also had a coordinator in place where necessary.

Over half (58%) the survey respondents agreed or strongly agreed that 'the planned integration of a Catholic perspective across the whole curriculum should be a key feature of the Catholic school'. A similar proportion said they integrated a Catholic perspective often or very often in their teaching with 40% saying they 'sometimes' did so. It proved quite a struggle however to find teachers who were willing to volunteer for the action research initiative. Eventually, teachers from five primary schools, one P-12 and one secondary school came forward. This meant that, over the period 2015–2016, the project team had direct ongoing engagement with 12 primary teachers and 10 secondary teachers of whom 7 participated in both years, while approximately seven other secondary teachers were tangentially involved. Three-quarters of these had fewer than 10 years' experience of working in Catholic Education, while all identified as Catholic and most rated religion as important or very important to how they live their lives. These participating teachers decided to focus on the CST principles and learning areas set out in Table 11.1 (p. 251).

Stewardship of Creation was the most popular option followed by Dignity of the Human Person and Subsidiarity and Participation.

Members of the research team observed that many of these teacher volunteers received minimal support from senior and middle management in their schools. Conscious of the importance of helping teachers find learning resources, the project team posted relevant materials on the project website (see https://www.acu.edu.au/772342). These included Caritas resources relevant to teaching particular CST principles to particular year levels and suggestions regarding children's literature appropriate to the treatment of CST principles.

Two seminars were held (May and November) in 2016 that provided opportunities for participating teachers to disseminate their experiences of integrating CST across the curriculum to the wider community.

Evaluation

In keeping with their evidence-based approach to action research, members of the project team visited schools frequently to meet with participating teachers and, where possible, to observe classes. These teachers were encouraged to keep reflective journals and, where appropriate, to design appropriate pre- and post-tests with a view to establishing student outcomes. Both team members kept a diary record of their meetings with teachers and shared these reflections regularly. Such reflections served to illuminate the lessons and outcomes of the project. In addition to these observations, the project team drew on two other main sources of evidence:

- Detailed Qualtrics survey with a number of open-ended items sent to 18 teachers who participated directly in action research – 16 responses were received.
- Data from those who attended the November 2016 seminar.

The workshop component of the 'November seminar' provided an opportunity to harvest the opinions of 60 participants (including action research teachers) with regard to substantive issues that had been identified by the project team. Working individually and in groups, attendees considered the effectiveness and feasibility of the various models of integration, curriculum planning and assessment options. Having responded individually to closed and open survey items, workshop participants attempted to reach consensus through group and plenary discussion.

Frequency counts were computed for closed items in the participating teachers' and November seminar surveys, while open-ended responses in both surveys were coded. Following discussion and review, these codes were categorised into themes with reference to the main focus of the research (Bowen, 2009).

Findings

Our findings are presented under the following main headings: general reactions of action research teachers, effectiveness and feasibility of various models of curriculum integration and approaches to curriculum planning, inclusion of CST-related assessment tasks, links between Religious Education and integration of CST, the Australian Curriculum and CST, participating teacher outcomes and reflections, participating student outcomes, lessons learned and next steps.

General reactions of action research teachers

Participating teachers offered a variety of reasons for their involvement in what they commonly described as an 'interesting' project. These included their passion for social justice, their commitment to Catholic values and the

The integration of Catholic social teaching 251

'good fit' between a particular CST principle and the unit they were teaching, for example

> They fitted naturally with science units already in place, so those units were an ideal vehicle to be used to deliver the teaching of the particular CST principles. (Secondary teacher)

> This fitted very closely with the HASS curriculum – civics and citizenship strand. (Primary teacher)

As may be seen from Table 11.1, many of them decided to integrate CST into Humanities subjects – English, history and geography at secondary and history and social sciences (HASS) at primary. Some primary teachers adopted a multidisciplinary approach involving a range of subjects, including HASS, English, science, media and digital technologies. Secondary teachers worked with their own teaching specialisations, science, English and business and

Table 11.1 CST principles and learning areas focused on by participating teachers

School type	Catholic social teaching	Year, learning areas, number of teachers (N = 26)
Primary	Stewardship of Creation	Year 3, across whole primary curriculum (1)
		Year 3, HASS**, RE, English, Design and Technologies (1)
		Year 4, HASS, RE, English, Science, Health and Physical Education, Design, Digital Media (2)
		Year 4, HASS, Science (1)
		Year 6, English (1)
Primary	Common Good	Year 4, English, HASS (1)
Primary	Subsidiarity and Participation	Year 6, HASS (1)
		Year 3, HASS, English, RE, Health/PE (2)
Primary	Preferential Option for the Poor	Year 6, HASS, RE, English (1)
Primary	Dignity of the Human Person	Year 6, Visual Art
Secondary	Stewardship of Creation	Year 12, Biology (3)
		Year 8, English* (1)
		Year 9, Geography (3)
Secondary	Dignity of the Human Person	Year 8, English* (1)
		Year 10, Biology (4)
Secondary	Solidarity	Year 8, English* (1)
Secondary	Common Good	Year 9, History (3)
Secondary	Dignity of the Human Person and Stewardship of Creation	Year 12, Business Communication and Technologies (corporate social responsibility) (1)

* Same teacher taught three English Units, one per term.
** HASS, History and Social Sciences.

252 Jim Gleeson

communications technology. Further information regarding these interventions including a number of video recordings from the November 2016 seminar is available under action research activities at http://www.acu.edu.au/1280444.

Curriculum integration models: Effectiveness and feasibility

Over half the action research participants adopted an intradisciplinary model of integration (see above), while one-third took a multidisciplinary approach and one teacher chose interdisciplinary (Drake, 2012). Secondary teachers felt that an intradisciplinary approach was the only feasible option in that sector where 'subjects usually stand-alone'. Primary teachers who chose an intradisciplinary approach said they wanted to adopt 'the least challenging approach', 'to take small steps', 'to set achievable goals', while a secondary teacher saw this approach as 'a gentle shift that created interest in the integration rather than having students see it as another RE lesson'.

More adventurous primary teachers opted for a multidisciplinary approach for reasons such as 'learning about CST across more than one learning area would embed the knowledge more effectively' and 'stewardship [of creation] has clear links across the curriculum and my school prefers an integrated approach to learning'. These teachers reported very positive experiences: 'students were engaged and would often make connections across curriculum areas'; 'it was easily integrated and very effective'; 'CST was effective, but it got very BIG. With reflection and tweaking, I feel this could be better managed'.

When participating teachers were asked to identify the most effective approach to the integration of CST, they indicated strong support for a multidisciplinary approach.

> With such a busy curriculum, we don't have time to do a whole separate unit so aligning it with what you are already doing and just doing it more explicitly is much more feasible. (Primary)

> It ensures that the curriculum is the priority and is completely addressed. (Primary)

> A multidisciplinary approach enables students to see relevance across a number of learning areas. (Secondary)

Those who indicated their preference for an intradisciplinary model made comments such as

> It worked very well as our unit of work was already established, I just needed to add the CST work into it.

> It worked well, because I was able to plan thoroughly for the integration.

> It's a good and simple place to begin ... otherwise it gets too big.

The integration of Catholic social teaching 253

Meanwhile, the primary teacher advocating for an interdisciplinary model of integration felt that it

> ... helps the students understand that our Christian values should permeate everything we do ... if we want the students to make ethical decisions about scientific and technological advances then we must arm them with the knowledge and skills to do so.

Another primary teacher saw the integration of CST in terms of a journey from one model to the next:

> It is a process of development, a journey ... while working towards an interdisciplinary model I am not there yet but each year I expect to get a little closer to this optimum.

Notwithstanding their general preference for multidisciplinary integration, when action research teachers were asked to identify the *most feasible* model of integration, they mainly favoured an intradisciplinary approach. Some primary teachers however made interesting comments in support of multidisciplinary integration:

> Multidisciplinary ensures the curriculum is still addressed and allows for smarter teaching not harder teaching. (Primary)

> Multidisciplinary is the most feasible because it is easier for a teacher to manage amongst other competing curriculum demands. (Primary)

When November seminar participants were asked to nominate the most effective model of integration, they were more ambitious than the action research teachers, being equally divided between the merits of multidisciplinary and interdisciplinary integration with a slight preference for the former. Indicative responses included

> Interdisciplinary, linking all learning areas and interchanging skills, concepts, themes is the best teaching and learning for lower primary.

> Interdisciplinary means working smarter not harder!

> Multidisciplinary because my planning for primary involves working with many subjects in a connected way and CST would work with many subjects.

> Subject still remains the priority in multidisciplinary, however CST is addressed through different perspectives.

Some attendees however opted for an intradisciplinary approach with one respondent remarking that 'there are primary versus secondary differences ... interdisciplinary approaches are easier at primary'.

Just like the action researcher teachers themselves, November seminar attendees were also more conservative when it came to the question of feasibility. Half of them regarded multidisciplinary integration as feasible, while one-third felt that intradisciplinary was 'as good as it gets'. Respondents identified the pros and cons of both approaches, for example 'intra-disciplinary requires less time and can be more flexible, multidisciplinary is ideal but takes more time and coordination which isn't always realistic'; 'it depends on the knowledge/confidence of the teacher'. Indicative responses (favoured model in parentheses) included

> Many hands make light work! (Multidisciplinary)
>
> Any model is possible – it depends on the needs of staff and students and on resources. (Multidisciplinary)
>
> Liaising with other subjects takes too much time. (Intradisciplinary)
>
> … the difficulty of getting all teachers on board. (Intradisciplinary)
>
> The curriculum is already overloaded. (Intradisciplinary)

The importance of school context was also recognised, for example 'our school values integrated units'; 'our school takes a "connected" approach and this lends itself to implementing the CST easily across a number of learning areas'.

The emerging trend regarding models of integration is that action research teachers and November seminar participants were more conservative in their opinions regarding the feasibility of particular models of integration than they were about their effectiveness.

Approaches to curriculum planning: Effectiveness and feasibility

It was observed by members of the project team that participating teachers were very dependent on elaborate planning templates that included large numbers of prescribed 'learning outcomes' and associated assessment standards. Along with the general expectation that teachers would adhere to common units planned at the beginning of the school year with all students being assessed according to the same standards, this meant that teacher autonomy and flexibility were compromised when it came to integrating CST.

While it was up to each individual teacher to decide what CST principles, learning areas and units they would work with, the project team provided a curriculum planning template for CST integration. Although most survey respondents were very positive about the effectiveness of their planning, some expressed concerns about over-planning, for example 'I would not try to cover so much [next time] … planning less will allow for the discussion that naturally occurs'.

The integration of Catholic social teaching   255

Action researchers and November seminar participants were asked to indicate their preferences for the following approaches to planning for the integration of CST in terms of their effectiveness and feasibility:

A   Plan across 1–3 learning areas.
B   Plan across 1–3 learning areas and include assessment task(s).
C   Plan across more than three learning areas.
D   Plan across more than three learning areas and include assessment task(s)
E   Plan across all learning areas.
F   Plan across all learning areas and include assessment tasks.
G   Pre-planned teachable moments in some unit(s).

Most action research teachers, including all secondary teachers, saw planning for the integration of CST across 1–3 learning areas (options A or B), as the 'simplest' approach for teachers who 'lack experience'. Typical teacher responses included '[this approach is] very effective, it's easy to fit in and link CST', 'it was very effective, children gained a lot'. However, one primary teacher who favoured integration across all learning areas felt that 'the first four [options] are all 'tag ons', NOT a whole school approach. Which subjects get left out? Why?'

When asked about the *feasibility* of the various planning options, action research teachers generally favoured option C because of its relative ease of implementation. Teachers also expressed concerns regarding the inclusion of assessment tasks on the grounds that 'least invasive', 'simple' approaches were more feasible as reflected in the comment that 'with time restrictions it's best to start small'.

The preferred curriculum planning options of November seminar participants were fairly evenly spread across options C, D, E and F along with some support for option G, the compromise position of 'pre-planned teachable moments', for example

> Pre-planned teachable moments would be effective because that would equip staff with the tools to effectively address teachable moments as they arise. Less is more … if we try to implement across all or too many curriculum areas it might lose its impact and become tedious for both staff and students.

> Teachable moments increase authentic learning.

Just like the action research teachers, these respondents were more conservative when asked to identify the *most feasible approach* to planning for the integration of CST. Although many had seen integration across all units as the most effective approaches to curriculum planning, options A and B along with planned/unplanned teachable moments were seen as most feasible. Indicative comments included

> Fewer learning areas means less work and it's easier to coordinate.

> It is all feasible but the more people involved, the harder it gets.

> Start small, find links, expand ….

256 Jim Gleeson

Some respondents noted the importance of contextual factors such as 'time, knowledge of curriculum areas and knowledge of CST' on planning.

As in the case of curriculum integration models, while action research teachers and November seminar participants generally favoured the more ambitious curriculum planning options, they were more conservative about the feasibility of such approaches.

Inclusion of CST-related assessment tasks

The most contested curriculum planning issue to emerge was the inclusion of CST-related assessment task(s). The majority of action research teachers, particularly at primary level, favoured the inclusion of associated assessment tasks for purposes of feedback on student learning, for example

> The inclusion of an assessment task provides feedback to me on the effectiveness of my teaching and the students' level of understanding.

> Having an assessment task focuses the learning.

Other teachers, however, particularly advocates of teachable moments, noted the limitations of formal assessments. These included concerns regarding the authenticity of students' responses in such tests and the importance of affective outcomes and 'action for change' rather than test outcomes:

> Formal assessment can compromise the authenticity of student interactions and the evolution of views and standpoints.

> Not all learning can be assessed through formal assessment tasks. Throughout the unit the students became globally aware students who took ownership of the small actions that they can take to bring about more fair and just world. They pulled together as a class, showing a great deal more respect for each other's differences. They enjoyed being positive leaders for the rest of the school. They became less reliant on extrinsic rewards as motivation and they were very proud of their achievements.

The majority of November seminar participants also favoured the inclusion of pre-planned assessment tasks for a variety of reasons, with some taking an assessment-led view of teaching and learning:

> Assessment is the driving force of your teaching. An integrated approach works well with CST as many learning areas can be fused.

> Assessment is the starting point for planning activities. Connected units allow for greater consolidation and reflection of CST principles.

> When assessment tasks are planned at the beginning (backward planning) there is stronger commitment to the teaching process and student commitment. Most effect would come from all disciplines converging.

The integration of Catholic social teaching   257

Others saw the inclusion of CST-related assessment tasks as important 'for accountability purposes' or student motivation – 'When it's assessed, students see it as valid'.

Some November seminar participants were opposed to the inclusion of CST-related assessment tasks for reasons to do with authentic learning:

> I'm not sure that assessment is required when CST is not a curriculum area that we are required to report against. Pre-planned teachable moments would be effective because it would equip staff with the tools to effectively address teachable moments as they arise. Less is more … if we try to implement across all or too many curriculum areas it might lose its impact and become tedious for both staff and students. (Integration across 1–3 learning areas)

> Assessment adds a great deal of pressure … I would prefer a 'Head-Heart-hands' approach that would include some social justice project and action outcome. (Integrate across all learning areas)

> Assessment task integration sucks the life out of very rich underpinning theology. (Unplanned teachable moments)

> I don't think formal assessment is critical to effectiveness. However, informal monitoring of students' attitudes would be informative. (All learning areas).

> … assessment may hinder genuine student response. (All learning areas)

Links between Religious Education and integration of CST

Both action research participants and November seminar participants saw the relationship between RE and the integration of CST as either very important or important:

> The RE curriculum is a common subject that all students encounter each year in their schooling. It is the natural repository of Catholic moral thought, and the resources to present these. (Secondary action research participant)

> Including Religion in the interdisciplinary approach provided the students with a values base on which to focus all learnings in the other areas. It allowed the students to draw parallels with the words and actions of Jesus and their actions. (Primary action research participant)

Whereas project team members noted that synchronisation with the prescribed RE curriculum was problematic, November seminar participants generally felt that such synchronisation was feasible once the importance of forward planning was recognised at system and school levels:

> This needs to be planned at the start of the year.

> Connections beforehand are important to ensure a CST lens is used seamlessly.

In response to an open-ended question regarding the best approach to improving levels of integration between RE, CST and other learning areas, November seminar participants identified the following complementary approaches:

- Collaborative review of the RE curriculum to facilitate the integration of RE into other learning areas.
- Treating CST as another cross-curricular priority so that its relevance to RE is demonstrated by the inclusion of icons as with the Australian Curriculum.
- Explicit teaching of CST in RE lessons.
- RE teachers provide professional development for teachers from other secondary subject areas to help them see the links with CST.

Controversial issues in the classroom

Given the countercultural nature of CST, the treatment of controversial issues in the classroom is a particularly important aspect of curriculum implementation. Such issues had arisen in the case of half the participating teachers, for example land development versus sustainability, refugees and asylum seekers, treatment of Indigenous Australians and the Dignity of the Human Person. When teachers were asked to identify, from a list of six options, the roles they had adopted in such situations they chose either 'teacher simply presents all views objectively' or 'teacher as devil's advocate – neutral, covering all viewpoints, challenging existing beliefs'. Their clear preference was to remain neutral:

> I wanted to explain Christian responsibilities and gospel values to children whilst staying 'impartial' so as not to alienate families. (Primary)

> It was important for students to develop their own opinion regardless of what I thought. (Primary)

> I felt it was important to present all viewpoints. I was hesitant about declaring my own views because I was concerned that my teaching would be seen as bias. (Primary)

> Devil's advocate was adopted with older students to challenge their thinking. (Primary)

> At a grade 12 standard, I would be a chairperson at times to try and facilitate the discussions but it was also very important for me to challenge existing beliefs. Some students have an opinion based on what they hear at home or in the media without understanding anything else behind the issue. They need to be prepared to defend their position and justify their views based on evidence and reasoning which is what I was trying to achieve. (Secondary)

Participating teacher outcomes and reflections

Teachers reported increased levels of awareness and knowledge of CST, commenting frequently on the enthusiastic reactions of students, particularly at primary level. Some teachers remarked that the integration of CST created stronger links between learning areas. Action research participants also identified the need for a systemic approach both at the level of the whole school and of the wider Catholic Education system – 'a system-wide support is necessary for successful and sustainable implementation' (Secondary teacher).

Some expressed surprise at how easy it was to make links between CST and their particular units:

> I have discovered that opportunities to integrate CST exist in all learning areas. (Primary)

> I now realize how easily the CSTs can be integrated into units of work and how valuable they are for engaging children in discussion. (Visual Art teacher)

Many felt that their knowledge of CST and their teaching skills had developed as a result of having to focus on it in their teaching:

> I have learned more about the CSTs and how they can be linked in with our curriculum, not only in RE but in many other subjects. (Primary)

> I have learnt more about the specific principles of Subsidiarity and Participation. (Primary)

> I was able to develop my research skills, resourcing skills and presenting skills. I found this very worthwhile. (Primary)

Others commented on its impact on students and on its relevance to the world around them:

> I have discovered [CST] can make the subjects so much more engaging and purposeful for the students. It provided opportunities for students to see learning with real-life situations and how they can have an impact on the community beyond their immediate school environment. (Primary) CST makes the Gospel relevant to their lives today. (Primary)

> I have learnt that embedding CST into subject areas outside of Religion helps to create more authentic learning experiences and fosters the holistic development of the child. (Primary)

> CST is very important to help students maintain a healthy balance in the process of forming moral judgements. (Secondary)

The enthusiasm of secondary teachers with respect to the relevance of CST to their own subject areas is of particular interest:

> There is value in the dialogue between RE and science teachers.

> It linked in really easily with Corporate Social Responsibility in the 21st century. Because the link was simple and easy to see, I got less resistance from students. (Secondary)

Asked to identify the changes they would make if they were to teach the unit again, most teachers identified the need for more careful and detailed planning and more extensive resources, for example

> More in-depth planning with more dialogue between science teachers and theologically qualified RE teachers in order to better understand the ethical underpinnings of the principles of CST taught. (Secondary)

> I would use more resources and spend more time on 'fleshing out' the chosen CST. I would also like to integrate other CSTs into other units of work. (Primary)

Participating student outcomes

Drawing on their own evaluation strategies as well as classroom observations, most teachers were very positive about levels of student engagement and their heightened awareness and knowledge of CST and of the relevance of the various principles to the world around them. Secondary teachers focused on students' increased levels of knowledge and their ability to apply CST to relevant issues:

> Richer concepts of knowledge, a better framework to discuss science issues and their own possible responses to those issues.

> Students were able to analyse a corporation and evaluate, 'using criteria', the extent to which a company is adhering to the CST principle of Dignity of the Human Person. At the completion of the unit, more students were able to articulate links with CST when asked … Some of the better students could recognise 'Dignity of the Human Person' as a standard by which companies should abide.

Primary teachers focused mainly on their students' ability to apply CST at age-appropriate levels:

> They were able to identify all six of the CST principles by the end of the unit … students developed age-appropriate understandings of Subsidiarity and Participation and how these principles empower them to have an active voice in matters that affect their lives, as well as encourage them to be a voice for others. (Year 6)

> By the end of the unit the children found a real sense of purpose and a need to create change in the world beyond their own environment. They saw the need for communities to ensure that all members have a say and work collaboratively to ensure fairness and that all members have rights and responsibilities for themselves and each other. (Year 3)

> The students were able to relate their HASS work to the CST of Stewardship and begin to use this language. They became more aware of the environment around them both local and national. (Year 4)

The students deepened their understanding of *Laudato Si'* and of their role in the ongoing creation story. The students' level of ownership of their [various environmental projects increased and they came closer together as a class, being more respectful and understanding of each other. Greater respect for the environment seen in their ownership of picking up rubbish around the school and in the creek, without being asked. (Year 3)

The Australian Curriculum and the integration of Catholic social teaching

All action research teachers agreed that CST is relevant to the general capabilities and cross-curricular themes in the Australian Curriculum with two-thirds saying it was very relevant. Most teachers reported that they found it easy to integrate capabilities such as ethical and intercultural understanding and themes such as sustainability in their classes, while some had not explicitly attempted to do so:

I was able to address the general capabilities and cross-curricular themes very easily and very well. (Primary)

All general capabilities were naturally covered through the unit progression except for ICT … there was no difficulty in doing this. Cross-curricular priority of ATSI histories and cultures was also easily tied into this unit. (Primary)

[It was] a Year 12 subject I did not have to consider the Australian Curriculum. However I can still see the following links: our engagement with Asia is very important especially if we consider fashion brands and their use of cheap labour in Asian countries. Sustainability is also relevant as we considered whether profit trumps everything and the responsibility companies have to protect the environment. In terms of the general capabilities, I think the unit could link with creative and critical thinking, personal and social capability, ethical understanding and intercultural understanding. (Secondary)

We addressed implicitly literacy, personal and social capability, intercultural understanding and explicitly ethical understanding, and critical and creative thinking. (Secondary)

Lessons learned and next steps?

Participating teachers identified the importance of building in more time for follow-up student action, the importance of integrating children's literature, stronger links with Religious Education, the need for more explicit teaching of CST principles and recognition on the part of some teachers that their chosen principle was not a good choice:

Next time, I would complete this unit earlier in the year, so that the students would have more of an opportunity to be advocates within the school community and put their plans into action.

I would do more background teaching about the person of Jesus. ... I would integrate more children's literature [and] make more explicit links to the general capabilities.

I would dedicate more lessons to explicit teaching of CST rather than incorporating it into a lesson here or there.

Two-thirds of action research participants reported they continued to integrate CST after their formal engagement with the project ended. Others had moved schools or been allocated to a new grade or a new position. Six action research participants, two of whom were involved in a whole school approach, reported that they had been able to involve some other colleagues:

I shared the activities that I had prepared with two other teachers after completing the activities with my own class. They were impressed with the responses from their students.

Some teachers saw the involvement of original group and asked how to get involved.

Another participant remarked that 'this will be a part of my teaching practice from now on. Not as much in a planned way, more of grabbing opportunities through discussion.'

November seminar participants were asked to consider three possible strategies that might be undertaken during the project's final year:

- A further round of action research in new settings.
- The development of teaching materials.
- A whole school approach to the integration of CST.

Working individually and in groups, they identified the strengths, weaknesses, opportunities and threats associated with each of these options and nominated the best way forward for the following year. As may be seen from Table 11.2, workshop participants were unanimously of the view that a whole school approach was the most desirable way forward.

Whole school approach

Three of our participating schools (two primary schools and one P–12) expressed interest in adopting such an approach during 2017. Under the leadership of the Acting APRE, one of these schools implemented this approach with considerable success (see https://www.acu.edu.au/1669195 for this school's conference presentation as well as the approach adopted in Ontario Catholic schools). However, after this APRE had moved to another school in 2018, the teacher librarian remarked that

The whole school approach has certainly taken a back seat since the changing of the guard at the leadership level and we certainly miss

The integration of Catholic social teaching   263

Table 11.2 Strengths, weaknesses, opportunities and threats associated with project priorities

	Further round of action research	*Develop curriculum materials*	*Focus on whole school approach*
Strengths	Teacher ownership; school-based; evidence-based; professional development	Always welcome to time-poor teachers; development of a common language	Involves all staff; builds staff capacity and confidence; enables coverage of all CST principles, all learning areas and all year levels
Weaknesses	Leadership support? School willingness? Teacher workload?	These may become dated	Requires strong leadership, time commitment and adds to teacher workload
Opportunities	Teacher development Introduce new ideas	Development of cross-curricular links; getting parents involved	Strengthens school identity; develops a shared language and a collaborative approach; makes connections with the local and global community
Threats	School disruption; Parental reaction? Competition from other initiatives; Loss of momentum	Over-dependency on the part of teachers	Teacher readiness, willingness, knowledge? Counter-cultural nature of CST

> [our APRE's] gentle guiding hand … the curriculum is incredibly busy and so much is required of teachers that some things just have to give … Some teachers have continued with the whole school approach and there have been liturgies, fundraisers and posters around the school focusing on *Preferential Option for the Poor* and the previously agreed rota of common CST principles remains in place.

She went on to reflect that 'the best thing we have done is make sure that we have plenty of books that are rich texts to spark discussions and encourage students to see-judge & act'. The fate of the whole school approach at this school is entirely consistent with the lessons of curriculum reform regarding the crucial importance of leadership for meaningful curriculum change (Fullan, 2005, 2016).

According to its APRE, the second primary school that expressed interest in adopting a whole school approach is 'looking into the Catholic perspective in a few areas of the curriculum in the next few years' (Personal communication, June, 2018), drawing on the experience of the action research participants in the school. While a member of the project team facilitated two professional development sessions on CST in the P–12 school, we are not aware of any further developments there at whole school level.

Summary of findings

Participating teachers saw a natural fit between the various CST principles and their chosen learning areas. While they were very positive about their action research experiences and while they felt they had learned about CST in the process, they had also come to realise that their knowledge of CST was limited. They were very satisfied with the high levels of student engagement and reported that participating students had become more aware of CST and its relevance to the world around them.

While most regarded multidisciplinary integration as the most *effective* approach, some supported an intradisciplinary approach on the grounds that this was the easiest place to begin. When asked what model was the most *feasible*, however, most participating teachers opted for intradisciplinary integration. Although November seminar participants regarded interdisciplinary and multidisciplinary integration as the most *effective* approaches, they too were more conservative when it came to *feasibility*, opting for multi- and intradisciplinary approaches.

With regard to planning for the curriculum integration of CST, most action research teachers felt it was best to work with a small number (1–3) of learning areas. November seminar participants gave a wide variety of responses when asked about planning options ranging from integration across all learning areas to planned/unplanned teachable moments with two-thirds of them favouring an assessment-led approach. As with integration models, their responses were more conservative when it came to the question of feasibility with integration across a small number of learning areas (1–3) and teachable moments being most popular.

Both action research teachers and November seminar participants held rather diverse views regarding the desirability of incorporating CST-related assessment task(s) at the curriculum planning stage. This emerged as the most contentious aspect of the integration of CST with strong arguments advanced on both sides of the argument.

The important role of Religious Education in supporting the integration of CST across the curriculum was recognised both by action research and seminar participants, and some interesting strategies for the strengthening of that relationship were identified.

When controversial issues arose from the integration of CST principles, participating teachers adopted neutral, non-directive roles. All participating teachers recognised the relevance of CST to the general capabilities and cross-curricular themes of the Australian Curriculum and reported that they found it easy to put these links into action.

While action research teachers had limited experience of reflective practice, they identified the importance of system-wide and whole school support as well as the importance of careful lesson planning, relevant resources and more explicit treatment of CST in the classroom. Two-thirds of action research participants reported that they had continued with the integration of CST in 2017 and six of them had been able to involve some other colleagues.

Discussion of findings

While it has not been possible to conform to all of the canons of action research (a matter for another paper), this small-scale project shows clearly that it is possible to effectively integrate CST in a planned way across learning areas outside of Religious Education. From a curriculum development perspective, the main issues arising include the difficulty of achieving interdisciplinary integration that includes Religious Education, the (inevitable) gap between what teachers see as desirable and what they see as feasible, the pros and cons of (a) CST-related Assessment Tasks and (b) teachable moments versus pre-planned integration. Notwithstanding the potential of teachable moments, spontaneity does not preclude planning, first for how to ensure that such opportunities arise and second for how to maximise their potential. As noted earlier, advocates of teachable moments were less likely to support the inclusion of pre-planned assessment tasks.

It must be acknowledged that the innovation reported in this chapter consisted of a pilot phase that was conducted at no cost to participating schools with support from a project team and involving a small number of volunteer teachers over relatively brief periods of time. In terms of teachers' Stages of Concern (Hall & Hord, 2011) when engaging in curriculum innovation these teachers were naturally preoccupied with 'management concerns' – 'I seem to be spending all my time getting resources ready'; 'I'm not sure what's the most appropriate task'. With prompting from the team, some were beginning to raise more sustainable issues such as 'how is this affecting students? How might I relate with what colleagues are doing? What changes do I need to make?' What does emerge clearly, and unsurprisingly, from the data is that the successful integration of CST demands

- the enthusiasm and motivation of individual teachers;
- external support and facilitation using a partnership model such as that outlined earlier and
- relevant professional development for school leaders and teachers, appropriate teaching resource materials and the necessary space for curriculum planning.

If the outcomes of this pilot phase are to be effectively built on, however, the above conditions are necessary but not sufficient. The broader and more substantive issues include the fundamental importance of system and school-based leadership for sustainable curriculum change, understanding the

266 Jim Gleeson

relationship between CST and education for human rights and social justice and the growing influence of market values and performativity on Australian education. These issues are now briefly considered.

Sustainable curriculum change: The importance of leadership

The planned integration of CST represents an ambitious and challenging curriculum development initiative. While the potential of such integration has been identified in the course of the pilot project, the active support of system and school leaders is essential if this potential is to be realised. For example, it requires a school-based champion/coordinator, somebody who is passionate about the importance of such integration, and without such support the project will be seen as just another 'interesting experiment'. As Fullan (2005) puts it, 'if a system is to be mobilized in the direction of sustainability, leadership at all levels must be the primary engine ... To help put in place the eight elements of sustainability ... we need a system laced with leaders who are trained to think in bigger terms' (p. 27). Sustainable curriculum change also depends on school leaders and teachers who are willing to critically reflect on their planning and implementation and to respond appropriately on such reflections (Leitch & Day, 2000).

The environment in which the current pilot project took place does not inspire confidence in the dissemination of project lessons and outcomes. Notwithstanding the positive responses of teachers in our reconnaissance survey (Chapter 7) towards the integration of a Catholic perspective, it was extremely difficult to find schools and teachers who were willing to participate in the action research project. For example, none of the 30 teachers in a primary school that was actively and very effectively promoting environmental sustainability took up our invitation although they were enacting the CST principle of Stewardship of Creation. Such reluctance highlights the clear lesson of Fullan's (2016) findings about successful curriculum change where the principal is the 'learning leader' (p. 133), the change agent whose role is one of 'developing a new culture' (p. 134).

If the planned integration of CST is to become a key curriculum task for teachers in Catholic schools, certain issues must be addressed by school leaders. For example, the adoption of a whole school approach to the integration of CST, seen as essential by action research teachers and our seminar participants, represents a major leadership challenge. The abortive efforts of three project schools to adopt this whole school approach simply underline the necessity for the *active* support of *both* system and school leaders, including APREs and senior and middle leadership. Meanwhile, the need to achieve synchronisation between the teaching of particular CST principles and the Religious Education curriculum represents a challenge to what Hargreaves (2008, 2010) calls 'the persistence of presentism'[1] and the balkanised culture of schools (Pinar, Reynolds, Slattery, & Taubman, 2008).

Achieving the right balance between the respective roles of centralised and school-based leadership, between system leadership and school leadership, is difficult. As Fullan (2016) concludes 'top leaders cannot control complex systems and bottom-up change does not add up' (p. 260). The adoption of an overly centralised approach results in the standardisation and neutering of curriculum, while school-based approaches are problematic either because 'individual schools lack the capacity to manage change or because assessment of attempted changes cannot be tracked' (Fullan, 2007, p. 236). Furthermore, the dominance of positivistic models of research means that the status of practitioner-based research is low, both in academia and with policymakers:

> Action research is most often positioned at the bottom of the contemporary methodological hierarchy … because the goal of action research and change is often seen as slight … The research that is most valued as being 'impact'-full occurs at scale. Impacting on one person, a small group or a single institution is seen as insignificant. (Thomson, 2015, p. 309)

Social justice, human rights and Catholic social teaching

While participating teachers were very positive about the 'fit' between their respective units and their chosen CST principle, members of the project team found that teachers generally had difficulty moving beyond social justice/human rights education (see Burridge, Chapter 5) to CST *per se*. This is hardly surprising in view of the close triadic relationship between these three areas as illustrated in Figure 11.2.

The evidence gathered by Pollefeyt and Bouwens (2014) using their Melbourne scale indicates that the most dominant Catholic school identity models are 'Recontextualisation of a Catholic school identity' and 'Values Education in a Christian perspective'. Pollefeyt and Bouwens (2014) also found that an increasing number of students in Victoria, particularly at secondary level, favoured *Colourful and Colourless* school types

Figure 11.2 Triadic relationship between CST, social justice and human rights

where 'Christianity ceases to be the privileged conversational partner and Secularisation will emerge' (p. 293).

When teachers introduce CST principles from the perspectives of social justice and human rights with little or no reference to Catholic teaching, they fall into the 'Values Education' (Pollefeyt & Bouwens, 2014) model and their schools are likely to fit the *Colourful* category. It is significant that teachers in Queensland Catholic schools rated the generic quality, 'caring community', surely a characteristic that might reasonably be expected of *all* schools regardless of type, as a far more important feature of Catholic schools than more explicitly faith-based items, and that they saw the provision of a 'safe and nurturing environment' as being as important a purpose of Catholic schools as providing 'an authentic experience of a Catholic community' and 'education in the Catholic faith and tradition' (Gleeson, O'Gorman, & O'Neill, 2018). Similar patterns emerged from their study of pre-service teachers in a Catholic university (Chapter 9).

Pollefeyt and Bouwens (2014) believe that Values Education 'risks becoming a compromise model, reducing the Catholic faith to its ethical aspects and therefore "hollowing it out"' (p. 174). The shaded segment shown in Figure 11.2 represents the intersection of CST, human rights and social justice. At a time when the profile of students (Chambers, 2012) and teachers (Croke, 2007) in Catholic schools is becoming increasingly secular, there is an urgent need to explore this intersection from the perspective of classroom practice. Such an exploration would have particular relevance for the relationship between the Religious Education curriculum and the integration of CST across the curriculum, one of the unresolved issues arising from our action research. Meanwhile, the integration of CST across the formal curriculum can assist schools wishing to respond to their Leuven Enhancing Catholic School Identity research findings (Pollefeyt & Bouwens, 2010).

Prevailing neoliberal educational environment

As noted earlier, market values and performativity are having extremely influential impacts on education in Australia where the discussions leading to the development of the Australian Curriculum reflected 'global education trends and promised to raise the competitive edge of Australia's results from international tests' (Mills & McGregor, 2016, p. 116). Luke (2006) cynically remarks that 'market ideology has been infused into different levels of the educational system' (p. 122) to an extent that would make Australia eligible for International Monetary Fund funding. Research involving over 8,000 educators from all states and territories concluded that NAPLAN 'distort[s] teaching practices, constrain[s] the curriculum and narrows students' educational experiences' (Polesel, Rice, & Dulfer, 2014, p. 640).

While both our action research teachers and workshop participants were favourably disposed towards more challenging (multi- and interdisciplinary)

The synergy between CST and the general capabilities and cross-curricular themes of the Australian Curriculum presents obvious opportunities around ethical, human rights and environmental sustainability issues. Given the countercultural nature of CST, consideration of such issues inevitably results in the consideration of controversial issues in classrooms. Apart from challenging the dominant neoliberal orthodoxy, this can raise particular problems for teachers in Catholic schools who are expected to uphold 'official church teaching' as Higgins (1979) found in the case of the integrated Humanities Curriculum Project (Stenhouse, 1971) in Catholic schools in the UK.

models of curriculum integration and curriculum planning, they chose more conservative options when asked what about the *feasibility* of integrating CST across the curriculum in the prevailing environment. Although this may reflect their experiences of the organisational culture of schools, it is also indicative of the aforementioned climate of performativity. In an environment where academic attainment, legislative compliance, good governance and accountability are the dominant concerns (Biesta, 2009; Pascoe, 2007), the promotion of faith-based identity through curriculum integration is particularly challenging (Gleeson, 2015) for senior leaders both in Catholic Education Offices and in Catholic schools.

The synergy between CST and the general capabilities and cross-curricular themes of the Australian Curriculum presents obvious opportunities around ethical, human rights and environmental sustainability issues. Given the countercultural nature of CST, consideration of such issues inevitably results in the consideration of controversial issues in classrooms. Apart from challenging the dominant neoliberal orthodoxy, this can raise particular problems for teachers in Catholic schools who are expected to uphold 'official church teaching' as Higgins (1979) found in the case of the integrated Humanities Curriculum Project (Stenhouse, 1971) in Catholic schools in the UK.

The Outcomes-Based Education (OBE) movement of the 2000s (Donnelly, 2007; Queensland Department of Education and the Arts, 2005) provides part of the national backdrop for the current emphasis on performativity. In his paper 'Taylorism and the logic of learning outcomes', Stoller (2015) argues that Taylor's scientific management principles as manifested today in the Learning Outcomes Movement (LOM) in the United States are 'antithetical to the development of deep learning and democratic forms of education [while] restricting the creative capacities and unique potentials of students' (p. 318). As noted earlier, our action research teachers were quite dependent on centrally generated electronic planning templates that included large numbers of learning outcomes and achievement standards in the OBE/LOM traditions. Since action research is about process and exploration (Stenhouse, 1975) rather than product and measurement, this prevailing environment does not lend itself particularly well to the goals of the current study. Notwithstanding the tendency of teachers to adhere rigidly to pre-planned schemes of work, the well-established process versus product dilemma inevitably arose in the shape of the perceived efficacy of spontaneous 'teachable moments' which many teachers regarded as being particularly powerful.

The focus on learning outcomes rather than teaching is a common global denominator across curriculum reform in developed countries (Gleeson et al., forthcoming). Biesta (2006) argues that this new 'language of learning facilitates an *economic* understanding of the process of education … where the provider is there to *satisfy the customer* [and] makes it very difficult to raise questions about the content and purpose of education other than in terms of what the "customer" or the "market" wants' (p. 24). The alternative is to see learning as a response to '*difficult* questions ... that make it possible for students to come into the world as unique, individual beings' (Biesta, 2006, p. 25). This latter approach resonates very well with countercultural CST. As Biesta (2006) suggests, drawing on Derrida, it is by asking the difficult questions 'we challenge and possibly disturb who and where students are' (p. 29).

Conclusion

This small-scale action research project has provided strong evidence of the potential and significance of integrating CST across the curriculum in an environment where we all 'need to reconnect with the question of purpose in education' (Biesta, 2009, p. 33). The project team members were fortunate to work with a group of enthusiastic volunteer teachers whose levels of satisfaction and enjoyment were evident in their presentations at the dissemination seminars. However, it is one thing to work in a project environment with external support and an entirely different matter when it comes to developing a strategy and disseminating a programme for implementation across a whole school or education system.

The experience of the Identity and Curriculum in Catholic Education project highlights the very significant leadership implications of the integration of Catholic perspectives across the curriculum for Catholic Education Offices and school leaders. These include school cultural and school organisational issues along with the development of teachers' theological literacy and their reflective practice capabilities. At a macro level, there is need for research and scholarship with respect to the relationship between school curriculum and faith-based identity and the interface between humanistic (human rights, social justice education) and faith-based principles such as CST.

Note

1. Presentism means focusing on the short term. According Hargreaves (2010), this has been associated with conservatism (concentrating on small-scale rather than whole school changes), and individualism (performing teaching in isolation from other teachers).

References

Arbuckle, G. A. (2013). *Catholic identity or identities? Refounding ministries in chaotic times.* Minnesota: Liturgical Press.

Arthur, J. (2013). The de-Catholicising of the curriculum in English Catholic schools. *International Studies in Catholic Education, 5*(1), 83–98.

Ball, S. J. (1998). Big policies/small world: An introduction to international perspectives in education policy. *Comparative Education, 34*(2), 119–130.

Ball, S. J. (2012). *Global Education Inc.: New policy networks and the neo-liberal imaginary*. London: Routledge.

Beane, J. A. (1995). Curriculum integration and the disciplines of knowledge. *Phi Delta Kappan, 76*(8), 616–622.

Bell, J. 2003. *Doing your own research project*. Maidenhead: Open University Press.

Biesta, G. (2006). *Beyond learning: Democratic education for a human future*. Boulder: Paradigm.

Biesta, G. (2009). Good education in an age of measurement: On the need to reconnect with the question of purpose in education. *Educational Assessment, Evaluation and Accountability, 21*(1), 33–46.

Boeve, L. (2005). Religion after detraditionalization: Christian faith in a post-secular Europe. *Irish Theological Quarterly, 70*(2), 99–122. doi: 10.1177/002114000507000201.

Bowen, G. A. (2009). Document analysis as a qualitative research method. *Qualitative Research Journal, 9*(2), 27–40. https://doi.org/10.3316/QRJ0902027

Chambers, M. (2012). Students who are not Catholics in Catholic schools: Lessons from the Second Vatican Council about the Catholicity of schools. *International Studies in Catholic Education, 4*(2), 186–199.

Congregation for Catholic Education (CCE). (1997). *The Catholic school on the threshold of the third millennium*. Vatican City: Author

Congregation of Catholic Education (CCE). (2013). *Educating to intercultural dialogue in Catholic schools: Living in harmony for a civilization of love*. Vatican City: Author.

Congregation for Catholic Education (CCE). (2014). *Educating today and tomorrow: A renewing passion – Instrumentum laboris*. London: Catholic Truth Society.

Croke, B. (2007). Australian Catholic schools in a changing political and religious landscape. In G. Grace and J. O'Keefe (Eds.), *International handbook of Catholic education* (pp. 811–833). Dordrecht: Springer.

Dewey, J. (1938). *Experience and education*. New York: Macmillan.

Ditchburn, G. M. (2012). The Australian curriculum: Finding the hidden narrative? *Critical Studies in Education, 53*(3), 347–360. doi: 10.1080/17508487.2012.703137.

Donnelly, K. (2007). Australia's adoption of outcomes based education: A critique. *Issues in Educational Research, 17*(2), 183–206.

Dowling, A., Beavis, A., Underwood, C., Sadeghi, R., & O'Malley, K. (2009). *Who's coming to school today? Final report*. Brisbane: ACER, Brisbane Catholic Education.

Drake, S. (2012). *Creating standards-based integrated curriculum*. Thousand Oaks, CA: Corwin Press.

Fullan, M. (2005). *Leadership and sustainability*. London: Sage.

Fullan, M. (2007). *The new meaning of educational change* (4th ed.). New York: Teachers' College Press.

Fullan, M. (2016). *The new meaning of educational change* (5th ed.). New York: Teachers' College Press.

Gleeson, J. (2015). Critical challenges and dilemmas for Catholic education leadership internationally. *International Studies in Catholic Education, 7*(2), 145–161. doi: 10.1080/19422539.2015.1072955.

Gleeson, J., Klenowski, V., & Looney, A. (Forthcoming). Curriculum change in Australia and Ireland: A comparative study of recent reforms. *Journal of Curriculum Studies*.

Gleeson, J., O'Gorman, J., & O'Neill, M. (2018). The identity of Catholic schools as seen by teachers in Catholic schools in Queensland. *International Studies in Catholic Education, 10*(1), 44–65.

Goodson, I. F. (1993). *School subjects and curriculum change* (3rd ed.). London, New York and Philadelphia: Falmer.

Grace, G. (2010). Renewing spiritual capital: An urgent priority for the future of Catholic education internationally. *International Studies in Catholic Education, 2*(2), 117–128.

Grace, G. (2013). Catholic social teaching should permeate the Catholic secondary school curriculum: An agenda for reform. *International Studies in Catholic Education, 5*(1), 99–109.

Hall, G. E., & Hord, S. M. (2011). *Implementing change: Patterns, principles, and potholes* (3rd ed.). Upper Saddle River, NJ: Pearson.

Hargreaves, A. (1994). *Changing teachers, changing times: Teachers' work and culture in the postmodern age*. New York, NY: Teachers College Press.

Hargreaves, A. (2008). *The persistence of presentism and the struggle for lasting improvement*. London: Institute of Education.

Hargreaves, A. (2010) Presentism, individualism, and conservatism: The legacy of Dan Lortie's schoolteacher: A sociological study. *Curriculum Inquiry, 40*(1), 143–154. doi: 10.1111/j.1467-873X.2009.00472.x.

Higgins, T. (1979). *Teaching about controversial issues in Catholic schools* (No. 7). Norwich, England: University of East Anglia.

Hirst, P., & Peters, R. (1970). *The logic of education*. London: Routledge.

Institute for Catholic Education. (1996). *Curriculum matters: A resource for Catholic educators*. Toronto: Author.

Kliebard, H. M. (1995). The Tyler rationale revisited. *Journal of Curriculum Studies, 27*(1), 81–88. doi: 10.1080/0022027950270107.

Lane, D. A. (1991). *Catholic education and the school: Some theological reflections*. Dublin: Veritas.

Lane, D. A. (2015). *Catholic education in the light of Vatican II and Laudato Si*. Dublin: Veritas.

Leitch, R., & Day, C. (2000). Action research and reflective practice: Towards a holistic view. *Educational Action Research, 8*(1), 179–193. doi: 10.1080/09650790000200108.

Lingard, B. (2010). Policy borrowing, policy learning: Testing times in Australian schooling. *Critical Studies in Education, 51*(2), 129–147. doi: 10.1080/17508481003731026.

Luke, A. (2006). Teaching after the market. In L. Weis, C. McCarthy, & G. Dimitriadis (Eds.) *Ideology, curriculum, and the new sociology of education* (pp. 115–144). New York, NY: Routledge.

Luke, A. (2010). Will the Australian Curriculum up the intellectual ante in primary classrooms? *Curriculum Perspectives (Journal Edition), 30*(3), 5–10.

Mills, M., & McGregor, G. (2016). Learning not borrowing from the Queensland education system: Lessons on curricular, pedagogical and assessment reform. *The Curriculum Journal, 27*(1), 113–133. doi: 10.1080/09585176.2016.1147969.

Murray, D. (1991). *A special concern*. Dublin: Veritas.

Pascoe, S. (2007). Challenges for Catholic education in Australia. In G. Grace & J. O'Keefe (Eds.), *International handbook of Catholic education* (pp. 787–810). Dordrecht: Springer.

Pinar, W., Reynolds, W., Slattery, P., & Taubman, P. (2008). *Understanding curriculum: An introduction to the study of historical and contemporary curriculum discourses*. New York, NY: Peter Lang.

Polesel, J., Rice, S., & Dulfer, N. (2014). The impact of high-stakes testing on curriculum and pedagogy: A teacher perspective from Australia. *Journal of Education Policy, 29*(5), 640–657. doi: 10.1080/02680939.2013.865082.

Pollefeyt, D., & Bouwens, J. (2010). Framing the identity of Catholic schools: Empirical methodology for quantitative research on the Catholic identity of an education institute. *International Studies in Catholic Education, 2*(2), 193–211.

Pollefeyt, D., & Bouwens, J. (2014). *Identity in dialogue: Assessing and enhancing Catholic school identity. Research methodology and research results in Catholic schools in Victoria, Australia* (Vol. 1). Zürich: LIT Verlag Münster.

Queensland Department of Education and the Arts. (2005). *Smarter learning: The Queensland curriculum, assessment and reporting framework*. Brisbane: Department of Education and the Arts, Queensland Government. Retrieved from http://education.qld.gov.au/qcar/

Stenhouse, L. (1971). The humanities curriculum project: The rationale. *Theory into practice, 10*(3), 154–162. doi: 10.1080/00405847109542322.

Stenhouse, L. (1975). *An introduction to curriculum research and development*. London: Heinemann.

Stoller, A. (2015). Taylorism and the logic of learning outcomes. *Journal of Curriculum Studies, 47*(3), 317–333. doi: 10.1080/00220272.2015.1018328.

Thomson, P. (2015). Action research with/against impact. *Educational Action Research, 23*(3), 309–311.

Young, M. (2007). *Bringing knowledge back in: From social constructivism to social realism in the sociology of education*. London: Routledge.

Chapter 12

Identity and Curriculum in Catholic Education: Main lessons and issues arising[1]

Jim Gleeson

The genesis, purpose and main activities of the Identity and Curriculum in Catholic Education initiative (2013–2018) have already been outlined in the Introduction to this volume. Relevant contextual aspects of Catholic Education in general and Australian Catholic Education in particular have been explored in various chapters of this volume along with our understandings of curriculum integration and the integration of Catholic perspectives. The purpose of this concluding chapter is to identify the main outcomes of the initiative and to reflect on some of the more obvious issues arising and lessons learned.

The members of the project team[2] conducted surveys and interviews with a view to informing their school-based action research. The surveys and interviews, seen in terms of reconnaissance, set out to establish teachers' opinions regarding the faith-based identity, purposes and characteristics of Catholic schools. Cognisant of their importance for the future of Catholic schools in Queensland, we also conducted a longitudinal study of pre-service teachers' opinions regarding these same aspects of Catholic schools.

As indicated in the Introduction, our primary focus from the very beginning was on the planned integration of Catholic teaching across the curriculum in Queensland Catholic schools using an action research approach. For this purpose, we chose to narrow the definition of Catholic teaching to Catholic social teaching and to use Drake's (2012) ladder of curriculum integration.

This concluding chapter draws together the main findings of these various research activities and identifies the emerging issues and common themes. Two associated and related macro issues are then discussed – project governance and school/university partnerships.

Empirical research outcomes and emerging trends

As already outlined in Chapter 7, the vast majority of survey respondents believed that Catholic schools are different from other schools and that their distinctive identity is important. When asked to nominate the most important purposes and characteristics of Catholic schools, respondents were more likely to choose generic rather than faith-based items and this pattern was confirmed in our interview data. A majority chose 'school environment' as the main reason for their decision to work in Catholic schools, well ahead of 'faith commitment' and 'job-related reasons'. This pattern was further reinforced when 'the provision of a safe and nurturing environment' emerged as the most commonly chosen purpose of Catholic schools and when they overwhelmingly opted for 'caring community' as the most important characteristic of Catholic schools. It is also noteworthy that Australian Catholic University (ACU) student teachers were even more likely than our teacher respondents to place a premium on generic school purposes and characteristics such as 'safe and caring environment', 'caring community' and education for citizenship rather than explicitly faith-related school purposes and characteristics (Chapter 9).

Regression analysis of the survey data involved entry of five sets of teacher-related variables followed by two sets of school-related (see Table 7.1, Chapter 7) variables. High self-reported levels of religiosity consistently emerged as the strongest teacher-related predictor of the perceived importance of the faith-based identity, purposes and characteristics of Catholic schools. High self-ratings for knowledge of Catholic teaching, choosing to teach in Catholic schools because of one's faith commitment, being Catholic, having longer service in Catholic schools and being a primary teacher were also strong predictors of these outputs. Other strong predictors of the faith-based practices characteristics of Catholic schools included having added professional responsibilities and being female. When survey respondents were asked about their willingness to pursue professional development regarding the faith-based identity of Catholic schools, the strongest teacher-related predictors were having high levels of religiosity and added professional responsibilities, while the strongest school-related characteristics were the perceived importance of the given characteristics of Catholic schools and of their faith-based identity.

As reported and discussed in Chapter 8, teachers in US Catholic schools (Convey, 2012) were far more likely to rate these same characteristics of Catholic schools as essential.[3] While we can only speculate about the reasons for this finding, it is significant that US Catholic schools do not receive state funding, that teachers in these schools receive lower salaries than teachers in the public education sector and that there has been a strong focus on the faith development of these teachers for more than 40 years.

With reference to the integration of Catholic perspectives across the curriculum beyond Religious Education, the teacher survey and associated interviews (Chapter 10) provide rather contradictory evidence regarding the attitudes and opinions of teachers in Queensland Catholic schools. While survey respondents were broadly positive about the importance of integrating Catholic perspectives across the curriculum, and while more than half of them said they did so in their teaching, the interviews showed that such integration was seen in terms of availing of 'teachable moments' and/or giving personal witness ('I teach who I am'). Commendable as both of these approaches are, they fall far short of planned curriculum integration. It is noteworthy that survey respondents ranked the integration of Catholic perspective 11th of 15 given characteristics of Catholic schools in order of importance.

Interviewees also expressed concerns regarding the theological literacy levels of teachers, particularly younger teachers, when it came to introducing a faith perspective in dealing with curriculum topics. Our subsequent difficulties in finding schools and teachers willing to engage in associated action research, outlined earlier in Chapter 11 lend further credence to the credibility of our interviewees.

Regression analysis of our survey data found that the strongest teacher-related predictors of the perceived importance of planning for the curriculum integration of a Catholic perspective, of the practice of such integration and of teachers' confidence and willingness to do so were high levels of religiosity followed by high self-ratings for knowledge of Catholic teaching. When school-related variables were included in the regression, these same teacher-related variables remained statistically significant together with the perceived importance of faith-based school identity as well as the given practice- and community-related characteristics.

In summary then, our survey findings consistently indicate that the strongest teacher-related predictors of the perceived importance of the faith-related purposes, identity and characteristics of Catholic schools are high self-reported levels of religiosity and knowledge of Catholic teaching and choosing to teach in Catholic schools because of one's faith commitment. When the school-related identity and characteristics variables are added to the regression, these same teacher-related variables continue to be strong predictors of the perceived importance of the planned integration of a Catholic perspective across the curriculum and of teacher confidence and willingness to do so.

The overall message is as clear as it is predictable – those teachers whose faith matters to them are most likely to value faith-based school purposes, identity and characteristics and are most favourably disposed towards the integration of Catholic perspectives across the whole curriculum. The predictability of these findings is reassuring insofar as they offer strong empirical support for what many will already have accepted on the basis of anecdotal evidence, namely the importance of teachers' 'faith credentials'. However, they also highlight a worrying question about the availability of teachers with these beliefs and attitudes, particularly in light of the findings of our longitudinal study of ACU student teachers (Chapter 9). The corollary is that they also highlight the need for ongoing faith formation for teachers in Catholic schools. It is also a cause of concern that teachers' accounts of their classroom practice contrast sharply with their generally positive survey responses regarding the curriculum integration of a Catholic perspective (Chapter 10 above) – what might be called a rhetoric/reality dichotomy.

School-based action research (2015–2017): Main issues arising

The main goal of the Chair and his team was to explore the planned integration of Catholic social teaching across the curriculum using an action research approach. Strong evidence is provided in Chapter 11 of the effectiveness and feasibility of the planned integration of Catholic social teaching (CST) across a wide range of learning areas and the large attendance at our dissemination conference in November 2017 were particularly inspired by the accounts of teachers who participated in these action research activities.

In the first instance this initiative involved a partnership arrangement between individual schools and the university so as to ensure relevant teacher professional development, the availability of appropriate teaching resources and opportunities for curriculum planning. The success of the action research initiative was ultimately due to the enthusiasm and motivation of the individual teachers who volunteered to participate. These teachers saw a natural fit between the various CST principles and their chosen learning areas. While mostly integrating CST in one unit over one term, they were very positive about the outcomes for participating students and their resulting deeper knowledge of CST.

It is noteworthy that participating teachers as well as participants in our November 2016 dissemination seminar were less positive about the *feasibility* of disseminating progressive models of curriculum integration and planning (e.g. interdisciplinary) than they were about the *effectiveness* of such models. Three main issues emerged from the action research and these are now considered in turn:

- The importance of strong leadership at system and school levels.
- The relationship between education for social justice and human rights and Catholic social teaching.
- Curriculum-related issues including Australian Curriculum reforms.

System- and school-level leadership

The lack of support from system and school leaders was a major issue. Notwithstanding the positive dispositions of survey respondents towards the integration of a Catholic perspective, the project team's attempts to coax schools and teachers to volunteer for action research might be summed up in terms of 'attempting to play (Irish) handball against a haystack. You hear a dull thud and the ball doesn't come back to you'. And this was not-withstanding the fact that funding was available for teacher release and that professional support and academic credit at Master's level were available to participating teachers.

All successful curriculum development initiatives (Fullan, 2016) depend on the active support of senior leaders at district/system and school levels. As one participating secondary teacher who really understood the overall concept remarked, 'this very important work is only sustainable if there is at least school-wide integration with full time support of the leadership. Ideally there would be a Catholic Education system-wide philosophy and full support to make this integration sustainable'.

Against the background of pressing concerns with various practical issues such as school financing, the introduction of the Australian Curriculum and performance in the National Assessment Plan – Literacy and Numeracy (NAPLAN) test, scores, meant that system leaders and senior leaders in most participating schools did not become actively involved in the action research. The lack of leadership support within schools is reflected in the following vignettes:

Missed opportunity: Green school and Stewardship of Creation

Having identified the really impressive work being done in relation to environmental sustainability by teachers and students at 'Green' primary school (Geiger, Gleeson, & Effeney, 2015), the project team met with the school principal and the Assistant Principal Religious Education (APRE). Our message was that the wonderful work being done on environmental awareness provided a ready-made opportunity to integrate the Catholic social teaching principle, Stewardship of Creation, across the curriculum and that this would enhance the faith-based identity of Green School. We were afforded an opportunity to address a full staff meeting of over 30 teachers where we highlighted the potential synergy between their many wonderful environmental activities and the integration of the Catholic social teaching of stewardship across the learning areas of the Australian Curriculum. No viable expressions of interest were received!

There's no need, we're doing this already!

This was a very common response. For example, the Brisbane Catholic Education (BCE) representative who was accompanying the author on his visit to a particular primary school became quite adversarial as she listened to my explanation of the project to the leadership group who met with me. Interrupting my presentation mid-sentence, she declared that 'we are already doing all of this! What's the point?' This was a discomfiting experience for both the senior staff members present and the author. Needless to say, that school did not engage with us subsequently.

The 'lone wolf' syndrome

'Patricia' is a primary teacher who is really committed to environmental sustainability. Having engaged with our action research initiative, she was extremely effective in her implementation of an interdisciplinary approach to the integration of Stewardship of Creation across most learning areas with Year 3 students over two terms. Despite the presence of this wonderful role model in their midst, no other teachers in that school expressed interest in the action research project.

Leadership vacuum

The Acting Assistant Principal, Religious Education (APRE), provided strong leadership as coordinator of the whole school approach to the integration of Catholic social teaching at 'St Patrick's Catholic primary school' in 2017 (their presentation at the November 2017 conference is available on the project website[4]). The school principal however showed no interest whatsoever in this initiative and the whole school approach at St Patrick's has been floundering since the departure of the acting APRE to take up a position at another school.

It's just common sense!

A senior leader in a P-12 school remarked during an interview with the Chair that

> We're looking at the whole way we do curriculum in Years 7 to 9 and the way we do assessment and the pedagogical approach we use; everything is up for grabs in middle school. I think it's an opportune time for us to look at the integration of the faith-based aspects through the curriculum .... I don't think you push it for the sake of pushing it but where there are purposeful connections then it's just common sense.

This same leader subsequently ignored a number of invitations to become involved in the action research project.

When volunteer teacher interviewees were invited to comment on the difficulty of finding schools to participate in action research, they invariably returned to importance of leadership.

> If there was to be any real ground-breaking change, it would have to come from the top [Brisbane Catholic Education] down and be supported by principals. I don't know how successful that would be if it was made compulsory ... We're now ruled by the government [and] the church's

sway is very limited. So we're crunching numbers because Catholicism is not the number one priority anymore. (Female primary teacher)

Clearly the principal and the leadership team would need to be on board to start with …. Teachers need to see how and why it's going to better my teaching, my work … my students' education? So I think that it needs to be sold to teachers. (Female primary APRE)

I think its lack of spine … there is a leadership dimension to this … and I think that people are too scared of the politics of things, of not upsetting people … that's what I meant by spine. You've got to be out there and this is what we are. We're proud to be this; not oh well we'll modify it to suit your child or your family. (Female primary APRE)

That's a leadership matter! Sometimes people get so focused on the kids in their class that they don't want to think more widely …. (Male secondary teacher)

It's a question of leadership … The only way to instigate change or progress is from the top-down. Instead of recruiting individual teachers or schools, I'd try to recruit the head office and let it filter down from the top (male secondary teacher).

Participating action research teachers and attendees at the project Dissemination conference (November 2017) saw the most effective approach to the integration of CST in terms of a systematic whole school approach, where particular CST principles are the focus across all learning areas at the same time. Fullan (2016, p. 46) identifies the importance of a systemic approach for sustainable curriculum reform. Such an approach, as adopted in Ontario Catholic schools (see Chapter 6), requires strong commitment to the faith-based identity of Catholic schools along with strong leadership support at all levels of the system.

It is also important to recognise the need for collaborative approaches to addressing the various implementation issues highlighted already in Chapter 11. These include synchronising the Religious Education programme with the relevant Catholic social teaching principle(s); the stance to be adopted by the teacher when controversial issues arise in the classroom; how to combine spontaneous teachable moments with pre-planned lesson activities and the merits of including CST-related assessment tasks.

Indeed, the role of student assessment tasks in driving curriculum integration was one of the most hotly debated issues among action research teachers and the pros and cons have been well rehearsed in Chapter 11. According to Mockler (2016), the effectiveness of curriculum integration depends on authentic assessment which is the common ground between curriculum, pedagogy and assessment. Mockler and Groundwater-Smith (2015) remind us of the 'not insubstantial literature on "authentic assessment" with its emphasis on the seamless integration of content knowledge, pedagogy and assessment in authentic tasks' (p. 147), while Drake (2012) found that 'rich culminating assessment tasks' made most impact on students. At the same time it is important to allow individual teachers the flexibility to adopt their preferred approaches.

The heavy dependency of action research teachers on planning templates built around 'Content Descriptors' and 'Achievement Standards' was quite remarkable. This is indicative of a mindset where the focus is on curriculum as product rather than on the process of learning (Stenhouse, 1975; Taylor & Richards, 1989). Countercultural Catholic social teaching principles however, just like social justice and human rights education (see Burridge, Chapter 5), lend themselves to a process rather than a product-oriented model of curriculum design and implementation focused on measurable outcomes. Controversial issues inevitably arise in classrooms where the process model is employed and it is important that these are dealt with in an educationally valid way.

While the school-based actions described in Chapter 11 generally worked well it is important to note that these were one-off interventions with strong support from the project team. If teachers and/or whole staffs are to take seriously the integration of Catholic social teaching as an expression of the faith-based of Catholic schools, strong leadership at both system and school levels is a fundamental requirement.

As indicated earlier, it was decided to operationalise the meaning of 'Catholic teaching' in the project brief in terms of 'Catholic social teaching'. The arguments presented in Chapter 3 certainly highlight the need for Catholic and other faith-based school systems to actively consider the meaning and social implications of the new anthropology (Pope Francis, 2015; Lane, 2015, 2017a, 2017b) and its relevance for the school curriculum. The relationship between science and spirit, now recovering from the effects of Cartesian dualism, offers further options for curriculum integration. This is the world of quantum physics, a world where matter and energy are completely entangled (Lipton, 2016), a world where links between science and spirituality are emerging (Braden, 2018). The increasing emphasis on the relationship between well-being and curriculum (Buchanan, 2010; Henderson, 2010; Lovat, Toomey, & Clement 2010; Soutter, O'Steen, & Gilmore, 2012) offers further important possibilities. The scope for further investigation is indeed great.

The relationship between education for social justice, human rights and Catholic social teaching

Our observations indicate that participating action research teachers found it difficult to identify and negotiate the boundaries between social justice, human rights and faith-based aspects of Catholic social teaching principles. This issue also arose when ACU teacher educators attempted to enact the Mission statement of the university by embedding pre-chosen Catholic social teaching principles in their curriculum.

The close triadic relationship between these three areas reflects the relationship between values/citizenship education on the one hand and Catholic social teachings inspired by faith and Biblical notions of justice on the other (see Figure 11.2, Chapter 11). This observation is consistent with our survey findings that teachers and pre-service teachers generally were likely to endorse generic values ahead of more explicitly faith-based values. When CST principles such as Human Dignity, Preferential Option for the Poor, Common Good and Subsidiarity are considered from the perspectives of social justice and human rights, without reference to their underlying Christian foundations, this resembles ethics, citizenship and political education rather than the expression of faith-based school identity.

The instruments developed by the Enhancing Catholic School Identity Project (Pollefeyt & Bouwens, 2014) provide very valuable diagnostic tools for Catholic schools wishing to enhance their faith-based identities. The associated study of Catholic schools in Victoria identifies a real danger of the Catholic faith being reduced to its ethical aspects in what Pollefeyt and Bouwens call *Colourful* and *Colourless* schools (Pollefeyt & Bouwens, 2010), where secularisation prevails and Christianity is compromised. When such diagnostic reports leave school leaders searching for appropriate responses, the informed integration of Catholic social teaching across the curriculum can serve to bring together the humanist values of the secular world and the Catholic Christian values of the religious world.

The extent of social class differentiation and high levels of competition between schools, which is of considerable relevance to the whole question of education for social justice in Australia (see Chapter 1), challenges Catholic Education systems to review their priorities in the light of Gospel values and Catholic social teaching principles such as Preferential Option for the Poor.

As evidenced by Organisation for Economic Cooperation and Development's (OECD, 2010) meta-analysis of the 2009 Programme for International Student Assessment (PISA) results, such competition is having a deleterious effect on the academic achievement of disadvantaged students. The 2015 PISA results reflect a similar picture with Australia heading, for example, the 'above-average science performance ... below-average equity in education' category (OECD, 2016, p. 218). Perry and Southwell (2014) suggest that 'social segregation between Australian schools [which is] ... due to school choice and the federal government's policies for funding private schools ... [means that] social segregation between schools is much higher in Australia than in comparable countries' (p. 471). According to Kenway (2013), 'the government sector educates 66% of all students and takes 79% of the bottom SEA quarter. The Catholic sector educates 20% of all students and takes 15% of those from the bottom SEA quarter. The independent sector educates 14% and takes 6% of those in the bottom SEA quarter ... 57% of the Catholic sector and 44% of the government sector are in the top half of [the Index of Community Socio-Educational Advantage]' (p. 290).

Preston's (2018) report for the Australian Education Union on the social make-up of schools is based on 2016 Census data. She found that students from low-income families are highly concentrated in public schools, while those from high-income families are concentrated in Catholic and Independent schools with 75% of low-income students attending public schools compared to 15% in Catholic schools and 10% in Independent schools. Whereas 43% of students in public schools are from low-income families, just 26% of Catholic school students and 24% of Independent school students fall into this category and the emerging picture is one where Catholic schools are becoming much more like Independent schools than public schools.

Such discrepancies between the government and independent sectors raise important social justice issues for the Catholic Education sector while providing important, albeit confronting, context for the treatment of Catholic social teaching in that sector. Meanwhile, the profile of students (Chambers, 2012) and teachers (Croke, 2007) in Catholic schools in Australia is becoming increasingly secular, national education policies are influenced greatly by market values and school funding for particular sectors has become a political football. In such an environment, the social inequalities outlined both here in Chapter 1 above are becoming increasingly difficult to tackle. And yet, from the perspectives of Gospel values and faith-based school identity, it is important to recognise and proclaim the counter cultural nature of Catholic social teaching principles such as Preferential Option for Poor and the Common Good. Various documents produced by the Congregation for Catholic Education (CCE) provide strong support for such an undertaking. For example, the Congregation expresses concerns regarding 'the unequal distribution of resources, poverty, injustice and human rights denied' (CCE, 2013, para 66), the growing popularity of a 'merely functional view of education' (CCE, 2014, p. 12) and the hegemony of market values where governments are consumed by 'the demands deriving from the ever-changing economic situation' (p. 64). The Congregation also acknowledges the unique climate of Catholic school communities where the school's 'evangelical identity' (CCE, 2014, para 13) takes expression and where the 'principles of the gospel become [the school's] internal motivation and final goal' (CCE, 1997, para 34).

Curriculum-related issues

So how does this curriculum change initiative measure up to what Fullan (2016, p. 69) identifies as the characteristics of change?

- Is there a perceived need for this change?
- Is the purpose of the initiative clear?
- Is it overly complex?
- Is it practicable?

Our difficulties with finding schools and teachers willing to volunteer for action research are clear indicators that the planned integration of Catholic perspectives across the curriculum was not regarded as a priority need. Furthermore, it would appear that many teachers felt that such integration simply involved availing of 'teachable moments' when they arose and having good relationships with students (I teach who I am). This is a classic example of where the very ambitious intentions of three well-placed innovators (see Introduction) were not sufficient to bring school leaders and teachers onside through discussion and reflection at what Fullan (2016) calls the initiation stage.

Such discussion and negotiation would also have helped clarify the purpose of the exercise, rather than leaving it to the small project team to operationalise the original project goals in isolation. As Fullan (2016 p. 70) suggests, 'clarity about goals is a perennial problem in the change process … [where] precise needs are not clear at the beginning, especially with complex changes … people often become clearer during the implementation itself' (p. 70). Our experience however was that, although participating teachers certainly became clearer on the importance and relevance of integrating Catholic social teaching, this realisation had little impact on system or school leaders.

Fullan (2016) defines complexity in terms of the 'difficulty and extent of change required of the individuals responsible for implementation' (p. 71). Insofar as the proposed change involved an understanding of Catholic social teaching, its relevance to the formal curriculum and an understanding of the various levels or types of curriculum integration, this initiative certainly met Fullan's criteria for complexity. As Berman and McLaughlin (1978) concluded, although 'ambitious projects were less successful in absolute terms of the percent of project goals achieved, they typically stimulated more teacher change than projects attempting less … nothing ventured, nothing gained' (cited in Fullan, 2006, p. 72). While the current venture was certainly ambitious, its success in stimulating change was limited.

With regard to his fourth question of practicality, Fullan (2016, p. 72) expresses concerns in relation to the adoption of change on political grounds and/or without sufficient time for development. His revealing statement that 'ambitious projects are nearly always politically driven' is certainly true of the initiative under consideration which certainly was not afforded sufficient time or resources. The significance of Fullan's (2016) antidote, namely to adopt 'a whole-system perspective [resulting in] greater specificity of action and commitment across the system' (p. 72), was recognised by all action research participants and above all by the project team.

Fullan (2016, p. 73) also recognises the importance of wider contextual factors which he refers to as 'situational constraints or opportunities for effective change'. It so happened that our action research project was taking place at the same time as the Australian Curriculum was introducing general capabilities and cross-curricular themes. The Australian Curriculum,

Assessment and Reporting Authority (ACARA) defines general capabilities in terms of 'knowledge, skills, behaviours and dispositions that can be developed and applied across the curriculum to help students become successful learners, confident and creative individuals, and active and informed citizens' (ACARA, 2012, p. 15). It believes that cross-curricular themes 'provide students with the tools and language to engage with and better understand their world at a range of levels ... through development of considered and focused content that fits naturally within learning areas' (ACARA, 2012, p. 18). Against that background, it is hardly surprising that the Authority (ACARA, 2012) clearly recognises the importance of an integrated approach to curriculum:

> 21st century learning does not fit neatly into a curriculum solely organised by learning areas or subjects that reflect the disciplines. Increasingly, in a world where knowledge itself is constantly growing and evolving, students need to develop a set of knowledge, skills, behaviours and dispositions, or general capabilities that apply across subject- based content and equip them to be lifelong learners able to operate with confidence in a complex, information-rich, globalised world. (p. 15)

ACARA general capabilities such as ethical understanding, intercultural understanding and personal and social capability have obvious relevance to Catholic social teaching as do the cross-curricular themes of sustainability and Aboriginal and Torres Strait Island histories and cultures. The reformed curriculum provided a wonderful and timely opportunity for Catholic system and school leaders to embrace curriculum integration in a manner consistent with the Australian Curriculum while recognising the obvious relevance of these capabilities and themes to Catholic social teaching. Indeed, the possibility of introducing faith-based identity as an additional cross-cutting theme in Tasmanian Catholic schools has recently been identified by Bailey, Stretton, and Cunningham (2017) and Hindmarsh (2017).

The report of the review panel for the Australian Curriculum, chaired by David Gonski, has identified the 'lack of support surrounding the general capabilities' (Australian Government, 2018, p. 40) and the need to 'raise their status within curriculum delivery' (p. xii). Their report recognises that 'teaching and assessing the general capabilities, particularly in an embedded form, is a highly complex task' (p. 40) and acknowledges that it 'takes deep expertise to know how best to interweave the teaching of the general capabilities into different learning areas [along with] the risk that general capabilities are treated as a secondary aspect of learning, relative to subject-based knowledge' (p. 40). Our own observations in action research settings as well as our teacher feedback would also suggest that the general capabilities and cross-cutting themes have not gained much traction in schools.

Notwithstanding the potential of these ACARA innovations to facilitate the curriculum integration of Catholic social teaching, the general environment of Australian curriculum is heavily influenced by product-oriented (Taylor & Richards, 1989) rather than process-oriented (Stenhouse, 1975) approaches to curriculum design. For example, action research participants were extremely dependent on planning templates that contained large numbers of prescribed learning outcomes and associated achievement standards. This approach is indicative of outcomes based education (OBE) or standards based education that was popularised in Queensland and other Australian states during the 1990s (Donnelly, 2007). It is an approach that 'privileges particular beliefs about pedagogy, the nature of knowledge, theories of learning and what it means to be educated' (Australian Government, 2014, p. 76). From the perspective of the United States, it is typical of the logic of learning outcomes (Stoller, 2015, p. 317), what Au (2011) calls the "New Taylorism" of scientific management in education.

Having considered the main outcomes, lessons and issues arising from the empirical and action research outcomes, it is important to also consider some of the emergent macro-level issues arising from 5 years' experience of the Identity and Curriculum in Catholic Education initiative.

Emerging macro issues

As we have just seen, school leadership is a fundamental requirement for the successful integration of Catholic social teaching across the curriculum. Moving beyond the micro and meso levels, the macro-level leadership both of the Catholic Education partners and the host institution also emerged as a major issue. The second macro issue discussed here, project governance, is a particularly important aspect of partnership projects in general and school/ university partnerships in particular.

Macro-level leadership

As outlined earlier in the Introduction, the genesis and gestation of this initiative are inextricably linked with the alignment of three innovative individuals from Australian Catholic University, Queensland Catholic Education Commission (QCEC) and BCE in key leadership roles at a particular point in time, with all three committed to addressing the relationship between Catholic school identity and curriculum. For example, QCEC had recently published *Queensland Catholic Schools and Curriculum*

> to assist Catholic school communities to reflect and to conduct learning and teaching through a curriculum that is aligned with Catholic theology and philosophy of education [since] it is imperative that Catholic schools intentionally base their curriculum on the core beliefs, values and philosophy of the Catholic community. (QCEC, 2008, p. 1)

The journal *Curriculum Matters*, published by BCE, had also been publishing articles which suggested that practitioners were beginning to focus on translating such broad foundational principles into curriculum practice. For example, Rush (2008, p. 18), charting the relationships between Queensland Studies Authority's Early Learning Areas and the BCE Religious Education curriculum, reported that 'the sturdiest connection made was [between the Queensland State] Early Learning Areas (ELAs) and ... religious texts, religious knowledge, Catholic Christian beliefs and religious practices'. Writing in the same journal, Barry (2008, p. 12) explicitly argued that 'a faith that does justice entails integrating Catholic social teaching and social justice education across the curriculum and providing opportunities for students and staff to be involved in action for social justice'.

It was unfortunate that David Hutton's period as Executive Director of BCE had elapsed before the Chair's arrival in Brisbane in February 2013 and that Professor Emmitt's Deanship ended shortly afterwards. Her immediate successor had little interest in the initiative and the all-important links between the project and the Catholic Education community (such as the Project Advisory Committee) had been seriously damaged by the time her successor was appointed in 2015.

Meanwhile, senior leaders of the university were either unaware of or indifferent to the very existence of the Chair position although Professor Emmitt had discussed its establishment with the Vice-Chancellor in advance. While this might be regarded as understandable in the context of a large bureaucratic multi-campus institution, it does raise serious questions regarding the attitudes of senior university leaders to the faith-based identity of Catholic schools and the preparation of those graduates who will teach in Catholic schools. Furthermore, the 'outlier' positioning of the Chair in the University's organogram (see Introduction) meant that the position was effectively isolated from the School of Education and from the mainstream of the university and its professional networks.

For the Identity and Curriculum in Catholic Education initiative to be effective, it was imperative that it should enjoy a good working relationship with Catholic schools and those who control them. While the donors met their financial commitments in full,[5] their overall levels of involvement and interest in project activities were minimal, particularly after the Advisory Committee ceased to function. Real engagement with four of the five Catholic Education Offices was difficult because of their distance from Brisbane and, in any event, their financial stakes in the project were modest.

David Hutton's replacement as Director of BCE was both enthusiastic and supportive during the early stages of the project. Being unfamiliar with Australia and Queensland, the Chair greatly appreciated the fact that BCE provided and arranged opportunities for him to visit schools and receive feedback on the evolving project concept during the months after his arrival. While afforded great courtesy during these visits, the Chair had a growing sense that those who had dreamt of integrating Catholic perspectives across the whole curriculum were somewhat ahead of their constituents in their thinking. Consistent with Fullan's (2016) findings, these teachers tended to accommodate to the near occasion of change by saying that such practices were already in place. However, our teacher interviews suggest that such responses were based primarily on their use of unplanned 'teachable moments' and on their general adherence to the inherited values and traditions of their schools. The contribution of school charism to faith-based identity was an enduring theme of these visits and its significance was confirmed in the findings of the comparative study of the roles of secondary teachers as moral educators in Australia and Ireland (Gleeson & O'Flaherty, 2016).

The BCE School Service Centres and the BCE Curriculum team were of particular relevance to the work of the project. The Service Centres engaged directly with schools and could help identify teachers and schools who might collaborate in action research while the Curriculum team could advise on the most fruitful and appropriate learning areas. Notwithstanding the genuine efforts of the Director of the School Service Centre North, visits to the two Centres did not produce any tangible results while collaboration with the Curriculum team tapered off after a couple of helpful early meetings.

A well-attended seminar was held at ACU in December 2013 with a view to publicising the initiative and identifying partner collaborators and it was decided to hold the following series of workshops in 2014:

- Curriculum coordinators: How does Catholic Education engage with current social issues?
- Discussion of our survey findings: Teachers' opinions regarding certain aspects of Catholic Education.
- Identity and Curriculum in Catholic Education: Teachers of social sciences.
- Identity and Curriculum in Catholic Education: Teachers of Business and Economics.

These workshops had to be cancelled however due to issues with the distribution lists necessary for issuing invitations to the relevant curriculum coordinators and teachers.

As already noted, BCE had to contend with a number of pressing issues around this time. However, in the case of a new curriculum initiative requiring collaboration with schools and teachers, one rather obvious strategy would have been to invite the Chair to address school principals and/or senior leaders (e.g. curriculum co-ordinators, Assistant Principals Religious Education) about the existence and goals of the project at one of their regular gatherings. However, no such opportunity was afforded.

From mid-2014 onwards all interactions with BCE were mediated through their coordinator of research who filled that particular role for 1 day per week.

This coordinator's congeniality and supportiveness were greatly appreciated. He drafted letters to school principals seeking participation and made arrangements for BCE to manage and facilitate payment to schools from project funds of teacher 'release time'.

Following the demise of the Advisory Committee (see Introduction), there has been a lack of engagement and discussion regarding the identity and curriculum initiative with senior university and Catholic Education Office leaders. For example, when the Chair indicated in June 2016 his willingness to meet with the various donor bodies to discuss project outcomes, no expressions of interest ensued. Coming towards the end of the Chair's fixed-term contract, it seemed reasonable to expect some evidence-based discussion regarding the continuation or disestablishment of the Chair position at ACU along with a review of the original intention to integrate a Catholic perspective across the curriculum.[6] Instead of that, the 'Identity and Curriculum in Catholic Education' initiative and the ACU Chair position have simply disappeared into the vacuum that developed over its 5-year existence.

So what are the outcomes of the Identity and Curriculum in Catholic Education initiative? The establishment and filling of the associated Chair and the achievements of the project (2013–2018) are duly acknowledged and disseminated in the current publication and on the project website.[7] The concept of integrating a Catholic perspective across the curriculum provides the basis for Unit EDCU623, Social Justice and Identity and Curriculum, of the ACU Master's in Education programme. This Unit, which was developed in 2013 by Professors Emmitt, Goldburg and the author, and which addresses the main themes addressed in the current publication, had been completed by some 400 students up to November 2018. Its existence means that students from across Australia will have an opportunity to learn about the relevance of Catholic social teaching to the faith-based identity and curriculum of Catholic schools and to watch the exemplar videos that feature our participating teachers (see action research activities at http://www.acu.edu.au/1280444).

Another positive systemic outcome is that teachers who participated in the action research described in Chapter 11 have developed the capacity to 'train' other teachers should the need arise.

Project governance and school/university partnerships

The Identity and Curriculum in Catholic Education initiative was predicated on a school/university partnership. While much of the literature on such partnerships has to do with pre-service practicum placements, there is also a long history of the engagement of such partnerships in action research (Simons, Kushner, Jones, & James, 2003). What has emerged is that teachers engaged in collaborative school/university research partnerships value the access to research experience, the links with other practitioners and the 'prestige' of working with a university. It has been suggested by

Hargreaves (2003, p. 18) that such partnerships have the potential to transform education through 'networks of communities of teachers who are passionate about transferred innovation'.

The success of school/university research partnerships requires that they 'pose questions ... of mutual interest to all participants and ... instigate the need to exchange ideas and interpretations between the different constituencies' (Baumfield & Butterworth, 2007, p. 421). Some obvious issues of mutual interest to the main partners in the Identity and Curriculum in Catholic Education initiative included strengthening the faith-based identity of Catholic schools and realising the potential of the whole curriculum to enhance the expression of that identity. Such exchanges of ideas are contingent, however, on the existence of effective governance structures, what Baumfield and Butterworth (2007, p. 415) call 'the "irregular heartbeat" of a partnership organisation'. In the absence of such a beating heart, our initiative was bereft of the key requirements of successful school/university partnerships such as collegial conversations regarding clarity of purpose, emerging issues and coalitions of interest (Miller, 2001).

In their UK-based study of school/university partnerships for educational research, McLaughlin and Black-Hawkins (2007) have also recognised the critical importance of clarity of purposes and of the active involvement of school and system leaders:

> Engaging and maintaining the commitment of head teachers and other school leaders, who were strongly committed to the research work of the partnership, had a positive effect on the research activities taking place in their own schools... and provided a forum for them to present their research findings to the other members of the staff. (p. 337)

For such research partnerships to be effective, these authors also highlight the importance of open and trusting relationships, effective communications and opportunities for the dissemination of research findings. They also identify the importance of collecting relevant evidence and supporting participating teachers, both of which have been effectively provided for in the current instance.

At a very minimum, this particular school/university partnership needed to have a functioning advisory group that was actively committed to the goals of the project and representative of the main partners. Unfortunately, the lack of engagement on the part of the university, Catholic Education Offices and school leaders in the current project meant that many of the conditions for effective school/university partnerships, including the development of a shared purpose with teachers and schools, clearly did not exist. Given the dysfunctional nature of the partnership, it simply was not possible to take on board Grundy's (1998, p. 44) advice about the importance of establishing 'research programmes and researching communities rather than one-off projects'.

Conclusion

The research reported in Chapters 7–11 of this book provides baseline empirical data regarding the beliefs and values of teachers and pre-service teachers that can enable future policymakers go beyond merely anecdotal evidence. Our action research findings provide important lessons for faith-related curriculum development in Catholic schools. The commitment of those teachers who completed the survey, volunteered for interview and particularly of those who engaged in school-based action research has made this possible. Their efforts are sincerely appreciated.

The fundamental importance of strong leadership on the part of the host university, Catholic Education Offices, and schools emerges as the overarching issue from this analysis of the Identity and Curriculum in Catholic Education school/university partnership. The challenges of moving beyond human values to faith-based values, beyond social justice and human rights education to Catholic social teaching, also emerges as an important challenge for Catholic educators.

It is clear from Part 1 of this book and Chapter 11 that the curriculum integration of Catholic social teaching has the potential to counter the prevailing market-driven educational ideology while expressing the faith-based identity of Catholic schools. Given the neoliberal educational environment in which they exist, and their need to serve two competing masters, Catholic schools have to think smarter in order to preserve their core values. For example, instead of having to choose between NAPLAN achievement and the integration of Catholic social teaching, they need to realise that it is possible to achieve both goals through, for example, considered choice of English literature texts and data for mathematical analysis. They can also avail of the wonderful opportunity provided by the general capabilities and cross-curriculum themes of the recently introduced Australian Curriculum, which are of such relevance to Catholic social teaching.

It appears however that there is a palpable sense of apathy in relation to the integration of a faith-based perspective across the curriculum in Queensland Catholic schools. There is also a sense of what Fullan (2016, p. 70) calls 'false clarity' regarding the relationship between faith-based school identity and the curriculum of Catholic schools. Such false clarity occurs when change is 'interpreted in an oversimplified way [and when] the proposed change has more to it than people perceive or realise' (2016, p. 71). One possible way to address this issue is to adopt the Young Social Innovators (Ireland) model, presented by Rachel Collier at our November 2017 conference (see bottom of page https://www.acu.edu.au/1341703), with its obvious links with Catholic social teaching, curriculum learning areas and the See, Judge, Act paradigm introduced in Chapter 3 above.

Although the hegemony of neoliberal educational values represents a serious threat to faith-based schools, it also provides a wonderful opportunity for schools to uphold countercultural Catholic social teaching principles in a manner that is educationally valid and to clarify and honour the core values that provide their very *raison d'etre*. The Ontario Institute for Catholic Education has shown the way in this respect. Soon after securing full public funding for their schools, the Institute reflected that

> Like the Hebrew slaves emerging from the wilderness of Sinai, we saw in the distance a land flowing with milk and honey. If we remember our scriptures however, we will, recall that after they entered the promised land the former slaves gradually forgot who they were, where they had come from, and what sort of work they were called to do. They became pre-occupied with building palaces, collecting taxes and establishing a kingdom. As their material well-being grew, their unique religious identity and moral imperative was diminished. They lost touch with their roots. Over time they became virtually indistinguishable from their neighbours. They managed to survive as a people only by remembering their covenant with God in the desert, preserving and enshrining the covenant in their laws and institutions, and interpreting it in the context of their new conditions. They realized that they had been freed from being slaves to Pharaoh so that they might become servants of the Lord. Is there a lesson here for Catholic Education in the 1990's? (Institute for Catholic Education, 1996, p. 4)

This realisation motivated Ontario Catholic School Districts to investigate and implement the integration of Catholic teaching, particularly Catholic social teaching, across the school curriculum beyond Religious Education (see Chapter 6). Their motivation comes from a strong desire to uphold the distinctive faith-based character of Catholic schools.

Coming back to Australia, it is most encouraging to find that the former Executive Director of Tasmania Catholic Education Office, Trish Hindmarsh (2017, pp. 1–3), recognises the important task of the Catholic school in seeking to achieve a synthesis of culture and faith through the school curriculum because 'the potential of the formal curriculum to be a means of grace for students has always excited me … It is important to consciously plan for a high quality curriculum that takes full advantage of Catholic life and a Catholic worldview'. Hindmarsh goes on to include both Catholic social teaching principles and the Australian Curriculum general capabilities in her treatment of curriculum mapping as she encourages teachers to 'decide which faith-based concepts and values may be relevant' (2017, p. 22) to their curriculum planning and to engage in both reflective practice as individuals and theological reflection at the level of the whole school.

The ambitious and exploratory nature of the Identity and Curriculum in Catholic Education initiative required careful nurturing and strong governance. While the chief architects of this initiative were strategically placed to enable such support, their departure from office and the associated breakdown of governance added greatly to the difficulty of the challenge. In the event of a similar intervention being attempted in the future, it is important to consider the issues identified in this chapter at the planning stage and, most importantly, to proceed to implementation with the full support of senior institutional leaders. Whatever else the current project may have achieved, it has certainly highlighted the critically important role of leadership at university, Catholic Education Office/Institute, and school levels in critically interrogating the faith-based identity of Catholic schools from the ground up.

Notes

1. This chapter is an extended version of the author's presentation at the Project Dissemination Conference, ACU Leadership Centre, Elizabeth Street, Brisbane on 8 November 2017.
2. Peta Goldburg, Professor of Religious Education, Dr Maureen O'Neill, Research Assistant (p/t) and the author.
3. Particularly in the case of 'teachers of religion are Catholic', 'celebration of school liturgies', 'RE programs present the teachings of the Church', 'integration of Catholic teachings across the formal curriculum' and 'prayer in the daily life of school'.
4. https://www.acu.edu.au/1669195.
5. With one exception.
6. While the November 2017 dissemination conference was well attended and received very positive evaluations, no senior policymakers attended.
7. http://www.acu.edu.au/1280444

References

Au, W. (2011). Teaching under the new Taylorism: High-stakes testing and the standardization of the 21st century curriculum. *Journal of Curriculum Studies, 43*, 25–45.

Australian Curriculum, Assessment and Reporting Authority (ACARA). (2012). *The shape of the Australian curriculum.* Version 4.0. Sydney: Author.

Australian Government. (2014). *Review of the Australian curriculum: Final report.* Canberra: Australian Government.

Australian Government. (2018). *Through growth to achievement. The report of the review to achieve educational excellence in Australian schools.* Canberra: Review Panel.

Bailey, B., Stretton, A., & Cunningham, A. (2017). How will a fourth cross curriculum priority of Catholicity and an eighth general capability of Wisdom contribute to Catholic curriculum in Tasmanian Catholic schools? *eJournal of Catholic Education in Australasia, 3*(1), 5.

Barry, G. (2008). Features of Catholicism and their implications for the curriculum of a Catholic school. *Curriculum Matters, 7*(2), 9–12.

Baumfield, V., & Butterworth, M. (2007). Creating and translating knowledge about teaching and learning in collaborative school–university research partnerships: An analysis of what is exchanged across the partnerships, by whom and how. *Teachers and Teaching: Theory and Practice, 13*(4), 411–427. doi: 10.1080/13540600701391960.

Berman, P., & McLaughlin, M. (1978). Implementation of educational innovation. *Educational forum, 40*(3), 345–370.

Braden, G. (2018). Science and spirituality co-operating for our new world. *Holistic Bliss*, *102*, 20–21.

Buchanan, M.T. (2010). Attending to the spiritual dimension to enhance curriculum change. *Journal of Beliefs & Values, 31*(2), 191–201. doi: 10.1080/13617672.2010.503632.

Chambers, M. (2012). Students who are not Catholics in Catholic schools: Lessons from the second Vatican council about the Catholicity of schools. *International Studies in Catholic Education, 4*(2), 186–199. doi: 10.1080/19422539.2012.708174.

Congregation for Catholic Education (CCE). (1997). *The Catholic school on the threshold of the third millennium.* Vatican City: Author.

Congregation for Catholic Education (CCE). (2013). *Educating to intercultural dialogue in Catholic schools. Living in harmony for a civilization of love.* Vatican City: Author.

Congregation for Catholic Education (CCE). (2014). *Educating today and tomorrow: A renewing passion, Instrumentum laboris.* Vatican City: Author.

Convey, J. J. (2012). Perceptions of Catholic identity: Views of Catholic school administrators and teachers. *Catholic Education: A Journal of Inquiry and Practice, 16*(1), 187–214.

Croke, B. (2007). Australian Catholic schools in a changing political and religious landscape. In G. Grace & J. O'Keefe (Eds.), *International handbook of Catholic education – Challenges for school systems in the 21st century.* (pp. 811–834). Dordrecht: Springer.

Donnelly, K. (2007). Australia's adoption of outcomes based education: A critique. *Issues in Educational Research, 17*(2), 183–206.

Drake, S. (2012). *Creating standards-based integrated curriculum.* Thousand Oaks, CA: Corwin Press.

Fullan, M. (2016). *The new meaning of educational change* (5th ed.). London: Routledge.

Geiger, V., Gleeson, J., & Effeney, G. (2015). *Education for sustainability in BCE schools: An investigation of policy and practice.* Brisbane: Catholic Education Office.

Gleeson, J., & O'Flaherty, J. (2016). The teacher as moral educator: Comparative study of secondary teachers in Catholic schools in Australia and Ireland. *Teaching and Teacher Education, 55*, 45–56.

Grundy, S. (1998). Research partnerships. In *Action research in practice. Partnerships for social justice in education* (pp. 37–46). London: Routledge.

Hargreaves, D. (2003). *Working laterally: How innovation networks make an education epidemic.* Nottingham: DEMOS and NCSL DfES.

Henderson, D. (2010). Values, wellness and the social sciences curriculum. In T. Lovat, R. Toomey, & N. Clement (Eds.), *International research handbook on values education and student wellbeing* (pp. 273–289). Dordrecht: Springer.

Hindmarsh, T. (2017). *Educator's guide to Catholic curriculum. Learning for 'fullness of life'.* Mulgrave VA: Vaughan.

Institute for Catholic Education. (1996). *Curriculum matters: A resource for Catholic educators.* Toronto: Author.

Kenway, J. (2013). Challenging inequality in Australian schools: Gonski and beyond. *Discourse: Studies in the Cultural Politics of Education, 34*(2), pp. 286–308. Retrieved from http://dx.doi.org/10.1080/01596306.2013.770254

Lane, D. A. (2015). *Catholic education in the light of Vatican II and Laudato Si'.* Dublin: Veritas.

Lane, D. A. (2017a). Catholic education in the light of Vatican II: Anthropology and Catholic education. In *Vatican II and new thinking about Catholic education* (pp. 123–135). Oxford: Routledge.

Lane, D. A. (2017b). Anthropology in the service of bridges to hope. In *A dialogue of hope. Critical thinking for critical times* (pp. 63–77). Dublin: Messenger.

Lipton, B. (2016). *The biology of belief* (10th ed.). New York: Hay House.

Lovat, T., Toomey, R., & Clement, N. (Eds.). (2010). *International research handbook on values education and student wellbeing*. Dordrecht: Springer.

McLaughlin, C., & Black-Hawkins, K. (2007). School-university partnerships for educational research – distinctions, dilemmas and challenges. *The Curriculum Journal, 18*(3), 327–341. doi: 10.1080/09585170701589967.

Miller, L. (2001). School-university partnership as a venue for professional development. In *Teachers caught in the action* (pp. 102–117). New York: Teachers College Press.

Mockler, N., & Groundwater-Smith S. (2015). Curriculum, pedagogy, assessment and student voice. In *Engaging with student voice in research, education and community*. Cham: Springer.

Mockler, N. (2016). *Curriculum integration: What could it look like? What would it take?* Keynote presentation. Sydney: ACSA Symposium.

Organisation for Economic Co-operation and Development (OECD). (2010). *PISA 2009 results: What makes a school successful? Resources, policies and practices (IV)*. Retrieved from http://dx.doi.org/10.1787/9789264091559-en

Organisation for Economic Co-operation and Development (OECD) (2016), *PISA 2015 results (volume I): Excellence and equity in education, PISA*. Paris: Author. Retrieved from http://dx.doi.org/10.1787/9789264266490-en

Perry, L. B., & Southwell, L. (2014). Access to academic curriculum in Australian secondary schools: A case study of a highly marketised education system. *Journal of Education Policy, 29*(4), 467–485. doi: 10.1080/02680939.2013.846414.

Pollefeyt, D., & Bouwens, J. (2010). Framing the identity of Catholic schools: Empirical methodology for quantitative research on the Catholic identity of an education institute. *International Studies in Catholic Education, 2*(2), 193–211. doi: 10.1080/19422539.2010.504034.

Pollefeyt, D., & Bouwens, J. (2014). *Identity in dialogue. Assessing and enhancing Catholic school identity. Research methodology and research results in Catholic schools in Victoria, Australia* (Vol. l). Zurich and Berlin: LIT Verlag.

Pope Francis. (2015). *Encyclical letter Laudato Si' on care for our common home*. Retrieved from http://w2.vatican.va/content/francesco/en/encyclicals/documents/papa-francesco_20150524_enciclica-laudato-si.html

Preston, B. (2018). *The social make-up of schools. Family income, Indigenous status, family type, religion, languages spoken, disability, home internet access, housing tenure, and geographic mobility of students in public, Catholic and independent schools.* A report prepared for the Australian Education Union. Retrieved from http://www.aeufederal.org.au/application/files/7115/2090/2405/Preston2018.pdf

Queensland Catholic Education Commission (QCEC). (2008). *Queensland Catholic schools and curriculum*. Brisbane: Author.

Rush, K. 2008. From the sandpit up: Developing the religious education curriculum guidelines for the early years. *Curriculum Matters, 7*(2), 16–18.

Simons, H., Kushner, S., Jones, K., & James, D. (2003). From evidence-based practice to practice-based evidence: The idea of situated generalization. *Research Papers in Education, 18*(4), 347–364.

Soutter, A. K., O'Steen, B., & Gilmore, A. (2012) Wellbeing in the New Zealand curriculum. *Journal of Curriculum Studies, 44*(1), 111–142. doi: 10.1080/00220272.2011.620175.

Stenhouse, L. (1975). *An introduction to curriculum research and development*. London: Heinemann.

Stoller, A. (2015). Taylorism and the logic of learning outcomes, *Journal of Curriculum Studies, 47*(3), 317–333. doi: 10.1080/00220272.2015.1018328.

Taylor, P. H., & Richards, C. (1989). *An introduction to curriculum studies*. London: Routledge.

Appendix 1

Identity of Catholic schools: Outcome (criterion) variables

Catholic schools are different

The criterion variable was based on Question 16.1 of the survey and involved comparing Catholic and non-Catholic schools on a scale from 1 (same) to 11 (different). Summary statistics for the ordinary least squares (OLS) regression are shown in Table B7 (Appendix 2). Because the criterion variable was markedly negatively skewed, a multinomial regression was run as well. The criterion variable was collapsed to produce groups as nearly equal in size as was possible. This resulted in four groups. The overall model fit was statistically significant (χ^2 = 428.24, df = 120, p < .001, Naglekerke R^2 = .20). Statistically significant predictors were AGE (p = .001), RELIGIOSITY (p < .001) and ENVIRO (p < .001). AGE was not judged statistically significant in the OLS regression. KNOWTOT and COMIT were judged significant in the OLS regression but here the p values were .048 and .028, respectively, which do not meet the more stringent criterion for statistical significance employed here.

Catholic schools are important

The criterion variable was based on Question 16.2 of the survey and involved rating the importance of Catholic identity of their school on a scale from 1 (unimportant) to 11 (important). Summary statistics for the OLS regression are shown in Table B8 (Appendix 2). Because the criterion variable was markedly negatively skewed, a multinomial regression was run as well. The criterion variable was collapsed to produce groups as nearly equal in size as was possible. This resulted in three groups. The overall model fit was statistically significant (χ^2 = 838.05, df = 80, p < .001, Naglekerke R^2 = .38). Statistically significant predictors were ENVIRO (p < .001), COMIT (p < .001), RELIGION (p < .001), RELIGIOSITY (p < .001) and APPOINT (p = .002). Contrary to the findings with OLS regression, KNOWTOT (p = .016) did not reach the conservative criterion for statistical significance, and being a primary teacher was not statistically significant either (p = .08).

Reasons for working in Catholic schools

The criterion variables were based on Question 8 of the survey. Both were dichotomous. The first, ENVIRO, contrasted those who selected the option of school environment as their main reason with those who selected other options. The second, COMIT, contrasted those who selected the faith commitment option with those who selected other options. A logistic regression analysis was conducted for each criterion in turn and the results are summarised in Tables B2 and B3 (Appendix 2).

Purpose of Catholic schools

The criterion was dichotomous, whether participants endorsed the explicit Catholic purpose of Catholic schools (1) or whether they did not (0). A logistic regression analysis was performed on this criterion with the results as shown in Table B4 (Appendix 2).

Characteristics of Catholic schools

The criterion variables were participants' scores on the components identified in a principal components analysis (PCA) of the ratings of importance of 14 of the 15 characteristics listed in Question 15 of the survey. The item relating to integration was not included as it was used as a criterion variable in its own right in an analysis not reported here. The two components accounted for 49% of the variance and characteristics loaded (after Varimax rotation) as shown in Table 7.4 (Chapter 7). The distribution of scores on the each of the components was approximately normal and OLS regression was employed with results as shown in Table B5 and Table B6 (Appendix 2).

Importance of religion (religiosity)

Although not an outcome variable, the importance of this variable meant that a better understanding of it was of value. The results of an OLS regression using variables in Sets 1 and 2 plus RELIGION is shown in Table B15 (Appendix 2).

Appendix 2

Identity of Catholic schools: Regression analysis tables

Table A1 Sets of predictor variables used in the regression analyses

Set	Variable	Scoring	Survey question
Set 1	Demographics		
	GENDER	Male = 1, female = 2	1
	AGE	< 29 years =1 .... 60+ years = 5	2
	LEVEL	Primary = 1, primary and secondary = 2, secondary = 3	5_1
	LOS	< 5 years = 1 ... > 30 years = 5 (length of teaching service)	6
	APPOINT	1 = principal ... 6 = teacher (level of appointment)	9
Set 2	Role in Catholic school		
	RELTEACH	1 = teaches religion, 2 = does not	5_2
	CURMANG	1 = curriculum responsibilities, 2 = none	5_3
	LOSCATH	1 = < 5 years ... 5 > 30 years	7
Set 3	Religion and religiosity		
	RELIGION	1 = Catholic, 0 = other	10
	RELGIMP	0 = very important ... 5 = very unimportant	11
Set 4	Self-reported levels of knowledge		
	KNOWTOT	1 = knowledge of faith very poor ... 5 = knowledge very good	20
Set 5	Reasons for working in Catholic schools		
	ENVIRO	1 = working because of environment, 0 = other	8
	COMIT	1 = working because of faith commitment, 0 = other	8
Set 6	Catholic purpose and identity		
	PURPCATH2	1 = explicit Catholic purpose, 0 = other	14
	CATSCHDF	1 = Catholic schools same...11 Catholic schools different	16_1
	CATIDIMP	1 = Catholic identity not important...11 important	16_2
	PRACTICES	low scores = unimportant, high scores = important	17
	PEOPLE	low scores = unimportant, high scores = important	17

Appendix 2: Identity of Catholic schools: Regression analysis tables 299

Table AI (Continued)

Set	Variable	Scoring	Survey question
Set 7	Attitude to integration		
	INTEGRI	I = essential...5 = unimportant	17_7
	INTEGR2	lower scores indicate more positive attitude	19_1
	INTEGR3	lower scores indicate more positive attitude	19_2
Set 8	Confidence and willingness		
	CONFIDENCE	lower scores indicate greater confidence	21
	WILLINGNESS	lower scores indicate greater confidence	22
Set 9	Professional development		
	PDLIKE	I = strongly disagree; 5 = strongly agree	23_2

Table BI Regression statistics for the prediction of KNOWTOT

Model	Unstandardized coefficients		Standardized coefficients			Correlations		
	B	Std. error	Beta	t	Sig.	Zero-order	Partial	Part
(Constant)	4.203	.115		36.520	.000			
GENDER	.028	.028	.019	.990	.323	.030	.022	.019
AGE	.012	.017	.021	.688	.492	.150	.015	.013
LEVEL	.118	.025	.104	4.737	.000	−.041	.104	.089
RELTEACH	−.262	.031	−.188	−8.497	.000	−.225	−.184	−.160
CURMANG	−.048	.035	−.035	−1.365	.172	−.134	−.030	−.026
LOS	−.062	.021	−.123	−2.923	.004	.162	−.064	−.055
LOSCATH	.109	.019	.210	5.744	.000	.276	.125	.108
APPOINT	−.032	.013	−.062	−2.372	.018	−.210	−.052	−.045
RELGIMP	−.151	.011	−.293	−13.927	.000	−.388	−.293	−.263
RELIGION	.331	.037	.184	8.882	.000	.288	.192	.168

$R^2 = .264; F(10, 2,063) = 74.11, p < .001.$

Table B2 Regression statistics for the prediction of ENVIRO

	B	SE	Wald	df	Sig.	Exp(B)
GENDER	.212	.148	2.039	1	.153	1.236
AGE	.169	.099	2.933	1	.087	1.185
LEVEL	−.228	.136	2.794	1	.095	.796
RELTEACH	.039	.170	.053	1	.818	1.040
CURMANG	.018	.189	.009	1	.924	1.018
LOS	−.397	.108	13.574	1	.000	.672
LOSCATH	.276	.092	9.008	1	.003	1.318
APPOINT	−.056	.081	.478	1	.489	.946
RELGIMP	−.023	.061	.147	1	.701	.977
RELIGION	.239	.184	1.685	1	.194	1.270
KNOWTOT	.285	.117	5.929	1	.015	1.329
Constant	.909	.800	1.290	1	.256	2.481

Nagelkerke $R^2 = .045; \chi^2$ (10; $N = 2,074) = 49.85, p < .001.$

300   Appendix 2: Identity of Catholic schools: Regression analysis tables

Table B3 Regression statistics for the prediction of COMIT

	B	SE	Wald	df	Sig.	Exp(B)
GENDER	.269	.130	4.299	1	.038	1.309
AGE	−.030	.081	.133	1	.715	.971
LEVEL	−.447	.122	13.552	1	.000	.639
RELTEACH	−.484	.144	11.296	1	.001	.616
CURMANG	−.184	.168	1.202	1	.273	.832
LOS	−.155	.099	2.435	1	.119	.856
LOSCATH	.329	.090	13.281	1	.000	1.390
APPOINT	−.176	.083	4.472	1	.034	.839
RELGIMP	−.714	.060	142.766	1	.000	.489
RELIGION	2.660	.202	173.176	1	.000	14.298
KNOWTOT	.332	.103	10.446	1	.001	1.393
Constant	.097	.731	.017	1	.895	1.101

Nagelkerke $R^2 = .466; \chi^2 = (11; N = 2{,}074) = 862.26, p < .001$.

Table B4 Regression statistics for the prediction of PURPCATH2

		B	SE	Wald	df	Sig.	Exp(B)
Step 1	GENDER	−.020	.106	.036	1	.849	.980
	AGE	.034	.065	.272	1	.602	1.035
	LEVEL	.080	.094	.711	1	.399	1.083
	RELTEACH	−.163	.118	1.904	1	.168	.849
	CURMANG	−.261	.130	4.042	1	.044	.770
	LOS	−.109	.082	1.782	1	.182	.896
	LOSCATH	.245	.074	10.921	1	.001	1.278
	APPOINT	−.134	.050	7.049	1	.008	.875
	RELGIMP	−.180	.042	18.072	1	.000	.835
	RELIGION	.519	.152	11.623	1	.001	1.680
	KNOWTOT	.089	.083	1.133	1	.287	1.093
	Constant	−.034	.558	.004	1	.951	.967
Step 2	GENDER	−.050	.108	.218	1	.640	.951
	AGE	.041	.066	.379	1	.538	1.041
	LEVEL	.130	.096	1.845	1	.174	1.139
	RELTEACH	−.099	.120	.672	1	.412	.906
	CURMANG	−.240	.131	3.340	1	.068	.787
	LOS	−.103	.083	1.534	1	.216	.902
	LOSCATH	.219	.075	8.418	1	.004	1.244
	APPOINT	−.125	.051	6.093	1	.014	.882
	RELGIMP	−.106	.045	5.602	1	.018	.900
	RELIGION	.172	.164	1.095	1	.295	1.187
	KNOWTOT	.054	.085	.401	1	.527	1.055
	ENVIRO	−.127	.146	.749	1	.387	.881
	COMIT	.759	.124	37.420	1	.000	2.137
	Constant	−.264	.578	.209	1	.648	.768

Step 1: Nagelkerke $R^2 = .112; \chi^2 = (11; N = 2{,}074) = 179.79, p < .001$.

Step 2: Nagelkerke $R^2 = .135; \chi^2$ change $= (2; N = 2{,}074) = 39.20, p < .001$.

Overall: $\chi^2 = (13, N = 2{,}074) = 218.99, p < .001$.

Appendix 2: Identity of Catholic schools: Regression analysis tables   301

Table B5 Regression statistics for the prediction of PRACTICES

Model	Unstandardized coefficients		Standardized coefficients			Correlations		
	B	Std. error	Beta	t	Sig.	Zero-order	Partial	Part
1 (Constant)	.410	.237		1.732	.083			
GENDER	.184	.045	.083	4.072	.000	.100	.089	.082
AGE	−.072	.028	−.084	−2.585	.010	.023	−.057	−.052
LEVEL	−.050	.040	−.030	−1.252	.211	−.062	−.028	−.025
RELTEACH	−.157	.050	−.076	−3.127	.002	−.123	−.069	−.063
CURMANG	−.089	.056	−.044	−1.587	.113	−.115	−.035	−.032
LOS	.036	.034	.048	1.065	.287	.045	.023	.022
LOSCATH	−.052	.031	−.067	−1.689	.091	.062	−.037	−.034
APPOINT	−.078	.021	−.103	−3.646	.000	−.177	−.080	−.074
RELGIMP	−.196	.018	−.256	−10.825	.000	−.323	−.232	−.219
RELIGION	−.209	.061	−.078	−3.444	.001	.015	−.076	−.070
KNOWTOT	.214	.035	.143	6.064	.000	.245	.132	.123
2 (Constant)	.120	.239		.501	.616			
GENDER	.167	.045	.076	3.727	.000	.100	.082	.075
AGE	−.074	.028	−.087	−2.697	.007	.023	−.059	−.054
LEVEL	−.026	.040	−.015	−.649	.516	−.062	−.014	−.013
RELTEACH	−.135	.050	−.065	−2.705	.007	−.123	−.059	−.054
CURMANG	−.080	.055	−.039	−1.438	.151	−.115	−.032	−.029
LOS	.053	.034	.071	1.571	.116	.045	.035	.031
LOSCATH	−.074	.031	−.095	−2.421	.016	.062	−.053	−.049
APPOINT	−.073	.021	−.096	−3.456	.001	−.177	−.076	−.069
RELGIMP	−.168	.019	−.218	−8.963	.000	−.323	−.194	−.180
RELIGION	−.338	.064	−.126	−5.257	.000	.015	−.115	−.105
KNOWTOT	.192	.035	.129	5.486	.000	.245	.120	.110
ENVIRO	.229	.060	.077	3.787	.000	.103	.083	.076
COMIT	.275	.051	.135	5.397	.000	.232	.118	.108

Model 1: $R^2 = .155$; $F(11, 2,062) = 34.44$, $p < .001$.

Model 2: $R^2 = .173$; F Change $(2, 2,060) = 21.67$, $p < .001$.

Overall: $F(13, 2,073) = 33.06$, $p < .001$.

302 Appendix 2: Identity of Catholic schools: Regression analysis tables

Table B6 Regression statistics for the prediction of PEOPLE

Model	Unstandardized coefficients		Standardized coefficients			Correlations		
	B	Std. error	Beta	t	Sig.	Zero-order	Partial	Part
1 (Constant)	−.191	.238		−.800	.424			
GENDER	−.023	.046	−.010	−.506	.613	.010	−.011	−.010
AGE	.054	.028	.062	1.914	.056	.116	.042	.038
LEVEL	−.226	.040	−.130	−5.588	.000	−.186	−.122	−.111
RELTEACH	.002	.051	.001	.031	.975	−.140	.001	.001
CURMANG	−.077	.056	−.037	−1.373	.170	−.064	−.030	−.027
LOS	−.050	.034	−.065	−1.461	.144	.109	−.032	−.029
LOSCATH	.057	.031	.072	1.853	.064	.196	.041	.037
APPOINT	−.010	.022	−.013	−.453	.651	−.126	−.010	−.009
RELGIMP	−.138	.018	−.176	−7.578	.000	−.261	−.165	−.151
RELIGION	.705	.061	.256	11.504	.000	.325	.246	.229
KNOWTOT	.062	.036	.040	1.740	.082	.214	.038	.035
2 (Constant)	−.264	.242		−1.091	.275			
GENDER	−.033	.045	−.014	−.716	.474	.010	−.016	−.014
AGE	.056	.028	.064	1.996	.046	.116	.044	.040
LEVEL	−.210	.040	−.120	−5.190	.000	−.186	−.114	−.103
RELTEACH	.023	.051	.011	.451	.652	−.064	.010	.009
CURMANG	−.069	.056	−.033	−1.225	.221	−.064	−.027	−.024
LOS	−.047	.034	−.062	−1.386	.166	.109	−.031	−.027
LOSCATH	.047	.031	.059	1.507	.132	.196	.033	.030
APPOINT	−.007	.021	−.008	−.304	.761	−.126	−.007	−.006
RELGIMP	−.113	.019	−.143	−5.946	.000	−.261	−.130	−.118
RELIGION	.595	.065	.216	9.146	.000	.325	.198	.181
KNOWTOT	.050	.035	.033	1.423	.155	.214	.031	.028
ENVIRO	−.051	.061	−.017	−838	.402	.034	−.018	−.017
COMIT	.254	.052	.122	4.933	.000	.325	.108	.098

Model 1: $R^2 = .180$; $F(11, 2,062) = 41.17$, $p < .001$.

Model 2: $R^2 = .190$; F change $(2, 2,060) = 12.53$, $p < .001$.

Overall: $F(13, 2,073) = 37.15$, $p < .001$.

Appendix 2: Identity of Catholic schools: Regression analysis tables   303

Table B7 Regression statistics for the prediction of CATSCHDIF

| Model | Unstandardized coefficients | | Standardized coefficients | | | Correlations | | |
	B	Std. error	Beta	t	Sig.	Zero-order	Partial	Part
1 (Constant)	9.338	.447		20.896	.000			
GENDER	.208	.086	.052	2.431	.015	.057	.053	.052
AGE	.022	.053	.015	.423	.672	.067	.009	.009
LEVEL	−.065	.076	−.021	−.855	.393	−.041	−.019	−.018
RELTEACH	−.122	.095	−.033	−1.280	.201	−.073	−.028	−.027
CURMANG	−.213	.106	−.059	−2.021	.043	−.110	−.044	−.043
LOS	−.013	.064	−.010	−.208	.836	.070	−.005	−.004
LOSCATH	−.007	.058	−.005	−.125	.901	.100	−.003	−.003
APPOINT	−.078	.040	−.057	−1.929	.054	−.140	−.042	−.041
RELGIMP	−.164	.034	−.119	−4.782	.000	−.195	−.105	−.102
RELIGION	.222	.115	.046	1.930	.054	.106	.042	.041
KNOWTOT	.260	.067	.097	3.903	.000	.185	.086	.083
2 (Constant)	8.937	.455		19.636	.000			
GENDER	.188	.085	.047	2.205	.028	.057	.049	.047
AGE	.017	.052	.011	.322	.747	.067	.007	.007
LEVEL	−.039	.076	−.013	−.508	.611	−.041	−.011	−.011
RELTEACH	−.103	.095	−.027	−1.079	.281	−.073	−.024	−.023
CURMANG	−.205	.105	−.057	−1.952	.051	−.110	−.043	−.041
LOS	.011	.064	.008	.176	.860	.070	.004	.004
LOSCATH	−.034	.058	−.025	−.590	.555	.100	−.013	−.012
APPOINT	−.073	.040	−.053	−1.810	.070	−.140	−.040	−.038
RELGIMP	−.138	.036	−.100	−3.875	.000	.195	−.085	−082
RELIGION	.101	.122	.021	.823	.411	.106	.018	.017
KNOWTOT	.235	.067	.087	3.520	.000	.185	.077	.075
ENVIRO	.397	.115	.074	3.456	.001	.100	.076	.073
COMIT	.246	.097	.067	2.539	.011	.173	.056	.054

Model 1: $R^2 = .066$; $F(11, 2,062) = 13.32, p < .001$.

Model 2: $R^2 = .075$; F Change $(2, 2,060) = 9.17, p < .001$.

Overall: $F(13, 2,073) = 12.77, p < .001$.

304   Appendix 2: Identity of Catholic schools: Regression analysis tables

Table B8 Regression statistics for the prediction of CATIDIMP

Model	Unstandardized coefficients		Standardized coefficients			Correlations		
	B	Std. error	Beta	t	Sig.	Zero-order	Partial	Part
1 **(Constant)**	8.979	.496		18.089	.000			
GENDER	.131	.095	.027	1.379	.168	.054	.030	.027
AGE	.030	.058	.016	.516	.606	.099	.011	.010
LEVEL	−.341	.084	−.093	−4.046	.000	−.176	−.089	−.079
RELTEACH	−.331	.106	−.073	−3.138	.002	−.206	−.069	−.062
CURMANG	−.152	.117	−.035	−1.295	.195	−.074	−.029	−.025
LOS	−.083	.071	−.051	−1.167	.243	.100	−.026	−.023
LOSCATH	.099	.064	.059	1.533	.125	.187	.034	.030
APPOINT	−.058	.045	−.035	−1.287	.198	−.149	−.028	−.025
RELGIMP	−.387	.038	−.233	−10.170	.000	−.339	−.219	−.200
RELIGION	.943	.128	.162	7.385	.000	.270	.161	.145
KNOWTOT	.381	.074	.118	5.152	.000	.298	.113	.101
2 **(Constant)**	8.037	.495		16.234	.000			
GENDER	.076	.093	.016	.815	.415	.054	.018	.016
AGE	.022	.057	.012	.389	.697	.099	.009	.007
LEVEL	−.262	.083	−.071	−3.172	.002	−.176	−.070	−.061
RELTEACH	−.260	.103	−.058	−2.512	.012	−.206	−.055	−.048
CURMANG	−.122	.114	−.028	−1.069	.285	−.074	−.024	−.020
LOS	−.028	.070	−.017	−.404	.686	.100	−.009	−.008
LOSCATH	.027	.063	.016	.422	.673	.187	.009	.008
APPOINT	−.042	.044	−.026	−.968	.333	−.149	−.021	−.019
RELGIMP	−.294	.039	−.177	−7.603	.000	−.339	−.165	−.146
RELIGION	.526	.133	.090	3.956	.000	.270	.087	.076
KNOWTOT	.312	.073	.096	4.298	.000	.298	.094	.082
ENVIRO	.746	.125	.116	5.963	.000	.168	.130	.114
COMIT	.892	.105	.202	8.469	.000	.392	.183	.162

Model 1: $R^2 = .206$; $F(11, 2{,}062) = 48.63$.

Model 2: $R^2 = .245$; F Change $(2, 2{,}060) = 53.469$, $p < .001$.

Overall: $F(13, 2{,}073) = 51.47$, $p < .001$.

Appendix 2: Identity of Catholic schools: Regression analysis tables 305

Table B9 Regression statistics for the prediction of INTGRI

Model	Unstandardized coefficients		Standardized coefficients			Correlations		
	B	Std. error	Beta	t	Sig.	Zero-order	Partial	Part
1 (Constant)	2.771	.244		11.339	.000			
GENDER	.009	.046	.004	.192	.848	.022	.004	.004
AGE	−.002	.028	−.003	−.085	.932	.066	−.002	−.002
LEVEL	−.087	.041	−.052	−2.124	.034	−.093	−.047	−.044
RELTEACH	−.113	.051	−.055	−2.221	.026	−.121	−.049	−.046
CURMANG	−.096	.056	−.048	−1.705	.088	−.111	−.038	−.035
LOS	.011	.034	.014	.310	.756	.068	.007	.006
LOSCATH	−.040	.031	−.052	−1.272	.203	.103	−.028	−.026
APPOINT	−.062	.022	−.082	−2.852	.004	−.171	−.063	−.059
RELGIMP	−.145	.019	−.192	−7.623	.000	−.282	−.166	−.158
RELIGION	.086	.066	.032	1.313	.189	.129	.029	.027
KNOWTOT	.101	.036	.069	2.826	.005	.205	.062	.059
ENVIRO	.076	.062	.026	1.235	.217	.058	.027	.026
COMIT	.145	.052	.072	2.782	.005	.218	.061	.058
2 (Constant)	2.656	.254		10.439	.000			
GENDER	−.026	.043	−.012	−.599	.549	.022	−.013	−.011
AGE	.000	.026	.000	.005	.996	.066	.000	.000
LEVEL	−.014	.038	−.008	−.367	.713	−.093	−.008	−.007
RELTEACH	−.076	.047	−.037	−1.604	.109	−.121	−.035	−.031
CURMANG	−.050	.052	−.025	−.955	.340	−.111	−.021	−.018
LOS	.013	.032	.017	.402	.688	.068	.009	.008
LOSCATH	−.038	.029	−.050	−1.318	.188	.103	−.029	−.025
APPOINT	−.038	.020	−.050	−1.869	.062	−.171	−.041	−.036
RELGIMP	−.060	.018	−.079	−3.252	.001	−.282	−.072	−.062
RELIGION	−.013	.062	−.005	−.207	.836	.129	−.005	−.004
KNOWTOT	.028	.034	.019	.843	.399	.205	.019	.016
ENVIRO	.016	.058	.005	.273	.785	.058	.006	.005
COMIT	−.037	.050	−.018	−.749	.454	.218	−.017	−.014
PURPCATH2	.075	.040	.038	1.851	.064	.168	.041	.036
CATSCHDF	−.011	.012	−.020	−.963	.336	.140	−.021	−.018
CATIDIMP	.028	.011	.061	2.569	.010	.271	.057	.049
PRACTICES	.266	.022	.270	12.218	.000	.320	.260	.235
PEOPLE	.291	.021	.301	13.593	.000	.340	.287	.261

Model 1: $R^2 = .116$; $F(13, 2,060) = 20.77$, $p < .001$.

Model 2: $R^2 = .243$; F Change $(5, 2,055) = 68.98$, $p < .001$.

Overall: $F(18, 2,073) = 36.63$, $p < .001$.

306 Appendix 2: Identity of Catholic schools: Regression analysis tables

Table B10 Regression statistics for the prediction of INTGR2

Model	Unstandardized coefficients B	Std. error	Standardized coefficients Beta	t	Sig.	Correlations Zero-order	Partial	Part
1 (Constant)	3.520	.241		14.586	.000			
GENDER	.048	.045	.022	1.054	.292	.037	.023	.021
AGE	.010	.028	.012	.359	.719	.114	.008	.007
LEVEL	−.060	.040	−.035	−1.493	.136	−.079	−.033	−.030
RELTEACH	−.015	.050	−.007	−.290	.772	−.093	−.006	−.006
CURMANG	−.085	.056	−.042	−1.516	.130	−.125	−.033	−.031
LOS	−.053	.034	−.071	−1.565	.118	.113	−.034	−.032
LOSCATH	.055	.031	.071	1.796	.073	.176	.040	.036
APPOINT	−.045	.021	−.059	−2.089	.037	−.190	−.046	−.042
RELGIMP	−.193	.019	−.252	−10.262	.000	−.351	−.221	−.207
RELIGION	.067	.065	.025	1.030	.303	.140	.023	.021
KNOWTOT	.119	.035	.080	3.364	.001	.245	.074	.068
ENVIRO	.102	.061	.034	1.672	.095	.074	.037	.034
COMIT	.156	.051	.076	3.031	.002	.251	.067	.061
2 (Constant)	3.166	.264		12.002	.000			
GENDER	.028	.044	.013	.635	.526	.037	.014	.012
AGE	.010	.027	.011	.354	.723	.114	.008	.007
LEVEL	−.012	.040	−.007	−.303	.762	−.079	−.007	−.006
RELTEACH	.013	.049	.006	.257	.797	−.093	.006	.005
CURMANG	−.056	.054	−.028	−1.028	.304	−.125	−.023	−.020
LOS	−.050	.033	−.067	−1.525	.127	.113	−.034	−.030
LOSCATH	.055	.030	.070	1.814	.070	.176	.040	.036
APPOINT	−.031	.021	−.041	−1.483	.138	−.190	−.033	−.029
RELGIMP	−.139	.019	−.181	−7.296	.000	−.351	−.159	−.143
RELIGION	−.009	.065	−.003	−.145	.885	.140	−.003	−.003
KNOWTOT	.071	.035	.047	2.035	.042	.245	.045	.040
ENVIRO	.046	.060	.015	.770	.442	.074	.017	.015
COMIT	.031	.052	.015	.598	.550	.251	.013	.012
PURPCATH2	.036	.042	.018	.868	.385	.152	.019	.017
CATSCHDF	−.002	.012	−.004	−.204	.838	.153	−.005	−.004
CATIDIMP	.048	.011	.104	4.233	.000	.295	.093	.083
PRACTICES	.132	.023	.132	5.831	.000	.250	.128	.115
PEOPLE	.159	.022	.162	7.163	.000	.268	.156	.141

Model 1: $R^2 = .159$; $F(13, 2,060) = 30.06$, $p < .001$.

Model 2: $R^2 = .206$; F Change $(5, 2,055) = 24.32$, $p < .001$.

Overall: $F(18, 2,073) = 29.69$, $p < .001$.

Appendix 2: Identity of Catholic schools: Regression analysis tables 307

Table B11 Regression statistics for the prediction of INTGR3

Model		B	Std. error	Beta	t	Sig.	Zero-order	Partial	Part
		Unstandardized coefficients		Standardized coefficients			Correlations		
1	(Constant)	2.858	.188		15.166	.000			
	GENDER	.100	.035	.054	2.839	.005	.079	.062	.053
	AGE	.029	.022	.040	1.328	.184	.161	.029	.025
	LEVEL	−.030	.031	−.021	−.955	.340	−.103	−.021	−.018
	RELTEACH	−.218	.039	−.124	−5.545	.000	−.218	−.121	−.103
	CURMANG	−.126	.044	−.074	−2.885	.004	−.151	−.063	−.054
	LOS	−.009	.027	−.014	−.346	.729	.163	−.008	−.006
	LOSCATH	.017	.024	.026	.717	.474	.230	.016	.013
	APPOINT	−.033	.017	−.052	−1.992	.046	−.212	−.044	−.037
	RELGIMP	−.132	.015	−.202	−8.942	.000	−.402	−.193	−.167
	RELIGION	−.021	.051	−.009	−.423	.672	.176	−.009	−.008
	KNOWTOT	.320	.028	.253	11.613	.000	.424	.248	.216
	ENVIRO	.016	.048	.006	.339	.735	.063	.007	.006
	COMIT	.169	.040	.098	4.211	.000	.322	.092	.078
2	(Constant)	2.629	.209		12.553	.000			
	GENDER	.087	.035	.046	2.469	.014	.079	.054	.045
	AGE	.032	.022	.045	1.506	.132	.161	.033	.028
	LEVEL	−.015	.031	−.010	−.471	.638	−.103	−.010	−.009
	RELTEACH	−.198	.039	−.113	−5.085	.000	−.218	−.111	−.094
	CURMANG	−.112	.043	−.066	−2.596	.009	−.151	−.057	−.048
	LOS	−.010	.026	−.016	−.389	.697	.163	−.009	−.007
	LOSCATH	.019	.024	.029	.783	.434	.230	.017	.014
	APPOINT	−.025	.017	−.038	−1.487	.137	−.212	−.033	−.027
	RELGIMP	−.104	.015	−.161	−6.917	.000	−.402	−.151	−.127
	RELIGION	−.029	.051	−.013	−.555	.579	.176	−.012	−.010
	KNOWTOT	.294	.028	.232	10.642	.000	.424	.229	.196
	ENVIRO	−.022	.048	−.009	−.471	.637	.063	−.010	−.009
	COMIT	.103	.041	.059	2.510	.012	.322	.055	.046
	PURPCATH2	.046	.033	.028	1.396	.163	.170	.031	.026
	CATSCHDF	−.007	.010	−.016	−.783	.433	.159	−.017	−.014
	CATIDIMP	.034	.009	.087	3.768	.000	.316	.083	.069
	PRACTICES	.083	.018	.098	4.640	.000	.283	.102	.086
	PEOPLE	.028	.018	.034	1.595	.111	.202	.035	.029

Model 1: $R^2 = .285; F(13, 2,060) = 63.04, p < .001$.

Model 2: $R^2 = .302; F$ Change $(5, 2,055) = 10.29, p < .001$.

Overall: $F(18, 2,073) = 49.41, p < .001$.

308   Appendix 2: Identity of Catholic schools: Regression analysis tables

Table B12 Regression statistics for the prediction of CONFIDENCE

Model	Unstandardized coefficients		Standardized coefficients			Correlations		
	B	Std. error	Beta	t	Sig.	Zero-order	Partial	Part
1 (Constant)	1.800	.216		8.345	.000			
GENDER	−.050	.041	−.023	−1.213	.225	−.039	−.027	−.022
AGE	.031	.025	.036	1.212	.226	−.117	.027	.022
LEVEL	−.020	.037	−.012	−.544	.586	.032	−.012	−.010
RELTEACH	.135	.046	.065	2.960	.003	.159	.065	.055
CURMANG	.121	.051	.060	2.377	.018	.159	.053	.044
LOS	−.009	.031	−.012	−.289	.772	−.143	−.006	−.005
LOSCATH	−.026	.028	−.034	−.937	.349	−.210	−.021	−.017
APPOINT	.032	.019	.042	1.621	.105	.211	.036	.030
RELGIMP	.127	.016	.166	7.694	.000	.357	.168	.142
RELIGION	.018	.055	.007	.330	.741	−.157	.007	.006
KNOWTOT	−.618	.032	−.415	−19.309	.000	−.515	−.393	−.356
2 (Constant)	2.033	.246		8.269	.000			
GENDER	−.028	.041	−.013	−.675	.500	−.039	−.015	−.012
AGE	.026	.025	.030	1.022	.307	−.117	.023	.019
LEVEL	−.039	.037	−.023	−1.054	.292	.032	−.023	−.019
RELTEACH	.109	.046	.052	2.391	.017	.159	.053	.044
CURMANG	.106	.050	.053	2.096	.036	.159	.046	.038
LOS	−.012	.031	−.016	−.401	.689	−.143	−.009	−.007
LOSCATH	−.022	.028	−.029	−.802	.423	−.210	−.018	−.015
APPOINT	.020	.019	.027	1.050	.294	.211	.023	.019
RELGIMP	.093	.018	.121	5.280	.000	.357	.116	.096
RELIGION	.036	.060	.014	.610	.542	−.157	.014	.011
KNOWTOT	−.585	.032	−.393	−18.173	.000	−.515	−.374	−.332
ENVIRO	−.065	.055	−.022	−1.172	.241	−.088	−.026	−.021
COMIT	−.001	.048	−.001	−.024	.981	−.254	−.001	.000
PURPCATH2	−.051	.039	−.026	−1.319	.187	−.150	−.029	−.024
PRACTICES	−.108	.021	−.109	−5.179	.000	−.280	−.114	−.095
PEOPLE	−.016	.021	−.017	−.800	.424	−.158	−.018	−.015
CATSCHDF	.014	.011	.025	1.232	.218	−.139	.027	.023
CATIDIMP	−.027	.011	−.059	−2.584	.010	−.272	−.057	−.047

Model 1: $R^2 = .306$; $F(11, 2,038) = 81.63, p < .001$.

Model 2: $R^2 = .322$; F Change $(7, 2,031) = 7.00, p < .001$.

Overall: $F(18, 2,049) = 53.64, p < .001$.

Appendix 2: Identity of Catholic schools: Regression analysis tables 309

Table B13 Regression statistics for the prediction of WILLINGNESS

Model	Unstandardized coefficients B	Std. error	Standardized coefficients Beta	t	Sig.	Zero-order	Partial	Part
1 (Constant)	.468	.236		1.982	.048			
GENDER	−.080	.045	−.036	−1.773	.076	−.051	−.039	−.036
AGE	.027	.028	.031	.966	.334	−.072	.021	.019
LEVEL	−.015	.040	−.009	−.383	.702	.035	−.008	−.008
RELTEACH	.146	.050	.070	2.916	.004	.129	.064	.059
CURMANG	.032	.056	.016	.569	.569	.100	.013	.011
LOS	−.023	.034	−.031	−.693	.488	−.081	−.015	−.014
LOSCATH	.035	.031	.046	1.157	.248	−.109	.026	.023
APPOINT	.055	.021	.073	2.588	.010	.165	.057	.052
RELGIMP	.174	.018	.227	9.644	.000	.328	.208	.195
RELIGION	.072	.061	.027	1.183	.237	−.075	.026	.024
KNOWTOT	−.328	.035	−.220	−9.330	.000	−.322	−.202	−.188
2 (Constant)	.977	.260		3.749	.000			
GENDER	−.036	.044	−.016	−.821	.412	−.051	−.018	−.016
AGE	.019	.027	.022	.698	.485	−.072	.015	.014
LEVEL	−.071	.039	−.041	−1.806	.071	.035	−.040	−.035
RELTEACH	.089	.048	.043	1.826	.068	.129	.040	.035
CURMANG	−.007	.054	−.004	−.133	.894	.100	−.003	−.003
LOS	−.028	.033	−.037	−.843	.399	−.081	−.019	−.016
LOSCATH	.043	.030	.055	1.435	.151	−.109	.032	.028
APPOINT	.033	.021	.043	1.597	.110	.165	.035	.031
RELGIMP	.090	.019	.117	4.787	.000	.328	.105	.093
RELIGION	.193	.064	.072	3.014	.003	−.075	.066	.058
KNOWTOT	−.255	.034	−.171	−7.427	.000	−.322	−.162	−.144
ENVIRO	.018	.059	.006	.302	.762	−.054	.007	.006
COMIT	−.090	.051	−.044	−1.779	.075	−.242	−.039	−.035
PURPCATH2	−.052	.041	−.026	−1.258	.209	−.143	−.028	−.024
PRACTICES	−.207	.022	−.207	−9.272	.000	−.336	−.201	−.180
PEOPLE	−.106	.022	−.109	−4.870	.000	−.190	−.107	−.095
CATSCHDF	.003	.012	.006	.289	.773	−.156	.006	.006
CATIDIMP	−.047	.011	−.103	−4.247	.000	−.292	−.093	−.082

Model 1: $R^2 = .163, F(11, 2,055) = 36.25, p < .001$.

Model 2: $R^2 = .228; F$ Change $(7, 2,048) = 24.97, p < .001$.

Overall: $F(18, 2,066) = 25.23, p < .001$.

310　Appendix 2: Identity of Catholic schools: Regression analysis tables

Table B14　Regression statistics for PDLIKE

Model	Unstandardized coefficients		Standardized coefficients			Correlations		
	B	Std. error	Beta	t	Sig.	Zero-order	Partial	Part
I (Constant)	4.067	.236		17.268	.000			
GENDER	−.039	.039	−.019	−1.009	.313	.019	−.022	−.019
AGE	.032	.024	.041	1.346	.178	.045	.030	.025
LEVEL	.002	.035	.001	.049	.961	−.092	.001	.001
RELTEACH	−.115	.043	−.061	−2.683	.007	−.161	−.060	−.051
CURMANG	.059	.047	.032	1.245	.213	−.076	.028	.024
LOS	−.045	.029	−.066	−1.558	.119	.019	−.035	−.029
LOSCATH	−.043	.026	−.061	−1.635	.102	.064	−.036	−.031
APPOINT	−.073	.018	−.106	−4.009	.000	−.181	−.089	−.076
RELGIMP	−.076	.017	−.110	−4.580	.000	−.324	−.101	−.087
RELIGION	−.034	.056	−.014	−.599	.549	.114	−.013	−.011
KNOWTOT	−.016	.033	−.012	−.482	.630	.230	−.011	−.009
CATIDIMP	.034	.010	.080	3.400	.001	.297	.075	.064
CATSCHDF	−.004	.011	−.009	−.413	.680	.146	−.009	−.008
PRACTICES	.096	.020	.106	4.774	.000	.287	.106	.090
PEOPLE	.101	.019	.114	5.198	.000	.236	.115	.098
ENVIRO	.030	.052	.011	.581	.562	.067	.013	.011
COMIT	.103	.045	.056	2.304	.021	.267	.051	.044
PURPCATH2	.027	.037	.015	.735	.462	.143	.016	.014
CONFIDENCE	−.023	.025	−.025	−.905	.366	−.328	−.020	−.017
WILLINGNESS	−.245	.024	−.271	−10.337	.000	−.425	−.224	−.196

$R^2 = .275$; $F(20, 2{,}023) = 38.42$, $p < .001$.

Table B15　Regression statistics for RELGIMP

Model	Unstandardized coefficients		Standardized coefficients		
	B	Std. error	Beta	t	Sig.
I (Constant)	.570	.212		2.695	.007
GENDER	−.121	.057	−.042	−2.134	.033
AGE	−.287	.034	−.260	−8.358	.000
LEVEL	.135	.050	.061	2.697	.007
RELTEACH	.459	.061	.169	7.558	.000
CURMANG	−.011	.070	−.004	−.163	.870
LOS	.045	.042	.046	1.085	.278
LOSCATH	−.090	.037	−.089	−2.463	.014
APPOINT	.255	.026	.258	9.712	.000

$R^2 = .196$, $F(8, 2{,}096) = 63.90$, $p < .001$.

Appendix 3

Identity and curriculum in Catholic Education: Survey of teachers' opinions regarding certain aspects of Catholic Education

Ethics Register: 2013 281Q

Submission of the completed survey is taken as an indication of consent.

We really appreciate your time today in filling out this survey.

1. **What is your gender?**

    ☐ Male   ☐ Female

2. **Age**

    ☐ < 29 year   ☐ 30–39 year   ☐ 40–49 years

    ☐ 50–59 years   ☐ 60+ years

3. **What best describes the location of your school?**

    ☐ Greater Capital City (Brisbane only)
    ☐ Significant Urban Areas (Bundaberg, Cairns, Gladstone, Gold Coast, Hervey Bay, Mackay, Rockhampton, Sunshine Coast, Thuringowa, Toowoomba, Townsville)
    ☐ Other Regional Towns
    ☐ Remote

4. **Is your school under the direction of?**

    ☐ Archdiocese of Brisbane
    ☐ Diocese of Cairns
    ☐ Diocese of Rockhampton

312 Appendix 3: Teacher survey

☐ Diocese of Toowoomba
☐ Diocese of Townsville
☐ Religious Institution/Public Juridic Person (please specify)_____

5 **At what level of education do you <u>mainly</u> work?**

☐ Primary   ☐ Secondary

If secondary, what are your <u>main</u> subjects?_____
Do you teach Religion?

☐ Yes   ☐ No

Do you have an added responsibility for <u>curriculum management/leadership</u>?

☐ Yes   ☐ No

If yes, please specify what these responsibilities are: _____

6 **How many years have you been teaching?**

☐ <5 years   ☐ 5–10   ☐ 11–20   ☐ 21–30   ☐ >30

7 **How many years teaching experience do you have in Catholic Education?**

☐ <5 years   ☐ 5–10   ☐ 11–20   ☐ 21–30   ☐ > 30

8 **Please choose <u>up to</u> <u>three reasons</u> why you are working in a Catholic school** from the following list by placing ticks in the boxes alongside your chosen options. **Do not** select more than three options. In the right hand column please tick the **<u>one main</u>** reason why you are working in a Catholic school).

Items	Your reasons (tick <u>no more than three</u>)	Main reason (tick <u>one</u> only)
Convenient location		
Environment of Catholic schools		
It's a secure job		
My commitment to the Catholic faith		
The job came up when I needed it		
Other		

If you selected other, please specify:

Appendix 3: Teacher survey 313

9 **Which of the following describes your <u>role</u> in your current school?**

☐ Principal
☐ Deputy Principal
☐ Assistant Principal
☐ APRE
☐ PAR (Position of Added Responsibility)
☐ Teacher
☐ Other (please specify)_____

10 **What is your religion?** (Please select one)

☐ Anglican   ☐ Buddhism   ☐ Roman Catholic
☐ Hinduism   ☐ Islam   ☐ Judaism
☐ Other Christian (please specify)_____
☐ No religion   ☐ Other (please specify)_____

11 **How important is your religion to the way you live your life?**

☐ Very important
☐ Important
☐ Somewhat important
☐ Unimportant
☐ Very unimportant
☐ Not Applicable

12 **Please locate your <u>beliefs</u> and <u>values</u> about the <u>fundamental aims of education</u> by shading in one 'radio button' on each line, where the mid-point (0) means that you regard both statements as <u>equally important</u>.**

	5	0	5	
The primary purpose of schools is to educate the whole child		O O O O O O O O O O O		The primary purpose of schools is to help students get high grades and good jobs
The primary purpose of education is to promote economic growth		O O O O O O O O O O O		The primary purpose of education is to facilitate personal wellbeing and promote active citizenship

314 Appendix 3: Teacher survey

13 **Please locate your beliefs about <u>student learning</u> by shading in one 'radio button' on each line, where the mid-point (0) means that you regard both statements as equally valid.**

	5	0	5	
Students learn best by collaborating with other students	O O O O O O O O O O O			Competition is necessary to bring out the best in students
Only a few students are capable of high academic achievement	O O O O O O O O O O O			All students are capable of high academic achievement
Students are best served by streaming according to ability	O O O O O O O O O O O			Students are best served by mixed ability grouping
My role as a teacher is to facilitate students' own inquiry	O O O O O O O O O O O			Effective/good teachers demonstrate correct ways to solve problems

<u>Purposes and Characteristics of Catholic Schools</u>

14 **What do you understand as the <u>main purposes</u> of Catholic schools?** (Please rank the following items in order of importance. You are asked to select **<u>at least three</u>** and to rank them 1, 2, 3, etc. **in order of importance).**

Item	Ranking (1, 2, 3...) (Please rank at least 3 items)
Develop active and informed citizens	
Education in the Catholic faith and tradition	
Promote academic achievement	
Provide an authentic experience of a Catholic community	
Provide a safe and nurturing environment	
Teach Christian values	
Other	

If you selected <u>other</u>, please explain _____

Appendix 3: Teacher survey   315

15 How well does <u>your</u> school achieve each of these purposes?

	Very well	Well	Fairly well	Poorly	Very poorly
Develop active and informed citizens	☐	☐	☐	☐	☐
Education in the Catholic faith and tradition	☐	☐	☐	☐	☐
Promote academic achievement	☐	☐	☐	☐	☐
Provide an authentic experience of a Catholic community	☐	☐	☐	☐	☐
Provide a safe and nurturing environment	☐	☐	☐	☐	☐
Teach Christian values	☐	☐	☐	☐	☐

16 Please indicate <u>your</u> position on Catholic schools using the following 'radio buttons', where the mid-point (0) means that you regard both statements as equally true.

5   0   5

Catholic schools are no different to other schools   O O O O O O O O O O O   Catholic schools are different to other schools

The Catholic identity of my school is important to me   O O O O O O O O O O O   The Catholic identity of my school is not important to me

17 Using this table please

a **rate the importance of each of the <u>following characteristics</u> to the identity of a Catholic school in the A column**

b **using these ratings, identify <u>the six most important characteristics</u> of a Catholic school <u>in order of importance</u> in the B column (Please do not choose more than six and rank them 1, 2, 3, 4, 5, 6).**

316   Appendix 3: Teacher survey

Characteristics	A. Ratings				B. Rankings (Rank 6 only)
	Essential	Very important	Important	Unimportant	
Annual age-appropriate religious retreats are available to students					
Catholic symbols throughout the school					
Caring community					
Prayer is integral to the school's daily life for staff and students					
Religious Education programmes present the teachings of the Catholic Church					
Teachers of religion are Catholic					
The integration of Catholic teachings across ALL learning areas is intentionally planned					
The principal is Catholic					
The school community celebrates school liturgies frequently					
The school engages in outreach and social justice programmes					
The school is a community of faith					
The school has strong links with the wider Church					
The teachers of RE are accredited to teach RE					
The vast majority of students are Catholic					
The vast majority of teachers are Catholic					

Please check that you are happy with your choices.

Appendix 3: Teacher survey 317

18 Does <u>your</u> school have a particular charism?

☐ Yes   ☐ No   ☐ Don't know

If you answered yes,

a **what is the charism of your school?** _____
b **please indicate your position on the following scale using the 'radio buttons'. The mid-point means you regard both statements as equally true.**

5   0   5

There is a greater focus on the school's charism than on its broader Catholic identity   O O O O O O O O O O O   There is a greater focus on the school's broader Catholic identity than on its charism

19 **Please indicate your response to the following statements.**
The **planned integration** of a Catholic perspective across the **whole curriculum** should be a key feature of the Catholic school.

☐ Strongly Agree   ☐ Agree   ☐ Unsure

☐ Disagree   ☐ Strongly Disagree

Why did you choose this response? _____
When teaching my subjects I integrate a Catholic perspective.

☐ Always   ☐ Often   ☐ Sometimes   ☐ Rarely   ☐ Never

Knowledge of Catholic teaching

20 <u>**Please indicate your response to each of the following statements.**</u>

Statements	Response				
	(please tick <u>**only one**</u> response for each statement)				
	Very Good	**Good**	**Fair**	**Poor**	**Very Poor**
My knowledge of the **key teachings** of the Catholic Church is					
My knowledge of **Catholic social teaching** is					
My knowledge of **Catholic moral teaching** is					

318   Appendix 3: Teacher survey

Confidence with respect to integrating a Catholic perspective

21 Please indicate your response to each of the following statements.

Statements	Response (please tick **only one** response for each statement)				
	Strongly Agree	**Agree**	**Unsure**	**Disagree**	**Strongly Disagree**
I feel confident about **integrating a Catholic perspective** into **my whole curriculum planning.**					
I feel confident about **integrating a Catholic perspective** into **my pedagogy in a planned way.**					
I feel confident about **integrating Catholic social teaching** into **my whole curriculum planning.**					
I feel confident about **integrating Catholic social teaching** into **my pedagogy in a planned way.**					
I feel confident about **integrating Catholic moral teaching** into **my whole curriculum planning.**					
I feel confident about **integrating Catholic moral teaching** into **my pedagogy in a planned way.**					

Appendix 3: Teacher survey 319

Willingness to integrate a Catholic perspective

22 **Please indicate your response to each of the following statements.**

Statements	Response (please tick **only one** response for each statement)				
	Strongly agree	**Agree**	**Unsure**	**Disagree**	**Strongly disagree**
I am willing to integrate **a Catholic perspective** into **my whole Curriculum planning.**					
I am willing to integrate **a Catholic perspective** into **my pedagogy in a planned way.**					
I am willing to integrate **Catholic social teaching** into **my whole curriculum planning.**					
I am willing to integrate **Catholic social teaching** into **my pedagogy in a planned way.**					
I am willing to integrate **Catholic moral teaching** into **my whole curriculum planning.**					
I am willing to integrate **Catholic moral teaching** into **my pedagogy in a planned way.**					

320 Appendix 3: Teacher survey

23 **Please indicate your views about the available Formation/ Professional Development in the identity of Catholic schools.**
Formation/Professional Development in the **identity of Catholic schools** is given priority in the overall **Formation/Professional Development** available to me.

☐ Strongly Agree   ☐ Agree   ☐ Unsure

☐ Disagree   ☐ Strongly Disagree

I would like to pursue **Formation/Professional Development** about the identity of the Catholic schools.

☐ Strongly Agree   ☐ Agree   ☐ Unsure   ☐ Disagree

☐ Strongly Disagree

24 **In your opinion,** what are the **main issues** facing Catholic Education today?

_____

_____

_____

_____

Do you wish to make any other comments and /or to identify any problems you may have had with the survey?

_____

_____

_____

_____

Thank you very much for your time.
   If you are willing to participate in a 30 minute interview in relation to some of these general issues (not your survey responses which are anonymous) please indicate this by emailing jim.gleeson@acu.edu.au

Appendix 4

Survey of student teachers' opinions and attitudes regarding Catholic Education

Ethics Approval Number: 2013 307Q

The study has been reviewed by the Human Research Ethics Committee at Australian Catholic University.

It is a longitudinal study of student teachers' opinions and attitudes regarding Catholic Education, first administered in Semester 1, 2014.

Participation in this study is completely voluntary. You are not under any obligation to participate and you can withdraw from the study at any time without adverse consequences. Submission of the survey is taken as an expression of consent.

All individual responses are confidential and will only be seen by the Principal Investigator, Professor Jim Gleeson, and the members of the research team. No individual respondent will be identified in any reports arising from the study.

We want to establish student teachers' honest opinions on a range of issues. There are no right or wrong answers. Respondents are asked to answer all questions as truthfully as possible.

If you have any complaints or concerns about the conduct of the project, you may email at res.ethics@acu.edu.au. Other contact details for such complaints are provided on the Information Letter. Any complaint or concern will be treated in confidence and fully investigated. You will be informed of the outcome.

1 What are the last four digits of your student number? ☐
2 What is your gender? ☐ Male ☐ Female
3 Age ☐ < 18 years ☐ 18– 21 years ☐ 22 +
4 What course are you taking? ☐ B.Ed. (Early Childhood/Primary) ☐ B.Ed. (Primary)
5 What was your entry pathway into university? ☐ OP ☐ IB ☐ Rank Entry Score ☐ Other
   If it was an OP, what was your score? ☐

322 Appendix 4: Student survey

6 What is your religion? (Please tick one only)

☐ Anglican ☐ Buddhism ☐ Roman Catholic
☐ Hinduism ☐ Islam ☐ Judaism
☐ Other Christian ☐ No religion ☐ Other _____

7 How important is your religion to the way you live your life?

☐ Very Important

☐ Important

☐ Somewhat Important

☐ Unimportant

☐ Very Unimportant

☐ Not Applicable

8 If you chose **Roman Catholic at Question,** please indicate your response to each of the following statements. **If not, go to Question 9.**
My **knowledge** of **Catholic teaching** is:

☐ Very Good ☐ Good ☐ Fair ☐ Poor ☐ Very Poor

My **knowledge** of **Catholic social teaching** is:

☐ Very Good ☐ Good ☐ Fair ☐ Poor

☐ Very Poor

My **knowledge** of **Catholic moral teaching** is:

☐ Very Good ☐ Good ☐ Fair ☐ Poor

☐ Very Poor

My **knowledge** of **Scripture texts** is:

☐ Very Good ☐ Good ☐ Fair ☐ Poor

☐ Very Poor

9 What type of secondary school did you attend?

☐ State school
☐ Independent school
☐ Catholic school
☐ Other (please specify) _____

Appendix 4: Student survey 323

If you ticked Catholic school, did the school belong to?

☐ A religious institute
☐ Local diocese
☐ Other (please specify) _____
☐ Don't know

10 From the following list identify **at least three reasons** why you attended that particular school. (Please rank these reasons in order of importance by placing 1 beside the first reason, 2 beside the second reason, 3 beside the third reason, and so on.)

Reason	Ranking
Convenient location	
Financial grounds	
Friends were going there	
Only option available	
Quality of the facilities	
Religious grounds	
Reputation as a caring school	
Reputation for academic excellence	
Reputation for good discipline	
Other (please specify)	

11 **Purposes of schools:** please **rank at least three** of the following **purposes of schools** in order of importance. (Place 1 in front of your first preference, 2 in front of your second preference, 3 in front of your third preference, and so on.)

☐ Academic achievement

☐ Develop good citizens

☐ Provide a faith-based education

☐ Provide a safe and caring environment

☐ Teach values

☐ Other (please specify) _____

Why did you choose this ranking?

324 Appendix 4: Student survey

12 How well did **your** secondary school achieve each of these purposes? (Please put a tick in each row)

	Very Well	Well	Fairly well	Poorly	Very Poorly	Not Applicable
Academic achievement						
Develop good citizens						
Provide a faith-based education						
Provide a safe and caring environment						
Teach values						
Other						

13 What did you like **most** about your secondary school experience?

14 What did you like **least** about your secondary school experience?

Appendix 4: Student survey 325

15 **Identity of Catholic schools:** In your opinion how **important** is each of the following characteristics to the identity of a Catholic school? (Please fill one circle **only** for each column, i.e. one per item).

Characteristics	Ratings				
	Essential	Very important	Important	Unimportant	No opinion
Annual age-appropriate religious retreats are available to students	O	O	O	O	O
Catholic symbols throughout the school	O	O	O	O	O
Caring community	O	O	O	O	O
Prayer is integral to the school's daily life for staff and students	O	O	O	O	O
Religious Education programmes present the teachings of the Catholic Church	O	O	O	O	O
Teachers of religion are Catholic	O	O	O	O	O
The integration of Catholic teachings across ALL learning areas is intentionally planned	O	O	O	O	O
The principal is Catholic	O	O	O	O	O
The school community celebrates school liturgies frequently	O	O	O	O	O
The school engages in outreach and social justice programmes	O	O	O	O	O
The school is a community of faith	O	O	O	O	O
The school has strong links with the wider Church	O	O	O	O	O
The teachers of RE are accredited to teach RE	O	O	O	O	O
The vast majority of students are Catholic	O	O	O	O	O
The vast majority of teachers are Catholic	O	O	O	O	O

If you answered 'no opinion' to all items, please go to Question 17.

326 Appendix 4: Student survey

16 Using your **ratings from the previous question**, please **rank the six most important characteristics** of a Catholic school in order of importance. Please place one tick **only** in each column.
Note: You should have a **total of 6 ticks** when you have finished.
Hint: Go back and look at the items you rated in the previous question as Essential, Very Important.

Characteristics	Rankings					
	Most Important item	Second most important item	Third most important item	Fourth most important item	Fifth most important item	Sixth most important item
Annual age-appropriate religious retreats are available to students	O	O	O	O	O	O
Catholic symbols throughout the school	O	O	O	O	O	O
Caring community	O	O	O	O	O	O
Prayer is integral to the school's daily life for staff and students	O	O	O	O	O	O
Religious Education programmes present the teachings of the Catholic Church	O	O	O	O	O	O
Teachers of religion are Catholic	O	O	O	O	O	O
The integration of Catholic teachings across ALL learning areas is intentionally planned	O	O	O	O	O	O
The principal is Catholic	O	O	O	O	O	O
The school community celebrates school liturgies frequently	O	O	O	O	O	O
The school engages in outreach and social justice programmes	O	O	O	O	O	O
The school is a community of faith	O	O	O	O	O	O
The school has strong links with the wider Church	O	O	O	O	O	O
The teachers of RE are accredited to teach RE	O	O	O	O	O	O
The vast majority of students are Catholic	O	O	O	O	O	O
The vast majority of teachers are Catholic	O	O	O	O	O	O

Appendix 4: Student survey   327

17 What type of school would you ideally like to teach in after you qualify? (Please tick one only).

- ☐ State school
- ☐ Independent school
- ☐ Catholic school
- ☐ Other (please specify)_____
- ☐ Don't know

18 **In your opinion,** what are the **main issues** facing Catholic/Faith-based Education today?

_____

_____

_____

19 Please locate your **beliefs** and **values** about the fundamental aims of education by shading in the following radio buttons, where the mid-point (0) means that you regard both statements as equally important. **Note:** You should shade 1 bold button on each line.

	3			**0**			**3**	
The primary purpose of schools is to educate the whole child	◌	◌	◌	◌	◌	◌	◌	The primary purpose of schools is to help students get high grades and good jobs
The primary purpose of education is to promote economic growth	◌	◌	◌	◌	◌	◌	◌	The primary purpose of education is to facilitate personal well-being and promote active citizenship
The main purpose of education is to hand on beliefs and values to future generations	◌	◌	◌	◌	◌	◌	◌	The main purpose of education is to promote critical and independent thought

328 Appendix 4: Student survey

20 Please locate your beliefs about **student learning** by shading in the following radio buttons, where the mid-point (0) means that you regard both statements as equally valid.

Note: You should shade 1 bold button on each line.

	3		0		3		
Students learn best by collaborating with each other	○	○	○	○	○	○	○	Competition is necessary to bring out the best in students
Only a few students are capable of high academic achievement	○	○	○	○	○	○	○	All students are capable of high academic achievement
Students are best served by streaming according to ability	○	○	○	○	○	○	○	Students are best served by mixed ability grouping
The role of the teacher is to facilitate students' own inquiry	○	○	○	○	○	○	○	Good teachers demonstrate correct ways to solve problems

Thank you for taking the time to complete this survey. Your assistance is greatly appreciated and will be of considerable value to the Catholic Identity and Curriculum in Catholic Education Project team.

If you are willing to give an interview of no more than 30 minutes duration about 'Identity and Curriculum in Catholic Education' please email Professor Jim Gleeson at jim.gleeson@acu.edu.au

Index

Action Research; effectiveness and feasibility, 252–256; evaluation of, 244, 249, 250; for social justice (Outreach), 135–136, 287; cycle, 248; implementation of, 7–8, 249, 259, 270; integration of 244, 246–247, 264; lessons learned, 250, 261, 274, 276; school based, 277–281, 289, 291; student outcomes, 137, 249, 250, 260
ACU Vice-Chancellor, 4, 287
Added professional responsibilities, 139, 146–147, 149, 152, 155, 173, 222, 226, 275
Anthropocentrism, 37, 41, 64–67, 71
Anthropology, 20, 34, 40, 65–67, 69, 70–72, 127, 220, 281
Apostolic Letter, 36–37, 46, 49, 56
Apostolic tradition, 33
Apple, M., 73, 236
Assessment, 1, 13–14, 27, 71, 82, 91, 101, 103, 189, 190, 214, 221, 246, 250, 254–257, 264–265, 267, 278, 279–280, 282, 285; and Catholic Social Teaching, 251, 256–257, 265, 280
Australian Catholic University, 1, 11, 188, 195, 221, 239, 275, 286, 322
Australian Curriculum, 2, 71, 82, 102–106, 109, 111, 189, 190, 211, 219, 221, 235–237, 246, 250, 258, 261, 264, 268–269, 277, 278, 284–286, 291–292
Australian Curriculum Assessment and Reporting Authority ACARA, 71, 103–105, 190, 219, 221, 237, 240, 285–286
National Assessment Plan – Literacy and Numeracy (NAPLAN), 1, 14, 82, 189, 211, 246, 268, 278, 291
Australian education system, 110, 190

Authentic development, 37, 40, 53, 65
Authenticity of Catholic schools, 155, 234

Ball, S., 1, 11–14, 67, 70, 98, 162, 188–189, 213, 246
Between-schools competition, 25
Bonaventure, 64
Brisbane Catholic Education, 4, 6, 278
Byrne, M., 4–5, 135, 192

Cardijn, J., 47, 59, 63, 76–77, 79, 81
Caring community, 136, 144–146, 148, 173, 192, 204–207, 223, 268, 275, 316, 326–327
Caritas Australia, 108–109, 249
Caritas (Charity), 44, 47, 52,
Caritas in Veritate 2009, 8, 19, 37, 44, 53, 56, 86–95, 244
Catechism of the Catholic Church (CCC), 38
Catholic character, 20, 113, 115–116, 119, 120–122, 130, 150, 220, 245
Catholic Christian Tradition, 51, 80–81
Catholic curriculum
Corporation, 21, 113; Integration, 113, 128; Maps, 124–125; Ontario, 116–123, 130
Catholic Education in Australia, 3, 138, 166, 168, 188, 191, 235, 245, 274
Catholic Education in the USA, 134, 166, 191, 221,
Catholic Education Ontario, 8, 14, 20–21, 27, 58, 66, 75, 113–131, 164–165, 220–221, 235, 237, 245–246, 280, 292
Catholic Graduate Expectations, 20–21; Ontario Catholic School, 20 118, 121–122, 128, 130–131

330 Index

Catholic identity, 4, 6, 11, 22, 125, 133–134, 136, 142, 149, 153–154, 156–157, 163–165, 171–173, 175–176, 183, 213, 223, 227–228, 246, 296, 298, 315, 317, 329

Catholic School Identity, 151, 153, 163, 183, 191–192, 195, 227, 267–268, 282, 286

Catholic social movements, 33–34

Catholic Social Teaching (CST), 35–36, 58, 63, 78, 80, 86–87, 89, 91–94, 97, 108, 114, 123–125, 128–129, 137, 165, 195, 199, 210, 214, 220, 230, 236, 244, 249, 261, 267, 274, 277–289, 291–292, 318–320, 323; framework, 114, 125, 128–129; principles, 124, 214, 278, 280–283, 292

Catholic teachers, 92, 115, 121–122, 124, 131, 133, 137–139, 155, 157, 171–172, 177, 179, 181, 234

Catholic tradition, 48, 59–60, 90, 93, 118, 127, 150–151, 166, 212, 230, 237

Centimus Annus 1991, 37, 41, 43, 50, 71

Chair of Identity and Curriculum in Catholic Education, 3, 221, 246,

Characteristics of Catholic schools, 8, 134, 139, 141, 144–150, 154–155, 162–163, 166, 171–173, 179, 183, 188, 193, 200, 204, 210, 213, 224–225, 233–234, 247–248, 274–276, 297

Charity, 35, 44, 47, 51–52, 86–88, 164

Christian anthropology, 40, 67, 127

Christian social action, 88

Citizenship, 12, 59, 70, 72, 99, 103–104, 106, 128, 144, 148, 190, 203, 239, 252, 275, 282, 313, 328

Common good, 20–21, 24, 32, 35–36, 40, 42–44, 52, 55–59, 63, 68–69, 92, 94, 124, 129, 189, 195, 251, 282–283

Comparative perspectives from the United States and Queensland, Australia , 162

Components of Catholic school identity, 163

Congregation for Catholic Education, 2, 17, 54, 66, 134, 163, 191, 218, 244, 283

Conscientisation, 75

Consumerism, 41, 43, 50, 54, 64–65, 72, 90

Conundrums, 188, 207, 212

Convey, J., 8, 22, 137, 139, 145, 152–155, 162, 163, 165, 171–176, 178, 180–181, 193, 213, 221, 275

Counter-cultural, 8, 15, 19, 26, 73, 82, 86, 92, 232, 258, 263, 269, 270, 281, 292

Critical literacy, 21, 75, 221, 245

Critical pedagogy, 73–76, 81, 237, 238

Critical thinking, 98, 99, 106, 246, 261

Current trends in Australian education, 188

Curriculum integration, 6–7, 18–20, 22, 113, 120–122, 124–125, 127–128, 130, 164, 180, 219–220, 222, 228–229, 238, 244–245, 247, 274, 284–286; effectiveness and feasibility, 250–252, 256, 280–281; Faith-based identity, 219–222, 225–226, 269, 291; of Catholic Perspectives, 250–252, 254–256, 264, 274, 276–277

Curriculum Matters 1996, 118, 120, 122, 125

Curriculum policy, 11, 118–122, 124, 235

Curriculum-related issues, 277, 283

Data analysis, 173, 240

Defining Issues Test, 194

Dialogue, 19, 58, 65, 70–71, 87, 95, 99, 118, 156, 220, 244, 259–260

Dignitatis Humanae, 33

Dignity of the human person, 36, 38–39, 42, 57–58, 63, 69, 94, 249, 251, 258, 260

Dignity of work, 36–37, 40, 94, 128

Discourse; Curriculum, 1, 13, 22, 86, 91, 235; Educational, 11, 92, 151, 219; Policy, 12

Drake, S., 7, 19, 21, 219, 221, 247, 252, 274, 281

Drake, S. and Burns, R., 20–21

Ecological devastation, 43

Economic Justice for All (EJA), 45

Educating to Fraternal Humanism (EFH) 2017, 59

Emmitt, M., 4–6, 287, 289

Environmental sustainability, 72, 219, 237, 266, 269, 278–279

Enrolments, 22, 25, 104, 135, 137, 168–169, 193

Ethical understanding, 103, 105–106, 237, 240, 246, 261, 285

Experience of teaching in Catholic schools, 153

Index 331

Faith-based Education, 16, 162, 188, 201–202, 206; Predictors of, 152
Faith-based identity of Catholic schools, 141–142, 147–149, 154, 155, 171, 173, 195, 207, 209, 210, 218, 226, 239, 244–247, 275, 280, 287, 290–291
Faith-based schools, 108, 133, 151, 162, 209, 291
Francis of Assisi, 64
Freire, P., 16, 27, 53, 73, 75, 80, 98, 236
Fullan, M., 263, 266–267, 278, 280, 283–284, 288, 291

Gaudium et Spes, 31, 33
Giroux, H., 73–75, 81–82, 238
Globalisation, 12, 16, 54, 95, 180
Gospel values, 11, 22, 26, 82, 108, 148, 151, 212, 225, 229–230, 237, 246, 258, 282–283
Grace, G., 3, 7, 11, 19, 38, 67, 86, 88, 90, 92, 94–95, 127, 133–137, 153–156, 164–166, 184, 191, 220, 237–238, 244, 292
Great Depression, 34, 37, 42
Gustavo Gutierrez, 16, 47

Hollenbach, D., 47
Hughes, P. J., 26, 191
Human Dignity, 2, 31, 33, 35, 38–42, 45, 54, 56–57, 108, 129, 211, 282
Human rights, 8, 13, 16, 18, 24, 34–38, 40, 42, 46, 53–54, 56–58, 65, 94, 98–111, 136, 165, 239, 246, 266–270, 277, 281–283, 291; conventions, 100–101; Education in the School Curriculum, 101–102, 104
Hutton, D., 4–5, 287

I Teach Who I Am, 227–228, 231, 233, 248, 276, 284
Ideologies, 53, 57, 63, 76, 188
Individualism, 18, 54–55, 58, 66, 70, 72, 93, 270
Industrial revolution, 33–34, 38
Institute for Catholic Education (ICE), 3, 7, 20, 58, 75, 113, 131, 139, 164–165, 220, 237, 245–246, 292
Institutional identity of schools, 163
Instrumentum Laboris 2014, 24, 66, 69
Intercultural understanding, 105–106, 237, 240, 246, 261, 285
Intra-disciplinary integration, 227, 229

Justitia In Mundo 1971, 49

Laborem Exercens 1981, 37, 40
Lane, D., 1, 3, 19, 66–70, 72, 133, 136, 151, 162, 164, 209, 220, 244–245, 281
Latin America, 47, 79, 109
Laudato Si', 8, 36–37, 41, 43, 47, 50, 56, 58, 63–73, 75, 77, 79, 81–82, 220, 261
Lay Catholics, 115, 208
Leadership in Catholic Education, 4, 11, 27, 94–95, 106, 108, 110, 115–116, 153, 169, 176, 181–184, 207, 212–213, 223, 233, 262–263, 265–267, 270, 277–281, 286, 291, 293
Leuven Catholic Identity Project, 156, 162, 268
Levels of Moral Reasoning, 194, 200, 202–203, 207
Liberation theologians, 33, 47, 51, 63, 79
Liberation theology, 16, 34, 73, 94, 236
Longitudinal study of the attitudes of pre-service teachers, 188
Lucio Gera, 47

Managerialist culture, 13
Market values, 22, 26, 67, 136, 162, 180, 211, 213, 234, 235, 237, 246, 266, 268, 283
Mason, Singleton, and Webber, 191
Mater et Magistra 1961, 42, 45, 55, 77
Materialism, 16, 91, 236
Medellin Conference, 47
Mission integrity, 92, 94–95
Murray, D., 18–19, 72, 150, 164, 208, 211, 220, 245

Neoliberalism; education policies, 1, 8, 16, 25, 81–82; thinking, 22, 25, 74, 207, 236
New Testament, 32, 44–45, 48, 51
Non-governmental organisations (NGO), 13, 33, 71, 103, 107–109

Octogesima Adveniens (1971), 36–37, 46, 49, 56, 64
Old Testament, 32, 48
On Care of our Common Home, 37, 63–64
Ontario Bishops, 113, 116–117, 121, 126, 130
Ontario Catholic Education, 27, 58, 75, 113–114, 116, 118, 125, 128–131, 246

332 Index

Ontario Ministry of Education, 21, 66, 113–115, 126, 128, 131
Option the poor and vulnerable, 11, 21–22, 34–36, 44, 46–48, 52, 58, 63, 69, 129, 237, 249, 263, 282
Organisation for Economic Co-Operation and Development (OECD), 12–15, 17, 25–27, 69, 73, 137, 164, 189, 211, 282
Outcomes-based Education (OBE), 14, 269, 286

Pacem in Terris 1963, 37, 39–40, 42, 45–46, 55–56, 63, 220
Pastoral circle – Holland & Henriot, 59, 76, 80–81
Pastoral Constitution on the Church in the Modern World - Gaudium et Spes, 31, 33
People Characteristics, 144, 147–149, 225, 227, 231
Permeation, 20, 87, 93, 113, 120–121, 125–127, 220, 246
Philosophy of Education, 18, 69, 109, 116, 286
Pollefeyt, D. and Bouwens, J., 66, 133, 151, 209, 267–268, 282
Pope Benedict XIV, 34
Pope Benedict XVI, 37, 44, 53, 56–57, 64, 90, 93, 95, 210
Pope Francis, 1, 37, 41, 43, 47–48, 50, 53, 57, 63–67, 69–75, 81–82, 130, 133, 211, 220, 281
Pope John Paul II, 34, 37, 40–41, 43–44, 47, 49, 50–52, 64, 92
Pope John XXIII, 34, 37, 39–40, 42, 43, 45–46, 53, 55–56, 59, 63, 77, 220
Pope Leo XIII, 33–34, 37–39, 42, 45, 54
Pope Paul VI, 37, 40, 46–47, 49, 52–54, 56–57, 64, 92, 209
Pope Pius X, 34, 37, 39, 42, 45, 51, 55
Pope Pius XI, 34, 37, 39, 42, 45, 51, 55
Populorum Progressio 1967, 37, 40, 46, 52–54, 95
Practices Characteristics, 146, 148–149, 154, 225–227, 231, 275
Praxis, 60, 75–76, 80
Preferential option for the poor, 34–36, 44, 47–48, 52, 58, 63, 69, 237, 249, 263, 282
Pre-service teachers, 7, 8, 109–110, 153, 188, 192–195, 200, 202, 206–213, 239, 268, 274, 282, 291

Programme for International Student Assessment (PISA), 1, 14–15, 25, 27, 82, 101, 189, 246, 282
Project Advisory Committee, 6, 287
Project governance, 274, 286, 289
Promotion of peace, 36, 129
Purposes of Catholic schools, 139, 141, 143, 149, 222, 314
Purposes of schools, 200–201, 324

Quadragesimo Anno 1931, 37, 42, 55
Queensland Catholic Education, 1, 4–5, 139, 173, 186

Redemptor Hominis 1979, 49
Reign of God, 32, 51
Religious affiliation, religiosity and culture of young Australians, 169, 190, 192, 195–196, 206, 212
Religious Education, 3–6, 18, 23, 27, 59, 87, 91–92, 117, 120–121, 123–126, 128, 136, 138–139, 145–146, 154, 164, 167–168, 172, 195, 218, 220, 222, 233, 235, 246, 249, 250, 257, 261, 264–266, 268, 275, 278–280, 287, 288, 292, 326–327
Rerum Novarum (1891), 33–34, 36–42, 45, 54, 56

Safe and caring environment, 150, 192, 196, 199, 201, 202, 210, 275
Scientific-technical reason, 11
School-based action research, 244, 277, 291
School charism, 147, 151, 167, 212, 288
School choice, 133, 191–192, 196, 282
School culture; community and service, 164; symbols, rituals and liturgies, 165
School fees, 23, 167
School partnerships, 274, 286, 289, 290; University partnerships, 274, 286, 289, 290
Scripture, 31–33, 47, 51, 76, 80, 124, 128, 199, 210, 220, 292
Second Vatican Council, 31, 33–34, 43, 47, 66, 95, 163–164, 183, 209
Secularisation, 1, 154, 188, 192, 209, 234, 239, 244, 268, 282
Secularism, 16, 18, 119, 210
Segundo, J., 47
See, Judge, Act, 47, 59, 63, 76–79, 81, 291
Separation, 20, 113, 120–121, 164, 220, 246
Shape of the Australian Curriculum, 105

Social analysis, 47, 52, 63, 76–77, 79–81, 93
Social ecology, 50
Social encyclicals, 8, 31, 35–36, 47, 56, 63, 86, 93
Social justice, 4–5, 7, 27, 31–33, 35, 54, 59, 72, 74, 75, 77, 81–82, 88, 98–100, 104–105, 108–110, 120, 130, 135–137, 145–146, 148, 172, 190, 204–205, 207, 210, 225, 229, 230, 236–237, 239, 250–251, 257, 266–268, 270, 277, 281–283, 287, 289, 291, 326, 327
Social justice, human rights and Catholic social teaching, 267, 281
Solidarity, 17, 35–36, 45, 51–56, 58, 60, 73, 77, 88, 94, 212, 237, 239, 249
Sollicitudo Rei Socialis 1987, 43, 50, 52
Spring, J., 13, 16, 25, 41, 189, 236
St Vincent de Paul Society, 109
Standardised testing, 1, 13–15, 22, 70, 189
Stenhouse, 14, 17, 66, 68–69, 74, 219, 233, 235, 238, 269, 281, 286
Stewardship of creation, 21, 35–36, 48–51, 58, 63, 129, 249, 251, 266, 278–279
Student survey, 188, 193, 195, 200
Study of Religion (RE/SoR), 139, 140, 149, 173, 222, 226
Subsidiarity and participation, 36, 54, 58, 249, 251, 259–260
Survey; Catholic Education in the United States, 168, 171–174, 181, 183; Teachers' opinions regarding certain aspects of Catholic Education, 134, 138–139, 141–142, 144, 148–150, 152–154, 247, 249–251, 254, 266, 274–277, 282, 311–320

Student teachers' opinions and attitudes regarding Catholic Education, 188, 193–195, 200, 213, 218, 221–225, 227, 231–232, 233, 282, 321–328
Sustainable curriculum change, 263, 265–266

Teachable moments, 225, 227–228, 231, 233, 238, 248, 255–256, 265, 269, 276, 280, 284, 288
Teachers' knowledge of Catholic Teaching, 139, 142–143, 148, 150, 152–156, 199, 222–223, 226–227, 233, 239, 248, 275–276
Teachers' religiosity, 139, 142–143, 146–148, 150, 152–155, 173, 183, 190, 192, 222–224, 226–227, 233, 248, 275–276, 297, 298
Teaching controversial issues, 74–75, 107–108, 264, 269, 280, 281; in the classroom, 232, 237–238, 258
Theological reflection, 77–80, 292
Thomas Aquinas, 64

Universal Declaration of Human Rights (UDHR), 40, 100–101

Well-being, 15, 31, 42, 57, 68, 70, 72, 103, 126, 128, 203, 207, 281, 292, 328
Whole school approach, 108, 110, 255, 262–263, 266, 279–280
Working in Catholic Education, 139, 141

Young Christian Worker (YCW), 34, 63, 77
Young Social Innovators (Ireland), 291

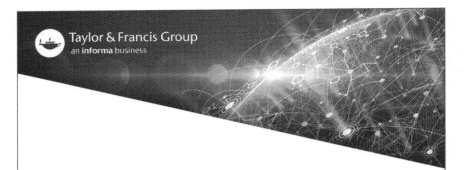

Printed in the United States
By Bookmasters